# A HISTORY OF PĀLI LITERATURE

# A HISTORY OF PĀLI LITERATURE

By

**BIMALA CHURN LAW,** Ph.D., M.A., B.L.

WITH A FOREWORD BY

**WILHELM GEIGER,** Ph.D.

**IN TWO VOLUMES**

VOL. II

GYAN

*Published by*

Gyan Publishing House
5, Ansari Road
Daryaganj, New Delhi-110002
Phone: 011-47034999, 9811692060
E-mail: books@gyanbooks.com

*Distribution Network*
gyanbooks.com
India, USA, Canada, UK, Australia, France



ISBN : 978-81-212-6866-0 (Set)
978-81-212-9917-6 (HB)
First Published, 1933

2nd Impression 2023

*Printed at:* Gyan Press, Delhi.



**A HISTORY OF PALI LITERATURE (Vol. II)**
Author: BIMALA CHURN LAW

# A HISTORY OF PĀLI LITERATURE

By

BIMALA CHURN LAW, Ph.D., M.A., B.L.,

Sir Asutosh Mookerjee Gold Medalist, Griffith Prizeman, Calcutta University;
Advocate, High Court, Calcutta; Author, *Some Kṣatriya Tribes of Ancient India, Ancient Mid-Indian Kṣatriya Tribes, The Life and Work of Buddhaghosa, Geography of Early Buddhism, Heaven and Hell in Buddhist Perspective, A Study of the Mahāvastu, Women in Buddhist Literature, Historical Gleanings, The Buddhist Conception of Spirits, The Law of Gift in British India*, etc., etc.,
Editor, *Buddhistic Studies*.

With a Foreword by
WILHELM GEIGER, Ph.D.,
Professor of Indo-Iranian Languages,
München University, Germany.

IN TWO VOLU

Vol. II.

1933

# CONTENTS

# POST-CANONICAL PĀLI LITERA'

## Introduction

In between the closing of the Pāli canon and the writing of the Pāli commentaries by Buddhadatta, Buddhaghosa, and Dhammapāla, there is a short but dark period of development of Pāli literature which has not as yet engaged adequate attention of scholars. Broadly speaking, this period extends from the beginning of the Christian era to the close of the 4th century A.D. The Nettipakaraṇa, the Peṭakopadesa, and the Milinda Pañha are undoubtedly the three extra-canonical and highly useful treatises that may be safely relegated to the earlier part of this period. There are a few other works, more or less, of a commentarial nature that are closely pre-supposed by the great commentaries of Buddhadatta, Buddhaghosa, and Dhammapāla. These comprise, among others, (1) certain earlier commentaries written in Sinhalese, such as the Mūla or Mahā-aṭṭhakathā, the Uttara Vihāra aṭṭhakathā (the Commentary of the dwellers in the "North Minster"), Mahāpaccariya, the Kurundiya or Mahākurunda aṭṭhakathā quoted by Buddhaghosa in his commentaries, (2) two other earlier commentaries, the Andhaka and the Saṅkhepa current in South India, particularly in Kañchipura or Conjeveram, and quoted by Buddhaghosa, (3) the Vinayavinicchaya by Buddhasīha, a fellow bhikkhu of Buddhadatta, pre-supposed by the Vinayavinicchaya of Buddhadatta and the Samantapāsādikā of Buddhaghosa, (4) the Sinhalese commentary on the canonical Jātaka book referred to and quoted by Buddhaghosa under the name of Jātaka-aṭṭhakathā, (5) certain views and interpretations of the schools of reciters quoted by Buddhaghosa in his commentaries, (6) the Dīpavaṁsa, the earlier Pāli chronicle quoted by Buddhaghosa in his commentary on the Kathāvatthu, and (7) the Aṭṭhakatha Mahāvaṁsa presupposed by Mahānāma's great chronicle of Ceylon.

The writings of Buddhadatta, Buddhaghosa, and Dhammapāla come necessarily after these earlier works in both Pāli and Sinhalese and occupy chronologically a place next to them. The Mahāvaṁsa or the great epic chronicle of Ceylon composed by Mahānāma, the Anāgatavaṁsa, a later supplement to the Buddhavaṁsa, and the Jātakatthavaṇṇanā written by a thera at the personal request of the elder Atthadassī, Buddhamitta of the Mahiṁsāsaka sect and Bhikkhu Buddhadeva of clear intellect, may be assigned to almost the same period of Buddhist literary activities in Ceylon which is covered by the writings of Buddhaghosa. Mahānāma's Mahāvaṁsa may be regarded as a Pāli model of certain chronicles the Pūjāvaliya and the rest written in Sinhalese. The commentaries on the books of the Vinaya, Sutta, and Abhidhamma Piṭakas were followed by certain ṭīkās to be chronologically discriminated as mūla and anu, Ānanda and Sāriputta being noted as authors of some of these mūla and anu ṭīkās. From the sixth or seventh century A.D. onwards we see also the beginning of a Pāli grammatical literature headed by Kaccāyana's Pāli Grammar as well as of Pāli lexicons headed by the Abhidhānappadīpikā. The literary processes connected with the commentaries and sub-commentaries and the compilations in the shape of handbooks continued resulting in the growth of a somewhat different type of later literature. The Abhidhammatthasaṅgaha and many other books of great authority written by the eminent Anuruddha and others are to be counted as remarkable literary output of this stage of the development of Pāli. The Narasīhagāthā quoted in the Nidānakathā of the Jātakatthavaṇṇanā, the Telakaṭāhagāthā ranking with the śatakas headed by the compositions of Bhartṛhari, the Jinacarita which is a kāvya attempted in Pāli less successfully on the model of Aśvaghoṣa's Buddhacarita, the Pajjamadhu, a Pāli poetical composition produced in Ceylon, the Pañcagatidīpana and the Saddhammopāyana, two similar poetical compositions of Ceylon and the Rasavāhinī, a book of interesting Buddhist folktales, written in simple prose, are some of the literary pieces that are included in our scheme of Post-Canonical Pāli literature. We are generally to exclude from our scheme various Pāli works on law, grammar, prosody, lexicography, and the commentaries written in Burma and Ceylon from the 15th century A.D. onwards. In dealing with the Post-Canonical Pāli literature we are first of all to take up the extra canonical works presupposed by the Pāli commentaries, next the Pāli commentaries, then the Pāli chronicles, Pāli Manuals, Pāli literary pieces, and lastly Pāli grammars, books on prosody and lexicons, the classification being arbitrary.

## CHAPTER IV

# EXTRA CANONICAL WORKS PRESUPPOSED BY PĀLI COMMENTARIES

Nettipakaraṇa.

The title *Nettipakaraṇa*[1] as explained by Dhammapāla, means exposition of that which leads to the knowledge of the Good Law. The Netti shows the methodical way of attaining textual knowledge. It contains much of the materials which are so grouped as to form a book by itself. The commentary on the Nettipakaraṇa says that without an able instructor it is impossible for men to be guided in the right understanding of the doctrines.

This treatise was translated into Burmese by Thera Mahāsīlavaṁsa in the fifteenth century of the Christian era, and again two centuries later, by a

---

[1] This work has been edited by Prof. E. Hardy for the P.T.S., London, and published by the said society in 1902. There is also a Burmese edition of this text. The text is not entirely free from inaccuracies but all such defects are pardonable when we remember that it is a pioneer work. The text edited by the P.T.S. is based on the following manuscripts :—

(i) Palm leaf manuscript of the India Office in Burmese character (see Catalogue of the Mandalay MSS. in the India Office Library by Prof. V. Fausboll, J.P.T.S., 1896);

(ii) Palm leaf manuscript of the India Office (Phayre collection), likewise written in Burmese character (see Catalogue of the Pāli MSS. in the India Office Library by H. Oldenberg);

(iii) Paper manuscript (brought from W. Subhuti by Prof. Rhys Davids) in Sinhalese character (Introduction, p. xxxv). Prof. Hardy has relied on the palm leaf manuscript of the India Office in Burmese character in noting readings whenever they are found to contribute to a better understanding of the text.

Nettipakaraṇa revised and edited by D. Sudassi thera and finally revised by Ven. Srisumaṅgala Ratanasāra, Colombo, 1923, should be consulted.

Mrs. Rhys Davids translates 'Nettipakaraṇa' as the '*Book of Guidance*' (Sākya or Buddhist Origins, p. 127).

dweller in the Pubbārāma-Vihāra. It was composed at the request of Thera Dhammarakkhita and highly praised by Mahākaccāna. The Mandalay manuscript ascribes its authorship to Mahākaccāna as every section bears a clear testimony to the authorship of Mahākaccāna who has been described here as Jambuvanavāsin, i.e., dweller in the rose-apple grove.

The Netti is essentially a Pāli treatise on the textual and exegetical methodology, a Buddhist treatment upon the whole of the Tantra Yuktis discussed in the Kauṭīliya Arthasaāstra, the Suśrutasaṁhitā, the Carakasaṁhitā, and the Aṣṭāṅga-Hṛdaya. The Netti and Jñānaprasthāna Śāstra have many points in common as they were written to serve a similar purpose. It stands in the same relation to the Pāli canon as Yāṣka's Nirukta to the Vedas. The scheme of methodology has been worked out in a progressive order, the thesis being developed or elaborated by gradual steps. To begin with we have the opening section, Saṅgahavāra, or the conspectus of the whole book which is a feature also of the Milinda Pañha. Then we have the Vibhāgavāra or the section presenting a systematic treatment in classified tables. This section comprises three tables or sub-sections :—(1) Uddesavāra, (2) Niddesavāra, and (3) Paṭiniddesavāra. The Uddesavāra merely presents a bare statement of the theses and as such it serves as a table of contents. It is followed by the Niddesavāra which briefly specifies the import or definitions of the theses awaiting detailed treatment in the section immediately following, we mean the Paṭiniddesavāra, which is but an elucidation and elaboration of the Niddesa scheme. The theses in the Uddesavāra are introduced in three separate tables or categories—(1) that of sixteen hāras (connected chains), (2) that of five nayas (modes of inspection), and (3) that of eighteen mūlapadas (main ethical topics). The sixteen hāras consist of desanā (the method of instruction), vicaya (the method of enquiry), yutti (the method of establishing connection in groups), padaṭṭhāna (the method of teaching with reference to the fundamentals), lakkhaṇa (the method of determining implications by characteristic marks), catuvyūha (the method of fourfold array), āvatta (the cyclical method), vibhatti (the method of classification), parivattana (the method of transformation), vevacana (the method of synonyms), paññatti (the method of determining signification), otaraṇa (the method of descending steps), sodhana (the method of rectification), adhiṭṭhāna (the method of determining positions), parikkhāra (the method of discriminating causal relations), and samāropana (the method of attribution).

The five nayas consist of the following modes of viewing things :—(1) nandiyāvatta, (2) tīpukkhala (by the triple lotus), (3) sīhavikkīḷita (the lion-like sport), (4) disālocana (broad vision), and (5) aṅkusa (focussing).

The eighteen mūlapadas comprise nine kusalas and nine akusalas. The nine akusalas are taṇhā (thirst), avijjā (ignorance), lobha (covetousness), dosa (hatred), moha (delusion), subhasaññā (false idea of purity), niccasaññā (false idea of permanence), attasaññā (false idea of personal identity), etc. The nine kusalas are samatha (tranquillity), vipassanā (insight), alobha (absence of covetousness), adosa (absence of hatred), amoha (absence of delusion), asubhasaññā (idea of impurity), dukkhasaññā (idea of discordance), aniccasaññā (idea of impermanence), and anattasaññā (idea of non-identity).

In the Niddesavāra, the reader is to expect nothing more than a general specification of the meaning of the topics proposed in the Uddesavāra for treatment. From the Niddesavāra the reader is led on to the next step, the Paṭiniddesavāra which contains four broad divisions, namely, (1) Hāravibhaṅga (explanations of the connected chains), (2) Hārasaṁpāta (discussions of the hāra projections), (3) Nayasamuṭṭhāna (exposition of the modes of inspection), and (4) the Sāsanapaṭṭhāna (the classification and interpretation of Buddha's instructions).

The treatise deals in detail with sixteen hāras in the specified order as follows:

The Desanāhāra directs the reader to notice six distinctive features in the Buddha's method of instructions, namely, assādaṁ (bright side), ādinavaṁ (dark side), nissaraṇaṁ (means of escape), phalaṁ (fruition), upāyaṁ (means of success), and ānattiṁ (the moral upshot). It also points out that Buddha's instructions are carefully adapted to four classes of hearers, namely (1) those of right intellect (understanding things by mere hints), (2) those needing short explanations, (3) those to be slowly led by elaborate expositions, and (4) those whose understanding does not go beneath the words. In the same connection it seeks to bring home the distinction between the three kinds of knowledge, sutamayī, cintāmayī, and bhāvanāmayī.

In the Vicayahāra the method of ruminating over the subjects of questions and thoughts and repetitions in thought is laid down, and this is elaborately illustrated with appropriate quotations from the canonical texts.

In the Yuttihāra we are introduced to the method of grouping together connected ideas and the right application of the method of reasoning or inference in interpreting the dharma.

The Padaṭṭhānahāra explains the doctrinal points by their fundamental characteristics and exemplifies them. *This hāra has an important bearing on the Milinda expositions.*

The Lakkhaṇahāra points out that when one of a group of matters characterised by the same mark is mentioned, the others must be taken as implied. For instance, when the sense of sight is mentioned in a passage, the implication should be that other senses received the same treatment.

The Catuvyūhahāra unfolds the method of understanding the doctrines by noting the following points :—

(1) the text, (2) the term, (3) the purport, (4) the introductory episode, and (5) the sequence, illustrating each of them with quotations from the canonical texts.

The Āvattahāra aptly illustrates with authoritative quotations how in the teachings of the Buddha all things turn round to form cycles of some fundamental ideas such as taṇhā, avijjā, the four Aryan truths and the like.

The Vibhattihāra explains the method of classifying Buddha's discussions according to their character, common or uncommon, or according to their values, inferior, superior or mediocre.

The Parivattanahāra contains an exposition of the method by which the Buddha tried to transform a bad thing into a good thing and transform also the life of a bad man.

The Vevacanahāra calls attention to the dictionary method of synonyms by which the Buddha tried to impress and clarify certain notions of the Dhamma. This section forms a landmark in the development of Indian lexicography.

In the Paññattihāra it is stated that though the Dhamma is one, the Lord has presented it in various forms. There are four noble truths beginning with dukkha. When these truths are realised then knowledge and wisdom come in and then the way to Bhāvanā is open to the knower. The elements may be compared but Nibbāna cannot be compared.

In the section on Otaraṇa the Netti illustrates how in the schemata of Buddha's doctrines diverse notions spontaneously descend under the burden of certain leading topics such as, indriyas, paṭiccasamuppāda, five khandhas and the like.

The Sodhanahāra illustrates the method by which the Buddha corrected the form of the questions in the replies offered by him.

The Adhiṭṭhānahāra explains in detail the method of determining the respective positions of different ideas according as they make for certain common notions. In the Adhiṭṭhānahāra the basis of all truth is given. The four truths beginning with dukkhaṁ are described and side by side avijjā is shown to be the cause working in opposite ways. There are also paths bringing about the extinction of dukkha, etc. The various kāyas and dhātus are also considered. Samādhi is the only means of removing evils.

In the Parikkhārahāra the Netti explains and exemplifies how one can distinguish between the causal elements, broadly between hetu and other causal relations. *This section has an important bearing on the Paṭṭhāna of the Abhidhamma Piṭaka.*

We come at last to the section called the Samāropanahāra. This section explains and illustrates the Buddha's method of fourfold attribution, (1) by way of fundamental ideas, (2) by way of synonyms, (3) by way of contemplation, and by way of getting rid of the immoral propensities.

Hāra Saṁpāta is a division which is dependent on the hāra as its purpose is to present the projections or main moral implications of the haras or the connected chains previously dealt with.

This division like the preceding one consists of sixteen parts exactly under the same headings.

In the Hāra Saṁpāta the commentator Dhammapāla has added and rearranged many new things. He cites the passages from the text and then puts a lay dissertation on them by way of questions and answers. *This division stands almost as an independent treatise by itself.*

Desanā hāra Saṁpāta—In this division it is laid down that Māra invades only a mind which is quite unprotected (pamādacitta), which is based on false beliefs, on idleness, etc.

Vicaya hāra Saṁpāta—In this section it is laid down that desire (taṇhā) is of two kinds : kusala and akusala. The one leads to nibbāna and the other to birth and suffering (saṁsāra). Mind is both kusala and akusala in nature. The real nature of things can only be seen in the fourth Jhāna stage. The various signs and nature of nibbāna and samādhi are described. Samādhi has five characteristics, namely, joy, happiness, consciousness, enlightenment, and right perception. There are ten objects of meditation (kasiṇāyatanāni), e.g., paṭhavī, āpo, etc. They are then attached to three objects, anicca (non-permanent), dukkha (suffering), and anatta (non-existence of soul).

A differentiation is brought about between an ordinary man and a man with knowledge. The former can do any kind of offence that may be possible. But the latter cannot. The former can even kill his father or mother, can destroy the stūpas but the latter cannot; when one practises the four Jhānas, and attains to Samādhi, his previous life and futurity are known to him.

In the Yutti-hāra-saṁpāta it is stated that sloth, stupor, and misery disappear from him who is well protected in mind, firm in resolution, and adheres to right seeing.

In the Padaṭṭhāna-hāra and Lakkhaṇa-hāra-saṁpāta, the padaṭṭhānas (reasonings) are described as belonging to one who is well restrained in mind, words, and actions and who by the proper attainment of padaṭṭhānas realises the highest path.

In the Catuvyūhahāra-saṁpāta, Āvattahāra-saṁpāta, Vibhatti-hāra-saṁpāta, etc., great stress is laid on right perception, mindfulness, and kusala deeds which lead to the knowledge of paṭicca-samuppāda.

The third division called the Nayasamuṭṭhāna contains a detailed treatment of the five specified modes of viewing things. Under the Nandiyāvatta mode, it is pointed out that the earlier extremity of the world cannot be known owing to avijjā (ignorance) which has taṇhā (desire) at the root. Those who walk in the field of pleasure are bound down in heretical beliefs and are unable to realise the truth. There are four noble truths—Dukkhaṁ, dukkhasamudayaṁ, dukkhanirodhaṁ, and dukkha-nirodhagāminipaṭipadā. There is a middle path (majjhima paṭipadā) which rejects the two extreme views and which is identified with the eightfold noble path (ariya aṭṭhaṅgiko maggo). He who has avoided diṭṭhi (false view) escapes from kāma (lust). Hence avoidance of desire (taṇhā) and ignorance (avijjā) leads to quietitude or calmness. Kamma is recognised as the cause of the world of sufferings. But consciousness and all that concerns consciousness may be seen in their increment in the ten vatthus. The ordinary enjoyment of food and touch, etc., is the cause of distress of a man with desire.

The various āsavas (sins) are next described. The sufferings of a man with attachments, faults, and wrong views are also narrated. The four paths, the four foundations of recollections, the four Jhānas, the four essentials (sammappadhānas), the four meditations, the four pleasure yielding states, etc., are also stated ; each of these is described as an antidote for the man with attachment, delusion, and wrong views.

Buddhas, Pacceka-Buddhas, the disciples, and all those who are devoid of attachment, hatred, delusion, etc., are like lions. Those who look to the right aspects, the senses, the counter forces of the views with as strong reasons as Buddhas, Pacceka-Buddhas, etc., are said to have seen things just like a lion. Human types are four in number. Each of these has to undergo some sort of training. To each of them is offered an advice as to taṇhā (desire), rāga (attachment), kusala (merit), etc. This is the way shown to be of the Tīpukkhalo and of the Aṅkusa described in the text.

Now turning to the fourth division, the Sāsanapaṭṭhāna, we get a treatment of the proper method of classification and interpretation of the texts of the Dhamma. That is to say, the Sāsanapaṭṭhāna embodies a classification of the Piṭaka passages according to their leading thoughts. It is suggested that the discourses of the Buddha can be classified according to the themes into :—(1) Saṅkilesabhāgiya (those dealing with saṅkilesa or impurity), (2)

Vāsanābhāgiya (those dealing with desire), (3) Nibbedhabhāgiya (those dealing with penetration), (4) Asekhabhāgiya (those dealing with the subject of a non-learner), (5) Saṅkilesabhāgiya and Vāsanābhāgiya, (6) Saṅkilesa and Nibbedhabhāgiya, (7) Saṅkilesa and Asekhabhāgiya, (8) Saṅkilesa and Nibbedha and Asekhabhāgiya, (9) Saṅkilesa and Vāsanā and Nibbedhabhāgiya, (10) Vāsanā and Nibbedhabhāgiya, (11) Taṇhāsaṅkilesabhāgiya, (12) Diṭṭhisaṅkilesabhāgiya, (13) Duccaritasaṅkilesabhāgiya, (14) Taṇhāvodānabhāgiya, (15) Diṭṭhivodānabhāgiya, (16) Duccaritavodānabhāgiya. Of these, saṅkilesas are of three kinds, taṇhā (desire), diṭṭhi (false view), and duccaritas (wrong actions).

Various padas, ślokas, and texts are cited while explaining each of these textual classifications.

The eighteen main padas are those which are worldly (lokikaṁ), unworldly (lokuttaraṁ), etc. In fact the chapter is made highly interesting by its numerous quotations from familiar texts and it does not enter deep into philosophical or logical arguments. But the classification and reclassifications are no doubt interesting as intellectual gymnastics.

That the Nettipakaraṇa is an earlier book than the Paṭṭhāṇa (Mahāpakaraṇa) has been ably shown by Mrs. Rhys Davids (J.R.A.S., 1925, pp. 111-112). She says that in the Netti there is a short chapter on parikkhāra, i.e., equipment. Usually applied to a monk's necessities of life, it is here applied to mean all that goes to bring about a happening, all the conditions to produce an effect. These are twofold—paccaya and hetu. Take now this happening: " A seeing something ". Here the eye is the dominant condition (adhipateyyapaccayatāya paccayo). The thing seen is the object condition (ārammaṇa paccayatāya paccayo). The light is the medium condition (Sannissāyatāya paccayo). But attention is the *hetu*. In conclusion it states: Whatever is sufficing condition (upanissaya) that is a causal antecedent (parikkhāra). "This simple exposition," says Mrs. Rhys Davids, "is a development of the yet simpler wording in the suttas. There no distinction is drawn between hetu and paccaya".

She then turns her attention to the Paṭṭhāna. Here at the start not only has a distinction been drawn but an elaborate classification of paccayas—twenty-four in kind, is drawn up as standardised knowledge.

Hetu is a species of paccaya, first and chief of them. Further, 'dominance', 'object', 'medium', 'sufficing condition', are classed as paccayas, Nos. 3, 2, 9, and 8. And further, the invariable way of assigning causal relation in a happening is not the Netti's way but (hetu, etc.)—paccayena paccayo. We may conclude from this that the writer of the Netti did not know the Paṭṭhāna. He did know some Abhidhamma. He alludes to a method in the Dhammasaṅgaṇi, to a definition in the Vibhaṅga but never to that notable scheme in the Paṭṭhāna.

Peṭakopadesa.

The Peṭakopadesa is another treatise on the textual and the exegetical methodology ascribed to Mahākaccāna and it is nothing but a different manipulation of the subject treated in the Nettipakaraṇa. Interest of this treatise, if it was at all a work of the same author, lies in the fact that it throws some new light here and there on the points somewhat obscure in the Netti. Its importance lies also in the fact that in places it has quoted the Pāli canonical passages mentioning the sources by such names as Saṁyuttaka (=Saṁyutta Nikāya) and Ekuttaraka (=Ekuttara or Aṅguttara Nikāya). Its importance arises no less from the fact that in it the four Ariyan truths are stated to be the central theme or essence of Buddhism, the point which gained much ground in the literature of the Sarvastivādin school. The importance of the last point will be realised all the more as we find how the discourses developed in the Netti in the course of formulating the textual and exegetical methodology centered round the four Ariyan truths. This work has not yet been edited. The P.T.S., London, has undertaken an edition of it. Specimen de Peṭakopadesa by R. Fuchs, Berlin, 1908 deserves mention.

Milinda Pañha—Introduction.

The Milinda Pañha or the questions of Milinda had originally been written in Northern India in Sanskrit or in some North Indian Prakrit by an author whose name has not, unfortunately enough, come down to us. But, the original text is now lost in the land of its origin as elsewhere; what now remains is the Pāli translation of the original which was made at a very early date in Ceylon. From Ceylon, it travelled to other countries, namely, Burma and Siam, which have derived their Buddhism from Ceylon, and where at a later date it was translated into respective local dialects. In China, too, there have been found two separate works entitled "The Book of the Bhikkhu Nāgasena Sūtra", but whether they are translations of the older recensions of the work than the one preserved in Pāli on of the Pāli recensions is difficult to ascertain. However, in the home of Southern Buddhism, the book is accepted as a standard authority, second only to the Pāli Piṭakas. Prof. Rhys Davids rightly observes, "It is not merely the only work composed among the Northern Buddhists which is regarded with reverence by the orthodox Buddhists of the Southern schools, it is the only one which has survived at all amongst them".[1]

Character of the book.

The book purports to discuss a good number of problems and disputed points of Buddhism; and this discussion is treated in the form of conversations between King Milinda of Sāgala and Thera Nāgasena. Milinda raises the questions and puts the dilemmas, and thus plays a subordinate part in comparison to that played by Nāgasena who answers the questions and solves the puzzles in detail.

[1] S.B.E., Vol. XXXV, Intro., p. xii.

Naturally, therefore, the didactic element predominates in the otherwise romantic account of the encounter between the two.

The two heroes.

Milinda who has been described as the King of the Yonas with his capital at Sāgala (Sākala=Sialkot), has long been identified with Menander, the Bactrian Greek King who had his sway in the Punjab. He was born, as our author makes him say, at Kalasi in Alasanda, i.e., Alexandria; and if we are to believe our author, he, resolved of all doubts as a result of his long conversations with Nāgasena, came to be converted to Buddhism. Nāgasena, however, cannot be identified with any amount of certainty.

Author.

The name of the author, as we have already said, has not come down to us. A close analysis of the book shows that a considerable number of place names refers to the Punjab and adjacent countries, and a few to the sea-coast, e.g., Surat, Bharukaccha, etc. Most of the rivers named refer again to the Punjab. It is, therefore, natural for us to conjecture that the author of the book resided in the far north-west of India or in the Punjab. Mrs. Rhys Davids has a theory of her own regarding the author of the Milinda Pañho. She thinks that the recorded conversations of Milinda and Nāgasena were edited in the new book form after Milinda's death, by special commission by a Brāhmaṇa of Buddhist Collegiate training, named Māṇava. She points out that the author was not a convinced Buddhist and that the detached first portion of the Milinda Pañha is in no way to be matched in style or ideas with the quite different dilemmas and the following portions. The first part is a set of jerky rather desultory talks breaking off and bearing marks of being genuine notes taken by recorders at the time. The latter portions are evidently written compositions, dummy conversations. "As to his name," says Mrs. Rhys Davids, "that is not by me made of any importance: it is, let us say, my playful guess:—a brāhmaṇa name like the Shakespeare hidden allusions, alluded to in a gāthā, which there was no reason for quoting save as a hint at the name".

Date.

It is somewhat difficult to ascertain exactly the date of the Book. Milinda or Menander is, however, ascribed to the last quarter of the 2nd century B.C. The book must, therefore, have been written after that date. On the other hand, it must have long been an important book of authority when Buddhaghosa, the celebrated Buddhist commentator, flourished in the 5th century A.D. For, he quoted from the book often in his commentaries, and that in such a manner that it follows that he regarded the book as a work of great authority. From a close analysis of the books referred to as quoted by the author of the Milinda Pañha, Prof. T. W. Rhys Davids, the learned editor and translator of Milinda Pañha, came to the conclusion that "the book is later than the canonical books of the Pāli Piṭakas (the author of the Milinda Pañha quotes a large number of passages from the Piṭaka texts), and on the other hand, not only older than the great commentaries, but the only book outside the canon, regarded in them as an authority which may be implicitly followed".[1]

Style and language.

The Milinda Pañha has a marked style of its own. Its language is most elegant, and studied against the background of ancient Indian prose, it is simply a masterpiece of writing. The formal exactness of the early Piṭakas as well as the studied ornamentation of later-day Pāli or Sanskrit-Buddhist treatises are alike absent from its pages. The charm of the style is captivating and there are passages that are eloquent in their meaning and gesture. The perorations with which the long discussions are often closed are supreme inventions by our author of the art of conversation as well as of writing. Its style

[1] S.B.E., Vol. XXXV, Intro., p. xxxviii.

and diction bear a close resemblance to and are somewhat maturer than those of the famous Hastigumpha inscription of Khāravela which is assigned by Dr. B. M. Barua to the second quarter of the 1st century A.D.[1]

Text.

At Sāgala, a city of wealth and affluence, ruled King Milinda versed in arts and sciences and skilled in casuistry. He had his doubts and puzzles with regard to Buddha's doctrines and utterances and other knotty problems of Buddhism. To resolve these doubts he went to Nāgasena, the famous arahat ; and then began a wonderful conversational discourse between the two. But before the discourse really begins, we are introduced by our author to the previous birth history (Pubba-yoga) of these two personages and then to the contents of various sorts of puzzles.

(*a*) Book I.

We are told that Nāgasena in a previous birth of his was one of the members of the religious brotherhood near the Ganges, where Milinda, in his turn, in a previous birth of his, was a novice. In accordance with his acts of merit in that birth and his aspirations, this novice after wandering from existence to existence came to be born at last as king of the city of Sāgala, a very learned, eloquent, and wise man. Now he had doubts and problems in his mind, and in vain did he seek the venerable Kassapa and Makkhali Gosāla to have them solved while all these were happening. The brother of the religious brotherhood who came to be born in a Brahman family was Nāgasena. When he was seven years old he learnt the three Vedas and all else that could be learnt in a Brahmanical house. Then he left the house, meditated in solitude for sometime and he was afterwards admitted into the order as a novice by a venerable Buddhist priest, Rohaṇa and was eventually converted into Buddhism. He was then

[1] Barua—*Old Brahmi Inscriptions*, p. 172.

sent to Pāṭaliputra to the venerable Buddhist sage Dhammarakkhita where he became an Arahat. Now while he was living there he was invited at the Guarded Slope in the Himalayas by an innumerable company of arahats who were being harassed by King Milinda who delighted in putting knotty questions and arguments this way and that. Nāgasena readily accepted the challenge of Milinda and went to Sāgala attended by a band of samaṇas. Just at that time Milinda had met Āyupāla, an Arahat of the Saṅkheyya monastery, whom too he confronted with his casuistry. Nāgasena who was then living at the same hermitage came now to the rescue of the Order. Milinda with five hundred Yonakas then repaired to Nāgasena, and after mutual exchanges of courtesy and compliments the conversational discourse began.

(*b*) Book II.

The first discourse turned on the distinguishing characteristics of moral qualities. Milinda enquired how Reverend Nāgasena was known and what was his name. Upon it Nāgasena initiated a discussion on the relation between name and individuality, and explained it thoroughly with the help of an instructive simile. The king then, obviously to test his knowledge, put to him a riddle and questioned him as to his seniority of years. Nāgasena fully vindicated himself, and the king then satisfied sought the permission of the Reverend Arahat to discuss with him. The Arahat in his turn told that he was agreeable to a discussion if he would only discuss as a scholar and not as a king. Then one by one Milinda put questions and Nāgasena solved them with his wonderful power of argumentation, simile, and illustration. He contended that there was no soul in the breath ; he explained one by one the aim of Buddhist renunciation, the Buddhist idea of reincarnation, the distinction between wisdom and reasoning, and wisdom and intelligence. He further contended that virtue was the basis of the five moral powers requisite for the attainment of nirvāṇa and that other moral powers were faith,[1] perseverance, mindfulness, and meditation which a recluse should develop in himself. The characteristic marks of each of these qualities were expounded in detail, and their power to put an end to evil dispositions. A very important metaphysical question is next discussed wherein Nāgasena wants to establish with the help mainly of illuminating illustrations that when a man is born, he remains neither the same nor the another; like a child and a growing man through different stages of life. "One comes into being" another passes away; and the rebirth is, as it were, simultaneous. In this connection it is discussed if a man who will not be reborn feel any painful sensation; and then what is after all reborn. A discourse is next initiated as to what is meant by "time", the root and the ultimate point of it. This leads to another discussion as to the origin and developments of qualities, as to other existence or non-existence of anything as soul, which in its turn most naturally leads to a further discussion as regards thought-perception and sight-perception, and lastly to the distinguishing characteristics of contact or phassa, sensation or vedanā, idea or saññā, purpose or cetanā, perception or viññāna, reflection or vitakka, and investigation or vicāra. In all these discourses and solutions, Milinda is fully convinced and is full of admiration for Nāgasena.

(c) Book III.

The second discourse turns on the question of removal of difficulties and dispelling of doubts in the way of attaining a life of renunciation. The various questions as to these doubts are not always related to one another, but all of them are instructive and helpful to solve doubts in the mind of Milinda, the King. He wants to know why really there is so much distinction between man and man, how renunciation is brought about, what is the character of the influence

---

[1] Cf. Summary of faith in the Nettipakaraṇa, p. 28.

of karma, and what is after all nirvāṇa, and whether all men attain it or not. The interesting point raised next is whether rebirth and transmigration are one and the same thing, and if there is a soul or any being that transmigrates from this body to another. Among other doubts that conflicted Milinda were if the body were very dear to the Buddhist recluse, if the Buddha had really thirty-two bodily marks of a great man, if the Buddha was pure in conduct, if ordination was a good thing. Milinda further enquired of Nāgasena what had been the real distinction between one full of passion, and one without passion, and lastly what was meant by an Arahat who recollected what was past and done long ago. Then there were also other difficulties of various kinds which were all solved by the venerable Nāgasena. Milinda was satisfied that he had propounded his questions rightly, and the replies had been made rightly. Nāgasena thought that the questions had been well-put and right replies had been given.

(*d*) Book IV.

This book deals with solutions of puzzles arising out of contradictory statements made by the Buddha. These puzzles were many and varied and were distributed in eighty-two dilemmas which were put by Milinda to Nāgasena, who, in his turn, gave satisfactory explanations to each of them. The contradictions in the Buddha's utterances were more apparent than real. About them strife was likely thereafter to arise, and it was difficult to find a teacher like Nāgasena. So an early solution of these dilemmas was imperative for the guidance of intending disciples of the Order. These dilemmas are particularly interesting as well as instructive and it is profitable to be acquainted here with a few examples. Milinda was puzzled by a dilemma—If the Buddha has really passed away, what is the good of paying honour to his relics ? Nāgasena said to him, " Blessed One, O King, is entirely set free from life and he accepts no gifts. If gods or men put up a building to contain the jewel treasure of the relics of a Tathāgata who does not accept their gift, still by that homage paid to the attainment of the supreme good under the form of the jewel treasure of his wisdom do they themselves attain to one or other of the three glorious states (Tisso Sampattiyo). There are other reasons too. For, gods and men by offering reverence to the relics, and the jewel treasure of the wisdom of a Tathāgata, though he has died away, and accepts it not, can cause goodness to arise in them, and by that goodness can assuage and can allay the fever and the torment of the threefold fire. And even if the Buddha has passed away, the possibility of receiving the three attainments is not removed. Beings, oppressed by the sorrow of becoming, can, when they desire the attainments, still receive them by means of the jewel treasure of his relics and of his doctrine, discipline, and teaching. Like the seeds which through the earth attain to higher developments are the gods and men who, through the jewel treasures of the relics and the wisdom of the Tathāgata—though he has passed away and consent not to it—being firmly rooted by the roots of merit, become like unto trees casting a goodly shade by means of the trunk of contemplation, the sap of true doctrine and the branches of righteousness, bearing the flowers of emancipation, and the fruits of monkhood. It is for all these reasons that even when the Buddha has passed away, an act done to him notwithstanding his not consenting thereto, is still of value and bears fruit."

A second dilemma that conflicted Milinda was, how can the Buddha be omniscient, when it is said that he reflects or thinks ? To solve this dilemma, Nāgasena analysed the thinking powers of men from the lowest individual full of lust, ill-will and delusion to the highest Buddha having all knowledge and bearing about in themselves the tenfold power and whose thinking powers are on every point brought quickly into play, and act with ease. He then classified these different kinds of thinking powers into seven classes. The thinking power of the Supreme Buddhas is of the last or seventh class, and its stuff is very fine, the dart is highly tempered and its discharge is highly powerful. It altogether outclasses the other six and is clear and active in its high quality that is beyond an ordinary man's comprehension. It is because the mind of the Blessed One is so clear and active that the Blessed One has worked so many wonders and miracles. For his knowledge is dependent on reflection, and it is on reflection that he knows whatever he wishes to know. It is more rapid than that, and more easy in action in the all-embracing knowledge of the Blessed One, more rapid than his reflection. His all-embracing knowledge is like the store-house of a great king who has stores of gold, silver and valuables, and all sorts of eatables ; it is with the help of reflection that the Blessed One grasps easily and at once whatever he wants from the big store-house of his knowledge.

A third dilemma was, why did the Blessed One admit Devadatta to the Order, if he knew of his machinations ? In giving a solution out of this dilemma Nāgasena told Milinda that the Blessed One was both full of mercy and wisdom. It was when he in his mercy and wisdom considered the life history of Devadatta that he perceived how having heaped up karma on karma, he would pass for an endless series of kalpas from torment to torment, and from perdition to perdition. And the Blessed One knew also that the infinite karma of that man would, because he had entered the Order, become finite, and the sorrow caused by the previous karma would also therefore become limited. But if that foolish person were not to enter the Order, then he would continue to heap up karma which would endure for a kalpa. And it was because he knew that that, in his mercy, he admitted him to the Order. And by doing so, the Blessed One acted like a clever physician, and made light the heavy sorrow of Devadatta who would have to suffer many hundreds of thousands of kalpas. For having caused schism in the Order, he (Devadatta) would no doubt suffer pain and misery in the purgatories, but that was not the fault of the Blessed One, but was the effect of his own karma. The Blessed One did in his case act like a surgeon who with all kind intent and for man's good smears a wound with burning ointment, cuts it with lancet, cauterises with caustic, and administers to it a salty wash. So did the Blessed One cause Devadatta to suffer such pain and misery that at the end he might be relieved of all pains and miseries. If he had not done so, Devadatta would have suffered torment in purgatory through a succession of existences, through hundreds of thousands of kalpas.

Of other puzzles that arose in Milinda's mind, mention may be made of three out of many. These were, for example, how was it that an Arahat could do no wrong; why did not the Buddha promulgate all the rules of the Order at once and how could Vessantara's giving away of his children be approved. Speaking as to the faults of the Arahat, Nāgasena told Milinda that the Arahats, like laymen, could be guilty of an offence, but their guilt was neither due to carelessness or thoughtlessness. Sins are of two kinds—those which are a breach of the ordinary moral law, and those which are a breach of the Rules of the Order. Now, an Arahat, in the true sense of the term, cannot be guilty of a moral offence; but it is possible for him to be guilty of any breach of the Rules of the Order of which he might have been ignorant. Next, speaking as to the method of promulgating the Rules from time to time and not all at once, Nāgasena quoted the authority of the Tathāgata; for the Tathāgata thought thus, "If I were to lay down the whole of the hundred and fifty rules at once the people would be filled with fear, those of them who were willing to enter the Order would refrain from doing so, they would not trust my words, and through their want of faith they would be liable to rebirth in states of woe. An occasion arises, therefore, illustrating it with a religious discourse, will I lay down, when the evil has become manifest, each Rule." As to the justification of King Vessantara's giving away his beloved sons in slavery to a Brāhmaṇa, and his dear wife to another man as wife, Nāgasena told Milinda that he who gave gifts in such a way as to bring even sorrow upon others, that giving of his brought forth fruit in happiness and it would lead to rebirths in states of bliss. Even if that be an excessive gift it was not harmful, rather it was praised, applauded, and approved by the wise in the world.

The last four dilemmas of Milinda are concerned with the difficult problem of Nirvāṇa. Is Nirvāṇa all bliss or partly pain ; the form, the figure, duration, etc., of Nirvāṇa, the realisation of Nirvāṇa, and the place of Nirvāṇa, these are the puzzles that inflicted the mind of the king. Nāgasena solved them all one by one to the satisfaction of Milinda. According to him Nirvāṇa is bliss unalloyed, there is no pain in it. It is true that those who are in quest of Nirvāṇa afflict their minds and bodies, restrain themselves in standing, walking and sitting, lying, and in food, suppress their sleep, keep their senses in subjection, abandon their very body and their life. But it is after they have thus, in pain, sought after Nirvāṇa, that they enjoy Nirvāṇa which is all bliss. By no metaphor, or explanation, or reason, or argument can its form or figure, or duration, or measure be made clear, even if it be a condition that exists. But there is something as to its qualities which can be explained. Nirvāṇa is untarnished by any evil dispositions. It allays the thirst of the craving after lusts, desire for future life, and the craving after worldly prosperity. It puts an end to grief, it is an ambrosia. Nirvāṇa is free from the dead bodies of evil dispositions, it is mighty and boundless, it is the abode of great men, and Nirvāṇa is all in blossom of purity, of knowledge and emancipation. Nirvāṇa is the support of life, for it puts an end to old age and death ; it increases the power of Iddhi (miracle) of all beings, it is the source to all beings of the beauty of holiness, it puts a stop to suffering in all beings, to the suffering arising from evil dispositions, and it overcomes in all beings the weakness which arises from hunger and all sorts of pain. Nirvāṇa is not born, neither does it grow old, it dies not, it passes not away, it has no rebirth, it is unconquerable, thieves carry it not off, it is not attached to anything, it is the sphere in which Arahat moves, nothing can obstruct it, and it is infinite. Nirvāṇa satisfies all desires, it causes delight and it is full of lustre. It is hard to attain to, it is unequalled in the beauty of its perfume, it is praised by all the Noble Ones. Nirvāṇa is beautiful in Righteousness, it has a pleasant taste. It is very exalted, it is immovable, it is accessible to all evil dispositions, it is a place where no evil dispositions can grow, it is free from desire to please and from resentment.

As to the time of Nirvāṇa, it is not past, nor future, nor present, nor produced, nor not produced, nor producible. Peaceful, blissful, and delicate, Nirvāṇa always exists. And it is that which he who orders his life aright, grasping the idea of all things according to the teaching of the conquerors realises by his wisdom. It is known by freedom from distress and danger, by confidence, by peace, by calm, by bliss, by happiness, by delicacy, by purity, and by freshness. Lastly as to the place of Nirvāṇa, there is no spot either in the East, or the South, or the West or the North, either above or below where Nirvāṇa is. Yet it exists just as fire exists even if there is no place where it is stored up. If a man rubs two sticks together, the fire comes out, so Nirvāṇa exists for a man who orders his life well. But there is such a place on which a man may stand, and ordering his life aright, he can realise Nirvāṇa, and such a place is virtue.

This book deals with solutions of problems of

inference. Milinda asked Nāgasena how they could know that Buddha had ever lived. Nāgasena told him that as the existence of ancient kings was known by their royal insignia, their crown, their slippers, and their fans, so was the existence of Buddha known by the royal insignia used by the Blessed One and by the thirty-five constituent qualities that make up Arahatship which formed the subject of discourse delivered by Gotama before his death to his disciples. By these can the whole world of gods and men know and believe that the Blessed One existed once. By this reason, by this argument, through this inference, can it be known that the Blessed One lived. Just at the sight of a beautiful and well-planned city, one can know the ability of the architect, so can one, on examining the City of Righteousness which the Buddha built up, come to know of his ability and existence.

(e) Book V.

The sixth book opens with an interesting discussion. Can laymen attain Nirvāṇa? Nāgasena told that even laymen and women could see face to face the condition of peace, the supreme good, Nirvāṇa. "But, what purpose then do extra vows serve?" asked Milinda again. To this Nāgasena replied that the keeping of vows implied a mode of livelihood without evil, it has blissful calm as its fruit, it avoided blame and it had such twenty-eight good qualities on account of which all the Buddhas alike longed for them and held them dear. And whosoever thoroughly carried out the vows, they became completely endowed with eighteen good qualities without a previous keeping of the vows by those who became endowed with these good qualities, there was no realisation of Arahatship; and there was no perception of the truth to those who were not purified by the virtues that depended on the keeping of the vows. Nāgasena next explained in detail with the help of a good number of similes the character that came as a result of keeping

(f) Book VI.

the vows for the good growth of the seed of renunciation and for the attainment of Nirvāṇa. But those who being unworthy take the vows incur a twofold punishment and suffer the loss of the good that may be in him. He shall receive disgrace and scorn and suffer torment in the purgatory. On the contrary, those who being worthy take the vows with the idea of upholding the truth deserve a twofold honour. For he comes near and dear to gods and men, and the whole religion of the recluses becomes his very own. Nāgasena then gave Milinda the details of the thirteen extra vows by which a man should bathe in the mighty waters of Nirvāṇa. Upasena the elder, practised all these purifying merits of the vows and Blessed One was delighted at his conduct. The thirty graces of the true recluse are detailed next and whosoever is endowed with these graces is said to have abounded in the peace and bliss of Nirvāṇa. Sāriputta, according to Nāgasena, was one like this who became in this life of such exalted virtue that he was the one who, after the Master, set rolling the royal chariot-wheel of the Kingdom of Righteousness in the religion of Gotama, the Blessed One.

(g) Book VII.

The seventh or the last book is concerned with a detailed list of the similes or qualities of Arahatship; of these similes thirty-eight have been lost and sixty-seven are still preserved. Any member of the Order who wishes to realise Arahatship must be endowed with these one hundred and five qualities. Milinda silently and reverently heard detailed descriptions of these qualities; and at the end he was full of admiration for the venerable Thera Nāgasena for his wonderful solution of the three hundred and four puzzles. He was filled with joy of heart; and all pride was suppressed within him. He ceased to have any more doubts and became aware of the virtue of the religion of the Buddhas. He then entreated Nāgasena to be accepted as a supporter of the Faith and as a true convert from that day onward as long as life should last. Milinda did homage to Nāgasena and had a vihāra built called the 'Milinda-Vihāra' which he handed over to Nāgasena.

The Milinda Pañha like the Bhagavat Gītā is the most interesting and instructive literary production of an age which is heroic. Its long narrative is composed of a long series of philosophical contest between two great heroes, King Milinda on the one hand and the Thera Nāgasena on the other. A pubba-yoga or prelude is skilfully devised to arouse a curiosity in the reader to witness the contest and watch the final result with a great eagerness. On the whole, the Milinda successfully employs a novel literary device to put together the isolated and disconnected controversies in the Kathāvatthu as representing different stages in the progress of the philosophical battle, and in doing so it has been in one place guilty of the literary plagiarism in respect of introducing King Milinda as a contemporary of the six heretical teachers on the model of the Sāmaññaphala Sutta.

Place and country names in the Milinda Pañha.

Alasanda (dīpa)—the island town of Alexandria on the Indus, founded by Alexander.

Yavana (Bactria)—That province watered by the Oxus or the Amu Daria and the premier satrapy of the Achæmenian kings later on came to be conquered by Alexander and in 321 B.C. fell to the share of Seleukos Nikator. Hundred years later the Bactrian Greeks threw off their allegiance to their Seleukidan lord, asserted independence, and gradually moved towards India to establish there an independent principality. Milinda or Menander was one of the kings of this line of Bactrian Greeks who came to establish their power in India.

Bharukaccha—an ancient seaport equivalent to modern Broach in the Kaira district in Guzrat; Barygaza of the Greek geographers.

Cīna (country)—China.

Gandhāra (raṭṭhaṁ)—an important ancient kingdom that had its capital at Puruṣapura or Peshwar in the North-western Frontier Province.

Kaliṅga—an ancient kingdom on the Orissan coast, identical with the modern Ganjam region. All older works, such as the Jātaka, Mahāvastu, and Dīgha Nikāya, mention a kingdom named Kaliṅga with its capital Dantapura ages before Buddha's time.

Kalasa (gāma)—a village situated in the Alasanda island on the Indus; the birthplace of Milinda.

Kajaṅgala—mentioned in very early Buddhist Pāli texts as a locality somewhere near Rajmahal.

Kasmīr (raṭṭhaṁ)—a famous kingdom in the North of India.

Kosala—an ancient province identical with South Bihar, capital Śrāvastī.

Kolopattanam—an ancient seaport probably on the Coromandel coast.

Magadha (raṭṭhaṁ)—an ancient kingdom identical with East Bihar; capital Pāṭaliputra.

Madhurā (nigamo)—an ancient city identical with modern Mathurā. Coins of Menander have been found here.

Nikumba (raṭṭhaṁ)—somewhere in the north-west of India.

Sāgala (nagaraṁ)—identical with Sākala, modern Sialkot, capital city of the King Milinda.

Sāketa—identical with ancient Ayodhyā country.

Saka country—the kingdom of the Sakas or Scythians in the time of Menander was confined to the Bactrian lands south of the Oseus and to Sogdiana to the north.

Sovīra—ancient Sauvīra, the country of the Sauvīra tribe adjacent to the Sindhu country.

Suraṭṭho (nigamo)—an ancient seaport identical with modern Surat.

Bārāṇasī—modern Benares.

Suvaṇṇabhūmī—identical probably with Lower Burma and Malay Peninsula.

Pāṭaliputra (nagaraṁ)—an ancient city, capital of Magadha near modern Patna.

Udicca—a country in the north-west of India.

Vaṅga—identical with East Bengal.

Vilāta—an ancient kingdom somewhere in the north-west of India.

Takkola—an ancient seaport near Thaton in Lower Burma.

Ujjenī—identical with ancient Ujjayinī, capital of the ancient Malwa country.

Greek (country)—ancient Greece in Eastern Europe.

Names of rivers in the Milinda Pañha.

1. Gaṅgā—The Ganges.

2. Acīravatī—an ancient river in Eastern India flowing through the Kosala country past Śrāvastī.

3. Yamunā—a tributary of the Ganges, the Isamos of the Greeks.

4. Sarabhū—identical with Sarayū, a tributary of the Ganges.

5. Mahī—a river south to the Vindhyas flowing into the Bay of Bengal. These five rivers are often mentioned together in the Piṭakas.

6. Sarassatī—an ancient tributary of the Indus.

7. Vitaṁsa—identical probably with Vitastā, a tributary of the Indus, the Hydaspes of the Greeks.

8. Candrabhāgā—identical with modern Chenab, a tributary of the Indus.

A. Books silently referred to :—

Books referred to and mentioned in the Milinda Pañha.

1. Dīgha Nikāya, 2. Kathāvatthu, 3. Aṅguttara Nikāya, 4. Mahāvagga, 5. Cullavagga, 6. Vessantara Jātaka, 7. Sivi Jātaka, 8. Majjhima Nikāya, 9. Sutta Vibhaṅga, 10. Cātuma Sutta, 11. Dhammacakka-pavattana Sutta, 12. Amba Jātaka, 13. Dummedha Jātaka, 14. Tittira Jātaka, 15. Khantivāda Jātaka, 16. Cūla-nandiya Jātaka, 17. Taccha-Sūkara Jātaka, 18. Cariyā-piṭaka, 19. Silavanāga Jātaka, 20. Sabbadāṭha Jātaka, 21. Apaṇṇaka Jātaka, 22. Nigrodha-miga Jātaka, 23. Mahāpaduma

Jātaka, 24. Ummagga Jātaka, 25. Sutta Nipāta, 26. Thera Gāthā, 27. Saṁyutta Nikāya, 28. Dhammapada, and 29. Nigrodha Jātaka.

Books or passages of books mentioned by name.

1. Vinaya, Sutta, Abhidhamma, 2. The Suttantas, 3. Dhamma-Saṅgaṇi, 4. Vibhaṅga, 5. Dhātu-Kathā, 6. Puggala Paññatti, 7. Kathā-Vatthu, 8. Yamaka, 9. Paṭṭhāna, 10. The Abhidhamma Piṭaka, 11. The Vinaya Piṭaka, 12. The Sutta Piṭaka, 13. Mahā-Samaya Suttanta—(Dīgha Nikāya), 14. Mahā-maṅgala Suttanta—(Sutta Nipāta), 15. Sama-cittapariyāya Suttanta—(unknown), 16. Rāhulvāda Suttanta (Majjhima), 17. Parābhava Suttanta—(Sutta Nipāta), 18. Saṁyutta Nikāya, 19. The Sutta Nipāta, 20. Ratana Sutta—(Sutta Nipāta), 21. Khandha Parittā—(not traced), 22. Mora Parittā, 23. Dhajagga Parittā—(Jātaka Book), 24. Āṭānāṭiya Parittā—(Dīgha Nikāya), 25. Aṅgulimāla Parittā—(Majjhima Nikāya), 26. The Pātimokkha, 27. Dhamma-dāyāda Sutta (Majjhima Nikāya), 28. Dakkhina Vibhaṅga of the Majjhima Nikāya, 29. Cariyā Piṭaka, 30. Navangaṁ Buddha Vacanaṁ, 31. Dīgha Nikāya, 32. Majjhima Nikāya, 33. Khuddaka Nikāya, 34. Mahā Rāhulovāda (Majjhima Nikāya), 35. Purā-bheda Suttanta (Sutta Nipāta), 36. Kalaha Vivāda Suttanta (Sutta Nipāta), 37. Cūla-Vyūha Suttanta (Sutta Nipāta), 38. Mahā-Vyūha Suttanta (Sutta Nipāta), 39. Tuvaṭaka Suttanta (Sutta Nipāta), 40. Sāriputta Suttanta (Sutta Nipāta), 41. Mahāsamaya Suttanta (Dīgha Nikāya), 42. Sakkha-Pañha Suttanta (Dīgha Nikāya), 43. Tirokuḍḍa Suttanta (Khuddaka Pāṭha), 44. Ekuttara Nikāya (Aṅguttara Nikāya), 45. Dhaniya Sutta (Sutta Nipāta), 46. Kummūpama Suttanta (Saṁyutta Nikāya), 47. Sacca Saṁyutta (Saṁyutta Nikāya), 48. Vidhura Puṇṇaka Jātaka, 49. Dhammapada, 50. Sutasoma Jātaka, 51. Kaṇha Jātaka, 52. Lomahaṁsana Pariyāya, 53. Cakkavāka Jātaka, 54. Culla Nārada Jātaka, 55. Lakkhaṇa Suttanta (Dīgha Nikāya), 56. Bhallāṭiya Jātaka, 57. Parinibbāna Suttanta (Dīgha Nikāya).

V. Trenckner's edition of the Milinda Pañha first published by Williams and Norgate in 1880 has been reprinted by the trustee of the James G. Forlong Fund, Royal Asiatic Society, in 1928 with a general index by C. J. Rylands and an index of gāthās by Mrs. Rhys Davids. There is another edition of this work by Hsaya Hbe, Rangoon, 1915. A Burmese word for word interpretation of this text by Ādiccavaṁsa, Rangoon, should be consulted. It has been translated into English by T. W. Rhys Davids and included in the Sacred Books of the East Series as Vols. XXXV-XXXVI. There is a Sinhalese translation of the Milinda Pañha by Hīnaṭi Kumbure under the title "Milinda prashnaya", Colombo, 1900.

The following books may be consulted :—

1. Le Bonheur du Nirvāṇa extrait du Milindapprashnaya ; ou Miroir des doctrines sacrees traduit du Pali par Lewis da Sylva Pandit. (Revue de l'histoire des religions, Paris, 1885.)

2. Deux Traductions chinoises du Milinda Pañha Par E. Specht arec introduction par S. Levi.

3. Chinese translations of the Milinda Pañha by Takakusu, J.R.A.S., 1896. This paper contains a number of Chinese translations in existence, the date of the two translations and the story of the discussions of King Milinda and Bhikkhu Nāgasena found in the Buddhist sūtra called Saṁyutta-Ratnapiṭaka.

4. Historical basis for the questions of King Menander from the Tibetan by L. A. Waddel, J.R.A.S., 1897. This paper points out that the Milinda Pañha is known to the Tibetans.

5. Nāgasena by Dr. T. W. Rhys Davids, J.R.A.S., 1891.

6. Milinda Questions by Mrs. Rhys Davids, 1930.

7. Critical and philological notes to the first chapter of the Milinda Pañha by V. Trenckner revised and edited by Dr. Anderson, J.P.T.S., 1908.

8. Paul Pelliot—Les noms propres dans les traductions chinoises du Milinda Pañha. (Journal Asiatic, Paris, 1914.)

9. There is a Bengali edition of this work published by the Bangīya Sāhitya Parishat, Calcutta, which can vie, if it can vie at all, in its uncritical method and blunders.

10. F. Otto Schrader, Die Fragen des Konig Menandros (Berlin, 1903).

11. Garbe, " Der Milindapañha, ein Kulturhistorischer Roman ", Indische Kulturgeschichte.

12. G. Cagnola, Dialoghi del Re Milinda (Italian translation of the Milinda Pañha).

13. Milinda by T. W. Rhys Davids (Encyclopædia of Religion and Ethics, pp. 631–633).

14. M. Winternitz, Geschichte der Indischen Litteratur (vol. 2., Leipzig, 1920).

Earlier Commentaries.

In the Gandhavaṁsa (pp. 58 foll. J.P.T.S., 1886) which is a comparatively modern Pāli compilation we have an interesting classification of the Buddhist teachers of India, Ceylon, and Burma connected with Pāli literature. This classification goes to divide the teachers chronologically into three orders: (1) Porāṇācariyas, (2) Aṭṭhakathācariyas, and (3) Gandhakāracariyas. By the Porāṇācariyas or ancient teachers are meant the distinguished and profoundly learned theras of old numbering about 2,200 Arhats, who as selected representatives of different sections of the orthodox saṁgha took part in the proceedings of the first three Buddhist Councils and rehearsed the canonical texts. These teachers are arbitrarily identified with the Aṭṭhakathācariyas or teachers commanding the commentarial authority. Buddhaghosa and others are, according to this classification, to be counted among the Gandhakāracariyas or teachers representing individual authorship. Such teachers are also to be known as Anekācariyas or different authors.

The Gandhavaṁsa expressly treats the earlier Sinhalese commentaries such as Kurundīya aṭṭhakathā and the Mahāpaccariya aṭṭhakathā presupposed by the writings of Buddhaghosa as remarkable productions of individual authorship.[1]

We may be prepared to appreciate this suggestive chronological classification in so far as it leads us to contemplate the beginning of individual authorship from a certain stage of literary development, a stage which is represented by Buddhadatta, Buddhaghosa, and Dhammapāla. In the first or early stage we have the various texts of the three Pāli piṭakas, all of which the Saṁgītikāras made their own by virtue of a joint rehearsal and canonisation. Though tradition ascribes the Kathāvatthu and the Parivārapāṭha to two different authors, namely, Moggaliputtatissa and the learned Dīpa, one need not be astonished to find that the claim of individual authorship has altogether merged in the interests of the Saṁgītikāras, and ultimately of the saṁgha as a whole.

The authority of the Milinda Pañha has been wrongly cited by Buddhaghosa and others with the stamp of individual authorship of thera Nāgasena. It is the same thing to ascribe the Milinda Pañha to the authorship of Nāgasena as to ascribe all the Pāli canonical texts to the authorship of the Buddha. As a matter of fact Nāgasena plays no more than the rôle of the more powerful of the two controversialists in the dramatic narrative of the Milinda Pañha —a position which is in many respects similar to that assigned to Vāsudeva in the dramatic conversational narrative of the Bhagavat Gītā.

The Gandhavaṁsa (p. 59) ascribes the Netti and the Peṭakopadesa along with four other treatises, exegetical and grammatical, to the authorship of Mahākaccāyana,—the venerable Mahākaccāyana who was one of the immediate disciples of the

[1] Gandhavaṁsa, p. 59—"Katame anekācariyehi katā Gandhācariyo kurundīgandhaṁ nāma akāsi. Aññataro ācariyo mahāpaccariyaṁ nāma aṭṭhakathaṁ akāsi. Aññataro ācariyo kurundīgandhassa aṭṭhakathaṁ akāsi".

Buddha, doing his missionary work in western India. This is a lump of anachronism which is too big for a critical scholarly mouth to swallow. As regards individual authorship, the Netti and the Peṭakopadesa stand in the same position as the Milinda Pañha. Have we in this respect to confront a different position with regard to the earlier Sinhalese commentaries under notice ? Highly doubtful is the source of information that has enabled the author of so modern a work as the Gandhavaṁsa to say that a certain individual author wrote out a treatise called Kurundīgandha, another author, the Mahapaccariya-aṭṭhakathā and another author, the Aṭṭhakathā of the Kurundīgandha.

Some earlier commentaries have been quoted by Buddhaghosa without even meaning to regard them as works of any individual authors. Even in cases where he has referred to them as personal authorities, he appears to have recourse to such an indefinite expression as aṭṭhakathācariyas.[1] On the other hand there are several statements in which Buddhaghosa and other commentators have regarded these earlier commentaries not as works of any individual authors but as authoritative books of interpretation of different monastic schools of teachers (cf. Samantapāsādikā, P.T.S., pp. 1-2 ; Atthasālinī, p. 2).

" Mahāvihāravāsīnaṁ dīpayanto vinicchayaṁ
Atthaṁ pakāsayissāmi āgamaṭṭhakathāsupi."

The earlier commentaries mentioned or cited by Buddhaghosa in his Samantapāsādikā, Atthasālinī, Sumaṅgalavilāsinī, and other commentaries are :—

(1) The Mahā Aṭṭhakathā.
(2) The Mahāpaccariya.
(3) The Kurundī or Kurundiya.[2]
(4) Andha Aṭṭhakathā.
(5) Saṁkhepa Aṭṭhakathā.

[1] Atthasālinī, pp. 85, 123, and 217
[2] Samantapāsādikā, p. 2, v. 10.

(6) Āgamaṭṭhakathā.[1]
(7) Ācariyānaṁ samānaṭṭhakathā.[2] (?)

According to the Saddhama Sangaha, the Mahā, the Mahāpaccari, and the Kurunda are the three earlier Sinhalese commentaries quoted by Buddhaghosa in his Samantapāsādikā while the Mahāaṭṭhakathā was made the basis of his commentaries on the first four nikayas.[3]

The Porāṇas and the Aṭṭhakathācariyas represent indeed a broad chronological classification of the pubbācariyas which may as well be inferred from Buddhaghosa's own statements. In the prologue of his Samantapāsādikā, he expressly says that the Mahā, the Mahāpaccari, and the Kurundī are the three earlier commentaries that were written in the native dialect of Sīhala (Ceylon) (saṁvaṇṇanā sīhaladīpakena vākyena, Samantapāsādikā, I, p. 2).

The Mahā-aṭṭhakathā otherwise known as the mūla aṭṭhakathā or simply the aṭṭhakathā is undoubtedly the old Sinhalese commentary on the three piṭakas developed in the school of the Mahāvihāra or Great Minster at Anurādhapura. There was a second monastery at Anurādhapura called Uttaravihāra or North Minster. A commentarial tradition was developed also in this school. The distinction between the traditions of Mahāvihāra and Uttaravihāra would seem to lie in the background of Buddhadatta's two Vinaya manuals—the Vinayavinicchaya and the Uttaravinicchaya. The name of Mahāpaccari or Great Raft can be so called "from its having been composed on a raft somewhere in Ceylon" (Saddhammasaṁgaha, p. 55). The suggested origin of the name is quite fanciful and therefore unreliable like the Mahā or mūla. The Mahāpaccari appears to have been a distinct compilation of a monastic school of Ceylon. The Kurundī was

1 Atthasālinī, p. 2.
2 *Ibid.*, p. 90.
3 Saddhama Sangaha, pp. 55-56, J.P.T.S., 1890.

so called because it was composed at the Kurundaveḷuvihāra in Ceylon (Saddhammasaṁgaha, p. 55).

The Andha-aṭṭhakathā represented a commentarial tradition handed down at Kañcipura (Conjeveram) in South India. Presumably it was written in some native dialect of the Deccan.

The Saṁkhepa aṭṭhakathā or short commentary is mentioned together with the Andha commentary and it is likely that like the latter it was a South Indian work.

The Āgamaṭṭhakathā referred to in Buddhaghosa's Atthasālinī is now taken to be an old general commentary on the āgamas or nikāyas.

Ācariyānaṁ Samānaṭṭhakathā has been catalogued by Mrs. Rhys Davids as though it were a separate commentary but the context of the passage in Buddhaghosa's Atthasālinī (p. 90) in which the term occurs, shows the matter to be otherwise. By this expression (Ettikā ācariyānaṁsamānaṭṭhakathā nāma, Atthasālinī, p. 90) Buddhaghosa appears simply to mean an explanation which is common to all the schools of interpretation. If so, there will be no justification whatever for regarding the term ācariyānaṁ samānaṭṭhakathā as a title of any commentary.

Jātaka-aṭṭhakathā.

Fausböll's edition of the Jātaka commentary now extant is known by the name of Jātakatthavaṇṇanā[1] containing about 550 Jātakas.[2] In the Jātakatthavaṇṇanā itself there is a reference to an older commentary namely, the Jātaka-aṭṭhakathā which, as rightly guessed by Prof. Rhys Davids, is "the older commentary of Elu, or old Singhalese, on which the present work is based".[3] This older commentary must have been the source from which

[1] Fausböll's Jātaka, Vol. I, p. 1—"......Jātakass' Atthavaṇṇanaṁ Mahāvihāravāsīnaṁ vācanāmagganissitaṁ bhāsissaṁ".

[2] Strictly speaking the total number of the Jātakas contained in it is 547.

[3] Buddhist Birth Stories, p. 173, f.n. 2; Fausböll's Jātaka, I, p. 62.

Buddhaghosa has quoted several birth stories in his commentaries. Judging by Buddhaghosa's narrations of the Jātakas bearing a close resemblance with those in the present Atthavaṇṇanā, we can say that the contents and arrangement of the Jātakas in the Aṭṭhakathā had not materially differed from those in the Atthavaṇṇanā. It is evident from Buddhaghosa's own statement in his Sumaṅgalavilāsinī that the total number of the Jātakas already came to be counted in his time as 550.[1] But as shown by Dr. B. M. Barua, the earlier total as mentioned in the Cullaniddesa (p. 80—"Bhagavā pañca jātaka-satāni bhāsanto attano ca paresañ ca atītaṁ ādisati"), which is a canonical commentary on the Khaggavisāṇa Sutta and the suttas of the Pārāyaṇavagga, was not 550 but 500 (pañcajātaka-satāni). He seems to think that the same inference as to the earlier total of the Jātakas may as well be drawn from an account of the Chinese pilgrim Fa-Hien stating that he witnessed representations of 500 Jātakas when he visited Ceylon in the beginning of the 5th century A.D.[2] The various literary processes by which the Jātakas were mechanically multiplied have been well discussed[3] and need no further orientation here.

Buddhasīha's Vinayavinicchaya.

The word vinicchaya means "investigation, trial, ascertainment, and decision". The meaning which suits the title of the work under notice is "decision". Certain decisions helping the right interpretation and application of the Vinaya rules and prescriptions embodied in the Vinaya Piṭaka grew up as a result of discussions among the theras of Ceylon and South India, the decisions of the Mahāvihāra school being generally regarded as the

---

[1] Sumaṅgalāvilāsinī, I, p. 24—"Apaṇṇaka-jātakādīni paññāsādhikāni pañca-jātaka-satāni Jātakan ti veditabbam".

[2] The Travels of Fa-hsien by H. A. Giles, p. 71—"repre[illegible] of the five hundred different forms in which the Bodhi[illegible] cessively appeared".

[3] B. M. Barua's paper—Multiplication of the Jātak[illegible]

most authoritative. These decisions referred to in the lump by Buddhaghosa as aṭṭhakathāvinicchayas were also incorporated in such Sinhalese commentaries as the Mahā (Mahāvihāra), the Mahākarundiya, and the Mahāpaccariya. It was binding on Buddhaghosa and other later commentators to see that the interpretations suggested by them were not only not inconsistent with the canonical texts but also with the aṭṭhakathāvinicchayas.[1] In many places of his Samantapāsādikā Buddhaghosa has termed even his own decisive interpretation as a Vinicchaya.[2] Even apart from the decisive interpretations in the earlier Sinhalese commentaries Buddhaghosa appears to have cited certain authoritative Vinayavinicchayas without mentioning the source from which he cited them. Looking out for the source we are apt to be led back to a treatise written by thera Buddhasīha which clearly bore the title of Vinayavinicchaya.

In the epilogue of his Vinayavinicchaya Buddhadatta expressly says that his own work was nothing but an abridged form of Buddhasīha's treatise. Buddhasīha himself is represented as a saddhivihārī or a fellow monk residing in the monastery erected by Veṇhudāsa or Kaṇhadāsa in the beautiful river port of Kāverī.[3]

No trace of Buddhasīha'a treatise lingers except perhaps in citations in Buddhaghosa's Samantapāsādikā. The treatise was in all probability written in prose while Buddhadatta's is a manual written entirely in verse.

Narasīhagāthā is the title of an interesting Pāli

---

[1] Samantapāsādikā, p. 539. In discarding a particular interpretation, Buddhaghosa says "aṭṭhakathā vinicchayehi na sameti", i.e., it does not tally with the decisions of the commentaries.

[2] Cf. Samantapāsādikā, p. 648: "Ayaṁ tāva anto dasāhaṁ adhiṭṭheti vikappetīti ettha adhiṭṭhāne *vinicchayo*". Again at p. 649 'ayaṁ vikappetīti imasmim pade *vinicchayo*'.

[3] Buddhadatta's Vinayavinicchaya, p. 229.

"vuttassa Buddhasīhena Vinayassa vinicchayo
Buddhasīhaṁ samuddissa mama saddhivihārikaṁ
kato 'yam pana bhikkhūnaṁ hitatthāya samāsato."

octade consisting of eight stanzas composed in an elegant style. The theme of this poem which became very popular throughout Ceylon is a description of 32 major bodily marks of the Buddha represented as a lion-like man (narasīha). The gāthās are characteristically put into the mouth of Rāhulamātā. Only the first stanza of the ancient octade is quoted in the Pāli Jātakanidānakathā (Fausböll, Jātaka, I, p. 89), the reading of which goes to show that its wording changed here and there in the octade as it comes down to us through the Buddhist literature of Ceylon.

Narasīhagāthā.

(*a*) Earlier reading—

" Siniddhanīlamudukuñcitakeso
suriyasunimmalatalābhinalāṭo
yuttatuṅgamudukāyatanāso
ramsijālavitato narasīho' ti."

(*b*) Later reading—

" Suddhanīlamudukuñcitakeso
suriyanimmalatalābhinalāṭo
yuttatuṅgamudukāyatanāso
ramsijālopitāte narasīho."

The octade may be regarded as an earlier specimen of the Sinhalese Pāli poetry.

The Dīpavaṁsa is the oldest known Pāli chronicle of Ceylon (dīpatthuti) and of Buddhism, the account of which is closed with the reign of King Mahāsena which may be assigned to the middle of the 4th century A.D. Buddhaghosa in his commentary on the Kathāvatthu, a book of the Abhidhamma Piṭaka, expressly quotes a number of verses from the Dīpavaṁsa as a traditional authority in support of a certain statement of his, from which it is easy to infer that the chronicle in its present form was extant in the 4th century A.D., if not earlier. It goes without saying that the tradition of both the kings and theras of Ceylon as well as of their Indian contemporaries grew up and accumulated gradually.

Dīpavaṁsa.

The stanzas quoted by Buddhaghosa may be traced *verbatim* in the Dīpavaṁsa (p. 36).[1]

Though a metrical composition, the verses of this earlier chronicle interspersed in places with certain prose passages some of which may be traced in such authoritative canonical texts as the Vinaya Cullavagga.[2] In the opening verses of the Dīpavaṁsa we are told that the chronicle embodied in it was handed down by tradition from man to man (vamsaṁ pavakkhāmi paramparāgataṁ). So we need not be astonished to find certain verses occurring in the Vinaya Parivārapāṭha and furnishing the traditional materials for the Dīpavaṁsa. The verses incorporated in the Parivārapāṭha may be just one of the isolated earlier specimens, there being many others that are probably now lost. Thus what we find in the Dīpavaṁsa is the first fruit of a methodical attempt at the composition of a systematic chronicle narrative on the basis of certain traditions, prevalent in both prose and verse. We need not dilate further on this subject as we have dealt with it in detail in the section on the Pāli chronicles.

**Aṭṭhakathā Mahāvaṁsa.**

The very name of the aṭṭhakathā Mahāvaṁsa may sound strange to the ears of those who are taught to think that the Pāli Mahāvaṁsa is the first work of its kind. To get rid of this predilection the reader may do well to acquaint himself with the

[1] Kathāvatthuppakarana-aṭṭhakathā, J.P.T.S., 1889, p. 3, " Vuttaṁ pi c' etaṁ Dīpavaṁse :
Nikkaḍḍhitā pāpabhikkhū therehi Vajjiputtakā
aññaṁ pakkhaṁ labhitvāna adhammavādī bahū janā.
Dasasahassā samāgantvā akaṁsu dhammasaṁgahaṁ
tasmāyaṁ dhammasaṁgīti mahāsaṁgīti vuccati."

[2] Dīpavaṁsa, p. 33
" tena kho pana samayena vassasatamhi nibbute bhagavati Vesālikā Vajjiputtakā Vesāliyaṁ dasa vatthūni dīpenti : kappati siṅgiloṇakappo, kappati dvaṅgulakappo, kappati gāmantarakappo, kappati āvāsakappo, kappati anumatikappo, kappati āciṇṇakappo, kappati amathitakappo, kappati jalogiṁ pātuṁ, kappati adasakaṁ nisīdanaṁ, kappati jātarūparajatan ti."
Cf. Vinaya Cullavagga, ch. xii, p. 294.

verses forming the prologue of the great chronicle. In these opening verses, the author says :

> " Mahāvaṁsaṁ pavakkhāmi nānānūnādhi-
> kārikaṁ.
> Porāṇehi kato p'eso ativitthārito kvaci,
> atīva kvaci saṁkhitto, anekapunaruttako.
> Vajjitaṁ tehi dosehi sukhaggahaṇadhāraṇaṁ"
> (Mahāvaṁsa, Chapter I).

Dr. Geiger translates " I will recite the Mahāvaṁsa, of varied contents and lacking nothing. That (Mahāvaṁsa) which was compiled by the ancient (sages) was here too long drawn out and there too closely knit ; and contained many repetitions. Attend ye now to this (Mahāvaṁsa) that is free from such faults." (Geiger's translation of the Mahāvaṁsa, p. 1.) Thus the author of the Pāli Mahāvaṁsa himself alludes to an earlier chronicle and claims that the chronicle composed by him was nothing but a thoroughly revised version of the earlier compilation. Here the question arises whether by the earlier compilations the author of the Pāli Mahāvaṁsa intended to mean the Dīpavaṁsa or some other work, especially only bearing the title of Mahāvaṁsa. There are two arguments that may be placed in favour of the Dīpavaṁsa : (1) that the faults—" here too long drawn out and there too closely knit ; and contained many repetitions " are well applicable to the Dīpavaṁsa ; and (2) that the narrative of the Pāli Mahāvaṁsa, precisely like that of the Dīpavaṁsa is closed with an account of the reign of King Mahāsena of Ceylon. Undoubtedly the Dīpavaṁsa is the earlier chronicle on which the Mahāvaṁsa narrative was mainly based. But there are many points of difference, which are in some cases material. These cannot be satisfactorily accounted for without bringing in a somewhat different authority. Fortunately Dr. Geiger in his instructive dissertation on the Dīpavaṁsa and the Mahāvaṁsa has convincingly proved the existence of an earlier great chronicle in Sinhalese.

He has been able to ascertain that the earlier form of the great chronicle was a part of a commentary written in old Sinhalese prose mingled with Pāli verses. The commentary could be found in different monasteries of Ceylon and it is just the other earlier work that served as a basis of the Pāli Mahāvaṁsa ascribed to Thera Mahānāma (Geiger, Mahāvaṁsa tr., intro., p. x).

The Schools of reciters: their views and interpretations.

Among the important citizens of the ideal Dhammanagara the Milinda Pañha mentions some six schools of reciters of the Buddhist holy texts, namely, (1) Jātakabhāṇakā, the reciters of the Jātakas, (2) Dīghabhāṇakā, the reciters of the Dīgha Nikāya, (3) Majjhimabhāṇakā, the reciters of the Majjhima Nikāya, (4) Saṁyuttabhāṇakā, the reciters of the Saṁyutta Nikāya, (5) Aṅguttarabhāṇakā, the reciters of the Aṅguttara Nikāya, and (6) the Khuddakabhāṇakā, the reciters of the Khuddaka Nikāya. To this list may be added Dhammapadabhāṇakā, the reciters of the Dhammapada, mentioned in Buddhaghosa's Atthasālinī (p. 18). Bhāṇaka or a reciter of the Buddhist holy texts is met with in a large number of Buddhist votive inscriptions at Bharaut and Sāñci as a distinctive epithet of the monks. Buddhaghosa in the introduction to his Sumaṅgalavilāsinī records a remarkable tradition accounting for the origin of the different schools of the bhāṇakās. The same tradition is met with in the Mahābodhivaṁsa with a slight variation. According to this tradition, it so happened that during the session of the first Buddhist Council as soon as the Vinaya was recited and the Vinaya texts were compiled, the preservation of the Vinaya traditions and texts by regular recitations was entrusted to the care of the venerable Upāli while in the course of rehearsal of the Dhammapada, the Dīghāgama or the Dīgha Nikāya came to be compiled, the preservation of this text was entrusted to the care of the venerable Ānanda; in a similar way the preservation of the Majjhimāgama or the

Majjhima Nikāya was entrusted to the care of the disciples of Sāriputta; that of Saṁyuttāgama or the Saṁyutta Nikāya was entrusted to the care of the venerable Kassapa, that of the Ekuttarāgama was entrusted to the care of the venerable Anuruddha. Thus one is to conceive the rise of the five schools of bhāṇakās, to wit, Vinayabhāṇakā, Dīghabhāṇakā, Majjhimabhāṇakā, Saṁyuttabhāṇakā, and Aṅguttarabhāṇakā (Barua and Sinha, Bharut Inscriptions, p. 9; Sumaṅgalavilāsinī, I, pp. 13–15).

With the progress of time, anyhow by the time of Buddhaghosa the schools of reciters appear to have developed into some distinct schools of opinion and interpretation. No other reasonable inference may be drawn from Buddhaghosa's citations of their authorities.[1] The individual teachers of Ceylon[2] whose views have been quoted and discussed here and there by Buddhaghosa in his various commentaries may be supposed to have belonged to this or that school of reciters[3] and we need not consider their case separately here.

[1] Sumaṅgalavilāsinī, I. p. 15. "Tato paraṁ Jātakaṁ Mahāniddeso Cūla-niddeso Paṭi-sambhidā-maggo Sutta-nipāto Dhammapadaṁ Udānaṁ Itivuttakaṁ Vimāna-peta-vatthu Thera-therīgāthā ti imaṁ tantiṁ saṁgāyitvā Khuddaka-gantho nāma ayan ti ca vatvā, Abhidhamma-piṭakasmiṁ yeva saṁgahaṁ āropayiṁsūti Dīgha-bhāṇakā vadanti, Majjhima-bhāṇakā pana Cariyā-piṭaka-Apadāna-Buddhavaṁsesu saddhiṁ sabbam pi taṁ Khuddaka-ganthaṁ suttanta-piṭake pariyāpannan ti vadanti."

Atthasālinī, p. 18—" Dhammapadabhāṇakā pana
Anekajātisaṁsāraṁ sandhāvissaṁ anibbisaṁ
gahakārakaṁ gavesanto. Dukkhā jāti punappunaṁ.
Gahakāraka diṭṭho 'si puna gehaṁ na kāhasi,
Sabbā te phāsukā bhaggā gahakūṭaṁ visaṅkhitaṁ,
visaṅkhāragataṁ cittaṁ taṇhānaṁ khayam ajjhagā ti
Idaṁ paṭhamabuddhavacanaṁ nāmā ti vadanti ".

See for other references Atthasālinī, pp. 151, 399, 420 noticed for the first time by Mrs. Rhys Davids in her Buddhist Manual of Psychological Ethics, p. xxx.

[2] We mean such teachers as Tipiṭaka Cūḷanāga thera in the Atthasālinī, pp. 229, 230, 266, 267, 284 and the Tipiṭaka Mahādhammarakkhita thera in the *ibid.*, pp. 267, 278, 286, 287.

[3] Cf. Visuddhimagga, p. 313.
Saṁyuttabhāṇaka-Cūḷa-Sīvathera.

CHAPTER V

# PĀLI COMMENTARIES

Before proceeding to deal with the Pāli commentaries it would be interesting to record here biographical sketches of three of the most celebrated Buddhist scholiasts.

Buddhadatta.

Buddhadatta, a contemporary of Buddhaghosa, was a celebrity of the Mahāvihāra of Ceylon and was an inhabitant of the Kāverī region in the kingdom of the Choḷas. He was born in Uragapura (modern Uraiyūr)[1] and flourished during the reign of King Accutavikkanta of the Kalamba (Kadamba) dynasty. His works which were all written in the famous monastery erected by Kaṇhadāsa (Kiṣṇadāsa) or Veṇhudāsa (Viṣṇudāsa), evidently a new Vaiṣṇava reformer of the Deccan,[2] on the banks of the river Kāverī are so far as known to comprise the following:

(1) Uttaravinicchaya
(2) Vinayavinicchaya
(3) Abhidhammāvatāra
(4) Rūpārūpavibhāga
} Known as Buddhadatta's Manuals.

and (5) Madhuratthavilāsinī, a commentary on the Buddhavaṁsa.

He was a patriotic poet of considerable reputation. It is stated in the Vinayavinicchaya that when Buddhadatta was going to India from Ceylon, he was met by Buddhaghosa who was then proceeding to Ceylon at the request of the Buddhist monks of India with the object of translating the Sinhalese commentaries into Pāli. Hearing of the mission of Buddhaghosa of whose deep learning he was fully convinced and delighted thereat Buddhadatta spoke

---

1 Barua, Religion of Asoka; Bhandarkar, Asoka, 2nd Ed., p. 42.

2 Skandapurāṇa, Brahmakhaṇḍa.

thus, "When you finish the commentaries, please send them up to me so that I may summarise your labours". Buddhaghosa said that he would gladly comply with this request and the Pāli commentaries were accordingly placed in the hands of Buddhadatta who summed up the commentaries on the Abhidhamma in the Abhidhammāvatāra and those on the Vinaya in the Vinayavinicchaya (*vide* Buddhadatta's Manuals or Summaries of Abhidhamma, edited by A. P. Buddhadatta, for the P.T.S. in 1915, p. xix). Buddhadatta was no doubt a great scholar. From the Vinayavinicchaya commentary we know that he was highly esteemed by the eminent commentators, Sāriputta Saṅgharāja, Buddhaghosa, and other great scholars of the period for his scholarly attainments (cf. Mādisāpi kavī honti Buddhadatte divaṅgate).

Buddhadatta opens his scheme with a fourfold division of the compendium, e.g., mind, mental properties, material quality, and Nibbāna; while Buddhaghosa expounds his psychology in terms of the five Khandhas. In this respect Buddhadatta's representation is perhaps better than that of Buddhaghosa.[1]

There is no reason to disbelieve the statement that the two teachers met each other. It is clear that they drew materials from the same source. This fact well explains why the Visuddhimagga and the Abhidhammāvatāra have so many points in common. Buddhadatta has rendered invaluable service to the study of the Abhidhamma tradition which has survived in Theravada Buddhism to the present day. The legendary account is that Buddhadatta put in a condensed shape that which Buddhaghosa handed on in Pāli from the Sinhalese commentaries. "But the psychology and philosophy are presented through the prism of a second vigorous intellect, under fresh aspects, in a style often less discursive and more graphic than that of the

---

[1] Mrs. Rhys Davids, Buddhist Psychology, Second Ed., p. 174.

great commentator, and with a strikingly rich vocabulary."

As we have already pointed out that when on sea Buddhadatta met Buddhaghosa and learnt that the latter was going to Ceylon to render the Sinhalese commentaries into Pāli. He requested Buddhaghosa to send him the commentaries when finished so that he might summarise his labours. Buddhaghosa complied with his request. Buddhadatta then summed up the commentaries on the Abhidhamma in the Abhidhammāvatāra and then on the Vinaya in the Vinayavinicchaya. Mrs. Rhys Davids says, "It is probably right to conclude that they both were but handing on an analytical formula which had evolved between their own time and that of the final closing of the Abhidhamma Piṭaka (Buddhist Psychology, Second Ed., p. 179).

Like Buddhaghosa, Buddhadatta employed the simile of the purblind and the lame to explain the relation between Nāma and Rūpa (Abhidhammāvatāra, P.T.S., p. 115). Buddhadatta's division of the term into Samūha and Asamūha is another interesting point (*ibid.*, p. 83). It will be remembered that such a division of terms as this was far in advance of the older classification embodied in the Puggalapaññatti commentary (P.T.S., p. 173).

Supposing that Kumāragupta I of the Imperial Gupta dynasty was a contemporary King of Ceylon and that Buddhaghosa was a contemporary of Thera Buddhadatta it follows that King Accutavikkanta of the Kalamba dynasty was a contemporary of Kumāragupta I.

According to Rev. A. P. Buddhadatta, Buddhadatta was either older than Buddhaghosa or of the same age with him. "Ayaṁpana Buddhadattācariyo Buddhaghosācariyena samāna vassiko vā thokaṁ vuḍḍhataro vā ti sallakkhema" (Viññāpanaṁ, pp. xiii-xiv, Buddhadatta's Manuals, 1915). This statement is however doubtful. In the Buddhaghosuppatti (p. 50) we find Buddhadatta addressing Buddhaghosa by the epithet 'Āvusa' which is applied to one who is younger in age. The passage runs thus "Āvuso Buddhaghosa, aham tayā pubbe Laṅkādīpe Bhagavato sāsanaṁ kātum āgatomhī ti vatvā, ahaṁ appāyuko......". This shows that according to the tradition recorded in the Buddhaghosuppatti, Buddhaghosa was younger than Buddhadatta.

The different accounts of the comparative age of Buddhadatta and Buddhaghosa are hardly reconcilable. The account given in the introduction of the Abhidhammāvatāra clearly shows that Buddhadatta lived to write abridgments of some of Buddhaghosa's works. This goes against the legend contained in the Buddhaghosuppatti that Buddhadatta left Ceylon earlier than Buddhaghosa without translating the Sinhalese Aṭṭhakathā apprehending that he was not to live long.

Buddhaghosa.

In the history of Pāli literature, the name of Buddhaghosa stands out pre-eminent as one of the greatest commentators and exegetists. He is one of those Indian celebrities who have left for us no other records of their career than their teachings and works to be appraised for what they are worth. So far as his life history is concerned we have nothing except his commentaries and a few legends and traditions, and it is not an easy matter to separate the few grains of biographical detail from the mass of extraneous matter gathered in them. Besides the meagre references that Buddhaghosa himself has made to the details of his life in his great commentaries, the earliest connected account of his life is that contained in the second part of Chapter XXXVII of the great Ceylonese chronicle, the Mahāvaṁsa. This section, however, is considered to be later than the remaining portions of the Chronicle, having been added by Dhammakitti, a Ceylonese Śramaṇa of the middle of the 13th century A.D. This compilation though made after the lapse of more than eight hundred years is not altogether unworthy of credence, and is very probably derived from older materials.

Buddhaghosa, according to this account, was a brahmin youth born in the neighbourhood of the terrace of the great Bo-tree in Magadha. After he had accomplished himself in the "Vijjā" and the "Sippa" and achieved the knowledge of the three "Vedas", he established himself in the character of a disputant, in a certain Vihāra. There he was once met by a Buddhist thera who convinced the brahmin youth of the superiority of the Buddha's doctrine and converted him to the Buddhist faith. As he was as profound in his 'ghosa' or eloquence as the Buddha, they conferred on him the appellation of Buddhaghosa or the voice of the Buddha. He had already composed an original work called 'Ñānodayaṁ' and written the chapter called "Atthasālinī" on the Dhammasaṅgaṇi. He went to Ceylon to study the Sinhalese Aṭṭhakathā in order to undertake the compilation of a "Paritta-aṭṭhakathā" or a general commentary on the Piṭakattaya. He visited the island in the reign of King Mahānāma, and there at the Mahāpadhāna Hall in the Mahāvihāra at Anurādhapura, he listened to the Aṭṭhakathā and the Theravāda, became thoroughly convinced of the true meaning of the doctrine of the Lord of Dhamma, and then sought the permission of the priesthood to translate the Aṭṭhakathā. In order to convince them of his qualifications he composed the commentary called "Visuddhimaggam" out of only two gāthās which the priests had given him as a test. Most successfully he came out of the test to the rejoicings of the priesthood; and taking up his residence in the secluded Ganthākāra Vihāra at Anurādhapura, he translated according to the grammatical rules of the Magadhas, the whole of the Sinhalese Aṭṭhakathā (into Pāli). Thereafter, the object of his mission being fulfilled, he returned to Jambudvīpa to worship the Bo-tree at Uruvelā in Magadha.

The most important service that Dhammakitti (the author of the supplementary chapter of the Mahāvaṁsa from which the above account is compiled)[1] renders to our knowledge of the great sage is that he fixes definitely the time when Buddhaghosa lived. The King Mahānāma as the Ceylonese chronicle shows, reigned in the first half of the 5th century A.D. ; and as Buddhaghosa visited Ceylon and worked there during this period we can be certain about the age he lived in. This date is also substantiated by internal evidence derived from the commentaries of Buddhaghosa himself. He shows his acquaintance with the Milinda Pañha as also to other post-canonical Buddhist works, such as the Peṭakopadesa and Anāgatavaṁsa besides some ancient Aṭṭhakathās, and other works which are no longer extant.[2] It is to be observed that in none of these cases there is the least reason for thinking that any of the works quoted from or referred to by Buddhaghosa was of a later date than that allotted to him by Dhammakitti. The Burmese tradition as recorded by Bishop Bigandet also points to the beginning of the 5th century A.D. as the time when the great commentator is said to have visited the shores of Suvaṇṇabhūmi.[3]

Dhammakitti's account of Buddhaghosa's proficiency in the Vedas and other branches of brahmanical learning is also substantially correct. It is confirmed by internal evidence from the great exegete's own commentaries ; they reveal that he was acquainted with the four Vedas as also with the details of Vedic sacrifices. But the Vedic texts were not the only brahmanical works known to Buddhaghosa. He reveals his knowledge of " Itihāsa ", of the brahmanical sūtras as also of the different systems of Hindu Philosophy.

Besides these comparatively authentic accounts of the life of the great commentator, there is a mass

---

1 The account given by Dhammakitti of the life of Buddhaghosa agrees generally with what the great exegetist has said about himself in his own commentaries, specially in the Nidānakathā or story of the origin of the works at their respective beginnings. For details see my " Buddhaghosa ", pp. 15–24.

2 For details, see my " Buddhaghosa ", pp. 9-10.

3 Buddhaghosa's Parables by Capt. T. Rogers, p. xvi, f.n. i.

of legendary accounts of his life. Such legends are found in the Buddhaghosuppatti, also known as the Mahābuddhaghosassa Nidānavatthu by the priest Mahāmaṅgala who lived in Ceylon evidently after the time when the Mahāvaṁsa account was written. Other late works of the Southern school such as the Gandhavaṁsa, the Sāsanavaṁsa, and the Saddhammasangaha furnish some additional details. But the accounts of all these works are of the nature of legends in which fact and fiction are often hopelessly blended together. In their kernel, however, they agree in more important points with Dhammakitti's account in the Mahāvaṁsa. Of further points we learn that Buddhaghosa's father was one Kesī, a brahmin preceptor who used to instruct the king of the realm in the Vedas ; Kesī was, however, later on converted by his son. The Buddhaghosuppatti refers to Buddhaghosa's deep knowledge of Sanskrit displayed before the Ceylonese monks as also to his quick wisdom.

Some are of opinion that after having completed his work in Ceylon, Buddhaghosa came to Burma to propagate the Buddhist faith. The Burmese ascribe the new era in their religion to the time when he visited their country from Ceylon. He is said to have brought over from that island to Burma, a copy of Kaccāyana's Pāli Grammar which he translated into Burmese. He is also credited with having written a commentary on it. A volume of Parables in Burmese language is also attributed to him. The Burmese code of Manu, too, is said to have been introduced into Burma from Ceylon by the same Buddhist scholar. But the code itself is silent on this point. The Chronicles of Ceylon to which we owe the information about Buddhaghosa, and which must have been well-informed on the subject, give no account of his journey to Burma. All serious scholars doubt this tradition.[1]

Buddhaghosa was not only a metaphysician.

---

[1] Hackmann's Buddhism as a Religion, p. 68.

His scholarship was wide and deep and of an encyclopædic character. His works reveal his knowledge of Astronomy, Grammar, Geography, of the Indian sects and tribes and kings and nobles of Buddhist India, of the fauna and flora of the country, of ancient manners and customs of the land, and of the history of Ceylon.

The quality and bulk of the work produced in a single life time show that Buddhaghosa must have been toiling steadily and indefatigably, year in and year out, working out the mission with which he was entrusted by his teacher, immured in a cell of the great monastery at Anurādhapura. Such a life is necessarily devoid of events, and we cannot expect to find in it the variety and fulness of the life-story of a great political figure. Born in Northern India, brought up in brahmanic traditions, versed in Sanskrit lore and an adherent of the system of Patañjali, it is really surprising to know how he acquired such a thorough mastery over the Pāli language and literature and over Buddhist religion and philosophy. His was a useful career, and as long as Buddhism remains a living faith among mankind, Buddhaghosa will not cease to be remembered with reverence and gratitude by Buddhist peoples and schools.[1]

Dhammapāla.

An inhabitant of South India, Dhammapāla dwelt at Padaratittha in the realm of the Damiḷas. He was also a celebrity of the Mahāvihāra. He seems to have based his commentaries on the Sinhalese Aṭṭhakathās which were not preserved in the main land. T. W. Rhys Davids is of the opinion that Dhammapāla and Buddhaghosa seem to have been educated at the same University. In support of this view he refers to the published works of the two writers, a careful study of which shows that they hold very

[1] For a fuller and more detailed treatment read my book, "The Life and Work of Buddhaghosa", Thacker Spink & Co., Calcutta, 1923.

similar views, they appeal to the same authorities, they have the same method of exegesis, they have reached the same stage in philological and etymological science and they have the same lack of any knowledge of the simplest rules of the higher criticism. The conclusion follows that as far as we can at present judge, they must have been trained in the same school (Hastings' Ency. of R. and E., Vol. IV, 701).

It seems probable that Dhammapāla was born at Kāñcipura, the capital of the Tamil country. Hiuen Tsang who visited Kāñcipura in the 7th century A.D. was told by the brethren there that Dhammapāla had been born here at Kāñcipura.

The Gandhavaṁsa (p. 60) enumerates the following works ascribed to Dhammapāla: (1) Nettipakaraṇa-aṭṭhakathā, (2) Itivuttaka-aṭṭhakathā, (3) Udāna-aṭṭhakathā, (4) Cariyāpiṭaka-aṭṭhakathā, (5) Thera and Therī-gāthā-aṭṭhakathā, (6) Vimalavilāsinī or the Vimānavatthu-aṭṭhakathā, (7) Vimalavilāsinī, or the Petavatthu-aṭṭhakathā, (8) Paramatthamañjūsā, (9) Līnattha-pakāsinī on the four aṭṭhakathās of the four nikāyas, (10) Līnatthapakāsinī on the Jātaka-aṭṭhakathā, (11) Nettittha-kathāyaṭīkā, (12) Paramattha-dīpanī, and (13) Līnatthavaṇṇanā.

From his works it appears that Dhammapāla was well read and well informed. His explanation of terms is very clear. His commentaries throw considerable light on the social, religious, moral, and philosophical ideas of time like the commentaries of Buddhaghosa. In his commentaries Dhammapāla follows a regular scheme. First comes an introduction to the whole collection of poems, giving the traditional account of how it came to be put together. Then each poem is taken separately. After explaining how, when, and by whom it was composed each clause in the poem is quoted and explained philologically and exegetically.

Mrs. Rhys Davids in her introduction to the translation of the Therīgāthā (PSS. of the Sisters,

p. xvi) says " In the 5th or 6th century A.D. either before or just after Buddaghosa had flourished, and written his great commentaries on the prose works of the Vinaya and Sutta Piṭakas, Dhammapāla of Kāñcipura, now Conjeeveram, wrote down in Pāli the unwritten expository material constituting the then extant three Aṭṭhakathās on the Psalms and incorporated it into his commentary on three other books of the Canon, naming the whole 'Paramatthadīpanī or Elucidation of the Ultimate Meaning'. He not only gives the ākhyāna in each Psalm but adds a paraphrase in the Pāli of his day, of the more archaic idiom in which the gathas were compiled." She further points out that the presentation of verses, solemn or otherwise, in a framework of prose narrative is essentially the historical Buddhist way of imparting canonical poetry. Dhammapāla's chronicles are, for the most part, unduplicated in any other extant work; but not seldom they run on all fours, not only with parallel chronicles in Buddhaghosa's commentaries, but also with a prose framework of poems in Sutta Nipāta or Saṁyutta Nikāya, not to mention the Jātaka (PSS. of the Brethren, p. xxv).

Origin and growth of the commentaries.

According to Indian tradition, a commentary means reading new meanings back into old texts according to one's own education and outlook. It explains the words and judgments of others as accurately and faithfully as possible; and this remark applies to all commentaries, Sanskrit as well as Pāli. The commentary or bhāṣya, as it is called in Sanskrit, implies, as suggested by the great Sanskrit poet Māgha in his famous kāvya, 'Śiśupālabadha', an amplification of a condensed utterance or expression which is rich in meaning and significance :

" Saṁkhiptasyāpyatosyaiva vākyasyārthagarīyasaḥ
Suvistaratarāvācobhāṣyabhūtā bhavantu me"
(ii. 24);

but at the same time an element of originality is also implied by its definition as given by Bharata in his lexicography. "Those who are versed in the bhāṣyas call that a bhāṣya wherein the meaning of a condensed saying (sūtra) is presented in words that follow the text and where, moreover, the own words of the commentator himself are given."

> "Sūtrārtho varṇyate yatra padaiḥ sūtrānusāribhiḥ
> Svapadāni ca varṇyante bhāṣyam bhāṣyavidoviduḥ
> Iti Liṅgādisaṁgrahaṭikāyāṁ Bharataḥ"—
> (Śabdakalpadruma).

The need for an accurate interpretation of the Buddha's words which formed the guiding principle of life and action of the members of the Saṁgha, was felt from the very first, even during the life time of the Master. There was at that time the advantage of referring a disputed question for solution to the Master himself, and therein we can trace the first stage in the origin of the Buddhistic comments. The Buddhist and Jaina texts tell us that the itinerant teachers of the time wandered about in the country, engaging themselves wherever they stopped in serious discussions on matters relating to religion, philosophy, ethics, morals, and polity. Discussions about the interpretation of the abstruse utterances of the great teachers were frequent and the *raison d'être* of the development of the Buddhist literature, particularly of the commentaries, is to be traced in these discussions. There are numerous interesting passages in the Tripiṭaka, telling us how from time to time contemporary events suggested manifold topics of discussion among the bhikkhus, or how their peace was disturbed by grave doubts calling for explanations either from the Buddha himself or from his disciples. Whenever an interested sophist spoke vehemently in many ways in dispraise of the Buddha, the Doctrine, and the Order (Dīgha, I);

whenever another such sophist misinterpreted the Buddha's opinion (Majjhima, Vol. III, pp. 207-8), whenever a furious discussion broke out in any contemporary brotherhood (Majjhima, Vol. II, Sāmagāma Sutta), or whenever a bhikkhu behaved improperly, the bhikkhus generally assembled under the pavilion to discuss the subject, or were exhorted by the Buddha or by his disciples to safeguard their interests by presenting a strong defence of their case. The Dīgha and Majjhima Nikāyas contain many illuminating expositions of the Buddha, e.g., Mahākammavibhaṅga. the Saḷāyatanavibhaṅga, (Majjhima, Vol. III, pp. 207–222), etc. Then we have from Thera Sāriputta, the chief disciple of the Buddha, a body of expositions of the four Aryan truths, the Saccavibhaṅga. We have also to consider other renowned and profoundly learned disciples of the Buddha, among whom were some women, who in their own way helped forward the process of development of the commentaries. Mahākaccāyana wrote some exegetical works like Kaccāyanagandho, Mahāniruttigandho, etc. We have similar contributions from Mahākoṭṭhita, Moggallāna, Ānanda, Dhammadinnā, and Khemā, but it is needless to multiply instances.

There is another class of ancient Buddhist literature, the porāṇas, of which our knowledge is at present based only upon some extracts in the aṭṭhakathās. We are told in the Gandhavaṁsa that those who are Porāṇācariyā are also Aṭṭhakathācariyā, or teachers who wrote the aṭṭhakathās, and were evidently the earliest contributors to the commentary literature. A number of quotations made by Buddhaghosa may be found in his works concerning the views of the porāṇas. It shall be noted here that the porāṇas do not represent a consistent school of philosophical thought. Each teacher must have been responsible for himself alone, and it is hopeless to discover any organic connection among the numerous short and long passages attributed to the porāṇas in Buddhaghosa's writings (*vide* my "The Life and Work of Buddhaghosa," Chap. III. There is a paper on the origin of the Buddhist arthakathās with introduction by R. C. Childers, J.R.A.S., 1871, pp. 289–302, which should be consulted).

Works of three great Pāli commentators.

The works of Buddhadatta, Buddhaghosa, and Dhammapāla are the most important Pāli commentaries. They are rich in materials for reconstructing a secular and religious history of ancient India. They also throw a flood of light on the philosophical, psychological, and metaphysical aspects of the period with which they deal. A large variety of information is available from these commentaries and hence their importance is very great. Thanks to the indefatigable labours of the Pāli Text Society, London, for printing and publishing a major portion of the Pāli commentaries and making them accessible to the reading public. Besides, there are some other Pāli commentaries, such as the Saddhammapajjotikā or a commentary on the Niddesa written by Upasena; Saddhammapakāsinī, a commentary on the Paṭisaṁbhidāmagga written by Mahānāma Thera of Anurādhapura, and the Visuddhajanavilāsinī or a commentary on the Apadāna written by an unknown author.

## A. Works of Buddhadatta

Abhidhammāvatāra and Rūpārūpavibhāga.

The Abhidhammāvatāra was written by Buddhadatta; and it has been in continuous use amongst the students of the Buddhist scriptures. Buddhadatta was held as a personage of exceptionally high scholarly attainments by Buddhaghosa and others. It is interesting to note the incidents which led to the writing of this work. Buddhadatta was going from Ceylon to India when he was met by Buddhaghosa who was then proceeding to Ceylon for the purpose of rendering the Sinhalese commentaries into Pāli. Knowing the mission of Buddhaghosa, Buddhadatta was highly pleased and spoke thus, "When you finish the commentaries, please send them up to me that I may summarise your labours". Buddhaghosa consented to comply with his request and the Pāli commentaries were accordingly placed in the hands of Buddhadatta who summed up the commentaries on the Abhidhamma in the Abhidhammāvatāra and that on the Vinaya in the Vinayavinicchaya.[1] He was the author of the Rūpārūpavibhāga and of the commentary on the Buddhavaṁsa. The Abhidhammāvatāra is written partly in prose and partly in verse. It discusses the following points :—

citta, nibbāna, cetasika (that which relates to the mind), ārammaṇa (object ideation), vipāka citta (consequence of mindfulness), rūpa (form), paññatti (designation), etc.

The Rūpārūpavibhāga deals with rūpa, arūpa, citta, cetasika, etc. It is written in prose. Rev. A. P. Buddhadatta has edited Buddhadatta's Manuals or summaries of Abhidhamma (Abhidhammāvatāra and Rūpārūpavibhāga) for the first time for the P.T.S., London.

Vinayavinicchaya and Uttaravinicchaya.

The Vinayavinicchaya and Uttaravinicchaya containing the summaries of the Vinaya Piṭaka have been edited by the Rev. A. P. Buddhadatta of Ceylon, and published by the Pāli Text Society of London. These two treatises on the Vinaya seem to have been composed, after the Samantapāsādikā, in an abridged form, in verses. The Vinayavinicchaya contains thirty-one chapters whereas the Uttaravinicchaya contains twenty-three chapters. The author of these treatises was a distinguished thera named Buddhadatta who was a native of Uragapur (or modern Uraiyur) on the banks of the Kāverī in the Chola Kingdom of South India. The Vinayavinicchaya was composed while he was residing in a monastery built by Piṇḍidāsa

---

[1] *Vide* Buddhadatta's Manuals, p. xix.

in the neighbourhood of Bhūtamaṅgala, a prosperous town on the banks of the Kāverī, during the reign of King Acyutavikrama of the Kalamba clan. According to the editor of these treatises Buddhadatta and Buddhaghosa were contemporaries; but the former was senior to the latter. Buddhadatta came to Ceylon earlier, studied the Sinhalese commentaries and summarised them in Pāli.

There are two Pāli commentaries of these two treatises. The commentary on the Vinayavinicchaya is known as the Vinayasāratthadīpanī and that on the Uttaravinacchaya as the Uttaralīnatthapakāsinī supposed to have been written by Vācissara Mahāsāmi. There is also a Sinhalese commentary on the Vinayavinicchaya written by King Parākramavāhu II but this work is now extinct.

The Vinayavinicchaya opens with the Pārājikakathā in verses and is followed by the Saṅghādisesakathā, Aniyatakathā, Nissaggiya-Pācittiyakathā, Paṭidesaniyakathā, and the Sekhiyakathā. Thus the Bhikkhuvibhaṅga is closed. Then this treatise deals with the Bhikkhunivibhaṅga under the following heads: Pārājikakathā, Saṅghādisesakathā, Nissaggiya-Pācittiyakathā and Paṭidesaniyakathā. Then khandhakakathā, kammakathā, pakiṇṇakathā, and kammaṭṭhānakathā are narrated in verses. The treatise consists of 3,183 verses which are written in simple language and marked by good diction.

The Uttaravinicchayakathā consists of 969 verses. Under the Mahāvibhaṅga it treats of the Pārājikakathā, Paṭidesaniyakathā and Sekhiyakathā. Under the Bhikkhunīvibhaṅga it deals with Pārājikakathā, Saṅghādisesakathā, Nissaggiyakathā, Pācittiyakathā, Catuvipattikathā, Adhikaraṇappaccayakathā, Khandhakapucchā, Āpattisamuṭṭhānakathā, Ekuttaranaya, Sedamocakagāthā, Sādhāraṇāsādhāraṇakathā, Lakkhaṇakathā, and Sabbasaṅkalananaya.

The Madhuratthavilāsinī is a commentary on the Buddhavaṁsa. The author was Buddhadatta

Thera. Spence Hardy mentions a commentary on the Buddhavaṁsa by Buddhaghosa. This is probably the Aṭṭhakathā called the Madhuratthavilāsinī whose authorship is assigned by Grimbolt not to Buddhaghosa but to a Buddhist monk living at the mouth of the Kāverī in South India.[1] There is a valuable edition of this commentary by Yogirala Paññananda Thera revised by Mahāgoḍa Siri Ñānissara Thera, Colombo, 1922.

## B. Works of Buddhaghosa

Visuddhimagga.

The Visuddhimagga[2] was written by Buddhaghosa at the request of the Thera Sanghapāla, it is generally believed, in Ceylon in the beginning of the 5th century A.D., when King Mahānāman was on the throne at Anurādhapura. Buddhaghosa, on reaching the Mahāvihāra (Anurādhapura) entered the Mahāpadhāna Hall, according to the account of the Mahāvaṁsa, the great Ceylonese Chronicle, and listened to the Sinhalese Aṭṭhakathā and the Theravāda, from the beginning to the end, and became thoroughly convinced that they conveyed the true meaning of the doctrines of the Lord of Dhamma. Thereupon paying reverential respect to the priesthood, he thus petitioned: "I am desirous of translating the Aṭṭhakathā; give me access to all your books". The Ceylonese priesthood for the purpose of testing his qualification, gave only two gāthās saying, "Hence prove thy qualification; having satisfied ourselves on this point, we will then let thee have all our books". From these (taking these gāthās for his text), and consulting the Piṭakattaya, together with the Aṭṭhakathā and condensing them into an abridged form, he composed the commentary called the "Visuddhimaggaṁ".

---

[1] Indian Antiquary, April, 1890, Vol. XIX, p. 119.

[2] The Visuddhimaggagaṇṭhi, a Burmese Pāli work, explains the difficult passages of the Visuddhimagga (Bode, Pāli Literature of Burma, p. 19, f.n.).

The Mahāvaṁsa account of the circumstances that led to the composition of the " Visuddhimagga " agrees substantially with what Buddhaghosa has written about himself in the Nidānakathā or story of the origin of the works at their respective beginnings. Thus in the Nidānakathā to his Visuddhimagga, Buddhaghosa at the very beginning quotes the following gāthā of Buddha's own saying :—

" Sīle patiṭṭhāya naro sapañño,
Cittaṁ paññaṁ ca bhāvayam,
Ātāpī nipako bhikkhu,
So imam vijaṭaye jaṭanti."

(After having been established in precepts, a wise person should think of samādhi and paññā, an active and wise bhikkhu disentangles this lock.)

Next he proceeds to record the circumstances under which he wrote his compendium of Buddhism (i.e., the Visuddhimagga). " The real meaning of Sīla, etc., is described by means of this stanza uttered by the great sage. Having acquired ordination in the Order of the Jina and the benefit of the Sīla, etc., which is tranquil and which is the straight path to purity, the yogis who are desirous of obtaining purity, not knowing purity as it is, do not get purity though they exert. I shall speak of the Visuddhimagga according to the instruction of the dwellers of the Mahāvihāra, which is pleasing to them, and which is the correct interpretation : Let all the holy men who are desirous of obtaining purity listen to what I say, attentively " (Visuddhimagga, P.T.S., Vol. I, p. 2).

At the end of the work again, Buddhaghosa returns to that very gāthā which he has adopted as his text for writing the Visuddhimagga, and after referring to his promise quoted above, thus delivers himself : " The interpretation of the meanings of the Sīla, etc., has been told in the aṭṭhakathās on the five nikāyas. All of them being taken into consideration, the interpretation gradually becomes manifest, being free from all faults due to confusion; and it is for this reason that the Visuddhimagga should be liked by the Yogis who are desirous of obtaining purity and who have pure wisdom."

Thus, according to Buddhaghosa, the whole of his Visuddhimagga was written as a commentary on that one gāthā uttered by the Master. Evidently it was this gāthā which the writer of the Mahāvaṁsa account had in his mind when he wrote that the Visuddhimagga was written as a comment on and expansion of the two gāthās which were set by the Sinhalese Saṁgha residing at the Mahāvihāra to test Buddhaghosa's learning and efficiency. The Visuddhimagga is in fact an abridged edition of the three piṭakas, the Vinaya, the Sutta, and the Abhidhamma, whose main arguments and conclusions are here condensed into a single treatise. In the gāthā itself, of which the Visuddhimagga is a commentary, there is however no mention either of the word "Visuddhi" or "Magga"; but there is mention of sīla, samādhi, and paññā. Strict observance of the sīlas leads to the purification or visuddhi of the kāya or body, while the practice of samādhi leads to the purity of soul and the thinking of paññā to perfect Wisdom. A wise man alone is capable of disentangling the net of cravings and desires and is fit to attain Nirvāṇa. The disentangling of the lock, as it is called, is the final goal, it is called "visuddhi"; and sīla, samādhi, and paññā are the ways or "magga" to attain to it. As the ways or "magga" to attain to Purity or "visuddhi" have been explained in the book, it is called "Visuddhimagga" or "Path of Purity".

The vocabulary of the text is astonishingly rich as compared with the archaic simplicity of the piṭakas. The quotations in the Visuddhimagga from the piṭakas, the Sinhalese commentaries, the porāṇas, etc., are numerous; in other words it is an abridged compilation of the three piṭakas together with quotations from aṭṭhakathās. The work deals with kusala, akusala, avyākatadhammas, āyatana, dhātu, satipaṭṭhānas, kammas, pakati and many other topics of Buddhist philosophy, and may be said to contain, in fact, the whole of the Buddhist philosophy in a nutshell. Sīla (conduct, precept), samādhi (concentration) and paññā (wisdom) are the three essential matters which are dealt with in this work. In the chapter on sīla are explained cetanāsīla, cetasika sīla and saṁvarasīla. The advantage of sīla is also mentioned therein. There are in it Pātimokkhasaṁvarasīla and Indriyasaṁvarasīla. Pātimokkha (monastic rule) is saṁvara (restraint) which purports to speak of restraint in form, sound, smell, contact, etc. It is interesting to read the section dealing with various kinds of precepts as well as the section on Dhutaṅgas.

The subject of concentration is next discussed—its nature, its advantages and disadvantages. Meditation comes in next for explanation—the four stages of meditation : meditation on fire, wind, water, delight, demerits, etc. The section on meditation on demerits is important containing the discussion of a variety of topics, viz.: Buddhānussati (recollection of the Buddha), Dhammānussati (recollection of dhamma), Saṁghānussati (recollection of saṁgha), cāgānussati (recollection of self-sacrifice), devatānussati (recollection of gods), purity on account of recollection, maraṇasati, kāyagatāsati, upasamānussati, mettābhāvanā, karuṇābhāvanā, upekkhābhāvanā, ākāsānañcāyatana-kammaṭṭhāna, akiñcaññāyatanakammaṭṭhānaṁ, nevasaññānāsaññāyatanakammaṭṭhānam, and āhārepaṭikūlasaññābhāvanā. Ten iddhis or miraculous powers next come in for systematic treatment. There is one section on abhiññā (supernatural knowledge) in which is discussed the nature and definition of wisdom, its characteristics, and the advantage of contemplating on it. Rūpa, vedanā, saññā, and saṁkhāra come one after the other for elucidation ; points worth considering in this connection are those on āyatana (abode), indriya (senses), sacca (truth), dukkha (suffering), paṭiccasamuppāda (dependent origination) and nāmarūpa (name and form).

Maggāmagga Ñāṇadassanavisuddhi is this: this is the right path and this is not the right path, the knowledge which has been well acquired is what is called maggāmaggañāṇadassanavisuddhi. Further may be noted the discussions of the nine important forms, viz.: delight, knowledge, faith, thorough grasp, happiness, emancipation, knowledge of all the four paths, right realisation of the truth and lastly removal of all sins.

The Visuddhimagga is really an encyclopædia of Buddhism, a good abstract of Buddhist doctrines and metaphysics and a vast treasure house of Buddhist lore. It has earned for its author an everlasting fame. The Sumaṅgalavilāsinī records the contents of the Visuddhimagga in a nutshell. The contents may be stated as follows:—nature of the sīlakathā, dhātudhamma, kammaṭṭhānaṁ together with all the cariyāvidhāni, jhānāni, the whole scope of the samāpatti, the whole of abhiññā, the exposition of the paññā, the khandha, the dhātu, the āyatanāni, indriyāni, cattāriariyasaccāni, paccayākārā, the pure and comprehensive nayā, maggā and vipassanabhāvanā.

Buddhaghosa is strong in his attacks on Pakativāda, i.e., the Sāṁkhya and Yoga systems which believe in the dual principles of Puruṣa and Prakriti. He showed an extravagant zeal for differentiating the Buddhist conception of avijjā from the Prakritivādin's conception of Prakriti as the root cause of things (Visuddhimagga, Vol. II, p. 525). The Visuddhimagga points out that the relation between phassa and its object is the relation between eye and form, ear and sound, mind and object of thought (p. 463). Vedanā is of five kinds, sukhaṁ, dukkhaṁ, somanassaṁ, domanassaṁ and upekkhā (*Ibid.*, Vol. II, p. 460). Saññā is only perception of external appearance of an object, while viññāna means thorough knowledge of the thing (*Ibid.*, Vol. II, p. 462). According to the Visuddhimagga

(Chap. XIV) we have 51 Saṁkhāras (confections) beginning with phassa (contact) and ending in vicikicchā (doubt). Kamma, according to Buddhaghosa, means consciousness of good or bad, merit and demerit (Visuddhimagga, Vol. II, p. 614). Kamma is of four kinds: kamma which produces result in this life and in the next life, kamma which produces result from time to time and past kamma (*Ibid.*, p. 601). There is no kamma, he says, in vipāka and no vipāka in kamma. Each of them is void by itself, at the same time there is no vipāka without kamma. A kamma is thus void of its vipāka (consequence) which comes through kamma. Vipāka comes into origin on account of kamma (*Ibid.*, Vol. II, p. 603). Consciousness is due to saṁkhāra which is produced by ignorance (*Ibid.*, p. 600). Saṁkhāras owed their existence in the past and will owe their existence in future to avijjā (*Ibid.*, 522 f.). The Visuddhimagga enumerates the twelve āyatanas as cakkhu, rūpa, sota, saddā, jhāna, gandha, jihvā, rasa, kāya, phoṭṭabba, māna, and dhamma (*Ibid.*, Vol. II, p. 481). The sense organs are due to kamma and it is kamma which differentiates them (*Ibid.*, pp. 444-445). In the section on rūpakkhandha, Buddhaghosa has divided rūpa into two, viz.: bhūtarūpa and upādārūpa. By bhūtarūpa four great elements are implied whereas by upādārūpa are implied twenty-four kinds (*Ibid.*, Vol. II, p. 259; *Ibid.*, pp. 443-444).

The Visuddhimagga contains a description of the evil effects of the violation of sīla (Vol. I, pp. 6–58). Buddhaghosa takes the word "Inda" in the sense of the Buddha (Visuddhimagga, p. 491). In his Visuddhimagga (Vol. II, Ch. XVI) he mentions twenty-two indriyas beginning from cakkhundriya or organ of the eye and ending with aññātavindriya. Upekkhā (indifference) according to him is of ten kinds beginning from chaḷaṅga (six senses) and ending with parisuddhi (purification) (Visuddhimagga, Vol. I, p. 160). The advantages of practising meditation are the five kinds of happy living (*Ibid.*, Vol. I, p. 84 foll.). Nirvāṇa includes absence of passion, destruction of pride, killing of thirst, freedom from attachment and destruction of all sensual pleasures. These are the attributes of Nirvāṇa (Visuddhimagga, Vol. I, p. 293) which can be attained, it is suggested, through meditation, wisdom, precept, steadfastness, etc. (Vol. I, p. 3).

Buddhaghosa had a fair knowledge of Anatomy as is evident from his account of the thirty-two parts of the body recorded in his Visuddhimagga[1] (Vol. I, pp. 249–265).

Samantapāsādikā.

The Samanatapāsādikā[2] is a voluminous commentary on the five books of the Vinaya Piṭaka. It was written by Buddhaghosa at the request of the Thera Buddhasiri. The principal contents of the book are as follows :— (1) The cause that led to the holding of the Buddhist council, (2) Selection of members for the Council, (3) The Council cannot be held without Ānanda, (4) Place of the Council, (5) What Ānanda did with Gandhakuṭi, (6) Eighteen Mahāvihāras, (7) Building of a nice pandal for the meeting, (8) Recital of the first and last words of the Buddha, (9) Classification of the Vinaya, Sutta, and the Abhidhamma, (10) How Vinaya was handed down to the third Council, (11) Life of Moggali Brāhmaṇa, (12) Account of Aśoka, (13) Preachers sent by Aśoka, (14) Discussions on pītisukha and jhānas, (15) Importance of Vajjibhūmi and Vajjiputtaka, (16) Various kinds of pregnancy, (17) Account of Mahāvana at Vesālī, (18) Importance of Bharukaccha as a port, (19)

---

[1] There is a book called Paramatthamañjūsā which is a scholium on Visuddhimagga. Besides the P.T.S. edition of the Visuddhimagga there is an incomplete edition of this work in Bengali by Gopaldas Choudhury and Samaṇa Puṇṇānanda, 1923.

Read H. C. Warren's paper on Buddhaghosa's Visuddhimagga (9th International Congress of Orientalists, London, 1893).

[2] Read "Pāli Elements in Chinese Buddhism", a translation of Buddhaghosa's Samantapāsādikā, a commentary on the Vinaya, found in the Chinese Tripiṭaka by J. Takakusu, B.A. ; J.R.A.S., 1897.

Account of Kuṭāgārasālā at Mahāvana at Vaisālī, (20) Discussions on kammaṭṭhāna, sati, samādhi, paṭisambhidā, citta, viññāna, indriya and four pārājikadhammas, etc. Unlike other commentaries of this nature, Samantapāsādikā is free from any elaborate tangle of similes and metaphors, and is written in an easy language.[1]

The facts and contents of historical and geographical interest in this commentary may in short be stated as follows :—

Once when they were much troubled on account of a famine at Verañjā, the bhikkhus wanted to repair to another place. The Buddha, therefore, crossed the Ganges at Prayāg direct from Verañjā and reached Benares (Vol. I, 201).

King Ajātasattu ruled Magadha for 24 years (Vol. I, 72). He bore the cost of repairing at Rājagaha 18 Mahāvihāras which were deserted by the bhikkhus after the parinibbāṇa of the Buddha (Vol. I, 9).

The Blessed One passed away in the eighth year of Ajātasattu's reign (Vol. I, p. 72).

The missionaries who were sent to various places to preach the dhamma of Aśoka were all natives of Magadha.

Udaya Bhadda was one of the kings of Magadha who reigned for 25 years. He was succeeded by Susunāga who ruled for 18 years. Kālāsoka had ten sons who ruled for 23 years. Then came the Nandas who ruled over the country for the same period. The Nanda dynasty was overthrown by Candgutta who ruled the kingdom for 24 years and he was succeeded by Bindusāra who sat on the Magadhan throne for 18 years. He was succeeded by Aśoka who also followed his father for some time

[1] Portions of this work have been edited by Drs. Takakusu and Nagai for the P.T.S., London. Siamese, Sinhalese, and Burmese editions are available respectively in Siam, Ceylon, and Burma. A portion of the Pāli Samantapāsādikā was rendered into Chinese by Saṁghabhadra in the 5th century A.D. (See Nariman's Literary History of Sanskrit Buddhism, p. 263.)

in making donations to non-Buddhist ascetics and institutions. But being displeased with them he stopped further charities to them, and gave charities to the Buddhist bhikkhus alone (Vol. I, 44). Asoka's income from the four gates of the city of Pāṭaliputta was 4,00,000 kahāpanas daily. In the sabhā (council) he used to get 1,00,000 kahāpanas daily (Vol. I, 52). Rājagaha was a good place having accommodation for a large number of bhikkhus (Vol. I, 8). Asoka is said to have enjoyed undivided sovereignty over all Jambudīpa after slaying all his brothers except Tissa. He reigned without coronation for four years (Vol. I, 41).

Two other kings of Magadha are mentioned in the Samantapāsādikā, Anuruddha, and Muṇḍa (Vol. I, 72-73). Anuruddha succeeded his father Udāyi Bhadda and reigned for 18 years. Then came Nāga Dāsaka who reigned for 24 years. Nāga Dāsaka was banished by the citizens who anointed the minister named Susunāga as King (Vol. I, 72-73).

Bimbisāra is stated to have hundred sons (p. 41), and Asoka is said to have built 84,000 vihāras in the whole of Jambudīpa (p. 115). Reference is made to Pāṭaliputta (p. 35) where the King Dhammāsoka would appear and rule the whole of Jambudīpa.

There were eighteen Mahāvihāras at Rājagaha (p. 9). On one occasion Mahākassapa asked Ānanda about dhamma (p. 15).

This commentary records the first and the last words of the Master (p. 17).

The different classifications of the Vinaya, Sutta, and Abhidhamma Piṭakas (p. 18) are detailed in this commentary. It contains also an interesting account of how Vinaya was handed down till the third council (p. 32).

Then we have accounts of the Thera Moggaliputta Tissa (p. 37), who once went to a mountain named Ahogaṅgā. In order to refute the doctrines of others, the thera composed the Kathāvatthuppakaraṇa (p. 61). The commentary then gives an account of the missionaries sent to different countries by Moggaliputtatissatthera (63-64).

The Samantapāsādikā refers to Kusīnārā, a town of the Mallas, where between the two Sāla trees, on the full moon day of the month of Vesākha, the Blessed One passed away (p. 4).

There are references to Campā and Gaggarā (p. 121), and to many other places, e.g., Verañjā (once visited by famine), Sāvatthī, Tambapaṇṇi, Suvaṇṇabhūmi, Uttarāpathaka visited by traders in horses (p. 175); Uttara-kuru, Kapilavatthu inhabited by many good families (p. 241), Bhaddiya, a city (p. 280), etc. Further, we are referred to the river Ganges, Bārāṇasi (which was once reached by the Buddha after crossing the Ganges), Soreyya, Vesālī, and Mahāvana (p. 201). Mention is made of a village of the Vajjis (p. 207). We are told of the kings of the Licchavigaṇa (p. 212). There is a reference to Uppalavaṇṇā, a beautiful daughter of a banker of Sāvatthī (p. 272). The commentary speaks of the Gijjhakūṭa mountain at Rājagaha where once the Blessed One dwelt (p. 285) and where Dabba, a Mallian, was once seen with a bhikkhu named Mettiya (p. 598), of Isigili, a mountain, and Kāsi-Kosala countries (p. 286). Bimbisāra is mentioned here as the Lord of the Magadhas who had an army of troops (p. 297).

There was a golden cetiya (dagoba) built by Prince Uttara (Samantapāsādikā, Vol. III, p. 544). A banker named Ghosita built a monastery which was named after him (*Ibid.*, p. 574). Veḷuvana was a garden surrounded by *lapis lazuli* and it was beautiful and of blue colour having a vault with a wall 18 cubits in circumference (*Ibid.*, p. 575). During the reign of King Bhātiya there arose a dispute regarding the doctrine between the theras of Mahāvihāra and Abhayagiri (*Ibid.*, 582). Kiṭāgiri is described as a janapada (*Ibid.*, 613). Sāvatthī is described as a city containing 57 hundred thousand families and Rājagaha is mentioned as a city inhabited by 18 koṭis of human beings (*Ibid.*, p. 614).

There is a reference to the Gotamaka Cetiya in Vesālī visited by the Buddha (*Ibid.*, p. 636). There is a reference to the Mahā-aṭṭhakathā and Kurundaṭṭhakathā (p. 299).

Kaṅkhāvitaraṇī.

The Kaṅkhāvitaraṇī is a masterly commentary on the Pātimokkha, a book of the Vinaya Piṭaka [1]; and was written by Buddhaghosa in his own initiative some time between 410 and 432 A.D. A manuscript of an ancient Sinhalese glossary on this work is preserved in the Government Oriental Library, Colombo. The work is remarkable for the restraint and mature judgment that characterise Buddhaghosa's style. While commenting on the precepts of the Pātimokkha, he has incidentally brought in much new information throwing light on the later development of the monastic life of the Buddhists.

Commentaries on the Sutta Piṭaka—(1) Sumaṅgalavilāsinī, the commentary on the Dīgha Nikāya.

The Sumaṅgalavilāsinī [2] is a famous commentary on the Dīgha Nikāya, written by the celebrated Buddhist exegete Buddhaghosa at the request of the Saṅghathera Dāṭha. It is rich in historical information and folklore, and abounds in narratives which throw a flood of light on the social, political, philosophical, and religious history of India at the time of the Buddha. A vivid picture of sports and pastimes as well as valuable geographical and other data of ancient days are carefully provided in it.[3] The book gives us a glimpse of the erudite learning of Buddhaghosa who flourished in the 5th century A.D. Its language is a bit less confused than that of his other commentaries.

In the introductory verses of his Sumaṅgalavilāsinī, Buddhaghosa makes the following reference

[1] We have Sinhalese and Burmese editions of this work.

[2] Read Paṭhamasāratthamañjūsā which is a scholium on the Sumaṅgalavilāsinī.

[3] The whole work has been printed and published in Burma, two of the sermons in two parts have been published in Ceylon and there is also an excellent Sinhalese edition in three parts.

to the history of the composition of his commentaries. Thus he observes :—"Through the influence of serene mind and merit which are due to the salutation of the Three Refuges and which put an end to obstacles, in order to explain the meaning of the Dīgha Nikāya containing long suttas, which is a good āgama, described by the Buddhas and minor Buddhas, which brings faith, the Aṭṭhakathās have been sung and afterwards resung from the beginning by five hundred theras, and are brought to the island of Laṅkā by the wise Mahinda and put in the language of the island of Laṅkā for the welfare of its inhabitants. Discarding the Sinhalese language and rendering the Aṭṭhakathās into a good language which is like Tanti and which is free from faults and not rejecting the explanations of the theras who are the dwellers of the Mahāvihāra, who are the lamps of the group of theras and who are good interpreters, I shall explain the meanings, avoiding repetitions, for the delight of the good men and for the long existence of Dhamma."

Here also Buddhaghosa refers to his Visuddhimagga (S.V., pt. I, p. 2) thus :—" I shall not again discuss what has been well told in the Visuddhimagga. Standing in the midst of the four āgamas, the Visuddhimagga will explain the meaning which has been told there, this being done, you will understand the meaning of the Dīgha Nikāya taking it along with this Aṭṭhakathā " (i.e., Sumaṅgalavilāsinī).

There are according to Buddhaghosa four kinds of suttas :—(1) Attajjhāsayo, i.e., sutta delivered by the Buddha of his own accord ; (2) Parajjhāsayo, i.e., sutta delivered to suit the intention of others ; (3) Pucchāvasiko, i.e., sutta delivered in answer to the question of the Supremely Enlightened One ; (4) Aṭṭhuppatiko, i.e., sutta delivered in course of delivering other suttas.

The examples of each class are given below :— (1) e.g., Mahāsatipaṭṭhāna, Ākaṅkheyya Suttaṁ, Vatthasuttaṁ, etc., (2) e.g., Cūlarāhulavāda, Mahārāhulavāda, Dhammacakkapavattana, etc., (3) e.g.,

Mārasaṁyutta, Devatāsaṁyutta, Sakkapañhasuttam, Sāmaññaphalasuttam, etc., (4) e.g., Dhammadāyāda, Cullasīhanāda, Aggikkhandūpama, Brahmajālasutta (Sumaṅgalavilāsinī, pp. 50-51).

The Sumaṅgalavilāsinī furnishes us with some information regarding a bhikkhu's daily life. In the day time a bhikkhu should free his mind from all obstacles by walking up and down and sitting. In the first watch of the night he should lie down and in the last watch he should walk up and down and sit. Early in the morning he should go and cleanse the space surrounding the cetiya and the Bodhi-tree. He should give water to the root of the Bo-tree, and keep water for drinking and washing. He should then perform all his duties towards his teacher. After finishing ablution, he should enter his own dwelling place, take his rest on the ground and think of kammaṭṭhāna. At the time of going for alms, he should sit up from meditation, and after taking his alms-bowl and garment he should first of all go to the Bodhi-tree and after saluting it he should go to the Cetiya. After he has saluted the Cetiya, he should enter the village for alms and after having finished begging for alms, he should give religious instruction to many persons so desirous of hearing it. Then he should return to the vihāra (S.V., pt. I, pp. 186-187).

The Sumaṅgalavilāsinī gives the following reasons for calling Buddha the Tathāgata[1] :—

1. He has come in the same way.
2. He has gone in the same way.
3. He is endowed with the sign of Tathā (truth).
4. He is supremely enlightened in Tathādhamma (truth).
5. He has seen Tathā (truth).
6. He preaches Tathā (truth).

[1] Read two interesting papers on the Tathāgata, one by R. Chalmers, J.R.A.S., 1898, pp. 311 foll. ; another by Dr. Walleser in the Journal of the Taisho University, 1930.

7. He does Tathā (truthfully).
8. He overcomes all.

These reasons are explained in detail as follows :—

1. As previous Buddhas, e.g., Vipassin, Sikhi, Vessabhu, Kakusandha, Konāgamana, Kassapa, came, as the previous Buddhas obtained Buddhahood by fulfilling ten Pāramitās (perfections),[1] by sacrificing body, eyes, wealth, kingdom, son, and wife, by practising the following kinds of cariyas : Lokatthacariya, i.e., exertion for knowledge ; Buddhatthacariya, exertion for Buddhahood, and by practising four sammappadhānas (four kinds of right exertion), four iddhipādas (four miracles), five indriyas (five senses), five balas (five potentialities), seven bojjhaṅgas (seven supreme knowledges), and the Noble Eightfold Path (ariya atthaṅgika maggo).

2. The Buddha Gautama walked seven steps towards the north just after his birth as Vipassi, Kassapa, and other Buddhas did. He looked all round by sitting under a white umbrella and made the following declaration :—

> " I am the first in the world, I am the chief in the world, I am the most prominent in the world. This is my last birth, there is no future birth to me."

The Buddha Gautama destroyed desire for sensual pleasures by renunciation, destroyed hatred by non-hatred, torpor by steadfastness, doubt by the analysis of Dhamma, ignorance by knowledge, etc., like the former Buddhas, e.g., Vipassi, Kassapa, and others.

3. The Buddha fully realised the true characteristics " Tathālakkhaṇam " of four elements, sky,

---

[1] The ten perfections are the following :—
dāna (charity), sīla (precepts), nekkhamma (renunciation), adiṭṭhāna (determination), sacca (truth), mettā (compassion), upekkhā (indifference), khanti (forbearance), viriya (energy), and paññā (wisdom).

consciousness, forms, sensation, perception, confections, discursive thought, decisive thought, joy, happiness, and emancipation.

4. The Buddha realised four sublime truths known as tathādhamma, suffering, origin of suffering, cessation of suffering, and the path leading to the cessation of suffering. He also realised dependent origination (paṭiccasamuppāda).

5. The Buddha saw all the forms which include four elements which are produced by the combination of four elements in the human world as well as in the world of gods. He heard, knew, touched, tasted, and thought of all that were in existence in the human world as well as in the world of gods.

6. From the time of his enlightenment by conquering Māra till the time of his parinibbāṇa, what he preached, was complete and perfect in meaning and exposition and to the point, and leading to the destruction of passion, hatred and delusion, and was true.

7. His bodily action was in agreement with his action and speech and *vice versa.* He did what he said and *vice versa.*

8. He overcame everything commencing from the highest Brahmaloka to the Avīci hell and endless lokadhātus (worldly elements) all around by sīla (precepts), samādhi (concentration), paññā (wisdom), and vimutti (emancipation). There was no equal to him and he was the unsurpassed king of kings, god of gods, chief of all Sakkas, and chief of all Brahmās (S.V., pt. I, pp. 59–68).

The Buddha had to perform fivefold duties :—(1) Duties before meal, (2) Duties after meal, (3) Duties in the first watch, (4) middle watch, and the (5) last watch of night.

1. Duties before meal included the following :—Ablution early in the morning, and sitting alone till the time of begging ; at the time of begging alms he used to robe himself ; tieing his waist with belt and taking his alms-bowl he used to go for alms

sometimes alone, sometimes surrounded by the bhikkhusaṅgha in villages or towns, sometimes in natural posture, and sometimes by showing miracles, e.g., wind cleaning the street which he was to traverse.

After collecting alms and partaking of them he used to preach to the dāyakas (alms-givers) according to their intelligence.

After hearing religious instruction, some of the dāyakas used to take refuge in the three gems, some used to establish themselves in the five precepts, some used to attain fruition of the first, second, and third stages of sanctification and some after renouncing the world used to attain Arahatship. After preaching the dhamma he used to return waiting for the arrival of the bhikkhus from begging tour. After they had all returned he used to enter Gandhakūṭi (perfumed chamber).

2. Duties after meal :—His attendant used to prepare seat for him in the Gandhakūṭi and he after sitting on it, used to wash his feet. Standing on the step of the staircase of a Gandhakūṭi, he used to instruct the bhikkhus to perform their duties diligently. He spoke thus, "The appearance of the Buddha is rare, it is difficult to be born as human being, good opportunity is also difficult to be obtained, ordination as bhikkhus is also difficult to be had, and the hearing of the Saddhamma (true law) is also difficult to be obtained". Some of the bhikkhus used to seek his instructions in kammaṭṭhānas (objects of meditation). The Blessed One used to give instructions in the Kammaṭṭhānas suitable to their nature. The bhikkhus used to return to their dwelling-place or to the forest after saluting the Buddha. Some used to return to the Cātummahārājika Heaven or to the Paranimmitavasavattī Heaven.[1] After giving instructions, the Blessed One used to enter the Gandhakūṭi and lie

[1] See my book, "Heaven and Hell in Buddhist Perspective", pp. 7, 15, etc.

down on the right side. He used to see the world with his eye of wisdom after refreshing himself. He then used to give instructions to the people who assembled in the preaching hall with scented flowers, etc., and then the people after listening to the religious instructions, used to return after saluting the Buddha.

3. In the first watch of the night if he desired to bathe himself, he used to get up from his seat and enter the bath-room and bathed himself with water supplied by the attendant who made ready the seat for him in the Gandhakūṭi. The Blessed One used to put on red coloured under-garment tieing his waist with belt. Then he used to put on the upper garment keeping one shoulder open, and then he used to sit on his seat alone in a mood of meditation. The bhikkhus used to come from all sides to worship him. Some bhikkhus used to ask him questions, some used to ask his instructions on kammaṭṭhāna, and some used to request him to give religious instructions. The Buddha used to satisfy the bhikkhus by fulfilling their desires. Thus he used to spend the first watch of the night.

4. Duties in the middle watch:—After the bhikkhus had left him, the devatās used to come from 10,000 lokadhātus (world cycles), and the Blessed One used to spend the middle watch in answering the questions of the devas.

5. Duties in the last watch of the night:—The last watch of the night was divided into three parts. He used to spend the first part by walking up and down, the second part by lying down on the right hand side in the Gandhakūṭi, and the last part by seeing with his eyes the person who acquired competency in knowing dhamma on account of the acquisition of merit by serving the previous Buddhas (S.V., pt. I, pp. 45–48).

The Buddha performed double miracles[1] at the gate of the city of Sāvatthī in the seventh

---

[1] The so-called Yamaka-pāṭihāriya.

year after his enlightenment at the foot of Gaṇḍambaka tree, e.g., fire was burning on the upper part of the body and water flowing down from the lower part, fire coming out of one of the pores of the skin of the body and water of six colours coming out of another pore of the skin of the body, six kind of rays coming out of the body of the Buddha and illuminating all the ten thousand Cakkavāḷas (world cycles).

Buddhaghosa describes the Buddha's fulfilment of ten perfections (pāramitās) during four asaṅkha kalpas and 1,00,000 kalpas. He renounced the world at the age of twenty-nine, took ordination on the bank of the Anoma river. For six years he exerted simultaneously. On the Vaisākha full-moon day he took honeyed rice-gruel offered by Sujātā at Uruvelā and in the evening he entered the Bodhi terrace by the south gate and thrice went round the Aśvattha tree. Going to the north-east side of the tree he spread a seat of grass and seated on it crosslegged facing the east and keeping the Bo-tree at the back, he first of all meditated upon mettā (friendliness, love).

At dusk he defeated Māra and in the first watch of the night he acquired the knowledge of previous birth, in the middle watch he acquired celestial insight and in early morning he acquired the knowledge of dependent origination and attained the fourth stage of meditation on inhalation and exhalation. Depending on the fourth stage of meditation, he increased insight and successively acquired all the qualities of the Buddha (S.V., pt. I, pp. 57-58).

The Buddha used to take two kinds of journey tarita (quick) and atarita (slow). In order to convert a fit person who was at a distance, he used to travel long distance within a short time as we find in the case of the Buddha going to receive Mahākassapa who was at a distance of three gāvutas in a moment. The Buddha also took tarita journey for Ālavaka, Aṅgulimāla, Pukkusādi,

Mahākappina, Dhaniya, and Tissasāmaṇera, a pupil of Sāriputta.

The Buddha daily used to take a short journey in order to do good to the people by preaching to them and accepting their offerings, etc. This was known as atarita journey. The atarita journey was divided into three maṇḍalas, e.g., mahāmaṇḍala, majjhimamaṇḍala, and antomaṇḍala. The mahāmaṇḍala was extended over an area of 900 yojanas, Majjhimamaṇḍala 600 yojanas, and antomaṇḍala 300 yojanas. He had to start on the day following the Mahāpavāraṇā (i.e., last day of the lent); if he had to undertake the mahāmaṇḍala journey he had to start at the beginning of Agrahāyaṇa and in case of antomaṇḍala journey, he could start at any time suitable to him (S.V., pt. I, pp. 239–242).

Among the Buddha's contemporaries were Jīvaka Komārabhacca, Tissasāmaṇera, Pokkharasāti, and Ambaṭṭha. It will not perhaps be out of place to record here a few interesting facts about them.

Jīvaka Komārabhaṇḍa was reared up by Abhayakumāra, one of the sons of Bimbisāra, so he was called Komāra-bhaṇḍa. Once Bimbisāra and Abhayakumāra saw from the roof of the palace, Jīvaka lying down on the floor at the gate of the palace surrounded by vultures, crows, etc. The king asked, "What is that?" He was told that it was a baby. The king asked if it were alive. The reply was in the affirmative. Hence he was called Jīvaka (S.V., pt. I, p. 133).

Once Jīvaka caused the Buddha to take some purgative. When the Buddha became all right in health, Jīvaka offered the Buddha a pair of valuable clothes. The Buddha accepted his offering and gave him suitable instructions with the result that he was established in the fruition of the first stage of sanctification. He offered his mango-garden to the Buddha for his residence with his pupils, as Jīvaka thought that it would be difficult for him to go to the Veḷuvana where the Buddha used to live for attending on him and which was far from his house. In the mango-garden, Jīvaka prepared rooms for spending day and night for the Buddha and his bhikkhus. Wells, etc., were sunk for them. The garden was surrounded by a wall and a Gandhakūṭi (perfumed house) was built for the Buddha in the Mango-garden (S.V., pt. I, p. 133).

Tissasāmaṇera :—Once Sāriputta wanted to go to his pupil. The Buddha expressed his willingness to go with him and ordered Ānanda to inform 20,000 bhikkhus who were possessed of supernatural powers that the Blessed One would go to see Tissa. The Buddha with Sāriputta, Ānanda, and 20,000 khīṇāsava-bhikkhus (the monks who were free from sins) traversed the path of 2,000 yojanas through sky and got down at the gate of the village where Tissa was and they robed themselves. The villagers received them all and offered them rice gruel. After the Buddha had finished his meal, Tissa returned from alms-begging and offered food to the Buddha, which he (Tissa) had received on his begging tour. The Buddha visited Tissa's dwelling place.

Pokkharasādi :—His body was like the white lotus or like the silver gate of Devanagara. His head was very beautiful and popular. At the time of Kassapa Buddha, he was well-versed in the three Vedas and in consequence of his offering charity to the Buddha, he was reborn in the Devaloka. As he did not like to enter the womb of a human being, he was reborn in a lotus in a big lake near the Himavanta. An ascetic who lived near the lake reared him up. He made the child learn the three Vedas and the child became very much learned, and was regarded as the foremost brahmin in the Jambudīpa. He showed his skill in arts to the king of Kosala. The king being pleased with him gave him the city of Ukkaṭṭha as Brahmottara property (i.e., the property offered to the brahmin) (S.V., pt. I, pp. 244-245).

Ambaṭṭha :— He was the chief disciple of Pokkharasādi or Pokkharasāti. He was sent to the

Buddha to see whether the Buddha deserved the praises offered to him. He attempted in various ways to defeat the Buddha but in vain. He also expressed his opinion that no samaṇadhamma could be practised by living in such a vihāra. He came back to his teacher after being defeated (S.V., pt. I, p. 253).

The Sumaṅgalavilāsinī supplies us with some new interesting geographical informations, some of them being more or less fanciful in their origin.

Aṅga :—On account of the beauty of their body, some princes were known as Aṅgas. The place was named Aṅga because those princes used to dwell there (S.V., pt. I, p. 279).

Not far from the city of Aṅga, there was the tank of Gaggarā, so called because it was dug by a queen named Gaggarā. On its bank all round, there was a great forest of Campaka trees decorated with flowers of five colours, blue, etc. This account of Campā has, however, hardly any geographical value. Buddhaghosa also gives us his own interpretation of the term Aṅga. According to him, it is so called because of the beauty of the princes of the country. The explanation seems to be rather fanciful (S.V., pt. I, p. 279).

Dakṣiṇāpatha or the Deccan :—Buddhaghosa defines Dakkhiṇāpatha or the Deccan as the tract of land lying to the south of the Ganges (S.V., pt. I, p. 265). Many ascetics used to live there and one of the forefathers of Ambaṭṭha went there and learnt ambaṭṭhavijjā, a science through the influence of which the weapon once raised could be brought down. He came to Okkāka and showed his skill and secured a post under him (S.V., pt. I, p. 265).

Ghositārāma :—In the past there was a kingdom named Addila. In this kingdom a poor man named Kotūhaḷaka while going to another place at the time of famine, being unable to carry his son, threw him on the way. The mother out of affection went back and brought the child and returned to the village of gopālas (cowherds) who gave them milk-rice to eat. Kotūhaḷaka could not digest the milk and died at night of cholera and was reborn in the womb of a bitch. The young dog was the favourite of the head of the cowherds, who used to worship a paccekabuddha. The cowherd used to give a handful of cooked rice to the young dog which followed the gopālas to the hermitage of the paccekabuddha. The young dog used to inform the paccekabuddha by barking that rice was ready and used to drive away wild beasts on the way by barking. As the young dog served the paccekabuddha, he was reborn after death in heaven and was named Ghosadevaputta who, fallen from heaven, was reborn in a family at Kosambī. The banker of Kosambī being childless brought him up and when a legitimate child was born to the banker, he attempted to kill Ghosa seven times but on account of the accumulation of merit Ghosaka could not be killed. He was saved by the instrumentality of a banker's daughter whom he eventually married. After the death of the banker who attempted to kill him, he succeeded him and was known as Ghosakaseṭṭhi. At Kosambī there were two other bankers named Kukkuṭa and Pāvāriya. At this time five hundred ascetics came to Kosambī and the three bankers, Ghosaka, Kukkuṭa, and Pāvāriya built hermitages in their respective gardens for the ascetics and supported them. Once the ascetics while coming from the Himalayan region through a forest became very much hungry and thirsty, and sat under a big banian tree thinking that there must have been a powerful devatā residing in the tree who would surely help them. The presiding deity of the tree helped the ascetics with water to quench their thirst. The deity when asked as to how he (deity) acquired such splendour, replied that he was a servant in the house of a banker Anāthapiṇḍika who supported the Buddha at Jetavana. On a sabbath day the servant went out to walk in the morning and returned in the evening. He enquired of the other servants of the house and learning that they had accepted uposatha, he went to Anāthapiṇḍika and took precepts. But he could not observe the precepts fully and in consequence of the merit accumulated due to the observance of half the uposatha at night, he became the deity of this tree endowed with great splendour. They went to Kosambī and informed the seṭṭhis of this matter. The ascetics went to the Buddha and acquired ordination and Arahatship. The seṭṭhis afterwards went to the Buddha and invited the Buddha to Kosambī. After returning to Kosambī, they built three hermitages and one of them was known as Ghositārāma (S.V., pt. I, pp. 317–319).

Kosala :—The Porāṇas say that prince Mahāpanāda did not laugh even after seeing or hearing objects that are likely to rouse laughter. The father of the prince promised that he would decorate with various kinds of ornaments the person who would be able to make his son laugh. Many, including even the cultivators, gave up their ploughs and came to make the son laugh. They tried in various ways but in vain. At last, Sakka the chief of the gods sent a theatrical party to show him a celestial drama to make the prince laugh. The prince laughed and men returned to their respective abodes. While they were returning home they were asked on the way, " Kacci bho kusalaṁ, kacci bho kusalaṁ " (are you all right ?). From this word kusalaṁ, the country came to be known as Kosala (S.V., pt. I, p. 239).

Rājagaha :—A name of the town in which Mandhāta and Mahāgovinda took their abode. At the time of the Buddha it was a town, at other times it was empty (S.V., pt. I, p. 132).

The Sumaṅgalavilāsinī serves as a glossary of important terms, a few of which may be enumerated here.

Adinnādānā :—It strictly means accepting that which is not given. It also means stealing the property of others, the thing which can be used by others according to their wish and by using which they are not liable to be punished, if that thing be taken with the intention of stealing it, then he is guilty of theft ; if the thing stolen be of greater value, then the offence will be greater and if it is of less value the offence will be less. If the thing stolen belongs to a person of greater quality, the offence will be greater and if it belongs to a person of less quality, the offence will be less.

One is guilty of theft if the following conditions are there :—

(1) the thing stolen must belong to others ;
(2) the thief must be conscious at the time of stealing, that the thing which he is stealing belongs to others ;
(3) he must have the intention to steal ;
(4) he must make effort to steal and that effort must bring about the theft of the thing belonging to others (S.V., Vol. I, p. 71).

Musāvāda :—It means application of word or bodily deed to bring about dissension. Consciousness due to the application of word or bodily deed with the intention of bringing about dissension is called speaking falsehood.

Musā in another sense means :—

(1) the thing not happened before,
(2) untrue thing.

Vāda means making known thing which is untrue to be true and a thing unhappened before to have happened.

Musāvāda is nothing but consciousness of the person who is willing to make known a thing which is untrue to be true and an unhappened thing to have happened.

Buddhaghosa cites some examples in this connection :

If a witness gives false evidence, he becomes liable to greater fault ; if a bhikkhu makes exaggeration humorously he will be liable to less fault ;

and if a bhikkhu says that he has seen a thing not seen by him, that he has heard of a thing unheard by him, he will surely be liable to greater fault.

One is guilty of falsehood if the following conditions are there :—

1. His subject or object must be false.
2. He must have the intention of creating disunion or dissension.
3. He must make the effort created by that intention.
4. His act of creating disunion must be known to the parties concerned. He must commit the offence himself. Buddhaghosa is of opinion that if a person instigates others to commit falsehood, and instigates others to do the offence by letters or by writing on walls, etc., and if he himself commits the offence, in all these cases, the nature of offence must be the same (*Ibid.*, p. 72).

Pharusāvācā :—According to Buddhaghosa, Pharusāvācā really means intention to wound the feelings of others. It means harsh words (S.V., pt. I, p. 75). According to him a thoughtless speech should be pleasing to the ear, producing love, appealing to the heart and agreeable to many (S.V., pt. I, pp. 75-76).

Pisuṇāvācā :—The person to whom the word is spoken takes a favourable view of the speaker but unfavourable view of the person about whom it is spoken. It is nothing but consciousness of the person who speaks to make himself closely acquainted with the person to whom the word is spoken and the person about whom it is spoken.

One is guilty of pisuṇāvācā if the following conditions be fulfilled :—

1. He must have the intention of creating dissension and making himself frie "
2. He must have the effort to intention.

3. The act of creating disunion must be known to the parties concerned.
4. The persons before whom the dissension is created must be in existence (S.V., pt. I, p. 74).

There are references to the following sports and pastimes in the Sumaṅgalavilāsinī :—

Aṭṭhapadaṁ : Dice.

Ākāsaṁ : A kind of pastime which is played after imagining a kind of dice-board in the sky.

Caṇḍālaṁ : Sporting with an iron ball.

Ghaṭikaṁ : A sport in which large sticks are beaten by short ones.

Vamsaṁ : Sporting with a bamboo which is turned in various ways.

Parihārapathaṁ : A kind of sport which is played on the ground on which many paths having fences are prepared to puzzle the player (S.V., pt. I, pp. 84-85).

References to various kinds of seats are found in this work :—

Āsandiṁ : A big seat.

Goṇakaṁ : A carpet with long hairs.

Koseyyaṁ : A silk seat bedecked with gems.

Kuttakaṁ : A kind of woollen seat in which sixteen dancing girls can dance together.

Pallaṅkaṁ : A seat having feet with figure of deer, etc.

Paṭalikā : Thick woollen seat with various designs of flowers.

Paṭikā : Woollen seat.

Vikatikā : A seat having the figure of lion or tiger.

Dhopanaṁ : It is a ceremony among the southern Indian people who wash the bones of their dead relatives after digging them out and after having besmeared them with scents and collecting all the bones in one place. On a certain auspicious day they eat up various kinds of food and drink collected for the occasion while crying for their departed relatives (S.V., pt. I, pp. 84–87).

A person is called Puthujjano because various kinds of sins are committed by him. His view is that the body which is soul is not gone. He is so called because he is merged in various kinds of ogha (floods) and because he is burnt by various kinds of heat. As he is attached to five kinds of sensual pleasures and as he is covered by five hindrances and as he does innumerable low deeds, so he is called puthujjano. As he is separated by Ariyas from the sīla (precepts), suta (learning), etc., he is called puthujjano (*Ibid.*, p. 59).

Rājā :—He is so called because he pleases (rañjeti) his subjects.

Sīlas :—Porāṇas say that sīla (precept) is the ornament of a Yogī and sīla is the object of decoration of a Yogī. The Yogīs being adorned with sīlas have acquired perfection in matters of decoration. One should observe sīlas just as a kiki bird protects her egg. One should observe sīlas properly just as one eyed man protects his only eye (S.V., pt. I, pp. 55-56). Buddhaghosa says that all good deeds are based on sīlas just as all the trees and vegetables grow on the earth (S.V., pt. I, p. 56).

*Cullasīla* :—Pāṇātipāta means slaughter of life. Pāṇa ordinarily means living beings but in reality it is vitality. The thought of killing vitality is what is called pāṇātipāta. To kill a lower animal which is devoid of good qualities and a small being, brings small amount of sin and to kill a big creature full of sins brings large amount of sin because a good amount of effort is needed to kill a big animal whereas to kill a small animal, little effort is required. To kill with great effort a creature having good qualities brings about much sin, whereas to kill with the same effort a creature having no quality or having quality not of great amount brings about less sin. If the body and the quality possessed by it be of equal standard, there will be a difference in the acquisition of sin according to greatness or smallness of kilesas (sins).

One will be guilty of life-slaughter if the following conditions be fulfilled :—

(1) there must be a living being ;
(2) the killer must be conscious at the time of killing that he is going to kill a living being ;
(3) he must have the intention to kill ;
(4) then he must make the effort to kill ;
(5) the effect of that effort must lie in the death of the being living.

The six kinds of efforts are :—

Sāhatthika (killing by own hand), āṇattika (order to kill), nissaggika (throwing with the intention that living being should die), vijjāmaya (killing by magic), iddhimaya (killing by miracle), thāvara (killing by instruction written on immovable pillars), etc. (*Ibid.*, pt. I, p. 70).

The Sumaṅgalavilāsinī contains some more interesting historical materials. It speaks of the origin of the Śākyas which is traced back to King Okkāka (i.e., Ikṣvāku). King Okkāka had five queens. By the chief queen, he had four sons and five daughters. After the death of the chief queen, the king married another young lady who extorted from him the promise to place her son upon the throne. The king thereupon requested his sons to leave the kingdom. The princes accordingly left the kingdom accompanied by their sisters and going to a forest near the Himalayas, began to search for a site for building up a city. In course of their search, they met the sage Kapila who said that they should build a town in the place where he (the sage) lived. The prince built the town and named it Kapilavatthu (Kapilavastu). In course of time the four brothers married the four sisters, excepting the eldest one and they came to be known as the Śākyas (pt. I, pp. 258–260). The only grain of fact hidden in this fanciful story of the origin of the Śākyas seems to be that there was a tradition which traced their descent from King Okkāka or Ikṣvāku. Buddhaghosa in his great commentaries, though a very reliable guide as regards exposition and exegesis and the unravelling of metaphysical tangles, becomes quite the reverse when any point of history or tradition comes up. Here he accepts the wildest theories and takes as gospel truth even the most improbable stories. Sister-marriage was not in vogue in ancient India even in the earliest times of which we have any record, as the story of Yama and Yamī in the Rigveda amply demonstrates. It was a revolting idea to the Indians from the time of the Rigveda downwards. Yet we see that Buddhaghosa in the case of the Licchavis and again here in that of the Śākyas, tries to explain the origin by sister-marriage. Perhaps Buddhaghosa was actuated by the idea of purity of birth by a union between brothers and sisters as in the case of the Pharaohs of Egypt. The great Ceylonese chronicle, the Mahāvaṁsa, also traces the origin of the Śākyas to the same King Okkāka and goes further back to Mahāsammata of the same dynasty.

When the Buddha was at Kosambī, he delivered the Jāliya Sutta at the Ghositārāma before a large gathering of people including a number of seṭṭhis among whom there were Kukkuṭa, Pāvāriya, and Ghosaka who built three monasteries for the Buddha. Ghosaka built the Ghositārāma, Kukkuṭa built the Kukkuṭārāma, and Pāvāriya built Pāvārika-ambavana (S.V., pt. I, pp. 317–319).

On one occasion the whole of Rājagaha was illumined and decorated and was full of festivities and enjoyments. Ajātasattu with his ministers went to the terrace and saw the festivities going on in the city. The moon-lit night was really very pleasing; and the thought arose within him of approaching a Samaṇa or Brāhmaṇa who could bring solace to his tortured mind (*Ibid.*, pt. I, pp. 140-141). Hearing of the great virtues of the Buddha from Jīvaka, the greatest physician of the day, Ajātasattu came to the ambavana where the Enlightened One was staying much afraid though he was of the Master for his (Ajātasattu's) many mischievous deeds against the latter (*Ibid.*, pt. I, 151-152). Ajātasattu asked the Blessed One whether he could show him the effect of leading the life of a Samaṇa. The Buddha did so by delivering to the repentant king a discourse on various virtues of the life of a samaṇa or ascetic as narrated in the Sāmaññaphala Suttanta of the Dīgha Nikāya (*Ibid.*, I, pp. 158 foll.). Buddhaghosa says that according to Gosāla things happen exactly as they are to happen (*Ibid.*, pp. 160–165).

In the Sumaṅgalavilāsinī Buddhaghosa has conjured up a myth in order to explain the conduct of the parricidal prince Ajātasattu. He avers that Ajātasattu was even before his birth an enemy of King Bimbisāra. The circumstances that preceded Ajātasattu's birth and augured the impending evil, as recorded in the Sumaṅgalavilāsinī, are appealing. When the would-be parricide was in his mother's womb, the queen, it is said, felt a craving for sipping blood from the right arm of the king. She, however, dared not speak out her inhuman desire. Worried by this, she looked pale and emaciated. The king asked her the cause of her getting weak. At last she spoke out and the king then sent for his surgeon who drew blood out of his right arm for the queen. The blood was diluted with water and the queen was asked to drink up the horrible potion. The soothsayers, however, warned that the child would be an enemy to the king and would kill him in consequence of the queen's drinking the king's blood. The queen, horrified at the prospect, tried to effect miscarriage but she was prevented by the king who urged that a sinful act would be abhorred by the people of Jambudīpa, and that voluntary abortion was against all national tradition of India.

The queen, it is said, thought of destroying the child at the time of delivery. But the attendants took away the child as soon as it came out of the mother's womb. When the child had grown up, he was presented before the queen whose maternal affection towards the lad got the upper hand and she could no longer think of killing him. In due course the king made him his viceregent (pt. I, p. 134). Ajātasattu took advantage of this and kept his father confined in a room which was very hot and full of smoke. None else was allowed to enter into that room except Ajātasattu's mother who used to take some food for the unfortunate king, but she was afterwards prevented from doing that even. In spite of the prohibitive injunction, she used to bring food for Bimbisāra concealing it in several parts of her body; but she was one day found out and was ordered not to enter the room with any kind of food. Thenceforth she used to enter the king's apartment with her body besmeared with a mixture of honey, butter, ghee, and oil. Bimbisāra got some sustenance by licking her body. This too was detected by the over-vigilant Ajātasattu and she was forbidden to enter into the room and asked to see the king from outside. The queen now reminded Bimbisāra that it was she who had requested him to kill Ajātasattu while in the womb. She further told him that it was the last occasion on which she had been permitted to meet him and she begged his pardon and took leave (S.V., pt. I, pp. 135-136). Bimbisāra was now prevented from taking any food but he was still alive and the commentator informs us that the inhuman practices of Ajātasattu increased in their barbarity. Bimbisāra, it is said, was meditating on the fruition of the path and was walking up and down and his appearance became very bright. Ajātasattu was informed of this and he ordered that his walking up and down must be stopped and ordered his barber to go and cut the feet of his father and to put salt and oil thereupon and then to heat them on the fire of Khadira charcoal. The barber went to Bimbisāra who thought that his son had come to realise his folly and become kind to him. The barber when asked by the king about his mission, intimated to him the order of King Ajātasattu. The barber carried out the ghastly operations required by the royal order. Bimbisāra breathed his last with the words, "Buddha and Dhamma". After death Bimbisāra was reborn in the Cātummahārājika heaven as an attendant of Vessavana named Javanavasabha (*Ibid.*, I, p. 137).

On the day Bimbisāra died, a son was born to Ajātasattu. Both the reports, one conveying the news of the death of his father, and the other, that of the birth of his child were received by his ministers at the same time. The ministers first of all handed over the letter conveying the news of the birth of his child to King Ajātasattu. On receipt of the letter the king's mind was filled with filial affection and at that moment all the virtues of his father rose up before his mind's eye and he realised that similar filial affection arose in his father's mind when the latter received the news of his (Ajātasattu's) birth. Ajātasattu at once ordered the release of his father but it was too late. On hearing of his father's death, he cried and went to his mother and asked her if his father had any affection for him. The mother replied, "When a boil appeared on your finger, you were crying and none could pacify you and you were taken to your father when he was administering justice at the royal court. Your father out of affection put your finger with the boil into his mouth and the boil was burst open. Out of filial affection he swallowed up the blood and pus instead of throwing them away." Ajātasattu heard this and shed hot tears. The dead body of his father was burnt. Shortly afterwards Devadatta went to Ajātasattu and urged him to order his men to go and kill the Buddha too. Devadatta sent Ajātasattu's men to kill the Master and himself took several steps to bring about his death. He himself went to the top of the Gijjhakūṭa mountain and hurled at the Buddha a big stone, then he set the mad elephant Nāḷagiri against the Enlightened One but all his attempts were baffled. All his gain and fame were lost, and he became very miserable (*Ibid.*, pt. I, pp. 138-139).

A conversation once took place between Brahmadatta and Suppiya, a paribbājaka. Suppiya said that the Buddha was a propounder of non-action, annihilation, and self-mortification. He further said that the Buddha was of low birth and he did not possess any super-human knowledge. Brahmadatta, on the other hand, was of opinion that he should not follow his teacher in performing evil deed. He said that if his teacher worked with fire, it did not behove him to do so ; if his teacher played with a black snake, it was not intended that he should also do like that. He further said, " All beings enjoy the fruits of their karma. Karma is their own, father is not responsible for his son's deeds and son is not responsible for his father's deeds. So also mother, brother, sister, pupil, and others are not responsible for one another's action. Three jewels (Triratana) namely, the Buddha, Dhamma, and Saṁgha are abused by me. To rebuke an ariya (elect) is a great sin." Brahmadatta spoke highly of the Master thus : " The Buddha is the Blessed One, an arahat (saint), supremely wise, etc. " He also spoke highly of the Dhamma and the Saṁgha. Thus Suppiya and his pupil Brahmadatta were holding contrary views. In the evening all of them arrived in the garden of the king named Ambalaṭṭhika. In that garden the king had a beautiful garden-house. The Buddha took his residence at that house for one night. Suppiya also took shelter in the garden. At night bhikkhus were seated surrounding the Buddha calmly and without the least noise. In the first watch of the night the bhikkhus sat in the maṇḍalamāla (sitting-hall) of the house. The Buddha went to the spot and asked them about the topic of their discussion.

The bhikkhus told him that they were discussing the contrary views of Suppiya and Brahmadatta and the endless virtues of the Buddha. The Buddha then solved their topics of discussion by the long discourse known as the Brahmajāla Suttanta (S.V., pt. I, pp. 26–44).

The Sumaṅgalavilāsinī furnishes us with an account which embodies the tradition regarding the recital of the Dīgha Nikāya in the First Council.

One week after the parinibbāṇa of the Buddha at the sālavana of the Mallas near Kusīnārā, on the full-moon day in the month of Vaiśākha, a monk named Subhadda who took ordination in old age spoke thus, "Friend, you need not lament, you need not grieve. We are free from the Mahāsamaṇa who used to trouble us by asking us to perform this or that act." Hearing this Mahākassapa thought that in order to save the monks from such people and to save the saddhamma from destruction, it was necessary to hold a council. He addressed the assembly of monks to rehearse the Dhamma and Vinaya. On the 21st day after the Buddha's parinibbāṇa, five hundred theras who were all Arahats and possessed of analytical knowledge were selected.

The people worshipped the dead body of the Buddha with incense, garland, etc., for a week. It was placed on a funeral pyre but there was no fire for a week and in the third week since his death, his bones, etc., were worshipped in the Mote-hall and the relics were divided on the fifth day of the bright half of the month of Jaiṣṭha. At the time of the distribution of relics many bhikkhus were assembled among whom five hundred were selected. The five hundred bhikkhus were given time for 40 days to remove all their hindrances in order to enable them to take part in the proposed rehearsal. Mahākassapa with the five hundred bhikkhus went to Rājagaha. Other Mahātheras with their own retinue went to different places. At this time a Mahāthera named Purāṇa with 700 bhikkhus consoled the people of Kusīnārā. Ānanda with five hundred bhikkhus returned to Jetavana at Sāvatthī. The people at Sāvatthī seeing Ānanda coming there thought that the Buddha would be in their midst; but being disappointed in this and learning the news of the Master's parinibbāṇa they began to cry. Ānanda worshipped the Gandhakūṭi where the Buddha used to dwell, opened its door and cleansed it. While cleansing the Gandhakūṭi, he cried saying, "The Blessed One, this is the time of your taking bath, preaching, instructing the bhikkhus, this is the time of your lying down, sleeping, washing your mouth, and face". He went to Subha's house for alms where he preached Subhasuttaṁ of the Dīgha Nikāya. After leaving the bhikkhus at Jetavana, he went to Rājagaha to take part in the proposed rehearsal. Other bhikkhus who were selected to take part in the rehearsal also came to Rājagaha. All the selected bhikkhus observed uposatha on the full-moon day of the month of Āṣāḍha and spent the rainy season. The bhikkhus approached Ajātasattu and requested him to repair eighteen mahāvihāras of Rājagaha. The king had them repaired. He also built a beautiful and well-decorated pandal near the Vebhāra mountain at the foot of the Sattapaṇṇi cave, for them. This pandal was like that built by Vissakammā in heaven. Five hundred seats were prepared in this pandal for five hundred bhikkhus. The seat of the President was on the south facing the north. In the middle there was a dhammāsana in which Ānanda and Upāli took their seats and preached Dhamma and Vinaya. Then Dhamma and Vinaya were repeated simultaneously by the five hundred bhikkhus. The question arose as to the competency of Ānanda to take part. He was not an Arahat. Hearing this Ānanda became ashamed and after exertion he acquired saintship at night. All the theras were present while Ānanda's seat was vacant. Some said that Ānanda came to the spot after coming through the sky and some were of opinion that he came through the earth. Mahākassapa declared the attainment of Arahatship by Ānanda by shouting "Sādhu, Sādhu". Mahākassapa asked whether Dhamma was to be rehearsed first or the Vinaya. The opinion of the assembly was that Vinaya should be rehearsed first as the existence of the Buddhasāsana depended on Vinaya. The question arose as to who would answer the questions of Vinaya. It was decided that Upāli would be the first person to answer such questions. Mahākassapa taking the consent of the assembly asked him where the first pārājikā rule was enacted. The reply was that at Vaiśālī it was enacted concerning Sudiṇṇa Kalandakaputto on the subject of methunadhamma (sexual intercourse). All the questions were put to Upāli who answered them and all the bhikkhus repeated and remembered them. The question arose whether Ānanda was competent to answer the questions of Vinaya. In the opinion of the assembly Ānanda was competent, but Upāli was selected because the Buddha gave him the first place among the Vinayadhara bhikkhus. Ānanda was selected by the assembly to answer the questions on Dhamma. The Dīgha Nikāya of the Sutta Piṭaka was taken up first for rehearsal. The Brahmajālasutta was first rehearsed by Ānanda and the assembly recited it in chorus. All the suttas of the five Nikāyas were then rehearsed one after another (S.V., pt. I, pp. 2–25).

The Sumaṅgalavilāsinī further records some interesting information. Ujuññā is the name of a town. Kaṇṇakatthala is the name of a beautiful spot. Migadāya is so called because it was given for the freedom of deer (S.V., pt. II, p. 349). The Blessed One who was dwelling in a great monastery at Gijjhakūṭa, listening to the conversation held between the paribbājaka Nigrodha and the disciple Sandhāna, went through the sky and came to them and answered the questions put to by Nigrodha (*Ibid.*, p. 362). The kingdom of Gandhāra built by the sage Gandhāra is a trading centre (p. 389). Sālavatika is the name of a village. It is called

Sālavatika because it is surrounded on all sides by the sāla trees appearing like a fence (p. 395). Manasākaṭa is the name of a village (p. 399). Ambavana is a thicket of mangoe-trees. It is a beautiful spot having sands scattered on the ground like silver leaves and on the top having thick branches and leaves of the mangoe-trees. Here the Exalted One lived finding delight in solitude (p. 399). In the interior of Jetavana there are four big houses, e.g., Karerikuṭi, Kosambakuṭi, Gandhakuṭi, and Salaḷaghara. Salaḷaghara was built by King Pasenadi and the rest by Anāthapiṇḍika (p. 407). There is a reference to trees, e.g., sāla, sirīsa, udumbara or fig tree, banyan, and assattha (p. 416). Jambudīpa is great and it is 10,000 yojanas in extent. There is also Majjhimadesa and in the east there is Kajaṅgala country (p. 429). There is a reference to seven gems, e.g., cakka (wheel), hatthi (elephant), assa (horse), mani (jewel), itthī (woman), gahapati or householder, paināyaka or leader (p. 444). Cātummahārājika heaven contains 90,00,000 gods who obtain celestial happiness (p. 472). The Ābhassara gods are those whose bodies shed lustre (p. 510) and whose lease of life is 8 kalpas (p. 511). Gijjhakūṭa is so called because it has a pinnacle like a vulture and vultures dwell in it (p. 516). Sārandada cetiya has been described here as a vihāra (p. 521). Sunīdha and Vassakāra were endowed with great riches (p. 540). Nādika has been described as a village of relatives. Near the lake Nādika, there are two villages belonging to the sons of Cullapīti-Mahāpīti (p. 543). Māra engages creatures to do mischief to others and kill them (p. 555). There are lakes, e.g., Kharassarā, Khaṇḍassarā, Kākassarā, Bhaggassarā, etc. (p. 560). There is a reference to weavers in Benares who produce soft and beautiful garments (p. 563). Buddhaghosa understands sūkara-maddava by the flesh of a grown-up hog neither too young nor too old. It is soft and glossy (p. 568). Buddhaghosa refers to four kinds of bed, e.g., the bed of one who is merged in sensual pleasures, the bed of the departed spirit, the bed of a lion, and the bed of the Tathāgata (p. 574). There is a mention of the three piṭakas, five nikāyas, nine aṅgas, and 84,000 dhammakkhandhas (p. 591). Buddhaghosa interprets "aṭṭha Malla-pāmokkhā" in the sense that the eight Mallarājās were middle-aged and were endowed with strength (p. 596). Makuṭabandhana is a cetiya of the Mallas and is a sālā (covered hall) which gives satisfaction and blessings to the Malla chief (p. 596). Rājagaha is 25 yojanas in extent from Kusīnārā (p. 609). Jambudīpa is 10,000 yojanas in extent, Aparagoyāna is 7,000 yojanas in extent, and Uttarakuru is 8,000 yojanas in extent (p. 623). Jotipāla is so called on account of his lustre and rearing others up (p. 660). The Sākiyas and the Koliyas cultivated lands well because they confined the river Rohiṇī by a bund. This river flows between the territories of the Śākyas and the Koliyas (p. 672).

(2) Papañcasūdanī—the commentary on the Majjhima Nikāya.

The Papañcasūdanī is an extensive commentary on the Majjhima Nikāya written by Buddhaghosa at the request of a thera named Buddhamitta in the style more or less of the Sumaṅgalavilāsinī. In the commentary on the first ten suttas of the Majjhima Nikāya, Buddhaghosa[1] discusses the following topics: the four suttanikkhepas, balabojjhaṅga, Dhammacakka, the origin of all the dhammas, Nibbāṇa, earth, Tathāgata, Abhisambuddha, destruction of sin, false belief, saddhā, faith, four puggalas, obstacles in the path leading to Nibbāṇa, contact, old age, death, suffering, right recollection, mindfulness, pleasing sensation, and lastly emancipation.[2]

The Papañcasūdanī furnishes us with some

[1] This commentary by Buddhaghosa has been edited for the P.T.S., London, by J. H. Woods and D. Kosambi.

[2] There is a printed Burmese edition of this work published by the P. G. Mundine Pitaka Press, Rangoon (J.R.A.S., 1894); and also an excellent Siamese edition of this commentary printed and published in three volumes.

interesting historical and geographical details. There was a janapada named Kuru and the kings of that province used to be called Kurus (p. 225), of whose origin a fanciful story is told in the commentary. King Mahāmandhātā was a cakravarttī-rājā, a title which he had acquired for his having had a cakraratana with the help of which he could go to any place he liked. He conquered Pubbavideha, Aparagoyāna, Uttarakuru besides the devalokas. While returning from Uttarakuru, a large number of the inhabitants of that country followed Mahāmandhātā to Jambudīpa and the place in Jambudīpa where they settled became known as Kururaṭṭham including provinces, villages, towns, etc. It is in this sense that the word Kurusu (i.e., among the Kurus) occurs in the Pāli-Buddhist Literature (pp. 225-226).

There is also another fanciful explanation of the origin of the name of Sāvatthī. Sāvatthī was a place where one could get, it is asserted, whatever he wanted ; hence it is called Sāvatthī (Sabbaatthī). In answer to a question by some merchants as to what the place contained, it was told " sabbam atthi " (there is everything). Hence it is called Sāvatthī (vol. I, p. 59). The commentary refers incidentally to Gaṅgā and Yamunā (p. 12), to Sāvatthī, Jetavana, and Giribbaja which is so called because it stands like a cow-pen surrounded by a mountain (p. 151). It also refers to four more rivers of India besides Gaṅgā and Yamunā, e.g., Bāhukā, Sundarikā, Sarassatī, and Bāhumatī (p. 178), and to a mountain named Cittala. It relates the activities of Gautama Buddha among the Kurus (p. 225), at the Bodhi tree, and at Lumbinīvana (p. 13). It is pointed out that the abode of Tāvatiṁsa gods is beautiful ; that the four great kings were the employees of Sakka, king of gods ; that Vejayanta palace is one thousand yojanas in extent and that the Sudhamma or the mote-hall of the gods is 500 yojanas in length and the chariot of the Vejayanta heaven is 150 yojanas in extent (p. 225). In this book we find that there are two kinds of Buddha's instructions; Sammutidesanā and Paramatthadesanā. The Paramatthadesanā includes anicca (impermanent), dukkhaṁ (suffering), anatta (impermanent), khandha (constituents), dhātu (elements), āyatana (sphere), and satipaṭṭhāna (right recollection) (p. 137). A most important information is found in this book of Damiḷabhāsā and Andhabhāsā, i.e., the languages of the Tamils and the Andhras who may now roughly be said to be represented by the Telegus (p. 138). Tree worship was in practice; there were trees, it is said, which were worthy of worship in villages and countries (p. 119). Cultivation and cow-keeping are the main occupations of a householder and they are for his good (p. 111). Five kinds of medicines are mentioned, e.g., sappi (clarified butter, ghee), navanīta (butter), tela (oil), madhu (honey), and phāṇita (molasses) (p. 90). In this text, Māra is called Pajāpatī because he lords over a large assembly (p. 33). There are four kinds of paṭhavī (earth):—earth with signs, earth with load, earth with sense object, and earth with selection (p. 25).

The Papañcasūdanī (Vol. II) further narrates that the Himavanta (Himalayas) is 3,000 yojanas in width (p. 6). Vesālī is so called because it expanded itself (p. 19). Rājagaha is 60,000 yojanas in distance from Kapilavatthu (p. 152). Nādikā has been referred to as a lake (p. 235). Ghositārāma is so called because the ārāma or monastery was built by the banker, named Ghosita (p. 390). Jambudīpa is mentioned here as a forest and Pubba-Videha, an island (p. 423).

(3) Sāratthapakāsinī—the commentary on the Saṁyutta Nikāya.

The Sāratthapakāsinī is a commentary on the Saṁyutta Nikāya written by Buddhaghosa at the request of a thera named Jotipāla.

It has been published in two volumes by the P.T.S. under the able editorship of F. L. Woodward. The following are the manuscripts and printed editions available :—

(1) Palm-leaf manuscript in Sinhalese character at the Adyar Oriental Library, Madras.
(2) Incomplete Sinhalese printed edition by Vajirasara and Ñāninda Theras, Colombo, 1900–1911.
(3) Simon Hewavitarne Bequest edition of 1924, Vol. I, revised and edited by W. P. Mahāthera.
(4) A beautifully written palm-leaf manuscript in Sinhalese character.

In this commentary the word 'guru' is always used in this world (loke) as referring to the Buddha. The Blessed One is described as the possessor of ten potentialities (dasa baladharo) (Vol. I, p. 12). The commentator speaks of a land where the cows graze near the Ganges and the Yamunā (*Ibid.*, p. 13). Aṅga and Magadha are described as having plenty of food (p. 15). There is a reference to the four Buddhas (cattāro Buddhā): sabbaññu Buddha (all knowing), pacceko Buddha (individual), catusacco Buddha (master of four truths), and suta Buddha (Buddha who has heard) (*Ibid.*, p. 25).

Saddhamma is explained in this commentary as the term which includes the five sīlas, ten sīlas, and four objects of recollection or mindfulness (p. 55). The Mahāvana is described here as a big natural forest extending up to the Himalayas (p. 67). Pañcaveda is meant here as the five Vedas including the Itihāsa (p. 81). By vimuttacitta the commentator means a mind which is free from the Kammaṭṭhānas (p. 104). Nāthaputta is explained here as Nāthassaputta or the son of Nātha (p. 130). Mallikā is mentioned as the daughter of a poor garland-maker (p. 140). According to the commentator, Kisāgotamī was kisa or lean because she had not got much flesh (p. 190). Loka refers to the khandhaloka (the world of constituents), dhātu loka (the world of elements), āyatana loka (the world of abode), sampattibhavaloka (the world of prosperity), and vipattibhavaloka (the world of adversity) (p. 201).

There is a reference to the Mandākinīpokkharaṇī which is 50 yojanas in extent (p. 281) and to the Kailāsa mountain inhabited by a celestial being named Nāgadanta (p. 282). Gayā is mentioned here as a village (p. 302). Sīha-nāda is explained as great uproar (Vol. II, 46). Gaṅgā and Yamunā are mentioned as two great rivers (p. 54). Dakkhiṇagiri is a janapada on the southern side of the hill encircling Rājagaha (p. 176). There is a reference to cow-killer who kills cows and severs the flesh from the bone (p. 218).

(4) Manorathapūraṇī—the commentary on the Aṅguttara Nikāya.

The Manorathapūraṇī[1] is a commentary on the Aṅguttara Nikāya written by Buddhaghosa at the request of a thera named Bhaddanta.[2]

The Manorathapūraṇī deals with the following topics: sloth and stupor, haughtiness, desire for sensual pleasures, friendliness, mental emancipation, suffering, right realisation, functions of the mind, bojjhaṅga (supreme knowledge), thirty-two signs of a great man, puggala (human types), Tathāgata, realisation of the four paṭisambhidās or analytical knowledge, accounts of Aññakoṇḍañña, Sāriputta and Moggallāna, Mahākassapa, Anuruddha, Bhaddiya, Piṇḍolabhāradvāja, Puṇṇa-Mantāniputta, Mahākaccāna, Culla-Mahā-Panthaka, Subhūti, Revata, Kaṅkhārevata, Soṇa Koḷivisa, Soṇa Kuṭikaṇṇa, Sīvali, Vakkali, Rāhula-Raṭṭhapāla, Kuṇḍadhāna, Vaṅgīsa, Upasena, Dabba, Pilindavaccha, Bāhiya-Dārucīriya, Kumāra Kassapa, Mahākoṭṭhita, Ānanda, Uruvela Kassapa, Kāḷudāyī, Bakkula, Sobhita, Upāli, Nanda, Nandaka, Mahākappina, Sāgata, Rādha, Mogharāja, Mahā-

---

[1] There is a ṭikā on the Manorathapūraṇī written by a pupil of Sumedha Thera who flourished in the reign of Parākramabāhu. This work is also known as the Cātutthasāratthamañjūsā.

[2] Dr. Max Wallesar has edited the first volume of this work for the P.T.S., London. The complete work has been printed and published in Ceylon, Burma, and Siam.

pajāpatī Gotamī, Khemā, Uppalavaṇṇā, Paṭācārā, Dhammadinnā, Nandā, Sonā, Sakulā, Bhaddā-Kuṇḍalakesā, Bhaddā-Kāpilāni, Bhaddā-Kaccānā, Kisāgotamī, Sigālakamātā, Tapassa-Bhallikā, Sudatta Gahapati, Citta Gahapati, Hatthaka, Mahānāma Sakka, Ugga Gahapati, Sūra, Jīvaka Komārabhacca, Nakulapitā Gahapati, Sujātā Senānidhītā, Visākhā Migāramātā, Khujjuttarā-Sāmāvatī, Uttarā Nandamātā, Suppavāsā Koliyadhitā, Suppiyā, Kātiyāni, Nakulamātā Gahapatānī, Kāliupāsikā.[1]

This commentary contains an interesting account of the theras and therīs. As to the account of the therīs contained in this commentary, the readers are referred to my work, "Women in Buddhist Literature", Chap. VIII. An account of some of the prominent theras is given below.

*Anuruddha* was the foremost among those who had the divine eye. At the time of the Buddha's visit to Kapilavatthu, the Sakiyan princes, Anuruddha, brother of Mahānāma, Bhaddiya, Ānanda, Bhagu, Kimbila, and Devadatta followed by the barber Upāli renounced the worldly life with the intention of becoming monks. They asked admission into the congregation and the Master ordained them (Manorathapūraṇī, P.T.S., Vol. I, pt. I, pp. 183–192).

*Piṇḍola-Bhāradvāja* was also one of the eminent of the bhikkhus. He was born in a brahmin family at Rājagaha. He was versed in the three Vedas. He was called Piṇḍola, for wherever he went he asked for food. He once heard the Master preaching the Norm at Rājagaha. Full of faith he asked for admission into the Order. The Blessed One ordained him, as he soon attained arahatship (*Ibid.*, pp. 196–199).

*Puṇṇa-Mantāniputta* was the son of a brāhmaṇī named Mantānī. He was born in a brahmin family

[1] *Vide* "Women Leaders of the Buddhist Reformation", published in the J.R.A.S., 1893; it is an English translation of some portions of the Manorathapūraṇī.

at Donavatthunagara which was not far off the city of Kapilavatthu. He was the nephew of the thera Aññakoṇḍañña, one of the five bhikkhus who were converted by the Master at Isipatana where he first set rolling the wheel of Law. It was through Aññakoṇḍañña that Puṇṇa was inspired with faith in the Buddha. He received ordination and in due course attained arahatship. He had five hundred disciples who also attained arahatship under his guidance. He was also declared by the Lord as one of the foremost of the bhikkhus (*Ibid.*, pp. 199–204).

*Mahākaccāna* was the foremost among those who could fully explain the brief utterances of the Tathāgata. He was born as the son of a chaplain at Ujjenī. At the request of the King Caṇḍapajjota, Mahākaccāna went to the place where the Buddha was in order to bring the Blessed One to Ujjenī. Mahākaccāna heard the Master preaching the Norm. At the end of the discourse he won arahatship. He informed the Buddha of king's desire. The Blessed One did not grant his request, but bade him go back to Ujjenī and assured him that the king would be glad to see him alone. The king was highly pleased with Mahākaccāna for his attainments (*Ibid.*, pp. 204–209).

*Revata* was the foremost among those who were dwellers in a forest. He was the younger brother of Sāriputta. He received ordination from the bhikkhus and performed the duties of a monk in the forest. He attained arahatship in time (*Ibid.*, pp. 223–230).

*Soṇa-Koḷivīsa* was the foremost among those who put forth great efforts (āraddhaviriyāni). He was born in a Seṭṭhikula. He was brought up in great luxury. Once he heard the Master preaching the doctrine. He took permission from his parents and received ordination. He perceived that the highest end could not be attained in luxury. So he put forth great efforts and suffered every sort of mortifications. But he could not attain arahatship.

He desired to return to the worldly life and perform meritorious acts. The Lord came to know the thera's thought, and exhorted him. The thera in due course won arahatship (*Ibid.*, pp. 231–237).

*Rāhula-Raṭṭhapāla.* Rāhula was the foremost of the Sāmaṇeras, and Raṭṭhapāla of the youths who left the world in search of 'amata'. Rāhula was the son of the Buddha and Raṭṭhapāla was born in a seṭṭhi family of the kingdom of Kuru. At the time of the Buddha's visit to Kapilavatthu Rāhula received ordination from the Buddha. In course of time he attained arahatship.

Once the Lord visited the Thullakoṭṭhita-nigama (in the Kururaṭṭha)—the place of Raṭṭhapāla's birth. Raṭṭhapāla took permission from his parents and received ordination from the Master and went with the Buddha to Sāvatthī. He attained arahatship. In order to see his parents he once went to Thullakoṭṭhita-nigama and admonished them. Then he came back to the place where the Buddha was (*Ibid.*, pp. 251–260).

*Vaṅgīsa* was born in a brāhmaṇa family at Sāvatthī. He was versed in the three Vedas. He learnt the 'chavasīsa mantam' by which he could tell the place of birth of deceased persons. He travelled into different places and gained his living by this sippa. He once met Buddha and had conversation with him. The result was that Vaṅgīsa received ordination. He soon attained arahatship. Whenever he visited the Buddha he visited him with a hymn of praise. Accordingly he was reckoned as the foremost of the Paṭibhānavantānaṁ or those possessed of intelligence or ready wit (*Ibid.*, pp. 266–270).

*Kumāra Kassapa* was born at Rājagaha. His mother, when she was pregnant, received ordination and became a Sāmaṇerī. As the rearing up a child was not consistent with the life of a Sāmaṇerī, the child was reared up by Pasenadi, King of Kosala. When he grew up he received ordination, eventually won arahatship, and shined among the preachers. Accordingly he was reckoned as the foremost of the 'cittakathikānaṁ' or a wise speaker, an orator or a preacher (*Ibid.*, pp. 283–285).

*Mahākoṭṭhita* was the foremost among those who possessed analytical knowledge. He was born in a brahmin family at Sāvatthī. He learned the three Vedas. He once heard the Master preaching the Norm. Full of faith he received ordination and attained arahatship through analytical knowledge (*Ibid.*, pp. 285-286).

*Ānanda* was the foremost among those who were vastly learned in the doctrine. He with Anuruddha, Bhaddiya, Bhagu, Kimbila, and Devadatta followed by Upāli received ordination from the Master. He was the personal attendant of the Buddha, and attained arahatship just before the work of the First Buddhist Council began (*Ibid.*, pp. 286–296).

*Uruvela Kassapa* was the foremost of those who had great followings. He with his two brothers became ascetics of the Jaṭila sect. All the three had a good number of followers. The Lord first converted the eldest brother, Uruvela Kassapa, by showing him his supernatural powers. The next two brothers naturally followed suit (*Ibid.*, pp. 297–300).

*Upāli* was the foremost of those who knew the Vinaya rules. He was a barber. The Sakiyan princes Anuruddha, Ānanda, and others with their attendant Upāli, the barber, visited the Blessed One with the intention of becoming monks. They asked for admission into the Order, and in order to curb their pride, they requested that the barber should be first ordained. Their request was granted (*Ibid.*, pp. 311-312).

Commentaries on the Khuddaka Nikāya:—the Khuddakapāṭha Commentary.

Buddhaghosa wrote commentaries on three books of the Khuddaka Nikāya, e.g., (1) Khuddakapāṭha, (2) Dhammapada, and (3) Sutta Nipāta.

Khuddakapāṭha Aṭṭhakathā is known as the Paramatthajotikā.[1]

Like other commentaries of Buddhaghosa, the Paramatthajotikā, too, contains a good deal of interesting information. To start with, there is a very interesting but mythical origin of the Licchavis which is summarised as follows :—

"There was an embryo in the womb of the chief queen of Benares. Being aware of it, she informed the king who performed the rites and ceremonies for the protection of it. With the embryo thus perfectly protected, the queen entered the delivery chamber when it was fully mature. With ladies of great religious merit, the delivery took place at the dawn of day. A lump of flesh of the colour of lac and of bandhu and jīvaka flowers came out of her womb. Then the other queens thought that to tell the king that the chief queen was delivered of a mere lump of flesh while a son, resplendent like gold, was expected, would bring the displeasure of the king upon them all ; therefore, they, out of fear of exciting displeasure of the king, put that lump of flesh into a casket, and after shutting it up, put the royal seal upon it, and placed it on the flowing waters of the Ganges. As soon as it was abandoned, a god wishing to provide for its safety, wrote with a piece of good cinnabar on a slip of gold the words, 'the child of the chief queen of the King of Benares' and tied it to the casket. Then he placed it on the flowing current of the Ganges at a place where there was no danger from aquatic monsters. At that time an ascetic was travelling along the shore of the Ganges close by a settlement of cowherds. When he came down to the Ganges in the morning and saw a vessel coming on, he caught hold of it, thinking that it

---

[1] There is a valuable edition of the Commentary on the Khuddakapāṭha by Welipitiya Dewananda Thera and revised by Mahāgoḍa Siri Ñānissara Thera, Colombo, 1922.

It includes the commentaries on Jātaka, Sutta Nipāta, Dhammapada, and Khuddakapāṭha.

contained rags (paṁsukula), but seeing the tablet with the words written thereon and also the seal and mark of the King of Benares, he opened it and saw that piece of flesh. Seeing it, he thus thought within himself: 'It may be an embryo and there is nothing stinking or putrid in it', and taking it to his hermitage, he placed it on a pure place. Then after half a month had passed, the lump broke up into two pieces of flesh; the ascetic nursed them with still greater care. After the lapse of another half month, each of the pieces of flesh developed fine pimples for the head and the two arms and legs. After half a month from that time, one of the pieces of flesh became a son resplendent like gold, and the other became a girl. The ascetic was filled with paternal affection for the babies, and milk came out of his thumb. From that time forward, he obtained milk from rice; the rice he ate himself and gave the babies the milk to drink. Whatever got into the stomach of these two infants looked as if put into a vessel of precious transparent stone (maṇi), so that they seem to have had no skin (nicchavi); others said, 'The two (the skin and the thing in the stomach) are attached to each other (līnā-chavi) as if they were sewn up together, so that these infants owing to their being nicchavi, i.e., having no skin, or on account of their being līnā-chavi, i.e., attached skin or same skin, came to be designated as Licchavis. The ascetic having to nurse these two children had to enter the village in the early morning for alms and to return when the day was far advanced. The cowherds coming to know this conduct of his, told him, 'Reverend Sir, it is a great trouble for an ascetic to nurse and bring up children; kindly make over the children to us, we shall nurse them, do you please attend to your own business'. The ascetic assented gladly to their proposal. On the next day, the cowherds levelled the road, scattered flowers, unfurled banners, and came to the hermitage with music. The ascetic handed over the two children with these words: 'The children are possessed of great virtue and goodness, bring them up with great care and when they are grown up, marry them to each other; please the king and getting a piece of land, measure out a city, and install the prince there'. 'All right, sir', promised they, and taking away the children, they brought them up. The children, when grown up, used to beat with fists and kicks the children of the cowherds whenever there was a quarrel in the midst of their sports. They cried and when asked by their parents, 'Why do you cry?' They said, 'These nurslings of the hermit, without father and mother, beat us very hard'. Then the parents of these other children would say, 'These children harrass the others and trouble them, they are not to be kept, they must be abandoned' (vijjitabbā). Thenceforward that country measuring three hundred yojanas is called Vajji. Then the cowherds securing the good will and permission of the king, obtained that country, and measuring out a town there, they anointed the boy, King. After giving marriage of the boy, who was then sixteen years of age, with the girl the king made it a rule: 'No bride is to be brought in from the outside, nor is any girl from here to be given away to any one'. The first time they had two children —a boy and a girl, and thus a couple of children was born to them for sixteen times. Then as these children were growing up, one couple after another, and there was no room in the city for their gardens, pleasure groves, residential houses and attendants, three walls were thrown up round the city at a distance of a quarter of a yojana from each other; as the city was thus again and again made larger and still larger (visālikatā), it came to be called Vesālī. This is the history of Vesālī" (Paramatthajotikā on the Khuddakapāṭha, P.T.S., pp. 158–160).

In the Khuddakapāṭha Commentary we read that at Sāvatthī, there was a householder who was rich and wealthy. He had faith in the Buddha. One day he fed the Buddha along with the Bhikkhusaṁgha. Once King Pasenadi being in need of money sent for the householder who replied that he was concealing the treasures and he would see the king with them afterwards (pp. 216-217).

While the Buddha was at Sāvatthī, many bhikkhus of different places went to him to learn kammaṭṭhāna (objects of meditation). Buddha taught them kammaṭṭhāna suitable to their nature. Five hundred bhikkhus learnt kammaṭṭhāna from him and went to a forest by the side of the Himalayas to practise it. The tree deities of the place became frightened at seeing them there and tried to drive them out in various ways. The bhikkhus being troubled by them went to the Buddha to whom they related the story of their trouble. The Buddha said that they cherished no friendly feelings (mettā) towards the deities and that was the cause of trouble. Accordingly the Buddha taught them mettasuttam and asked them to practise it. Afterwards the deities became their friends (pp. 231 foll.).

The Khuddakapāṭha Commentary [1] furnishes us with many new and important materials concerning religious and political history of ancient India. It has references to the hermitage of Anāthapiṇḍika at Jetavana (p. 23), Kapilavatthu (p. 23), 18 great monasteries in Rājagaha (p. 94), Sattapaṇṇi cave (p. 95), Vesālī (p. 161), Magadha, Gayāsīsa (p. 204), Gaṅgā (p. 163), Bimbisāra (p. 163), Licchavi (p. 163), Upāli (p. 97), Mahākassapa (p. 91), Ānanda (p. 92), Mahāgovinda (p. 128), Visākhā, Dhammadinnā (p. 204), Mallikā (p. 129), etc.

In this commentary, the explanations are disproportionate to the short readings of the text. Its style is heavy and laboured, and its disquisitions are in many places redundant. It seems, therefore,

[1] The Khuddakapāṭha Commentary has been edited for the P.T.S. by Helmer Smith from a collation by Mabel Hunt.

highly doubtful if this work can really claim to have been written by Buddhaghosa.

Dhammapada-atthakathā.

The Dhammapada-aṭṭhakathā [1] is a voluminous work which explains the stanzas of the Dhammapada and contains a mass of illustrative tales of the nature of the Jātakas. It derives a considerable number of its stories from the four nikāyas, the Vinaya, the Udāna, the works of Buddhaghosa, and the Jātaka Book. But it is more intimately related to the Jātaka Book, for over fifty stories of the Dhammapada Commentary are either derivatives of Jātaka stories or close parallels. In addition many other Jātaka stories are referred to and many Jātaka stanzas are quoted. So it is certain that the Jātaka Book is earlier than the Dhammapada Commentary.

The Dhammapada-aṭṭhakathā is a commentary on the stanzas of the Dhammapada which is an anthology of 423 sayings of the Buddha in verses. An analysis of each story in the Dhammapada Commentary shows that each story consists of eight subdivisions : (1) Citation of the stanza (gāthā) to which the story relates, (2) mention of the person or persons with reference to whom the story was told, (3) story proper, or, more strictly, story of the present (Paccuppanna-vatthu), closing with the utterance of the (4) stanza or stanzas, (5) word-for-word commentary or gloss on the stanza, (6) brief statement of the spiritual benefits which accrued to the hearer or hearers, (7) story of the past, or, more accurately, story of previous existences (atīta-vatthu), and (8) identification of the personages of the story of the past with those of the story of the present. Sometimes the story of the past

[1] Prof. H. C. Norman has edited the complete volume for the P.T.S. ; Mr. E. W. Burlingame has translated it into English under the title of 'Buddhist Legends' in three parts (Harvard Oriental Series edited by Lanman, Vols. 28, 29, and 30) ; C. Duroiselle has translated it into English in the periodical *Buddhism*, Vol. II, Rangoon, 1905–1908.

precedes the story of the present, and not infrequently more than one story of the past is given (Buddhist Legends, pt. I, pp. 28-29).

Mr. Burlingame in his Introduction to stories of Dhammapada Commentary (Buddhist Legends, pt. I, p. 26), has rightly said that the Dhammapada-aṭṭhakathā (as a matter of fact all other Pāli aṭṭhakathās) is in name and form a commentary. But in point of fact it has become nothing more or less than a huge collection of legends and folk-tales. The exegesis of the text has become a matter of secondary importance altogether and is relegated to the background.

The Jātaka Book consists of 550 stories relating to previous births of the Buddha. Our present edition (Fausböll's edition) is not an edition of the text but of the commentary.

Each Jātaka consists of the following subdivisions: a verse together with a commentary without which the verse will be unintelligible, a framework of story stating when and where and on what occasion the story is supposed to have been spoken by the Buddha; and finally the conclusion in which the characters of the story are identified with the Buddha and his contemporaries in a previous birth.

We have pointed out the characteristics of a Jātaka story and also of a Dhammapada-aṭṭhakathā story and it is not unreasonable to say that in general character and structure of parts, the Jātaka Book and the Dhammapada-aṭṭhakathā do not differ.

Doubts have been raised whether the work can really be attributed to Buddhaghosa. The colophon, however, definitely ascribes the authorship to the celebrated commentator, and there is hardly any reason to doubt its authority. The scheme of the commentary is systematic and can easily be followed. Each story has been amplified by a good story, and at the end of each story interpretations of words have been given. The language is easily intelligible. The work as a whole is full of materials which, however, should be properly and carefully read and utilised for the study of social, religious, political, and economic conditions of India in the 5th century A.D. Besides, there are in this work humorous tales, animal stories, e.g., the story of Pārileyyaka, legends of saints, e.g., Visākhā, Paṭācārā, etc. Some stories of the Dhammapada are derived from the Vinaya Piṭaka, e.g., Devadatta, Bodhirājakumāra, Channa, etc. ; some from Udāna, e.g., Mahākassapa, Sāmāvatī, Visākhā, Soṇa Kotikaṇṇa, Sundarī, Nanda, Suppavāsā, etc. Some of the Jātaka stories correspond to some of the stories of the Dhammapada Commentary, e.g., Devadhamma, Kulāvaka, Telapatta, Sālittaka, Babbu, Godha, Cullapalobhana, Ananusociya, Kesava, Sāliya, Kusa, Ghata, etc. The Dhammapada Commentary, Therīgāthā Commentary, and the Aṅguttara Nikāya Commentary have some of the stories in common, e.g., Kuṇḍalakesī, Paṭācārā, Nandā, Khemā, Dhammadinnā, etc. Mr. Burlingame is able to point out that from the Saṁyutta are derived seventeen stories, fifteen of them almost word for word (Buddhist Legends, pt. I, pp. 45-46). Milinda Pañha contains some of the stories mentioned in this work, e.g., Maṭṭhakuṇḍali, Sumana, Ekasāṭaka brāhmaṇa, Pesakāradhītā, Sirimā, etc. (*vide* Buddhist Legends, pt. I, pp. 60–62). Parallels to the stories of this work are found in the Divyāvadāna and Tibetan Kandjur (*Ibid.*, pp. 63-64). Buddhaghosa says in the prologue of the Dhammapada-aṭṭhakathā that he translated the Sinhalese commentaries into Māgadhī (tanti) adding notes of his own at the request of the thera named Kumārakassapa (Dhammapada Commentary, Vol. I, pp. 1 and 2). Buddhaghosa often mixes up fact and fable without exercising any discrimination whatsoever as we find in the story of King Parantapa of Kosambī (Dhammapada-aṭṭhakathā, Vol. I, pt. II). The commentator also records the account of the elopement of Vāsavadattā with Udayana as we find it in Bhāsa's Svapnavāsavadattā. Udayana had another wife named Māgandiyā, the daughter of a brahmin, in the Kuru kingdom (Udenavatthu, pp. 161 ff.) Anāthapiṇḍika built a vihāra known as the Jetavana Vihāra for the Buddha at the expense of 54 Koṭis of Kahāpaṇa (Dhammapada Commentary, Vol. I, pp. 4-5). A girl of Anāthapiṇḍika's family went to the kingdom of Sātavāhana and there she offered alms to a bhikkhu. A great thera informed King Sātavāhana of it and eventually the girl was made the chief queen of the monarch (*Ibid.*, Burmese edition, p. 333). Buddhaghosa refers to flying through the air on the back of a garuḍa-bird made of wood and sufficient for the accommodation of three or four persons (*Ibid.*, Vol. III, pp. 134 ff.). In the Dhammapada Commentary, Buddhaghosa makes mention of a bird called Hatthiliṅga which is described as an animal possessing the strength of five elephants. It was in the habit of looking back on the track already trodden (Vol. I, pt. II). Buddhaghosa refers to the Mahāvihāra in Ceylon (Dhammapada Commentary, Vol. IV, p. 74) where, presumably his commentaries were written. Prof. Hardy points out (J.R.A.S., 1898, pp. 741–794) that the story of the merchant Ghosaka as related by Buddhaghosa in his Manorathapūraṇī, the commentary on the Aṅguttara Nikāya, differs from the same story told in the Dhammapada-aṭṭhakathā. It should be borne in mind that Buddhaghosa was not the writer of an independent commentary on the canonical texts, but he was for the most part translating or compiling from various Sinhalese commentaries, sometimes from the Mahā-aṭṭhakathā, sometimes from the Mahāpaccari, and sometimes from the Kuruṇḍa-aṭṭhakathā. Buddhaghosa cannot, therefore, be held responsible for variations in the narratives which might have been due to the differences in the authorship of the great old commentaries which were the embodiments of joint labours of a large number of Buddhist sages and scholars who had been working at the interpretation of the Master's sayings ever since they were uttered.

The Dhammapada-aṭṭhakathā abounds in references to kings, e.g., Bimbisāra, Ajātasattu, Pasenadi ; to Acelakas, Nigaṇṭhas, Ājivakas, Jaṭilas, Micchādiṭṭhikas ; to lakes, e.g., Anotattadaha ; to principal cities, e.g., Takkasīlā, Kapilavatthu, Kururaṭṭha, Kosambī, Kosala, Bārāṇasī, Soreyya, Magadha, Rājagaha, Sāvatthī, Vesālī ; to mountains, e.g., the Himalayas, Sineru, Gandhamādana, Gijjhakūṭa ; to principal Buddhist women, e.g., Mahāpajāpatī Gotamī, Khemā, Yasodharā, Sumanādevī, Māyādevī, Mallikā, Paṭācārā, Sujātā, Rāhulamātā, Vāsuladattā, Visākhā, Suppavāsā, Dinnā, Kisāgotamī, Rūpanandā ; to the heavens, e.g., Tāvatiṁsa, Tusita ; to forests and tanks, e.g., Veḷuvana, Mahāvana, Jetavana, Maṅgalapokkharaṇī ; to rivers, e.g., Gaṅgā, Rohiṇī (Vol. II, p. 99) ; to the famous physician Jīvaka ; to ancient Indian tribes, e.g., Licchavis, Mallas ; to distinguished persons, e.g., Siddhattha, Sāriputta, Mahinda, Rāhula, Ānanda, Vessavana, Soṇa Kūṭikaṇṇa, Moggallāna, and Meṇḍaka.

In the Dhammapada-aṭṭhakathā we read that there lived at Kosambī a householder's son, Kosambivāsī Tissa Thera, who took ordination from the Buddha. His supporter offered his son who was seven years old to Tissa. The boy was made a sāmaṇera by Tissa and as the hair of the sāmaṇera was being cut, he attained arahatship (Vol. II, pp. 182–185).

Buddhaghosa records legend which has some points of agreement with a story in the Skandapurāṇa (Ch. 5, Brahmakhaṇḍa). It is recorded that there lived at Kosambī a king named Parantapa. One day he sat under the sun with his pregnant wife who was covered with a red blanket when a bird named Hatthiliṅga having the strength of five elephants, took her to be a lump of flesh, came to her, and took her away with its claws. The queen thought that before it could eat her, she would cry out and it would leave her. It was in the habit of looking back on the track. The queen also cried accordingly and the bird left her. At that time rain poured heavily and continued throughout the night. Early in the morning when the sun arose, a son was born to her. A hermit came to the spot where the son was born and saw the queen on the Nigrodha tree which was not far from his hermitage. When the queen introduced herself as a Kṣatriyāṇī, the hermit brought down the baby from the tree. The queen came to the hermitage of the sage who accompanied her with her infant son. The queen succeeded in tempting him to take her as his spouse and they lived as husband and wife. One day the hermit looked at the stars and saw the star of Parantapa disfigured. He informed her of the death of Parantapa of Kosambī. The queen cried and told him, "He is my husband and I am his queen. If my son had lived there, he would have become the king now." The hermit assured her that he would help her son to win the kingdom. Her son eventually became king and was known as Udayana. The new king married Sāmāvatī, a daughter of the treasurer of Kosambī. Buddhaghosa records moreover the account of the elopement of Vāsavadattā with Udayana as we find it in the Svapnavāsavadattā by Bhāṣa (Vol. I, pt. II).

The Dhammapada Commentary gives us details regarding the life of the Thera Mahākaccāyana. We are told that when he was dwelling at Avanti, the Buddha was residing at the palace of the renowned upāsikā at Sāvatthī, Visākhā Migaramātā; nevertheless, though separated by such a long distance from the Master, yet whenever any sermon was delivered by the latter on Dhamma, Mahākaccāyana used to be present. Therefore a seat was reserved for him by the bhikkhus (Vol. II, pp. 176-177). We also read in the same commentary that when Mahākaccāyana was living at the city of Kuraraghara in Avanti, an upāsaka named Soṇa Kūtikaṇṇo was pleased with him after listening to his religious sermon. The upāsaka requested him to give him ordination which was given (Vol. IV, p. 101). A nāga king named Erakapatta was taught by the Buddha at the foot of the Sattasirīsaka tree at Benares that it was very difficult to be born as a human being (Vol. III, p. 230). A trader of Benares used to trade by putting his goods on the back of an ass. Once he went to Taxila for trade and gave his ass rest there by taking down the goods from its back (Vol. I, p. 123). A trader of Benares was going to Sāvatthī with five hundred carts full of red cloth, but he could not cross the river as it was full of water, so he had to stay there to sell his goods (Vol. III, p. 429). At Benares there was a rich banker named Mahādhanaseṭṭhi. His parents taught him dancing and music. Another rich banker had a daughter who was trained in dancing and music and both of them were married. Mahādhanaseṭṭhi began to drink wine and was addicted to gambling, with the result that he lost his own wealth as well as his wife's. Afterwards he began to beg for alms (Vol. III, pp. 129 foll.). A king of Benares learnt a mantra from a young brahmin by paying him 1,000 kahāpaṇas as teacher's fee. The king saved his life from the hands of the barber who was instigated by the senapati to kill him by that mantra (Vol. I, pp. 251 foll.). A brahmin of Taxila sent his son Susīma to learn Vedic mantra from a teacher who was his father's friend. The teacher taught him well (Vol. III, p. 445). A young man of Benares went to Taxila to learn archery from a distinguished teacher and he was well versed in the art, and the teacher being satisfied gave his daughter in marriage to him (Vol. IV, p. 66). We read that a king of Benares went out in disguise to enquire whether any of his subjects spoke ill of him. For 1,000 kahāpaṇas he learnt from a young brahmin of Benares a mantra which enabled him to read the evil thoughts of people (Vol. I, pp. 251 foll.). In spite of the good government, the country was not free from crime. Cakkhupāla was a physician at Benares. He gave medicine to a woman who deceived him by telling a lie. He being angry with her gave her a medicine which made her blind (Vol. I, p. 20). Pasenadi, son of Mahākosala, was educated at Taxila and Mahāli, a Licchavi prince, and a Malla prince of Kusīnārā were his class-mates (Vol. I, pp. 337-338). Kosala was not inhabited by the seṭṭhis previous to Pasenadi of Kosala who asked Meṇḍakaseṭṭhi and Dhanañjayaseṭṭhi to settle in the country and they did settle there (Vol. I, pp. 384 foll.). Pasenadi of Kosala was enamoured of a beautiful woman and tried to win her by killing her husband, but he gave up this idea when warned by the Buddha (Vol. II, pp. 1 foll.). Some thieves were caught and brought before the king of Kosala. He ordered them to be bound in ropes and chains. They were thrown in prison. This information was given by the bhikkhus to the Buddha who was asked whether there was any stronger tie than this. Buddha replied, "attachment to wives, sons, and wealth is stronger than other ties" (Vol. IV, pp. 54-55). In Kosala a cowherd named Nanda was rich and wealthy. He used to go to Anāthapiṇḍika's house from time to time taking with him five kinds of preparations from cow's milk. He invited the Buddha who accepted the invitation. Nanda continued charities for a week. On the seventh day Buddha delivered a sermon on dāna, sīla, etc., upon which Nanda obtained the first stage of sanctification (Vol. I, pp. 322-323). Mahāsuvaṇṇa, a banker of Sāvatthī, had two sons, the first son became a bhikkhu under the Buddha and was known as Cakkhupāla (Vol. I, pp. 3 foll.). Maṭṭhakuṇḍali was the son of a rich and stingy brahmin of Sāvatthī. Only by saluting the Buddha he went to heaven (*Ibid.*, pp. 25 foll.). Thullatissa was the Buddha's father's sister's son and lived at Sāvatthī as a bhikkhu. He was pacified by the Buddha (*Ibid.*, pp. 37 foll.). Kāliyakkhinī was a Yakkhinī worshipped by the people of Sāvatthī. She could foretell drought and excessive rainfall (*Ibid.*, pp. 45 foll.). Sāvatthī contributed a fair number of the bhikkhus and bhikkhuṇīs who acquired fame and renown in the Buddhist congregation for the purity of their lives. Paṭācārā was the daughter of a rich banker of Sāvatthī. She afterwards became a bhikkhuṇī after great bereavements and came to be known as Paṭācārā (Vol. II, pp. 260 foll.). Kisāgotamī was the daughter of a seṭṭhi of Sāvatthī. After the death of her only child she went to the Buddha with the dead body and requested him to bring the dead to life. The Buddha delivered a sermon which led her to become a bhikkhuṇī (*Ibid.*, Vol. II, pp. 270 foll.). Anitthigandhakumāra fallen from the Brahmaloka was reborn in a rich family of Sāvatthī. He used to cry when touched by women. He was afterwards converted by the Buddha (*Ibid.*, Vol. III, pp. 281 foll.). Vakkali born in a brahmin family of Sāvatthī became a bhikkhu seeing the beauty of the Buddha's body (*Ibid.*, Vol. IV, p. 118). A servant of a brahmin of Sāvatthī became a bhikkhu and subsequently attained arahatship (*Ibid.*, Vol. IV, p. 167). Nanda was the son of Mahāpajāpatī Gotamī. He was made a bhikkhu by the Buddha at Sāvatthī (*Ibid.*, pp. 15 foll.).

The Dhammapada Commentary refers to the long continued jealousy of the heretics towards Buddhism. Moggallāna, one of the chief disciples of the Buddha, was struck by certain heretics with the help of some hired men (Vol. III, pp. 65 foll.). He used to dwell in Kullavālagāma in Magadha. At first he was very lazy, but being encouraged by the Buddha he exerted strenuously and fulfilled sāvakapāramī. It is to be noted that Sāriputta who was a Magadhan obtained pāramitā here (*Ibid.*, Vol. I, p. 96). The same commentary also gives us legends about Bimbisāra, King of Magadha, who went to see the most beautiful palace of Jotiya in the mythic land of Uttarakuru. Ajātasatru was his son. Both of them took their meals at Jotiya's palace. Jotiya presented Bimbisāra with a valuable gem, the light of which was enough to illuminate the whole house (Dh. Com., Vol. IV, pp. 209 foll.). A large number of heretics of the Saṁsāramocaka caste, who were opponents of Buddhism, employed some hired men to assault Moggallāna, one of the chief followers of the Buddha (Dh. Com., Vol. III, pp. 65 foll.). Two chief disciples of the Buddha went to Rājagaha and the inhabitants of Rājagaha showered charities upon them. A silk robe which was given in charity was given to Devadatta (*Ibid.*, Vol. I, pp. 77 foll.). A daughter of a banker of Rājagaha obtained Sotāpatti (*Ibid.*, Vol. III, p. 30). Sirimā was a beautiful prostitute of Rājagaha. She asked pardon of Uttarā, daughter of Puṇṇakaseṭṭhi for her faults, in the presence of the Buddha. She afterwards became one of his lay devotees and spent a large sum for him and his disciples (*Ibid.*, Vol. III, pp. 104 foll.). The mother of Kumārakassapa was the daughter of a banker of Rājagaha. When she grew up, she asked permission from her parents to receive ordination which was refused. She then went to her husband's place. She pleased her husband very much and got permission from him to receive ordination (*Ibid.*, Vol. III, pp. 144-145). A brahmin of Sāvatthī became an arahant of Gijjhakūṭa. He was very proud of seeing the beauty of the Buddha's body. The Buddha told, "No use seeing my body, see my Dhamma and you will see me" (*Ibid.*, Vol. IV, pp. 117-118).

This work further relates that Kuṇḍalakesī, a beautiful daughter of a banker of Rājagaha, remained unmarried till the age of sixteen. It is there incidentally pointed out that at this age women long for men (Vol. II, p. 217). Magha, a householder of Magadha, married his maternal uncle's daughter named Sujātā (Vol. I, p. 265). Ānanda was enamoured of the beauty of his father's sister's daughter named Uppalavaṇṇā and wanted to marry her (*Ibid.*, Vol. II, p. 49). Vepacitti, King of the Asuras, refused to give his daughter in marriage to any of the Asura princes. So he said, "My daughter shall choose for herself such a husband as she sees fit ". He then assembled the host of Asuras, made over a garland of flowers to his daughter and said to her, " Choose for yourself a husband who suits you ". The girl selected one as her husband and threw the wreath over his head (Dh. Com., Vol. I, pp. 278-279). We are informed by this commentary that a rich man's daughter, when she attained marriageable age, was lodged by her parents in an apartment of royal splendour on the topmost floor of a seven-storied palace, with a female slave to guard her. No male servant was kept in that house (Vol. II, p. 217). Daughters of noble families did not ordinarily come out of their house, but they travelled in chariots and the like while others entered an ordinary carriage or raised a parasol of a palmyra-leaf over their heads ; but if this was not available, they took the skirt of their undergarment and threw it over their shoulder (Vol. I, p. 391). From the instances cited above it is reasonable to hold that elopement and the preservation of chastity *inter alia* contributed largely to the observance of ' purdah ' by the tender sex before or after marriage. But there are exceptions, Visākhā, for example, while going to her father-in-law's house just after her marriage entered the city of Sāvatthī not under the ' purdah ' but standing up in a chariot uncovered showing herself to all the city (Vol. I, pp. 384 foll.). Daughters of respectable families, who did not ordinarily stir out, used to go on foot during a festival, with their own retinue, and bathe in the river (Vol. I, pp. 190-191 and 388). Instances of dowry being given by the bride's father are referred to in the Visākhāyavatthu of the Dhammapada Commentary (Vol. I). The Sāvatthian treasurer, Migāra, on the occasion of the marriage of his daughter, Visākhā, well-known in the Buddhist literature, gave her as dowry five hundred carts filled with vessels of gold, five hundred filled with vessels of silver, five hundred filled with copper vessels, five hundred filled with garments made of various kinds of silk, five hundred filled with ghee, five hundred filled with plows, plowshares, and other farm implements. Sixty thousand powerful bulls and sixty thousand milch cows, and some powerful bull-calves were also given to her.

Princess Vajirā was the daughter of Pasenadi of Kosala. She was given in marriage to Ajātasattu of Magadha. Kāsigāma was given to her by her father for bath and perfume money (Dh. Com., Vol. III, p. 266). The Sāvatthian treasurer, Migāra, gave his daughter, on her marriage, fifty crores of treasure to buy aromatic powders for the bath (*Ibid.*, I, p. 398). The custom of collecting presents (puṇṇākāram) on the occasion of a marriage ceremony is met with in the Dhammapada Commentary where we read that on the occasion of the marriage ceremony of Visākhā, daughter of Dhanañjaya seṭṭhi with the son of Migāra seṭṭhi, presents including a hundred each of all kinds of gifts were collected from hundred villages (Vol. I, pp. 384 foll.). After marriage the girl was sent to her father-in-law's house with the following directions [1]:—

1. Do not carry outside the indoor fire.
2. Do not carry inside the outdoor fire.
3. Give only to him that gives.
4. Do not give him that does not give.
5. Give both to him that gives and him that does not give.
6. Sit happily.
7. Eat happily.
8. Sleep happily.
9. Tend the fire.
10. Honour the household divinity.

[1] Antoaggi bahi na nīharitabbo, bahi aggi anto na pavesetabbo, dadantass' eva dātabbaṁ, adantassa na dātabbaṁ, dadantassāpi adantassāpi dātabbaṁ, sukhaṁ nisīditabbaṁ, sukhaṁ bhuñjitabbaṁ, sukhaṁ nipajjitabbaṁ, aggi paricaritabbo, antodevatā pi namassitabbā' ti idam dasavidhaṁ ovādaṁ (Dh. Com., I, 397-398).

These ten admonitions were interpreted as follows :—

1. If the mother-in-law or other female members of the household engage in a private conversation within the house, their conversation is not to be communicated to slaves, whether male or female, for such conversation is tattled about and causes quarrels.

2. The conversation of slaves and servants is not to be communicated to persons within the household ; as such conversation is talked about and causes quarrels.

3. This means that one should give only to those who return borrowed articles.

4. This means that one should not give to those who do not return borrowed articles.

5. This means that one should help poor kinsfolk and friends who look for succour, without considering their capability of repaying.

6. This means that a wife seeing her mother-in-law or her father-in-law should stand and not remain sitting.

7. This means that a wife should not eat before her mother-in-law, father-in-law, and husband have taken their meals. She should serve them first, and when she is sure that they have had all they care for, then and not till then may she herself eat.

8. This means that a wife should not go to bed before her mother-in-law, father-in-law, and husband. She should first perform all the duties which she owes them and then she may herself lie down to sleep.

9. This means that a wife should regard her mother-in-law, her father-in-law, or her husband as a flame of fire or as a serpent king.

10. When a monk after keeping residence in a remote lodging comes to the door of a house, and the housewife sees him, she must give to such a monk whatever food there is in the house both

hard and soft; and then she may eat (Dh. Com., Vol. I, pp. 403-404). A Magadhan householder, named Magha, had four wives at a time, viz., Nandā, Cittā, Sudhammā, and Sujātā (*Ibid.*, I, p. 269). The first wife of a householder of Sāvatthī being barren brought another wife for her husband. When her co-wife became pregnant, she was jealous and effected abortion by administering medicine. Thrice did this woman commit this heinous crime with the result that her co-wife succumbed at last to the effect of the abortive medicine. But the cruel woman did not escape the penalty for doing this sinful deed. She was beaten to death by her husband who declared her to be the cause of the death of his pregnant wife and destroyer of his line (Dh. Com., Vol. I, pp. 45 foll.).

Besides her household duties a slave woman had to husk paddy (Dh. Com., Vol. III, p. 321) and to go to market (*Ibid.*, Vol. I, p. 208).

Khujjuttarā, a maid-servant of Samāvatī, queen of Udena, King of Kosambī, had to buy flowers daily for eight kahāpaṇas for the queen. But she used to steal four kahāpaṇas daily. One day while she went to the garland-maker's house to buy flowers, she heard the sermon delivered by the Buddha. She obtained sotāpattiphalaṁ. Since then she discontinued stealing and bought flowers for eight kahāpaṇas. The queen questioned her how she had bought so many flowers for eight kahāpaṇas. The maid-servant could no longer conceal anything, as by this time her faith in the Buddha had become very strong. She confessed her guilt and said that after hearing the Buddha's sermon she had come to realise that stealing a thing is a sin. The queen asked her to repeat the Dhamma she had heard. Khujjuttarā did so in the presence of the queen and her five hundred female attendants. The queen did not reproach her for her stealing four kahāpaṇas daily, on the contrary, she praised her much for letting her hear the Buddha's Dhamma. Since then the maid-servant was regarded as a mother and teacher by the queen and her five hundred female attendants, who asked her to go to the Master daily to hear the Dhamma and repeat it to them. In course of time she mastered the Tripiṭaka (Dh. Com., Vol. I, pp. 208 foll.).

Sirimā was the youngest sister of Jīvaka, the well-known physician. She was a courtesan of unique beauty. She lived at Rājagaha. Once she was appointed for a fortnight by the female lay disciple, Uttarā, wife of the treasurer's son, Sumana, and daughter of the treasurer, Puṇṇaka, for one thousand pieces of money per night (Dh. Com., Vol. III, pp. 308-309) in order to minister to Uttarā's husband. One day she offended Uttarā, but desiring to be on good terms with her again, she begged pardon of her. Uttarā assured her that she would pardon her if the Exalted One would do the same. One day the Master and the congregation of monks came to Uttarā's house. When the Master had finished his meal, Sirimā begged his pardon. The Teacher pronounced thanksgiving and delivered discourse to which Sirimā listened attentively. Then she attained the first stage of sanctification. Since then she regularly gave alms to eight monks (Dh. Com., Vol. III, pp. 104 foll.). On her death, Sirimā's dead body was not burnt. It was kept in a charnel-house (āmakasusānaṁ) and watched by a guard against its being devoured by crows and dogs. King Bimbisāra informed the Buddha of her death, and the Buddha requested the king not to burn her dead body but to preserve it so that it could be seen by the bhikkhus daily for asubha-bhāvanā. The bhikkhus saw it daily and realised that the most beautiful body becomes rotten, worm-eaten, and finally the bones remain without flesh. The citizens, too, were compelled to behold Sirimā's dead body, for there stood the royal proclamation, " All who refuse to do so shall be fined eight pieces of money ". This was done with a view to impress on the citizens the idea of transitoriness of human beauty which is but skin-deep (Dh. Com., Vol. III, pp. 106–109).

Dinnā was an upāsikā of the Buddha. She was the queen of King Uggasena. A king promised to the deity of a nigrodha tree that he would worship the deity with blood of one hundred kings of Jambudīpa, if he got the throne after his father's death. He then defeated all the kings one by one and went to worship the deity, but the deity, seeing that many kings would be killed, took compassion for them and refused his worship on the ground that the queen of King Uggasena whom he defeated was not brought. The king had her brought and she preached a sermon on the avoidance of life-slaughter in their presence. The deity approved and the king refrained from life-slaughter and released the defeated and captured kings who praised Dinnā for her act. It was due to her that so many kings were saved (Dh. Com., Vol. II, pp. 15 foll.).

Kisāgotamī came of a respectable family at Sāvatthī. She was married to a rich banker's son who had 40 koṭis of wealth (Dh. Com., Vol. II, pp. 270–275). Bodhisatta was her maternal uncle's son. One day while the Bodhisatta was returning home after receiving the news of Rāhula's birth, he was seen by Kisāgotamī from her palace. Buddha's physical grace and charm gladdened the heart of Kisāgotamī and she uttered that the mother who had such a child and the father who had such a son and the wife who had such a husband were surely happy (nibbuta); but the Bodhisatta took the word nibbuta in the sense of nibbānaṁ. The Bodhisatta presented her with a pearl necklace for making him hear such an auspicious and sacred word (Dh. Com., Vol. I, p. 85). After the Bodhisatta had become the Buddha, Kisāgotamī once came through the sky to worship the Buddha ; but she saw that Sakka with his retinue was then seated before the Master. She, therefore, chose it not to descend and come near to the Buddha ;

but did her worship from the sky and went away. Being questioned by Sakka who had seen Kisāgotamī performing her worship, the Buddha answered that she was his daughter. Kisāgotamī was the foremost among the bhikkhunīs who used very rough and simple robes (Dh. Com., Vol. IV, pp. 156-157).

Once Pasenadi invited the Buddha to teach Dhamma to queens Mallikā and Vāsabhakhattiyā who were desirous of learning it. But as it was not possible for him to go everyday, the Buddha asked the king to engage Ānanda for the purpose. Mallikādevī in due course learnt it thoroughly well; but Vāsabhakhattiyā was inattentive and could hardly, therefore, learn it (Dh. Com., Vol. I, 382). Mallikā once induced her husband, King Pasenadi, to go to the Buddha and receive instructions from him, and thus saved the life of many living beings who were brought before the king for sacrifice to save the king himself from the evil effect of hearing four horrible sounds at midnight, and she made the following arrangements on the occasion of Pasenadi's offering unique gift to the Buddha and the Buddhists:—

1. She made a canopy with sāla wooden parts under which five hundred bhikkhus could sit within the parts and five hundred outside them.

2. Five hundred white umbrellas were raised by 500 elephants standing at the back of five hundred bhikkhus.

3. Golden boats were placed in the middle of the pandal and each khattiya daughter threw scents standing in the midst of two bhikkhus.

4. Each khattiya princess was found standing in the midst of two bhikkhus.

5. Golden boats were filled with scents and perfumes (Dh. Com., Vol. III, pp. 183 foll.).

Mallikādevī had, however, to suffer after death, in the Avīci hell, because she had once deceived her husband by telling a lie about her misconduct (Dh. Com., Vol. III, pp. 119 foll.).

The daughter of Queen Mallikā was also named Mallikā. She was the wife of General Bandhula, but was childless for a long time. Bandhula, therefore, once for all, sent her to her father's house, when on the way she went to the Jetavana to salute the Buddha and told the Master that her husband was sending her home as she was childless. The Buddha asked her to go back to her husband's house. Bandhula came eventually to know of this fact, and thought that the Buddha must have got the idea that she would be pregnant. The sign of pregnancy was soon visible in her and she desired to drink water and bathe in the well-guarded tank. Her husband made her bathe and drink water of the tank (Dh. Com., Vol. I, pp. 349–351).

Uttarā and her husband were serving a seṭṭhi at Rājagaha. Once the seṭṭhi went to attend a famous ceremony and Uttarā with her husband stayed at home. One morning, the husband of Uttarā had gone to the fields to till the soil, and Uttarā was going with cooked food to feed her husband there. On the way she met Sāriputta who had just got up from nirodhasamāpatti and offered the food to him with the result that she became the richest lady at Rājagaha and her husband became a seṭṭhi named Mahādhanaseṭṭhi (Dh. Com., Vol. III, pp. 302 foll.).

Puṇṇā was the maid-servant of a banker of Sāvatthī. Once while engaged in husking paddy at night, she went outside the house to take rest. At this time Dabba, a Mallian, was in charge of making arrangements for the sleeping accommodation of the bhikkhus who were guests. Puṇṇā with some cakes went out to enquire of the cause of their movements with lights at night, and met the Buddha who had come out on that way for alms. She offered all the cakes to the Buddha without keeping anything for her, and the Buddha accepted all of them. Puṇṇā was thinking whether Buddha would partake of her food; but the Buddha most unhesitatingly did partake of it in her house. The effect of this offer was that Puṇṇā obtained sotāpattiphalaṁ at the place where the offer was made (Dh. Com., Vol. III, pp. 321 foll.).

Rohiṇī was Anuruddha's sister. She was suffering from white leprosy, and did not go to her brother as she feared she might contaminate him. Anuruddha sent for her and asked her to build a rest-house for bhikkhus to get rid of her sin. She did so, and kept the rest-house clean even when it was under construction. After she had done it with great devotion for a long time, she eventually became free from her disease. Shortly afterwards the Buddha went to Kapilavatthu and sent for Rohiṇī. When she came, he told her that she had been the queen of Benares in her former birth. The king of Benares was at that time enamoured of the beauty of a dancing girl. The queen knowing this was jealous of the girl and to punish her she put something in her cloth and poured in bathing water which produced terrible itching all over the body. On account of this sin, she had got this disease. She however obtained sotāpattiphalaṁ and the colour of her body was golden (Dh. Com., Vol. III, pp. 295 foll.).

A cultivator's daughter was in charge of a paddy-field. She was once frying paddy in the field, when at that time Mahākassapa was engaged in meditation for a week in the Pipphali cave. Rising up from meditation he went to the girl for alms; and she with a delightful mind offered fried grains to him which he accepted. While the girl was returning from the presence of Mahākassapa to the spot where she was frying she was smitten by a poisonous snake and died instantly. After death she was reborn in the golden mansion of the Tāvatiṁsa heaven on account of this meritorious deed, and was named there as Lājadevadhītā who had come from heaven to get more merit by serving Mahākassapa. She used to cleanse his monastery and keep water ready for his use. But after two days, she was forbidden to serve him any more as she was found out to be a devī. She lamented much for not being able to serve the great arahat. The Buddha came to know of this and preached a sermon to her with the result that she obtained sotāpattiphalaṁ (Dh. Com., Vol. III, pp. 6–9).

The mother of Kumārakassapa had become pregnant before she renounced the worldly life; but she was herself unaware of it. After she had become a bhikkhunī it was known that she was pregnant. The matter was referred to the Buddha who asked Upāli to enquire into the matter. Upāli referred to Pasenadi, Anāthapiṇḍika, and Visākhā. Visākhā was afterwards solely entrusted to decide the matter. Visākhā found out that she had become pregnant before her renouncing the world (Dh. Com., Vol. III, pp. 144 foll.).

Rūpanandā was the Buddha's step-mother. She thought that her eldest brother had renounced the world and had become a Buddha. Her younger brother Nanda was a bhikkhu; Rāhulakumāra had also obtained ordination; her husband too had become a bhikkhu; and her mother Mahāpajāpatī Gotamī, a bhikkhunī. She, therefore, thought that as so many of her relatives had renounced the world, so she too must follow their path. She did not go before the Buddha as she was proud of her beauty while the Buddha used to preach impermanence and worthlessness of rūpa. The other bhikkhunīs and bhikkhus always used to praise Buddha in her presence and told her that all, in spite of their having different tastes, had become pleased on seeing the Buddha (Dh. Com., Vol. III, p. 115). Nandā, wife of Nandasena, a householder of Sāvatthī, had no faith in the Buddha. One day she thought of going to the Buddha with other bhikkhunīs, but she would not show herself to the Buddha. The Buddha came to know that with other bhikkhunīs Nandā too had come; and he desired to lower down the pride of her beauty. By his miraculous power, the Buddha created a most beautiful girl by his side who at once engaged herself in fanning the Buddha. Nandā saw the beauty of the girl, and readily discovered that her own beauty was much inferior. The attendant girl was seen gradually but miraculously attaining youth, the state of mother of one child, and the old age and disease and death. Nandā saw this happening before her eyes and gave up the pride of her beauty and came to realise the impermanence of physical beauty. The Buddha knowing the state of her mind delivered the sermon (Dh. Com., Vol. III, pp. 113 foll.).

Visākhā was the daughter of Dhanañjayaseṭṭhi, son of Meṇḍakaseṭṭhi, who lived in the city of Bhaddiya in the kingdom of Aṅga. The family of Meṇḍaka was greatly devoted to the Buddha. Dhanañjayaseṭṭhi at the request of Pasenadi, King of Kosala, went to his kingdom and settled at Sāketa. Visākhā was married to Puṇṇavaddhana, son of Migāraseṭṭhi, who was, however, a follower of the Nigaṇṭhas. After marriage, she lived with her father-in-law at Sāvatthī. One day Migāraseṭṭhi invited five hundred naked ascetics (nigaṇṭhas) and when they came he asked his daughter-in-law to come and salute the arahats. She came hearing about the arahats and seeing them, she said, " Such shameless creatures can't be arahats. Why has my father-in-law called me ? " Saying this she blamed her father-in-law and went to her residence. The naked ascetics seeing this, blamed the seṭṭhi and asked him to turn her out of the house as she was a follower of Samaṇa Gotama. But the seṭṭhi knowing that it was not possible to do so, apologised to them and sent them away. After this incident the seṭṭhi sitting on a valuable seat was drinking milk-porridge with honey from a golden pot and Visākhā stood there fanning him. At that time a Buddhist monk entered the house for alms and stood before him, but the seṭṭhi took no notice of him. Seeing that, Visākhā said to the thera " Go to another house, Sir, my father-in-law is eating a stale food ". At this the banker grew angry. He then stopped eating and ordered his men to drive her out. Thereupon, Visākhā said that he should examine her shortcomings. The seṭṭhi welcomed the idea and summoned her relations and told them that his daughter-in-law had said to a Buddhist monk that he was eating stale food while he was drinking milk porridge with honey. Visākhā's relations enquired about the truth of the statement. Visākhā said that she did not say so. She only said that her father-in-law was enjoying the fruition of his merit in the previous birth. In this way Visākhā explained away everything that was considered by her father-in-law to bring blame upon her. While she was found not guilty by her relations, she prepared to leave the house of her father-in-law. Thereupon the banker apologised and entreated his daughter-in-law to remain in the house. She, however, consented to remain on one condition only, namely, that she could be allowed to entertain the bhikkhus in the house at her will. Next day she invited the Buddha to her house. The naked ascetics knowing that the Buddha had entered the house of Migāra-seṭṭhi surrounded the house. Visākhā requested her father-in-law to come and serve the Buddha himself. The naked ascetics prevented him from going there. Thereupon Visākhā herself served the Buddha and his disciples and when their meal was finished, she again requested her father-in-law to come and listen to the sermon of the Buddha. The naked ascetics again said that it was extremely improper to go at that time, but when he went to listen to the Buddha's sermon, he saw that the naked ascetics had gone there earlier and placed the curtain and requested the seṭṭhi to sit outside it. The seṭṭhi sat outside the curtain, listened to the Buddha's sermon, obtained the fruition of the first stage of sanctification, went up to his daughter-in-law and said to her, " Henceforward you are my mother ". From that time Visākhā came to be known as Migāramātā or Migāra's mother. Migāra was converted to

Buddhism. Visākhā afterwards made a vihāra at Sāvatthī at the cost of twenty-seven crores of coins (Dh. Com., Vol. I, pt. II, pp. 384 foll.).

*Sutta Nipāta Commentary.*—The Sutta Nipāta Commentary written by Buddhaghosa is a mine of various sorts of valuable information—geographical, historical, religious, and otherwise. Illuminating definitions of rāga, taṇhā, māna, dosa, moha, anusaya, and akusalamūla ; and interpretations of the words, e.g., sati, brahmaloka, uposatha, saṅkappa, pamāda, jhāna, dhamma, gambhirapañña, musāvāda, pāṇātipāta, upadhi, etc., occur briskly in it sometimes systematically, sometimes at random. To give one example, the very interesting word 'Nibutta' is explained in connection with the account of Dhaniya, the cowherd. In connection with another account, namely, that of the Khaggavisāṇa Sutta, we are referred to three kinds of dramas. Besides mentioning mountains and mountain caves, e.g., Gandhamādana and Caṇḍagabbha, the commentator reveals his knowledge of geography when he makes mention of Bārāṇasī, Magadha, Sāvatthī, Kapilavatthu, Kosala, Nerañjarā, etc., nor does he seem to be deficient in his knowledge of history, for he mentions Bimbisāra, Sundarīparibbājaka, and Kosalarāja Pasenadi. Bimbisāra, we are informed, was called Māgadha, because he was the lord of the Magadhas. He was the possessor of a big army, hence he was called Seṇiya. It adds, besides, that Bimbisāra was so called because his colour was like that of excellent gold (p. 448). Rājagaha was ruled by famous kings like Mandhāta and Mahāgovinda. In the time of the Buddha, it became a city, and in other times, it came to be vacant and then inhabited by the yakkhas.

Interesting side-lights are thrown by other accounts, a few of which may profitably be recounted here. A carpenter of Benares prepared mechanical wooden birds by which he conquered a tract of land in the Himavanta and became the ruler of that land. His capital was known as

Kaṭṭhavāhanagara. He sent valuable presents to the king of Benares and made friendship with him. The king in return sent him the news of the advent of the Buddha Kassapa in Benares, but when they reached Benares the Buddha had obtained mahāparinibbāṇa. Afterwards, the yuvarāja with a bhikkhu and the relics of the Buddha went back to the Kaṭṭhanagara, and the bhikkhu was later on successful in converting the king and his subjects into Buddhism (Vol. II, pp. 575 foll.). A trader of Benares went to buy goods with 500 carts to a frontier country, and bought sandal wood (Vol. II, pp. 523 ff.).

There lived at Sāvatthī a paribbājaka, named Pasura, who was a great disputant. He planted a branch of a Jambu tree declaring that he who would be able to hold discussion with him, would uproot it. Sāriputta did uproot it. Pasura had a discussion with Sāriputta about sensual pleasures and eye-consciousness with the result that the paribbājaka was defeated. The paribbājaka went to the Jetavana in order to be ordained by Sāriputta and to learn Vādasattam (art of disputation). He met Lāludāyi at the Jetavana vihāra. Thinking that this Lāludāyi must be greatly wise, he took ordination from him. He defeated Lāludāyi in disputation and made him a paribbājaka even while he was wearing the dress of a bhikkhu. Pasura again went to Sāvatthī to hold discussion with Gautama. He held discussion with Gautama but was defeated. The Buddha then gave him instruction and he was converted into Buddhism (Vol. II, pp. 538 foll.).

*The Jātaka Commentary.*—As to the authorship of the Jātaka Commentary there is a great dispute which has not yet been settled. Some ascribe the authorship to Buddhaghosa.

Buddhaghosa wrote a commentary on the Dhammasaṅgaṇi known as the Atthasālinī.[1] It

[1] There is a scholium on the Atthasālinī called the Paṭhamaparamatthapakāsinī. Read Abhidhammakathā, a Pāli prose

Commentaries on the Abhidhamma Pitaka—*The Atthasālinī.*

simply gives the meaning of the terms that occur in the Dhammasaṅgaṇi. In some places word-for-word explanations have been given which are apparently tedious but are certainly useful to students of Buddhism.[1]

The Atthasālinī contains some historical and geographical information besides some explanations of certain technical terms of Buddhist psychology. It refers to some rivers, e.g., Aciravatī, Gaṅgā, Godāvarī, Nerañjarā, Mahī, Sarabhū, and Anomā. It also refers to some cities, islands, etc., e.g., Kāsipura, Penaṁbaṅgana, Kosala, Isipatana, Jambudīpa, Jetavana, Tambapaṇṇi, Aparagoyāna, Pāṭaliputta, Pubbavideha, Bandhumati, Bharukaccha, Rājagaha, Sāketa, Sāvatthī, Sīhaladīpa. There are references to some historical personages as well, e.g., Ajita, Aññakodañña, Abhayathera, Assagutta, Ānanda, Āḷāra Kālāma, Uttiya, Udāyi, Uddaka, Upaka, Kassapa, Channa, Duṭṭhagāmani, Abhaya, Dāsaka, Dipaṁkara, Nāgasena, Buddhaghosa, Bhaddaji, Mallikā, Mahākassapa, Mahinda, Moggaliputta Tissa, Revata, Vipassī, Vissakammā, Sāriputta, Sujātā, Sumanā, Sonaka, Metteyya, Piṅgalabuddharakkhita, Cakkana Upāsaka. Buddhaghosa in the introductory verses laid down that after he had already dealt with some subjects in his previous composition, the Visuddhimagga, he had only to supplement it by way of writing a commentary on

---

work being a guide to metaphysics of Buddhism for beginners extracted from the Atthasālinī. The Atthasālinī has been edited by Prof. E. Muller for the Pāli Text Society. A translation of this work has been brought out by Mr. Pe Maung Tin, and revised by Mrs. Rhys Davids. It is widely studied by students of Buddhism and by the Burmese monks ; and is often quoted by authors of the Abhidhamma works.

[1] Mr. Maung Tin speaks of the two Burmese translations of the Atthasālinī, namely, old Nissaya (MSS. Bernard Free Library, Rangoon) by Ariyālaṅkāra of the earlier part of the 19th century, and the new Nissaya printed in Kemmendine, Rangoon, 1905, by Pyi Sadaw of the middle of the 19th century. On the whole the translation will be useful in reading the text. In the Bernard Free Library, Rangoon, there are original manuscripts of the Atthasālinī.

the Dhammasaṅgaṇi. But though the Atthasālinī aims to be an exposition of the Dhammasaṅgaṇi, yet there is some anomaly in the contents and arrangements of the two books. There are some chapters of the text which the commentary omits and some chapters which it adds independently of the text itself. Unlike the Dhammasaṅgaṇi the chapters in the Atthasālinī are clearly marked so that the treatment is more scientific than that of the former. Buddhaghosa at the outset gives an introductory chapter. In this he deals with various questions, both literary and philosophical. His dissertation on literary subjects helps us to a great extent in fixing the chronology of the texts of the Sutta, Vinaya, and Abhidhamma. He says that the commentary on the Abhidhamma was sung in the First Council and was rehearsed in the succeeding Councils. Mahinda brought it to Ceylon and it was translated into Siṅhalese. Buddhaghosa defines Abhidhamma as one which excels all other dhammas in qualities. The chief difference between Suttanta and Abhidhamma is that in the Suttanta the five aggregates are classified partially while in the Abhidhamma this classification has been done according to three methods, namely, the Suttanta classification, the Abhidhamma classification, and Catechism. He shows that Suttanta classification is incomplete and defective. He next deals with the Abhidhamma books themselves which are seven in number and records that the very nature of the Kathāvatthu makes its position untenable in the very classification itself, for it dates from the incidents of the Third Council. But Buddhaghosa relying on the traditional number seven in the Abhidhamma class and showing the internal defects of Mahādhammapadaya or Mahādhātukathā as the possible substitutes for the Kathāvatthu, holds that the Kathāvatthu falls within Abhidhamma class particularly because Tissa followed the contents and method of the Teacher who himself foresaw this book.

The author then gives a table of contents of each of the seven Abhidhamma books after which he gives a history of the first Abhidhamma thought and compilation as emanating from the Buddha himself. To Sāriputta he attributes the origin of the number and order of the books. Buddhaghosa quotes many poetical passages as an introductory explanation of the Sutta, Vinaya, and Abhidhamma Piṭakas.

He says that the Abhidhamma is intended for those only who think that there is " I ", " This is mine ", and who fail to understand that the ultimate self is merely a collection of things. The main purpose of the Abhidhamma is, according to him, to lay a distinction between mind and matter and to train one in higher and metaphysical understanding.

The author then justifies the fact that the three piṭakas are the words of Buddha himself, for those bhikkhus who are well practised in Vinaya arrived at the three kinds of knowledge while those who are well versed in the Sutta arrive at the six kinds of super-knowledge and bhikkhus well cultivated in Abhidhamma arrive at the four analyses. He then explains why each of the nikāyas or groups is so called. The first one is Dīgha, because it contains 34 long suttas. The second one containing 152 suttas is called Majjhima, because they are of medium length. The Saṁyutta Nikāya contains seven thousand seven hundred and sixty-two suttas. The Aṅguttara contains nine thousand five hundred and fifty-seven suttas.

The Khuddaka is one which excludes the four nikāyas, the Vinaya, the Abhidhamma, and includes such books as Khuddakapāṭha, Dhammapada, etc. Then follows an enumeration of the nine Aṅgas, the eighty-four thousand units of texts. Buddhaghosa then says that the Abhidhamma is a piṭaka by piṭaka classification and holds it as a word of the Buddha. The Abhidhammikas claim to be the best expositors of the Dhamma. But the Abhidhamma is a field for the Buddha and not for others. The author quotes the Elder Tissabhuti who while seeking to trace the origin of the Abhidhamma at the place of the great enlightenment quoted Padesavihāra Sutta where the Buddha intuited all his qualities and possessions. He then recommends the introduction of the Abhidhamma to all its readers. The author then compares the introductory portions both of the Sutta and the Abhidhamma. He says that unlike the Sutta which has one, the Abhidhamma has two introductions, the one dealing with the life and equipment of the Buddha and the other with the events just before the Dhammacakkapavattana. The author then traces the history of Abhidhamma teaching in Ceylon. According to him, Abhidhamma, originated with faith and nurtured in the 550 Jātakas, was taught by the Buddha. It contained exactly Buddha's words and was handed down by the unbroken line of teachers till the Third Council beginning with Sāriputta and followed by the long line of disciples. An examination of the Atthasālinī shows that it was composed after the Samantapāsādikā to which it refers in pages 97 and 98 of the P.T.S. edition.

The Sammoha-vinodanī or the commentary on the Vibhaṅga (Vibhaṅga-aṭṭhakathā) written by Buddhaghosa has been edited for the P.T.S. by A. P. Buddhadatta Thera in 1923. This commentary was published in Burma several times, but in Ceylon about half of the book has been printed. In many places we find that this commentary and the Visuddhimagga comment on the same subjects. This book consists of 18 sections dealing with the expositions of five khandhas (e.g., rūpa, vedanā, saññā, saṅkhāra, and viññānaṁ), āyatanas (spheres), dhātus (elements), sacca (truth), indriyas (senses), paccayākāra (causes interdependent), satipaṭṭhāna (right recollection), sammappadhāna (right concentration), iddhipādas (bases of miracles), seven bojjhaṅgas (supreme knowledge), magga (the Noble Eightfold Path), jhāna (stages of meditation), appamañña (four appamaññas consisting in an unlimited or perfect exercise of the qualities of friendliness, compassion, good will, and equanimity), sikkhāpadas (precepts), paṭisambhidā (analytical knowledge), ñāna (true knowledge), khuddakavatthu (minor points), and dhammahadaya (religious heart). It should be noted that in the section on the dhātus, 32 parts of the body have been discussed. In the section dealing with truth, the noble truths (ariyasaccaṁ) are dealt with. In the section on the Paccayākāras we find a discussion of the topic of dependent origination. The Satipaṭṭhāna Vibhaṅga should be read along with the Mahāsatipaṭṭhāna Suttanta of the Dīgha Nikāya and Satipaṭṭhāna Suttanta of the Majjhima Nikāya. The Sammohavinodanī contains short notes on avijjā (ignorance), kāya (body), jāti (birth), jarā (old age), taṇhā (desire), domanassa (despair), nibbāna, nāma-rūpa (name and form), bhava (existence), bodhi (enlightenment), macchariya (sloth), marana (death), māyā (illusion), etc.

There is a ṭikā on the Sammohavinodanī known as the Sammohavinodanīlīnattha.

The Dhātukathāpakaraṇa-aṭṭhakathā is a commentary on the Dhātukathā written by Buddhaghosa. It has 14 sections containing interpretations of the five khandhas, twelve āyatanas (spheres), sixteen dhātus (elements), etc.

The Puggalapaññatti-aṭṭhakathā is a commentary on the Puggalapaññatti. This work has been edited for the P.T.S. by G. Landsberg and Mrs. Rhys Davids (J.P.T.S., 1913-1914). The available manuscripts are—(1) palm-leaf Sinhalese manuscript procured for the P.T.S. by Gooneratne, (2) paper Sinhalese manuscript, and (3) Pyi Gyi Mandyne Press edition, Rangoon, in Burmese character.

The Kathāvatthu-aṭṭhakathā is a commentary on the Kathāvatthupakaraṇa written by Buddhaghosa. According to this commentary (Kathāvatthu Commentary), two truths, dukkhaṁ and dukkhasamudayaṁ, are mundane (belonging to the world of re-birth) and the other two truths (nirodha and nirodhagāminipaṭipadā) are supramundane (belonging to the paths). Of the indriyas, ten belong to the region of sense-desire, nine to the next two worlds, and three to the supramundane. Samayavimutta, according to the commentator, applies to sotāpanna, sakadāgāmī, and anāgāmī, and asamayavimutta applies to sukkhavipassaka-khīnāsavas. Kuppadhamma is applied to an ordinary person who has attained eight samāpattis. It is also applied to a stream-attainer and to an once-returner. It means a person who is unsteady or not firmly established in the path. It is so called because in his case the mental conditions which are antagonistic to samādhi and vipassanā have not been completely stopped nor well washed off, and it is for this reason that their attainment perishes and falls away. Akuppa-dhamma is applied to an anāgāmī who has attained eight samāpattis and to a khīnāsava. It means a person who does not go astray. He is steady or firmly established in the path. Hindrances of samādhi and vipassanā in such a person are completely destroyed. His attainment is not broken or destroyed by useless talks or by any other unsuitable act committed through negligence. The commentary further narrates that the term 'Gotrabhu' is applied to a person who has reached the family, circle, or designation of Ariyas by surpassing the family, circle, or designation of ordinary persons through the knowledge acquired by meditation on Nirvāṇa. According to the commentary, by meditation on 'formlessness' a person is freed from rūpakāya (form) and by going through the sublime Eightfold Path he is freed from nāmakāya, therefore he is called ubhato-bhāgavimutto.

A person at first goes through different stages of meditation, then he realises nibbānaṁ. There are six classes of kāyasakkhi commencing from sotāpattiphalaṭṭha to arahattamaggaṭṭha.

Diṭṭhapatto.—He who thoroughly knows that this is suffering, this is the cause of suffering, this is the cessation of suffering, this is the path leading to the cessation of suffering, is one who has won vision.

Dhammānusārī.—It applies to one who has reached the first stage of sanctification because he moves by saddhā or faith.

Sattakkhattumparamo applies to one who obtains arahantship at the seventh birth.

After the realisation of the fruition of sotāpatti one is not reborn in a low family. He is reborn amongst devas and men six times only.

The term Ekabījī is applicable to a stream-attainer who is reborn once only.

Antarā-parinibbāyī applies to a person who obtains Nirvāṇa before reaching the middle of the term of life. Upahacca-parinibbāyī applies to a person who obtains parinibbāna after passing the middle of the term of life but does not reach the end. Asaṅkhāraparinibbāyī applies to a person who attains complete passing away of mental impurities. Sasaṅkhāra-parinibbāyī applies to a person who obtains the foregoing with instigation, with trouble, and with exertion.

Akaniṭṭhagāmī.—According to this commentary, a person goes to the highest Brahmaloka passing through four intermediate Brahma worlds, namely, Avīhā, Atappā, Sudassā, and Sudassī.

Kalyāṇamitta means a good or spiritual friend. Hīnādhimutto means low inclination. Paṇītādhimutto means "*having good inclination*".

The commentary says that the seven learners and average men are restrained from sin through fear, but the Khīnasavas have completely uprooted their fear, therefore they are called Abhayūparato.

A person who has first obtained knowledge of previous births and deva-sight and then arahantship is called a tevijjo, i.e., possessed of three vijjās, namely, pubbenivāsañānaṁ (knowledge of previous births), dibbacakkhuñānaṁ (knowledge of deva-sight), and arahantaphalañānaṁ (knowledge of arahantship). A person attaining arahantship first and then the other two is also called tevijjo.

Chaḷabhiñño.—A person possessing six supernormal faculties or super-knowledges, namely, iddhividhā (various sorts of magical power), dibbasota (deva-ear), paracetoñānaṁ (power of knowing another's thought), pubbenivāsañānaṁ (power of remembering previous births), dibbacakkhu (deva-sight), and āsavakkhayañānaṁ (knowledge of destruction of sinful tendencies) is called chaḷabhiñño.

Pubbakārī.—A person who does good to others before getting benefit from them.

Kataññakatavedī.—It means that a person who after having known that he has got some benefit from others does benefit to them afterwards. Kasambu means dirty and also bad smelling water.

The word samkittisu means samkittetvā katabhattesu. In time of famine an acelaka (naked ascetic) collects uncooked rice by begging from house to house and declaring the object of his begging; he then cooks rice to be distributed among the acelakas. A good acelaka does not accept any kind of food.

Anusotagāmī puggalo means putthujjano or ordinary person. According to this commentary, by a fifth person is to be understood the person who has exhausted the sinful tendencies.

The Yamakapakaraṇa-aṭṭhakathā is a commentary on the Yamaka written by Buddhaghosa. Strictly speaking, it is a commentary on the Mūla Yamaka, Khandha Yamaka, Āyatana Yamaka, Dhātu Yamaka, Sacca Yamaka, Saṁkhāra Yamaka, Anussaya Yamaka, Citta Yamaka, Dhamma Yamaka, and Indriya Yamaka.

The Mūla Yamaka deals with the essence of the teaching of Gotama. In it is included the kusalamūla. Mūla here means the cause.

The Khandha Yamaka deals with an account of the khandhas (aggregates), e.g., Rūpa, Viññāna, Vedanā, Saññā, and Saṁkhāra.

The Āyatana Yamaka deals with āyatana or space, e.g., cakkhu, sota, kāya, rūpa, rasa, phoṭṭabba, etc.

The Dhātu Yamaka contains an account of various dhātus or elements.

The Sacca Yamaka treats of the four Aryan truths.

The section on Saṁkhāra Yamaka deals with kāyasaṁkhāra, vacisaṁkhāra, etc.

The Anussaya Yamaka is a section on attachment, e.g., kāma, rāga, etc.

The Citta Yamaka deals with mind and mental states.

The Dhamma and Indriya Yamakas deal with kusala, akusala, and avyākata dhammas and senses respectively, e.g., manindriya, jīvitindriya, domanassindriya.

The Paṭṭhānapakaraṇa-aṭṭhakathā, edited by Mrs. Rhys Davids for the P.T.S., London, is a commentary on the Paṭṭhāna written by Buddhaghosa at the request of a monk named Cullabuddhaghosa (J.P.T.S., 1886).

### C. Works of Dhammapāla

The Vimānavatthu Commentary.

The Vimānavatthu Commentary is practically a collection of stories illustrating the Buddhist perspective of Heaven and Hell, or more correctly, the Buddhist idea of Heaven and Hell 'prevalent amongst the people of Northern India at the time of the Buddha and incorporated subsequently in the Buddhist Scriptures'.[1] These stories help us to form an idea of the various grades of heaven, the pleasures of the Tāvatiṁsa heaven, the joys and comforts of the dwellers in the Buddhist vimānas, location of the various vimānas, and the form of the vimāna and its comforts which are but proportionate to meritorious deeds.

---

[1] Ronaldshay—in his Foreword to the 'Heaven and Hell in Buddhist Perspective' by Dr. B. C. Law.

## *Synopses of Stories* [1]

1. *Pīṭhavimāna* (*pp.* 5-6).—A girl, a great believer in the Buddha, once made the gift of a wooden stool to a thera whom she had offered food. In consequence of this meritorious deed, the girl was reborn in the Tāvatiṁsa heaven where she enjoyed joys and comforts of the heaven.

As a reward of her offering a seat to a bhikkhu a woman of Sāvatthī obtained in heaven a vimāna made of Veḷuriya (lapis lazulis).

For presenting a pīṭha or a seat to an arhat whom she had offered food, a mistress of a house was reborn in the golden mansion of the Tāvatiṁsa heaven.

2. *Kuñjaravimāna* (*pp.* 31 *foll.*).—A daughter of a family of Rājagaha once entertained Sāriputta with a seat and various kinds of food and drink, and presented him with new clothes and a conch. In consequence of this meritorious deed, she was reborn in the golden mansion of the Tāvatiṁsa heaven.

3. *Nāvāvimāna* (*pp.* 40 *foll.*).—A woman for offering drinking water to some thirsty bhikkhus was reborn by virtue of her meritorious deed in the Tāvatiṁsa heaven. Another woman, too, for offering cold drink and oil to rub his feet with to a thera, was reborn after death in the same heaven.

A slave girl of a brahmin of the village of Thūna in Kosala ran the risk of being beaten by her master and offered a pot of water to the Buddha to drink water from. The Buddha quenched his thirst as well as that of his entire Order and yet returned the pot full of water to the slave girl. The girl after death was reborn in the Tāvatiṁsa heaven where she was given other objects of heavenly enjoyment.

4. *Dīpavimāna* (*pp.* 50-51).—For offering a light in the dusk before a preacher's seat, an

---

[1] For detailed summaries of these stories see my "Heaven and Hell in Buddhist Perspective", Sec. II, pp. 36–85.

upāsikā after death was reborn in the Tāvatiṁsa heaven in the Jotirasavimāna.

5. *Tiladakkhiṇavimāna* (*p.* 54).—For presenting to the Buddha a certain quantity of sesamum seeds in joined palms, a pregnant woman was reborn after death in the Tāvatiṁsa heaven.

6. *Patibbatāvimāna* (*pp.* 56-57).—A beautiful and faithful wife, as a reward of her sweetness and sincerity, charity, and faithfulness, was reborn after death in the Tāvatiṁsa heaven.

7. *Suṇisāvimāna* (*p.* 61).—For offering some portion of the cakes which she had got for her own use to an arahant, the daughter-in-law of a Sāvatthian family was reborn after death in the Tāvatiṁsa heaven.

8. *Uttarāvimāna* (*pp.* 62–74).—By offering to Sāriputta the whole of the food prepared and meant for her husband, Uttarā, the loving wife of Puṇṇa, the servant of a banker of Rājagaha, performed a meritorious deed as a result of which her husband became the richest man in the whole city and was made the Nagaraseṭṭhi ; and both the husband and wife attained the first stage of sanctification by their deeds of charity in the shape of gifts to the Buddha and the congregation.

Puṇṇa's daughter was also named Uttarā ; at one time she invited the Buddha and his disciples, listened to the Buddha's religious discourse, and then attained the second stage of sanctification, while her husband and other relatives, who had thus an opportunity of listening to the discourses of the Master, attained the first stage. Uttarā on her death was reborn in the Tāvatiṁsa heaven.

9. *Sirimāvimāna* (*pp.* 75 *foll.*).—For offering alms to eight bhikkhus daily, and spending sixteen kahāpaṇas on charity, Sirimā the courtesan was reborn after death as a celestial nymph.

10. *Kesakārivimāna* (*pp.* 86–89).—A daughter of Kesakāri, a brahmin of Benares, listened to the precepts of the Buddhist faith from a lay disciple, and, while meditating on those of impurities, attained

the first stage and was, after death, reborn as an attendant of Sakka.

11. *Dāsīvimāna* (*pp.* 91-92).—For serving four bhikkhus daily with hearty devotion and observing the true dhammas, a maid-servant was reborn after death as one of the beloved attendants of Sakka.

12. *Lakhumāvimāna* (*pp.* 97-98).—For preparing seats and supplying water to the bhikkhus in the āsanasālā daily, a woman called Lakhumā was established in the Sotāpatti and was, after death, reborn in the Tāvatiṁsa heaven.

13. *Acāmadāyikāvimāna* (*pp.* 100-101).—For offering her food and the ācāma which had been given her by the inmates of a house behind which she had taken shelter, to Mahākassapa, a woman of Rājagaha was reborn among the Nimmānaratidevas.

14. *Caṇḍālīvimāna* (*pp.* 105–107).—A caṇḍālī once at the exhortation of Mahāmoggallāna fell down at the feet of the Buddha and worshipped him. On account of this meritorious deed, she was, on her death, reborn in the Tāvatiṁsa heaven.

15. *Bhadditthivimāna* (*pp.* 109-110).—Bhaddā, usually known as Bhadditthī, once offered good food and drink to four disciples of the Master with their followers, served them in every way, listened to their discourses, embraced the faith, and received the five sīlas. She, after death, was reborn in the Tāvatiṁsa heaven and worshipped the Buddha when the Master went there.

16. *Soṇadinnāvimāna* (*p.* 115).—For serving bhikkhus, observing the precepts and the uposotha with perfect regularity, Sonadinnā, a devoted upāsikā of Nālandā, attained Sotāpatti and was reborn after death in the Tāvatiṁsa heaven.

17. *Uposathavimāna* (*p.* 115).—For similar meritorious deeds, Uposatha, another devoted upāsikā of Sāketa, was reborn after death in the Tāvatiṁsa heaven.

18. *Bhikkhādāyikavimāna* (*pp.* 118-119).—On account of her inviting the Buddha to have his

daily meal at her house and serving him in other ways, a woman of Uttaramadhurā in Sāvatthī was, after death, reborn in the Tāvatiṁsa heaven.

19. *Uḷāravimāna* (*pp.* 120-121).—For offering the cake of her mother-in-law's share to Mahāmoggallāna, a girl was reborn, after death, in the Tāvatiṁsa heaven.

20. *Ucchudāyikavimāna* (*p.* 124).—For similar reasons another girl also obtained the same good fortune.

21. *Pallaṅkavimāna* (*p.* 128).—A daughter of an upāsikā at Sāvatthī was reborn in the Tāvatiṁsa heaven for her having been virtuous, free from anger, devoted, and an observer of the Sabbath.

22. *Latāvimāna* (*pp.* 131-132).—As a result of her gentle behaviour and practising charity and observing the Sabbath, Latā, a daughter of an upāsaka of Sāvatthī, was reborn as a daughter of Vessavana Kuvera, and was appointed along with her four other sisters as a dancing girl by Sakka.

23. *Guttilavimāna* (*pp.* 137–148).—On account of various kinds of charity, 32 nymphs had become liberated from earthly life and came to be born as heavenly nymphs possessing splendour greater than that of other gods. When Guttila, the musician, saw them in Indra's court, he, as remuneration for his songs, prayed that all the bright goddesses would recount to him the good deeds that had brought them to the heavenly regions.

24. *Daddaḷhavimāna* (*pp.* 149 *foll.*).—The Daddaḷhavimāna illustrates that offering food and drink to the Saṁgha brings forth more merit than that to individual bhikkhus.

25. *Pesavatīvimāna* (*pp.* 156 *foll.*).—In consequence of the meritorious deed of offering her gold ornaments to be utilised for the erection of a stūpa, a girl was reborn in the devaloka, and from that devaloka she was reborn in the family of a householder in Magadha. In this birth of her, she showed her respect to the dead body of Sāriputta by worshipping it with scents, flowers, etc. And

when she died with her mind full of respect for the Buddha, she was reborn in the Tāvatiṁsa heaven.

26. *Mallikāvimāna* (*p.* 165).—For offering worship to the relic of the Buddha, Mallikā, daughter of the king of Kusīnārā, was reborn, after death, in the Tāvatiṁsa heaven.

27. *Visālakkhīvimāna* (*pp.* 169-170).—For daily sending garlands, perfumes, fruits, flowers, etc., to the stūpa over the relic of the Buddha, Sunandā, a daughter of the garland-maker of Rājagaha, was born after death as an attendant of Sakka, who, on one occasion, addressed her as Visālakkhi.

28. *Pāricchattakavimāna* (*p.* 173).—For worshipping the Buddha with Asoka flowers and showing respect to him in various ways, a certain woman was reborn in the Tāvatiṁsa heaven.

29. *Mañjeṭṭhakavimāna* (*pp.* 176-177).—As a result of her worshipping the Buddha with sāla flowers, a certain maid-servant was, after death, reborn in the Tāvatiṁsa heaven.

30. *Pabhassaravimāna* (*pp.* 178-179).—For welcoming Mahāmoggallāna to her house, offering him a seat, and worshipping him, a daughter of a certain upāsaka of Rājagaha was reborn, after death, in the Tāvatiṁsa heaven.

31. *Nāgavimāna* (*pp.* 181-182).—For offering a pair of clothes to the Buddha and listening to a religious discourse of the Master, an upāsikā of Benares was, after death, reborn in the Tāvatiṁsa heaven.

32. *Alomavimāna* (*p.* 184).—The good deed of offering some rotten cooked rice,—not finding anything better without salt—to the Buddha, brought a poor woman named Alomā to the Tāvatiṁsa heaven after death.

33. *Kañjikadāyikavimāna* (*pp.* 185-186).—For offering to the Buddha a medicated drink of rice-gruel that relieved the Master of his pain in the stomach, the wife of the Buddha's physician was reborn in the Tāvatiṁsa heaven after death.

34. *Vihāravimāna* (*pp.* 187–189).—Visākhā the great upāsikā of Sāvatthī once listened to a religious discourse of the Buddha and offered her mahālatā ornament to the Master for the construction of a vihāra, the merit whereof was given to her maid-servant. Visākhā was, on that account, reborn in the Nimmānarati heaven where he became chief queen to the King Sunimmita, and the maid-servant was reborn in the Tāvatiṁsa heaven.

35. *Caturitthivimāna* (*pp.* 195-196).—For making gifts to bhikkhus, four girls of the time of the Kassapa Buddha became celestial nymphs after death. At the time of Gautama Buddha they were in heaven.

36. *Ambavimāna* (*p.* 198).—For building a hermitage for bhikkhus and the Master, an upāsikā of Sāvatthī was, after death, reborn in the Tāvatiṁsa heaven.

37. *Pītavimāna* (*p.* 200).—While on his way to worship a stūpa, an upāsikā was killed by a milch-cow. She was reborn in the Tāvatiṁsa heaven.

38. *Vandanavimāna* (*p.* 205).—For making obeisance to a number of bhikkhus to whom she was filled with veneration and respect, a village woman was reborn in the Tāvatiṁsa heaven.

39. *Rajjumālavimāna* (*pp.* 206–209).—For being instrumental in inviting the Buddha to her mistress's house, a servant girl was reborn in the Tāvatiṁsa heaven after death.

40. *Maṇḍukadevaputtavimāna* (*pp.* 217-218).—A frog was trod upon by a cowherd while listening to a religious discourse of the Buddha. It was reborn, after death, in the Tāvatiṁsa heaven.

41. *Revatīvimāna* (*pp.* 220 *foll.*).—Revatī, wife of a householder of Sāvatthī, practised charity only when her husband was at home, and stopped all works of charity after the death of her husband. In consequence of this she had to experience suffering in different hells while enjoying blessings of the Tāvatiṁsa heaven.

42. *Chattamāṇavakavimāna* (*pp.* 229–233).—Knowing the impending death of Chatta, a son of a learned brāhmaṇa, the Buddha set out for him, and meeting him on the way converted him to the faith. For his devotion to the faith, Chatta, after death, was reborn in the Tāvatiṁsa heaven.

43. *Kakkaṭakarasadāyakavimāna* (*pp.* 243-244).—For offering to a bhikkhu rice and crab soup which relieved him of an acute pain in the ear, a farmer of Magadha was reborn after death in the Tāvatiṁsa heaven.

44. *Dvārapālakavimāna* (*pp.* 246-247).—For daily receiving bhikkhus with care and devotion and listening to their exhortations, a gatekeeper was converted to the faith, and was, after death, reborn in the Tāvatiṁsa heaven.

45. *Karaṇiyavimāna* (*p.* 248).—For inviting the Buddha to his house and offering him food and drink, an upāsaka was reborn, after death, in the Tāvatiṁsa heaven.

46. *Sūcivimāna* (*p.* 250).—For offering two needles to Sāriputta, a blacksmith was, after death, reborn in the Tāvatiṁsa heaven.

47. *Dutiyasūcivimāna* (*p.* 251).—For similar act of charity, a tailor acquired the same good fortune.

48. *Nāgavimāna* (*pp.* 252–254).—For obtaining with difficulty eight flowers with which he worshipped the stūpa, an upāsaka was reborn as a devaputta in various vimānas, and came to the Tāvatiṁsa heaven at the time of the Buddha Gautama.

49. *Dutiyanāgavimāna* (*pp.* 254-255).—An upāsaka of Rājagaha was reborn in the Tāvatiṁsa heaven on account of his charity and faithfulness and on account of his offering alms and drinks to the bhikkhus.

50. *Tatiyanāgavimāna* (*pp.* 255–257).—For offering rice with sugarcane juice and sugarcane pieces to three bhikkhus and then entertaining respectfully an offence for which he was beaten to death by his master, the keeper of a sugarcane

field at Rājagaha was reborn in the Mote-hall called Sudhamma of the gods.

51. *Cūḷarathavimāna* (*pp.* 259–270).—For receiving instruction in the faith from Mahākaccāyana, building a vihāra, and inviting a thera to come there, and for performing other meritorious deeds, Sujāta, the banished son of the king of Asoka, was reborn after death in the Tāvatiṁsa heaven.

52. *Mahārathavimāna* (*pp.* 270-271).—For having worshipped the Buddha Vipassi with a garland of gold, a devaputta named Gopāla was reborn at the time of Kassapa Buddha as the son of King Kikī of Benares. In this birth he made immense gifts and received the Dhamma from that Buddha, and was accordingly reborn, after death, in the Tāvatiṁsa heaven. Later, at the time of Gautama Buddha he learnt the principles of the faith from Mahāmoggallāna and became established in the Sotāpatti.

53. *Agāriyavimāna* (*p.* 286).—In consequence of their offering charity to bhikkhus, a rich couple of Rājagaha were reborn in the Tāvatiṁsa heaven, having a very large golden vimāna full of celestial comforts.

54. *Phaladāyakavimāna* (*pp.* 288-289).—For offering to Mahāmoggallāna four mangoes which were distributed by the Buddha to his four prominent disciples, and making over the merit of the gift to King Bimbisāra, a gardener, after death, was reborn in the Tāvatiṁsa heaven.

55. *Upassayadāyakavimāna* (*p.* 291).—For placing one room at the disposal of a bhikkhu for one night and for entertaining him with food and drink, an upāsaka of Rājagaha with his wife was, after death, reborn in the Tāvatiṁsa heaven.

56. *Bhikkhādāyakavimāna* (*pp.* 292-293).—As a reward of his offering food to a bhikkhu, a householder was reborn in the Tāvatiṁsa heaven.

57. *Yavapālakavimāna* (*p.* 294).—For offering food to a bhikkhu a boy, who was at that time himself very hungry, was born, after death, in the Tāvatiṁsa heaven.

58. *Kuṇḍalīvimāna* (*p.* 295).—For making arrangements for bhikkhus for their stay at night and offering plenty of food and drink an upāsaka, after death, was reborn in the Tāvatiṁsa heaven.

59. *Uttaravimāna* (*pp.* 297-298).—For listening to the Pāyāsi Sutta delivered by Kumārakassapa Thera and embracing the Buddhist faith, as also for practising charity on a poor scale, King Pāyāsi was, after death, reborn in the Cātummahārājika devaloka. But his officer who spent all his wealth in charity was reborn in the Tāvatiṁsa heaven.

60. *Cittalatāvimāna* (*p.* 299).—For serving other people, and for being faithful, obedient, and devoted to the three gems, a poor man of Sāvatthī was reborn in the Tāvatiṁsa heaven.

61. *Maṇithūṇavimāna* (*p.* 301).—For sweeping the path which the bhikkhus used when going out for alms, and for making all other arrangements for making their journey comfortable as well as for observing the precepts and offering charity, an upāsaka was reborn in the Tāvatiṁsa heaven.

62. *Suvaṇṇavimāna* (*p.* 302).—For offering to the Buddha an excellent gandhakūṭi provided with all necessary comforts, an upāsaka, after death, was reborn in the Tāvatiṁsa heaven.

63. *Ambavimāna* (*pp.* 305-306).—For inviting Sāriputta to his garden and offering him water for bath and drinking, a gardener was reborn in the Tāvatiṁsa heaven.

64. *Gopālavimāna* (*p.* 308).—A hungry cowherd of Rājagaha offered Mahāmoggallāna the sour gruel meant for him. He was, as a result, reborn after death in the Tāvatiṁsa heaven.

65. *Kaṇṭhakavimāna* (*pp.* 312–314).—The famous horse of Gautama, named Kaṇṭhaka, was, after death, reborn in the Tāvatiṁsa heaven for its past services to Gautama, its master.

66. *Anekavaṇṇavimāna* (*pp.* 318–320).—A bhikkhu who became a householder was in the habit of performing meritorious deeds, worshipping Caityas and listening to the discourses. He was, after

death, born in the devaloka and was more powerful than Sakka. At the time of Gautama Buddha, he was reborn in the Tāvatiṁsa heaven.

67. *Serīsakavimāna* (*pp.* 331 *foll.*).—In consequence of his failing to offer charities with a whole heart, King Pāyāsi could not reach the Tāvatiṁsa heaven, but was reborn in the lower heaven of Cātummahārājikas, in a vacant vimāna called Serisakavimāna.

68. *Sunikkhitavimāna* (*pp.* 352 *foll.*).—An upāsaka who was very much devoted to the worship of the Kassapa-Sammāsambuddha and his caitya, was reborn, after death, in a golden mansion in the Tāvatiṁsa heaven.

It will be seen from the above account of the vimānas or celestial mansions that the form of the vimāna and the comforts and pleasures provided therein are proportionate not only to the meritorious deeds done on earth, but also to the particular nature of the deeds themselves, as also to the desire of the dweller of the vimāna. It appears, furthermore, that most of the departed spirits go to the Tāvatiṁsa heaven. Only in rare cases do we read of a spirit passing to the regions of the higher gods, the Nimmānaratis. It is only in very exceptional cases indeed that spirits go to the Brahmaloka. Downward also we read only in one case of a king who went to the region of Cātummahārājikas for stinginess of making gifts.

Another thing that deserves notice is that the vimāna may not always be in the heavenly regions. This is specially the case with the spirits in the lower heavens who are not sufficiently purified or whose attachment to things on earth is still rather keen. The spirits could at will come down on earth in the vimānas, and in several cases they came to the Buddha in their vimānas to listen to his discourse.[1]

[1] For fuller and more critical observations on these anecdotes see my "Heaven and Hell in Buddhist Perspective", Chap. III, pp. 86–91.

"The joys of heaven," Lord Ronaldshay rightly observes, in his Foreword to my book on 'Heaven and Hell in Buddhist Perspective', "are represented as being obtainable by means of what is suspiciously like a mercenary bargain, entered into in a spirit which far from being selfless is, on the contrary, frankly selfish". This is quite obviously foreign to the lofty thought and teaching of Buddha himself.

*Petavatthu Commentary.*—The Paramatthadipanī[1] is a commentary on the Petavatthu, a work devoted entirely to the petas or spirits of the deceased. It was written by Dhammapāla of Kāñchipuram[2] in Southern India and it contains details of stories compiled from Buddhist tradition handed down orally as well as recorded in the ancient aṭṭhakathās (or commentaries) preserved in Ceylon. Dhammapāla's aṭṭhakathā is a great storehouse of information about the individual petas or spirits, and these stories enable us to form an idea of the Buddhist conception of spirits and the spirit world.

A short synoptical account of the stories of the Petavatthu Commentary may be catalogued as follows :—

1. *Khettūpamā Peta* (*pp.* 1–9).—A seṭṭhiputta who deserved to be reborn in the devaloka for a deed of charity towards Mahāmoggallāna was, however, born on a much lower plane as a tree spirit, owing to his affection towards Sulasā, a beautiful maiden of his town. As a tree spirit, he stole away Sulasā and kept her with him on the tree for some time.

2. *Sūkaramukhapeta* (*pp.* 9 *foll.*).—For having been unrestrained in speech, a bhikkhu was reborn

[1] Petavatthu Commentary edited by Son Dhammārāma Tissa Nāyaka Thera and Māpulagamacaṇḍajoti Thera ; finally revised by Mahāgoḍa Siri Ñānissara Thera Tripiṭaka Wāgiswarācārya and Pradhāna Nāyaka, Colombo. The Petavatthu with Sinhalese commentary by Jinavamsa Paññāsāra of Kosgoda, Colombo, 1893–1898, deserves mention.

[2] The commentary has been edited for the P.T.S. by Prof. E. Hardy.

as a peta with the face like that of a swine or sūkara.

3. *Pūtimukhapeta* (*pp.* 12 *foll.*).—A bhikkhu very much unrestrained in speech once created dissensions between two friends. As a punishment he was reborn as a peta under the name of pūtimukha, because his mouth used to give out a very bad smell on account of his having been wicked and unrestrained in speech.

4. *Piṭṭhadhitalikapeta* (*pp.* 16 *foll.*).—In course of a discourse the Buddha approved of making offering to the departed spirits; but added that sorrow, lamentation, and weeping were of no use to the petas, they only brought suffering to the living relatives.

5. *Tirokuḍḍapeta* (*pp.* 19 *foll.*).—Some people for their misdeeds were reborn as petas; but as they did not obtain any offering from their relatives, they were again born as petas. Bimbisāra, who was their former relative, however, gave a dinner to the whole Saṁgha and made over to the petas the merit thereof; and the Buddha approved of it.

6. *Pañchaputtakhādakapeta* (*pp.* 31 *foll.*).—For causing miscarriage to a pregnant woman, another woman was reborn as a petī of evil look and suffered untold miseries. She was, however, freed from her miserable condition only when her former husband transferred the merit of a pious deed of charity to the petī.

7. *Sattaputtakhādakapeta* (*pp.* 36-37).—The story of the misdeed and its retribution is just like the previous one.

8. *Goṇapeta* (*pp.* 38–42).—A son consoled his father who had become overpowered with grief at the death of his father by saying that he was weeping for one whose body was not even before him and could not even be seen or heard.

9. *Mahāpesakārapeta* (*pp.* 42–46).—The wife of the headman of a village was very malicious towards the bhikkhus whom her husband used to provide with cloth. The husband was reborn as a

tree-god while his wife came to live close by as a petī who suffered boundless miseries, anguish, and pain. She was however released from her poor lot when her former husband, the tree-god, transferred the merit of one of his deeds of charity to her.

10. *Khalātiyapeta* (*pp*. 46–53).—As a result of both good and evil deeds, a woman in her next life found herself seated in a golden vimāna, but on account of her having stolen clothings of invited guests, she was naked. But when the merit of a pious act of a body of merchants was transferred to her, she became draped in finest garments. Subsequently she sent some presents to the Buddha and was as a result reborn in a golden palace in the Tāvatiṁsa heaven.

11. *Nāgapeta* (*pp*. 53–61).—As a direct result of their unbelief and past misdeeds, husband and wife were reborn as a peta and petī respectively, and used to beat each other with iron clubs.

12. *Uragapeta* (*pp*. 61–66).—Dhammapāla, a brahmin of Benares, taught the members of his family not to lament at the death of anybody, and all of them acted accordingly. For this wise attitude they were rewarded by Sakka who was no other than their own son reborn in heaven as Sakka.

13. *Maṭṭakuṇḍalipeta* (*p*. 92).—The son of a miserly brahmin who was reborn as a god came down to console his father in the guise of a peta and asked him not to lament for one whose dead body was not even visible (cf. Dhammapada Commentary, Vol. I, p. 28).

14. *Saṭṭhikūṭasahassapeta* (*pp*. 282–286).—In consequence of various serious misdeeds, four sons of seṭṭhis of Rājagaha suffered in hell for 60,000 years, and then became petas suffering in Lohakumbhi hell (cf. Dhammapada Commentary, Vol. II, pp. 68–73).

15. *Bhogasaṁharapeta* (*pp*. 278-279).—For cheating people, four women came to be reborn as petīs and became overwhelmed with great pain.

16. *Akkharukkhapeta* (*pp.* 277-278).—On account of his act of help and charity done to an upāsaka, a man came to be reborn as a god living on earth.

17. *Ambapeta* (*pp.* 273 *foll.*).—An avaricious trader, after death, came to live as a peta; and he was not relieved of his miserable plight until his daughter transferred the merit of her meritorious deed to him.

18. *Pāṭaliputtapeta* (*pp.* 271 *foll.*).—An upāsaka on account of his attachment to a particular woman was reborn as a Vimānapeta where he with the help of his miraculous power enjoyed for some time the company of his lover.

19. *Gaṇapeta* (*pp.* 269 *foll.*).—A number of people of Sāvatthī, who formed a Gaṇa and who were unbelievers, unfaithful, misers, and doers of evil deeds, were reborn after their death as petas and on one occasion they related in detail the story of their suffering to Moggallāna.

20. *Guthakhādakapeta* (*pp.* 266–269).—A family bhikkhu was in the habit of speaking against other bhikkhus, and also induced a householder who had built for him a house to abuse them. Both of them on account of their misdeeds were reborn as petas.

21. *Sānuvāsipeta* (*pp.* 177–186).—The son of the king of Benares once insulted a Pacceka Buddha, for which sin, he, after death, was reborn in the Avīci hell. He was, however, reborn in the time of Gautama and eventually became a famous monk. But his relatives who all misbehaved with him came to be born after death as petas.

22. *Kumārapeta* (*pp.* 261–263).—Two princes of Kosala were, for committing adultery, reborn as petas. To relieve them of suffering, the Buddha asked the people to make offerings to the Saṁgha, and transfer the merit of the offerings to the petas.

23. *Dhātuvivaṇṇapeta* (*pp.* 212–215).—A wealthy householder, who was an unbeliever, and used to speak ill of the relics, was reborn as a peta.

24. *Ucchupeta* (*pp.* 257 *foll.*).—A sugarcane farmer for his beating an upāsaka with sugarcane-sticks was reborn as a peta. He, however, got rid of his sufferings, when he made an offering of a huge bundle of canes to the Buddha and Saṁgha; as a result of this offering, he was reborn in the Tāvatiṁsa heaven.

25. *Nandakapeta* (*pp.* 244–257).—Nandikā, the commander-in-chief of the king of Surattha, for his unbelief, was reborn as a peta and resided on a nigrodha tree. But when his daughter transferred the merit of one of her meritorious deeds, he became a believer.

26. *Ambasakkharapeta* (*pp.* 215 *foll.*).—A merchant of Vaisālī for joking concealed the garment of his associate and had to go naked in his next birth though he was reborn as a god living on earth. But impressed by his exhortations, King Ambasakkhara offered his garments to bhikkhus so that the naked might get clothes to wear.

27. *Kūṭavinicchayikapeta* (*pp.* 209 *foll.*).—For his past sins of speaking malicious words and cheating people, a judicial officer of King Bimbisāra had to eat the flesh taken out from his own body, though he was reborn as a devatā for having kept upasotha for one night.

28. *Dutiyaluddapeta* (*pp.* 207 *foll.*).—As a result of his cruelty by day, a hunter used to be bitten by dogs in the daytime though he was reborn as a Vimānapeta enjoying happiness at night for his having ceased hunting by night.

29. *Migaluddapeta* (*pp.* 204 *foll.*).—Like the previous one.

30. *Serinipeta* (*pp.* 201 *foll.*).—Serinī, an unbeliever, used to speak ill of the Samaṇas; she was, therefore, reborn as a petī in the petaloka suffering miserably. She was, however, at last freed from the petaloka by virtue of the merit transferred to him by the mother of an upāsaka.

31. *Kumārapeta* (*pp.* 194 *foll.*).—An envious and stingy person used to speak ill of the ascetics;

but he was eventually prevailed upon to worship the Buddha and make an offering. After death, the son was reborn in the womb of a prostitute who threw him into a cemetery. He was eventually picked up by a wealthy householder to whose wealth he became later on the sole heir.

32. *Bhūsapeta* (*pp.* 191 *foll.*).—A merchant of Sāvatthī used to cheat people in trade, his son was a sinner, his wife and daughter-in-law were also very greedy. They were all reborn, after death, as petas and petīs in the Vindhya forest where they suffered terribly and miserably.

33. *Rathakārapeta* (*pp.* 186 *foll.*).—For the good act of building a vihāra for a Saṁgha, a pious woman was reborn as a Vimānapetī on account of some of her past misdeeds.

34. *Abhijjamānapeta* (*pp.* 168 *foll.*).—A hunter who delighted in the cruel sport of hunting was reborn as a peta naked and fierce in appearance and never saw any food or drink. He was, however, clothed and fed as a result of the charity of the minister of King Bimbisāra of food and clothes to all upāsakas.

35. *Ubbarīpeta* (*pp.* 160 *foll.*).—At the death of her husband Cūḷani Brahmadatta, king of Pañcāla, Ubbarī was overpowered with grief and she wept bitterly. The Master who was then Bodhisattva came to her, and by a discourse on kamma and on the many births and deaths, as also by expounding the Dhamma, consoled her lacerated soul.

36. *Suttapeta* (*pp.* 144 *foll.*).—A boy who was an attendant of a paccekabuddha came to be reborn as a Vimānapeta on account of his attachment to a girl. By winning over her mother, the peta was, however, able to bring the girl to his abode where they lived together happily for some time.

37. *Uttaramātupeta* (*pp.* 140 *foll.*).—Uttarā, a woman, was stingy and a believer of false doctrines. She also used to curse those who were believers; she was accordingly, after death, reborn as a petī, and suffered terribly for 55 years, when she was

at last saved by the merit of a charity transferred to her by a thera.

38. *Saṁsāramocakapeta* (*pp.* 67 *foll.*). A girl of the Saṁsāramocaka caste who was a false believer was, however, made indirectly to salute a thera who wanted her to be saved from going to hell after death. She was reborn, therefore, as a petī, with some chance of salvation. The chance eventually came, and she was freed from the petaloka.

39. *Sāriputtattherassa Mātupetī* (*pp.* 78 *foll.*). A mischievous woman, who did not give food, drink, and habitation to the bhikkhus who came to her place as guests, was reborn as a petī and had to suffer miseries. She was, however, relieved of her sufferings and reborn in the devaloka by Sāriputta whose mother she had been in the fifth birth.

40. *Mattāpetī* (*pp.* 82 *foll.*).—Mattā, the barren wife of a householder of Sāvatthī, was very jealous of her husband and his second wife who were very loving and friendly towards each other, and daily made offerings to theras and bhikkhus. On account of her jealousy and other misdeeds, she was reborn as a petī and suffered terribly. She was, however, released from the petaloka by dint of the merit of the second wife being transferred to her.

41. *Nandāpeta* (*pp.* 89 *foll.*).—Nandā, the wife of a householder, was, as a result of her misdeeds, reborn as a petī. One day she appeared before her husband who according to her direction made gifts of charity to the bhikkhus and the petī was released from her miseries.

42. *Dhanapālapeta* (*pp.* 99 *foll.*).—Dhanapāla, a miserly and sceptic merchant, was reborn as a peta in a desert where he could not get a drop of water to drink or grain to eat. After suffering for 55 years, he was, however, saved from suffering by a caravan of merchants who made offerings on his account to the Buddha and his disciples.

43. *Cūḷaseṭṭhipeta* (*pp.* 105 *foll.*).—A stingy and sceptic householder of Benares was reborn after death as a peta with a body without flesh and

blood. The peta once approached King Ajātasattu, who, on his request and on his account, made offerings to the Buddha and hi( ʼisciples, and the peta was relieved of his suffering.

44. *Revatīpeta* (*pp.* 257).—An unbelieving and uncharitable wife of a believing and charitable householder was reborn, as a result of her misdeeds, as a petī. But when she was asked by her husband to approve, and did so, of the meritorious acts done by him, she became a devatā and resided with her husband in heaven.

45. *Aṅkurapeta* (*pp.* 111 *foll.*).—Aṅkura, the youngest son of the king of Uttaramadhurā, was a charitable man. He learnt a good lesson, first from a deity of a nigrodha tree, and later on from a peta, that one should make gifts with his own hands, because the man charged with work might not do it in the right spirit. After death, he was reborn in the Tāvatiṁsa heaven.

These stories were evidently compiled with a purpose. Each one of them has a lesson, a moral which wants to drive home to the mind of the reader the effect of kamma after death. A man after death is reborn in the Tāvatiṁsa heaven, or in the devaloka, and enjoys the good and healthy effects of kamma to the extent he during his life-time did good to others, especially to the Buddha and the bhikkhus of the Order, he was religiously and favourably minded towards Buddhism, he was charitable and he followed the right path by which of course was meant the Eightfold Path of Buddhism. But whosoever is guilty of misdeeds, of cruelty, of too much worldly attachment, of hatred or even lack of faith and devotion towards the Buddha's religion or towards anyone belonging to that religious Order, or was an unbeliever or believer in false doctrines by which was certainly meant any doctrine other than Buddhism, that individual comes to be reborn, after death, as a peta or petī; he then suffers as the spirit of his deceased existence. And not until he or she does some good works or anybody else does it on their account—religious or charitable in the Buddhist sense—that he or she is delivered of his or her life of a peta or petī.

Theragāthā Commentary.

The Theragāthā Commentary written by Dhammapāla [1] and known as Paramatthadipanī contains accounts of theras mentioned in the Theragāthā. The commentary refers to a number of important places of ancient India, e.g., Sāvatthī, Rājagaha, Kapilavatthu, Kosambī, Magadha, Campā, Vesālī, Avanti, Sāketa, Takkasīlā, Bharukaccha, etc. Kings and tribes are also frequently mentioned: Pasenadi, Bimbisāra, Candapajjota, Mallas, Vajjians, Sakians, etc., are a few of them. It is evident from a study of the contents of the commentary that the theras belonged to different castes, from the highest aristocracy to the lowest scavenger, but they looked to one another with fraternal affection and equanimity. Most of the theras lived contemporaneously with the Buddha. A brief summary of the principal theras is given below:—

*Subhūti* was a nephew of Anāthapiṇḍika. On the day when the Jeta grove, purchased by his uncle, was presented to the Exalted One, Subhūti was present. When he headed the Norm preached by the Blessed One, he realised the worthlessness of the worldly life. He left the world and developed his insight in the basis of love-jhāna and won arahatship. The Exalted One declared him to be the chief of his disciples in universal amity and chief among such as were held worthy of gifts.

*Koṭṭhita* the Great was born in a very wealthy clan of brahmins. He perfected himself in the accomplishments of a brahmin. He found faith

[1] It was edited by Suriyagoda Sumaṅgala Thera and Webada Saṃgharatana Thera, and finally revised by Mahāgoḍa Siri Ñāṇissara Thera; Simon Hewavitarane Bequest Series, published by the Trustees, B.E.C.E., 2461/1918. The Pāli Text Society has entrusted the editorship of this text to Dr. Przyluski and M. Durr.

in the Norm preached by the Exalted One and entered the Order. He gained insight, attained arahatship, and was ranked chief among those who were proficient in insight.

*Kaṅkhā-Revata* was born in a wealthy family of Sāvatthī. He found faith in the Norm and entered the Order. The Master pronounced him to be the chief of the bhikkhus who practised Jhāna.

*Puṇṇa of the Mantānis* was born in an eminent brahmin clan. He was sister's son of the Elder Kondañña. He accomplished the highest duties of a recluse, and in due course of time, the Master proclaimed Puṇṇa chief among the bhikkhus in preaching the Norm.

*Dāsaka* was born as the child of a slave of Anāthapiṇḍika who appointed him as gate-porter of the Jetavana vihāra. His master freed him as he was virtuous. He left the world and was ordained accordingly. But he was slothful. He was soon inspired by the Buddha. Not long after he realised arhatship.

*Abhaya* was the bastard son of King Bimbisāra. He was at first the follower of Nātaputta, the Jain leader. He had a conversation with the Master. After the king's death he left the world. He soon realised arhatship.

*Uttiya* was born as the son of a brahmin. He left the world and became a paribbājaka, a wanderer. One day in course of his journey he came where the Exalted One was preaching, and entered the Order. He attained arhatship in time.

*Suppiya* was born in a despised class, as one of a clan of watchman in a cemetery at Sāvatthī. He was converted by the Thera Sopāka. He entered the Order and attained to the highest.

*Gavampati* was born as one of the four lay-companions of the Thera Yasa. He left the world hearing Yasa's renunciation, and eventually won arhatship. Once the Lord with a great company of bhikkhus went to the Añjana grove. The accommodation being insufficient, the bhikkhus slept around the vihāra on the sand banks of the river Sarabhu. At night the stream rose in flood. But the Thera Gavampati, as he was asked by the Master, arrested the rising stream by his mystic power.[1]

*Vimala-kondañña* was the bastard son of King Bimbisāra. His mother was Ambapālī. He left the world for the Order and attained arhatship.

*Channa* was a slave of Suddhodana's household. He entered the Order when the Master returned after obtaining enlightenment to meet his kinsfolk. Out of his affection for the Lord, egoistic pride in 'our Buddha, our Doctrine' arose in him. He could not conquer this fondness nor perform his duty as a novice. He suffered the Brahmadaṇḍa as prescribed by the Buddha after the Lord's Mahāparinibbāṇa. Later on he attained arhatship.

*Tissa* was a ruler of the town of Roguva. He was an absent ally of King Bimbisāra. It was

[1] Mrs. Rhys Davids rightly calls him, "a very Moses in psychic power". She is perfectly right when she says that Gavampati has been lost in his last acts by the piṭaka tradition and we have to seek him in Chinese translations of possibly Mahāsaṅghika originals. (Sakya or Buddhist Origins by Mrs. Rhys Davids, p. 128.) Mrs. Rhys Davids further points out that the Thera Gavampati praised in the Anthology as of mighty iddhi but elsewhere coming into, she thinks but one brief sutta (Samyutta, V, 436), declined to come for less worthy motives: this is according to the Chinese recensions translated further by Prof. Przyluski (Le councile de Rājagriha, pt. I, pp. 8, 30, 66, and 116). She further adds, "there seemed to be nothing worth while in trying to help the world, now that the light of it had faded out, save in fading out also which he proceeded to do. It may well be that the failure lay not in Gavampati's will but in his physical inability to travel. But that it has been allowed to come in, as a serious reason for holding aloof from a Community in whom the mission spirit was still alive, is a sinister feature in the Compilers" (Sakya, pp. 348-349).

It may further be noted here that Gavampati lives still in Burmese Buddhist tradition where he has been acclaimed as the "Patron saint of the Mons" as well as the "patron saint of Pagan". He has been mentioned more than once in the Mon inscriptions of Pagan as one of those who assisted sage Bisṇu in the foundation of the city of Sisit or Śrīkṣetra, i.e., Old Prome. He thus becomes intimately associated with the Mon or Telaing tradition of Lower Burma as well. (E. P. Birminica.)

through Bimbisāra that he renounced the world and entered the Order. He won arhatship.

*Vacchagotta* was the son of a wealthy brahmin. He became a wandering recluse. He had a conversation with the Lord. He entered the Order and in due course acquired sixfold abhiññā.

*Yasa* was the son of a very wealthy councillor at Benares. Seeing the worthlessness of the worldly life he forsook it and went to the Buddha for ordination. He entered the Order and won arahatship.

*Piṇḍola-Bhāradvāja* was the son of the chaplain to King Udena of Kosambī. He was versed in the brahmanical lore. He entered the Order and acquired sixfold abhiññā. The Master pronounced him to be the chief among his disciples who were lion-roarers.

*Cunda the Great* was the son of a female brahmin named Rūpasārī, and younger brother of Sāriputta. He followed the latter into the Order and won arhatship.

*Dhammapāla* was born as a brahmin's son. Hearing from a certain thera about the Norm, he left the world and acquired sixfold abhiññā.

*Dhaniya* was born in a potter's family and practised the potter's craft. Seeing that the Buddha-Sāsana helps one to be free from the sorrows of rebirth, he entered the Order and in due course won arhatship.

*Upāli* was born in a barber's family. He left the world following Anuruddha and the other five nobles. In due time he won arahatship. The Master himself taught him the whole Vinaya Piṭaka. He was ranked first among those who knew the Vinaya.

*Rāhula* was born as the son of Princess Yosodharā. The circumstances of his entering the Order are recorded in the Khandhaka. He won arhatship.

*Soṇa-Kūṭikaṇṇa* was born in the country of Avanti in the family of a very wealthy councillor. He learned the Norm from the venerable Kaccāna the Great and entered the Order through him. He recited the sixteen aṭṭhakas and won arahatship.

*Kassapa of Uruvela* was born in a brahmin family. He learnt the three Vedas. Finding no vital truth in the scripture he became an ascetic. It is mentioned in the Vinaya texts how the Blessed One converted him and his two brothers having the family name Kassapa. This Kassapa was the chief of those bhikkhus who had great following.

*Māluṅkyā's son* was born as the son of the king of Kosala's valuer. His mother was named Māluṅkyā. He left the world as a wandering ascetic. On hearing the Master's teaching, he entered the Order and in due course won arahatship.

*Kaccāyana the Great* was born as the son of the chaplain to the King Candapajjota of Ujjenī. At his father's death he succeeded to the post of chaplain. The king coming to know the Buddha's advent asked him to bring the Master there. He went to the Master who taught him the Norm. Afterwards he won arahatship. As bidden by the Master he himself went to the king and established him in the faith and then returned to the Master.

*Kappina the Great* was born in a rājā's family in the border country at a town named Kukkuṭa. At his father's death he succeeded as rājā. At that time there was a brisk trade between Sāvatthī and Kukkuṭa. Once some traders, who were followers of the Buddha, were brought to the king. The king heard the excellence of the Norm from the traders and forthwith renounced the world. The Master who was then at Sāvatthī thought it a proper time to see Kappina. The Lord then came to the banks of the Candabhāgā where he met Kappina and his men. The Master preached the Norm and they all won arahatship.

It is interesting to note as what Mrs. Rhys Davids has rightly pointed out (Sakya, p. 39) that an unrest of enquiry (as in the Dīgha, Vol. II, 151) is noticeable in the commentarial tradition of another nobleman of North India, the rājā Kappina. Mrs. Rhys Davids remarks in this connection thus, "For us of European traditions the riding forth of the noble on a quest is familiar, but we do not find the Indian noble so doing in a similar tradition. We have the Jātaka quest of King Kusa after his lady, but it is as a very exceptional procedure. The Christian knight went on a worthy quest: the aid of those who needed him. Kappina's interest was said to be in the new in knowledge. The purpose of the Sakyan prince was the combined purpose of the new in knowledge in order to bring help to men" (Sakya, pp. 39-40). This remark of Mrs. Rhys Davids seems to be just and fair.

*Revata.*—When the Thera Revata had won arahatship he went from time to time with the great theras to visit the Master. Going thus one day to visit the Buddha he stayed not far from Sāvatthī in a forest. Now the police came round on the track of thieves. The thieves, however, dripped their booty near the thera and ran. The thera was arrested and taken to the king. The thera proved his incapability for stealing and taught the king the Norm.

*Anuruddha* was born in the house of Amitodana, the Sakiyan. His elder brother was Mahānāma, the Sakiyan, the son of the Master's paternal uncle. He was summoned with the Sakiyan rājās to form a guard for the Master. Under the tuition of the Master himself he won arahatship. The Master ranked him foremost among those who had attained the celestial eye.

*Sāriputta and Moggallāna the Great.*—The stories of Sāriputta and Moggallāna the Great are taken together. In the days of Gautama Buddha they were playmates named Upatissa (Sāriputta) and Kolita (Moggallāna). They were born as brahmins. Disgusted with the worldly life they left the world and became followers of the wanderer Sañjaya. In Sañjaya's teaching they found nothing genuine. Through Assaji, the bhikkhu, they found the Exalted One and were ordained by him. In course of time they won arahatship. Sāriputta was ranked chief among the disciples in wisdom and insight and Moggallāna was foremost in supernatural power of will.

*Ānanda* was born in the family of Amitodana, the Sakiyan. Ānanda renounced the world with Bhaddiya and others and was ordained by the Exalted One. He became the permanent body-servant to the Blessed One—a favour which was denied to Sāriputta and Moggallāna and others. He won arahatship after the death of the Buddha and just before the holding of the First Council.

*Kassapa the Great* was born in a brahmin family at the brahmin village of Mahā-tittha in Magadha and was named Pippali-māṇava. He had not the intention of marrying. But he was married to one Bhaddā Kapilānī. Both of them lived separately. When Pippali-māṇava's parents died, both of them decided to renounce the world. Kassapa was ordained by the Master himself. In no time he won arahatship. The Master pronounced him chief among those who undertook the extra austerities.

*Phussa* was born as the son of the ruler of a province. He shunned worldly desires. He heard a certain great thera preach the Norm and entered the Order. In due course he acquired sixfold abhiññā (supernatural knowledge).

*Aṅgulimāla* was born as the son of the brahmin Bhaggava, who was chaplain to the king of Kosala. As he was born in the conjunction of the thief's constellation, he became a thief. He made a garland of the fingerbones and hung it round his shoulder as if decked for sacrifice. Both the king and the people were tired of him. The king sent a strong force to capture the bandit. The Exalted One, however, converted the robber-chief.

*Añña-Kondañña* was born in the village of Donavatthu, not far from Kapilavatthu, in a very wealthy brahmin family. Añña-Kondañña and four others left the world in quest of Amata or Nirvāṇa.

Buddha after attaining enlightenment preached his wheel sermon at Tripatana to those five ascetics.

*Soṇa-Koḷivisa* was born at the city of Campā, in the family of a distinguished councillor. When the Blessed One had attained omniscience and began rolling the wheel of the Norm, and was staying at Rājagaha, Soṇa came to pay a visit to the Buddha. He heard the Master teach the Norm and obtained his parents' consent to enter the Order. In due course he attained arahatship.

*Kappa* was born in the kingdom of Magadha, as the son of a provincial hereditary rājā. He was addicted to self-indulgence and sensuality. The Master out of compassion for him preached the Norm to him. Kappa entered the Order and in due course won arahatship.

*Puṇṇa* (*Sunāparanta*) was born in the Sunāparanta country, at the port of Suppāraka, in the family of a burgess. Once he went to Sāvatthī with a great caravan of merchandise. There he heard the discourse of the Buddha. He entered the Order and in due course won arahatship.

*Nandaka* was born at Campā in a burgess's family. He was the younger brother of Bharata. When both of them heard that Soṇa-Koḷivisa had left the world, they also renounced the worldly life. Bharata soon won sixfold abhiññā. But Nandaka could not. Seeing an ox pulling a cart out of the bog after it had been fed with grass and water, Nandaka like the refreshed ox drew himself out of the swamp of Saṁsāra. Within a short time he won arahatship.

*Lakuṇṭaka-Bhaddiya* was born in a wealthy family. Hearing the Master preach he entered the Order and won arahatship.

*Kassapa of the River* was born in a clan of Magadha brahmins, as the brother of Uruvela-Kassapa. His religious inclination made him dislike domestic life, and he became an ascetic. How. Exalted One ordained him is recorded Khandhaka.

*Kassapa of Gayā* was born in a brahmin family. He left the world and with a company of disciples dwelt at Gayā. The story of his conversion by the Master is recorded in the Khandhaka.

*Therīgāthā Commentary.*—The Therīgāthā Commentary[1] called the Paramatthadīpanī written by the Thera Dhammapāla appends explanatory stories to the verses of the Therīgāthā. These stories give us accounts of women who gradually became therīs. A summary of accounts of some of the important therīs is given below :—

*Abhirūpanandā*—Nandā, so called for her great beauty and amiability, had to leave the world against her will owing to the sudden and untimely death of her beloved suitor Carabhūta. But as she was still very conscious of her beauty and always avoided the presence of the Buddha for fear of being rebuked on that account, she was one day urged upon to appear before the Buddha. And he, the Buddha, by his supernatural power transformed her into an old and fading figure. It had the desired effect and she became an arhat.

*Jentī.*—Born in a princely family at Vaisālī, she won arahatship after hearing the Dhamma preached by the Buddha ; and later developed the seven saṁbojjhaṅgas.

*Cittā.*—Born at Rājagaha, she one day, when of age, heard the Buddha preaching, and came to believe in his doctrine. She was ordained by Mahāpajāpatī, the Gotamī, and later on won arahatship.

*Sukkā.*—Born in a rich family at Rājagaha, Sukkā, when of age, came to believe in the Buddha's doctrine and became a lay disciple. But one day hearing Dhammadinnā preach she was much moved, became a follower of him, and later on attained arahatship with paṭisaṁbhidā (analytical knowledge). One day she gave to the bhikkhuṇīs a sermon so

[1] It has been edited by E. Muller for the P.T.S.

engrossing that even the tree-spirit heard her with rapt attention.

*Selā.*—Otherwise known as Āḷavikā for her having been born in the kingdom of Āḷavī, she one day heard the Master and became a lay disciple. Not long after she became an arhant, and came to live with the Buddha at Sāvatthī, Māra once tried in vain to seduce her to choose the sensuous life.

*Sīhā.*—Born at Vesālī as the daughter of General Sīha's sister, she one day heard the Master teaching the Norm and thereupon entered the Order. For seven years she tried in vain to attain arahatship and she intended to die. When she was about to kill herself, she succeeded in impelling her mind to insight which grew within and she won arahatship.

*Sundarī Nandā.*—Born in the royal family of the Sākyas, beautiful Nandā renounced the world, but was still proud of her beauty. Buddha compelled her to come before his presence and taught her in the same way as in the case of Abhirūpanandā, and preached to her about the frail beauty of the body. She afterwards became an arhant.

*Khemā.*—Beautiful Khemā was the consort of King Bimbisāra. Hearing that the Buddha was in the habit of speaking ill of beauty, she liked not to appear before him. One day, hearing the beauty of the Veluvana vihāra, she came to see it. It happened that the Buddha was then living there, and she was led before him. The Buddha then illustrated with the example of a beautiful celestial nymph passing from youth through middle and old age to death the vanity of physical beauty and the suffering therefrom. Khemā at once became a believer and came to attain arahatship.

*Anopamā.*—Daughter of a banker of Sāketa, and beautiful as she was, she was sued by many young men of influence. But thinking that there was no happiness in household life, she went to the Master, heard his teachings, and later on attained arahatship.

*Rohiṇī.*—Born at Vesālī in a prosperous brahmin family, she, when grown up, went to the Master and heard him preach. With her parents' permission she entered the Order and soon attained arahantship.

*Subhā.*—Beautiful Subhā, the daughter of a goldsmith of Rājagaha, saw the Master, who taught her the Dhamma. She then entered the Order under Mahāpajāpatī Gotamī and in course of time won arahantship.

*Tissā.*—Born at Kapilavastu among the Sākyas, she renounced the world and afterwards attained arhantship.

*Sumedhā.*—Daughter of King Koñca of Mantāvatī, she, on hearing the doctrine of the Buddha from the bhikkhuṇīs, renounced the world, and soon acquiring insight, attained arahantship.

*Candā.*—Coming of a brahmin family, she had to beg from door to door for food. One day she took her food from Therī Paṭācārā and other bhikkhuṇīs. She then listened to the discourses of Therī Paṭācārā, renounced the world, and afterwards succeeded in attaining arahantship with paṭisaṁbhidā (analytical knowledge).

*Guttā.*—Coming of a brahmin family of Sāvatthī, she, with her parents' consent, entered the Order under Mahāpajāpatī Gotamī, and eventually attained arahantship together with paṭisaṁbhidā.

*Cālā, Upacālā, and Sisupacālā.*—Born in Magadha, these three were younger sisters of Sāriputta. On their brother leaving the Order, they too followed suit and afterwards attained arhantship. In vain Māra tried to stir up sensual desires in them.

*Uppalavaṇṇā.*—Coming of a banker's family at Sāvatthī, Uppalavaṇṇā was sued by many bankers' sons and princes. But she renounced the world, received ordination, and gradually attained arhantship with paṭisaṁbhidā or analytical knowledge.

*Sumaṅgalamātā.*—Coming of a poor family at Sāvatthī, and wife of a basket-maker, she one day reflected on all she had suffered as a lay-woman. On this her sight quickened and she attained arhatship with analytical knowledge.

*Puṇṇā.*—Born of a domestic slave at Sāvatthī in the household of Anāthapiṇḍika, and with great merits acquired in her previous births, she obtained Sotāpattiphalaṁ, and afterwards defeated in debate a brahmin Udakasiddhika. Puṇṇā renounced the worldly life, entered the Order, and attained arahantship.

*Sundarī.*—Born at Benares, Sundarī lost her brother, upon which her father renounced the world and became an arhant. Sundarī then followed her father, left the world, entered the Order, and after hard striving attained arhantship with paṭisaṁbhidā.

*Vimalā.*—Born of a public-woman at Vesālī, Vimalā one day went to the house of Mahāmoggallāna to entice him. The venerable thera rebuking her, she was ashamed and became a believer and lay-sister. Some time after she entered the Order and gradually attained arhantship.

*Mittakālikā.*—Coming of a brahmin family in the Kuru kingdom, she, when of age, entered the Order of sisters. For seven years she strove hard and afterwards won arhantship with the analytical knowledge.

*Sakulā* (*Pakulā*).—Born of a brahmin family at Sāvatthī, she early became a believer, and one day hearing the preaching of an arahat became so much convinced that she entered the Order. Afterwards she attained arhantship and became foremost among the bhikkhuṇīs.

*Muttā.*—Coming of a brahmin family of Sāvatthī, she, when twenty years old, went to Mahāpajāpatī Gotamī and got ordination from her. She eventually became an arhant.

*Puṇṇā.*—Daughter of a leading burgess of Sāvatthī, she, when twenty years of age, heard the Great Pajāpati and renounced the world. In due course she attained arhantship.

*Dantikā.*—Coming of a purohita family, she, when of age, entered the Order under Mahāpajāpatī Gotamī at Rājagaha, and eventually attained arhantship with analytical knowledge.

*Vaḍḍhesī.*—Nurse of Mahāpajāpatī Gotamī, she renounced the world following her mistress. For twenty-five years she was harassed by the lusts of the senses. But one day hearing Dhammadinnā preach the Norm, she began to practise meditation and soon acquired the six supernatural powers.

*Uttamā.*—Coming of a householder's family at Bandhumati, she in her old age heard Paṭācārā preach and entered the Order and very soon became an arhant. Afterwards she converted thirty sisters who entered the Order, and they in their turn became arhants.

*Uttarā.*—Coming of a clansman's family at Sāvatthī, she, when grown up, heard Paṭācārā preach the Norm, became a believer, entered the Order, and became an arhant.

*Bhaddā Kuṇḍalakesā.*—Coming of the family of a banker at Rājagaha, she, when grown up, fell in love with one Satthuka, a purohit's son. But Satthuka was avaricious and wanted to have all the jewels with which Bhaddā had decked herself. In vain she pleaded that she herself and all her ornaments belonged to him. So when, Satthuka one day took Bhaddā to the precipice of a cliff to give an offering, the latter pushed him over the precipice and he died. Bhaddā then left the world, entered the Order of the Niganṭhas, and became an unequalled debator. One day she challenged Sāriputta to a debate but she was defeated, and went to the Buddha for refuge. Buddha discerned her maturity of knowledge, and she attained arhantship with analytical knowledge.

*Sāmā (I).*—Coming of a rich household at Kosambī and moved by the death of one of her dear friends, she went to listen to the Elder Ānanda and acquired insight. On the seventh day after this she became an arhat.

*Sāmā (II).*—Another Sāmā coming of a clansman's family heard in her old age a sermon through which her insight expanded and she won arhantship with paṭisaṁbhidā (analytical knowledge).

*Ubbirī.*—Coming of the family of a rich householder at Sāvatthī, beautiful Ubbirī was made a queen of the king of Kosala. But a few years after when her only daughter Jīva died, she wept bitterly, whereupon she was questioned and instructed by the Buddha. She was then established in insight and in due course won arhantship.

*Kisāgotamī.*—Coming of a poor family at Sāvatthī, she, on the death of her only child, went to the Buddha with the dead body, and requested him to bring the dead to life. The Buddha then delivered a sermon upon which she became a bhikkhuṇī, and later on an arhant.

*Paṭācārā.*—Coming of banker's family at Sāvatthī, she, when of age, eloped with her lover who afterwards became her husband. But unfortunately enough the husband died of snake-bite and her son was drowned while crossing a river. She lost her brother and parents. She then became mad and went naked. But upon Buddha's directing her to recover her shamelessness, she acquired consciousness; and instructed by the Master she was established in Sotāpattiphalaṁ. Afterwards she became an arhant.

*Vāsiṭṭhī.*—Coming of a clansman's family at Vesālī, she became mad with grief at the death of her only son. But when she came to Mithilā and saw the Buddha she got back her normal mind, and she listened to the outlines of the Norm preached by the Buddha. She then acquired insight and became an arhant.

*Dhammadinnā.*—Coming of a clansman's family at Rājagaha, Dhammadinnā was married to a seṭṭhī named Visākhā. But on his renouncing the world, she too followed and became a bhikkhuṇī in a village. By virtue of her merits acquired in a previous birth, she soon became an arhant and was later on ranked by the Buddha as the foremost among the sisters who could preach.

*Dhammā.*—Coming of a respectable family at Sāvatthī, Dhammā entered the Order on her husband's death and became an arhant with thorough knowledge of the Norm in form and meaning.

*Mettikā.*—Daughter of a rich brahmin of Rājagaha, Mettikā lived the life of a recluse and eventually attained arhantship.

*Abhayā.*—Coming of a respectable family at Ujjain, Abhayā renounced the world, entered the Order, and in course of time attained arhantship at Rājagaha.

*Soṇā.*—Born at Rājagaha as the daughter of a purohita, Soṇā in her advanced years became a lay disciple first and afterwards entered the Order. Within a short time she attained arhantship, and Māra tried in vain to deviate her from this path.

*Bhaddā Kāpilānī.*—Coming of a brāhmaṇa family of the Kosiya clan at Sāgala, she renounced the world along with her husband and dwelt five years in a hermitage. She was then ordained by Mahāpajāpatī Gotamī and soon won arhantship. She was later on ranked first among the bhikkhuṇīs who could remember previous births.

*Dhīrā.*—Born at Kapilavatthu in the noble clan of the Sākiyas, Dhīrā renounced the world with Mahāpajāpatī Gotamī and was troubled in heart at the Master's teaching. She strove for insight and eventually became an arhant.

*Saṅghā.*—Her story is exactly like that of Dhirā.

*Sumanā (I).*—Born at Kapilavatthu, Sumanā (I) renounced the world, was ordained by Mahāpajāpatī Gotamī, and became gradually an arhant.

*Sumanā (II).*—Born at Sāvatthī as the sister of the king of Kosala, Sumanā (II) after the death of her grandmother went to the vihāra, and there hearing the Buddha preach, asked for ordination in her old age. She eventually became an arhant with thorough knowledge of the Norm in form and in meaning.

*Aḍḍhakāsī.*—Born in the kingdom of Kāsī, Aḍḍhakāsī became a prostitute. But later on she left the world and became ordained by a messenger sent by the Buddha himself. She soon attained arhantship with knowledge of the Dhamma in form and meaning.

*Soṇā.*—Coming of a clansman's family at Sāvatthī, Soṇā, following her husband, renounced the world in her old age and entered the Order. Her knowledge gradually matured as a result of her hard strife, and she attained arhantship. She was ranked first among the bhikkhuṇīs for capacity of effort.

*Sujātā.*—Born at Sāketa in a treasurer's family, Sujātā one day visited the Buddha in the Aṅgana Grove where the Master expounded the Norm to her in an inspiring lesson. Her intelligence being ripe, she at once became an arhant and was admitted to the Order of bhikkhuṇīs.

*Vaḍḍhamātā.*—Born in a clansman's family at Bharukaccha, Vaḍḍhamātā, hearing a bhikkhu preach, became a believer and entered the Order and eventually became an arhant.

*Ambapālī.*—Born spontaneously at Vesālī in the king's gardens at the foot of a mango tree, beautiful Ambapālī was sued by many princes and afterwards became their courtesan. Later on, out of faith in the Master, she built a vihāra and handed it over to him and the Order. And when she heard her own son preach the Norm, she worked for insight and soon attained arhantship.

*Cāpā.*—Born in the Vaṅkahāra country as the daughter of the chief trapper, Cāpā, on the attainment of arhantship by her husband, renounced the world at Sāvatthī and attained arhantship.

*Subhā.*—Born at Rājagaha in the family of an eminent brahmin, beautiful Subhā received faith and became a lay disciple. Later on, she renounced the world, entered the Order under

Mahāpajāpatī Gotamī, exercised herself in insight, and soon attained arhantship with a thorough grasp of the Norm in form and meaning.

*Isidāsī.*—Born at Ujjain as the daughter of a wealthy and virtuous merchant, she was married several times, but finding each husband undesirable, she grew agitated and took orders under the Therī Jīnadattā. She strove for insight and not long after attained arhantship together with thorough grasp of the Norm in form and meaning.

Paramatthadīpanī.

The Paramatthadīpanī[1] is a commentary on the Cariyāpiṭaka. Its author was Dhammapāla. The British Museum has acquired a good manuscript of this commentary in Burmese character dated 1764 (*vide* J.R.A.S., 1904, 174). The P.T.S. has undertaken to edit this text. Dhammapāla also wrote commentaries on the Udāna and Itivuttaka. The Itivuttaka Commentary is being edited by the P.T.S.

[1] It includes the commentaries on the Cariyāpiṭaka, Thera-Therīgāthā, Petavatthu, Vimānavatthu, Itivuttaka, and Udāna.

CHAPTER VI

# PĀLI CHRONICLES

Dīpavaṁsa.

The Dīpavaṁsa[1] or the chronicle of the island of Laṅkā is the earliest known work of its kind. It puts together certain well-known traditions handed down among the Buddhists of Ceylon, sometimes in a clumsy manner. Its diction is in places unintelligible, and its narrative is dull and interrupted by repetitions. Though it is composed in verse, curiously enough the verses are, here and there, intervened by prose passages (cf. Dīpavaṁsa, pp. 33, 64-65). What inference should be drawn from the occurrence of the prose passages in a metrical composition is still a matter of dispute. The point to be settled is whether the traditions on which the Dīpavaṁsa narrative is based were prevalent all in prose or all in verse or in both prose and verse. Its authorship is unknown. The canonical model of this work is to be traced in a number of verses in the Parivārapāṭha of the Vinaya Piṭaka.[2] The Dīpavaṁsa is an authorita-

[1] Dr. Geiger has published a valuable treatise known as "Dīpavaṁsa und Mahāvaṁsa und die geschichtliche überlieferung in Ceylon," Leipzig, 1905. Translated into English by E. M. Coomaraswamy, Dīpavaṁsa and Mahāvaṁsa, Colombo, 1908. We invite our readers' attention to Dr. Geiger's interesting contribution to the Indian Antiquary, Vol. XXXV, p. 443, on the Dīpavaṁsa and the Mahāvaṁsa and the Historical tradition in Ceylon.

[2] Cf. Parivārapāṭha, Vinaya Piṭaka, Vol. V, p. 3.

"Tissatthero ca medhāvī Devatthero ca paṇḍito, |
punar eva Sumano medhāvī vinaye ca visārado,
bahussuto Cūlanāgo gajo va duppadhaṁsiyo, |
Dhammapālitanāmo ca Rohaṇe sādhupūjito,
tassa sisso mahāpañño Khemanāmo tipeṭakī |
dīpe tārakarājā va paññāya atirocatha.
Upatisso ca medhāvī Phussadevo mahākathī, |
punar eva Sumano medhāvī Pupphanāmo bahussuto
mahākathī Mahāsivo piṭake sabbatthakovido, |

tive work well known in Ceylon at the time of Buddhaghosa, and, as a matter of fact, the great Pāli commentator has copiously quoted from it in the introductory portion of his commentary on the Kathāvatthu. Dr. Oldenberg has edited and translated the book into English. He says that the Dīpavaṁsa and the Mahāvaṁsa are in the main nothing but two versions of the same substance, both being based on the historical introduction to the great commentary of the Mahāvihāra. The Dīpavaṁsa follows step by step and almost word for word the traces of the original. According to Oldenberg the Dīpavaṁsa cannot have been written before 302 A.D. because its narrative extends till that year. If we compare the language and the style in which the Dīpavaṁsa and the Mahāvaṁsa are written, it leaves no doubt as to the priority of the former. The Dīpavaṁsa was so popular in Ceylon that King Dhātusena ordered it to be recited in public at an annual festival held in honour of an image of Mahinda in the 5th century A.D. (*vide* Dīpavaṁsa, ed. by Oldenberg, Intro., pp. 8-9). An idea of its contents can be gathered from the summary given below.

The first chapter gives an account of Buddha's

punar eva Upāli medhāvī vinaye ca visārado,
Mahānāgo mahāpañño saddhammavaṁsakovido, |
punar eva Abhayo medhāvī piṭake sabbatthakovido,
Tissatthero ca medhāvī vinaye ca visārado, |
tassa sisso mahāpañño Pupphanāmo bahussuto
sāsanaṁ anurakkhanto Jambudīpe patiṭṭhito. |
Cūlābhayo ca medhāvī vinaye ca visārado
Tissatthero ca medhāvī saddhammavaṁsakovido |
Cūladevo ca medhāvī vinaye ca visārado
Sīvatthero ca medhāvī vinaye sabbatthakovido, |
ete nāgā mahāpaññā vinayaññū maggakovidā
vinayaṁ dīpe pakāsesuṁ piṭakaṁ Tambapaṇṇiyā 'ti."

Cf. also Dīpavaṁsa, p. 32.

Nibbute lokanāthasmiṁ vassāni soḷasaṁ tadā,
Ajātasattu catuvīsaṁ, Vijayassa soḷasaṁ ahū,
samasaṭṭhi tadā hoti vassaṁ Upālipaṇḍitaṁ,
Dāsako upasampanno Upālitherasantike.
yavatā buddhaseṭṭhassa dhammappatti pakāsitā
sabbaṁ Upāli vācesi navaṅgaṁ jinabhāsitaṁ.

first visit to the island of Laṅkā. Gotama obtained perfect enlightenment at the foot of the Bodhi-tree. He surveyed the whole world and perceived the island of Laṅkā, a dwelling-place fit for saints. He foresaw that Mahinda, the son of the Indian King Asoka, would go to the island and propagate the Buddhist faith there. Accordingly he placed a divine guard over the island. He visited Laṅkā and drove the Yakkhas, the inhabitants of the place, out of the island.

Buddha visited the island for the second time when the island was on the verge of being destroyed by a terrific war which ensued between the mountain-serpents and the sea-serpents. The Lord exhorted them to live in peace and all the serpents took their refuge in him.

His third visit to the island was in connection with an invitation he got from the Nāga King Maṇiakkhika of Kalyāṇī.

The Dīpavaṁsa then traces Buddha's descent from the Prince Mahāsammata, the first inaugurated king of the earth. Gotama Buddha was the son of Suddhodana, chief of Kapilavatthu and Rāhulabhadda was the son of Gotama. Mention is also made of many other kings who reigned before Suddhodana and after Mahāsammata.

A brief account of the first two Buddhist Councils and the different Buddhist schools that arose after the Second Council is also given. The First Council was held under the presidency of Mahākassapa and under the patronage of Ajātasattu. The first collection of Dhamma and Vinaya was made with the assistance of Upāli and Ānanda. The Second Council was held during the reign of Kālāsoka. The Vajjiputtas proclaimed the ten indulgences which had been forbidden by the Tathāgata. The Vajjiputtas seceded from the orthodox party and were called the Mahāsāṁghikas. They were the first schismatics. In imitation of them many heretics arose, e.g., the Gokulikas, the Ekavyohārikas, the Bahussutiyas, etc. In all there were eighteen sects [1]—seventeen heretical and one orthodox. Besides these there were other minor schools.

The Dīpavaṁsa further deals with the reign of the great Indian King Asoka, the grandson of Candagutta and son of Bimbisāra, and the notable events that took place in his time. It was during his reign that Mahinda went to Ceylon and spread Buddhism there with the help of the Ceylonese King Devānaṁpiyatissa who was a contemporary of Asoka the Great. It is said that this great king built 84,000 vihāras all over the Jambudīpa. The Third Buddhist Council was held under the presidency of Thera Moggaliputta Tissa and under the patronage of Asoka. After the Council was over the thera sent Buddhist missionaries to different countries (Gandhāra, Mahisa, Aparantaka, Mahāraṭṭha, Yona, Himavata, Suvaṇṇabhūmi, and Laṅkā) for the propagation of Buddha's religion.

The Dīpavaṁsa gives a brief account of the colonisation of Ceylon by Vijaya, son of the king of Vaṅga, and also a systematic account of kings of Ceylon who ruled after Vijaya and their activities in promoting the cause of Buddhism. Sīhabāhu, king of Vaṅga, enraged at the bad conduct of Vijaya, his eldest son, banished him from his kingdom. Vijaya with a number of followers went on board a ship and sailed away on the sea. They in course of their journey through the waters visited the seaport towns of Suppāra and Bharukaccha and later on came to Laṅkādīpa. Vijaya and his followers set on colonising this country and built many cities. Vijaya became the first crowned king of the island. After Vijaya we find a long list of kings among whom Devānaṁpiyatissa stands out pre-eminent.

[1] *Vide* Mrs. Rhys Davids, 'The sects of the Buddhists,' J.R.A.S., 1891, pp. 409 foll.; schools of Buddhist belief, J.R.A.S., 1892, pp. 1 foll. Cf. Mahāvaṁsa, chap. 5, Mahābodhivaṁsa, pp. 96-97, Sāsanavaṁsa, p. 14, Kathāvatthupakaraṇa-aṭṭhakathā, pp. 2, 3, 5.

It was during the reign of Devānaṁpiyatissa that Buddhism was first introduced into Laṅkā through Mahinda who at the instance of Thera Moggaliputta Tissa, the President of the Third Council, went to Ceylon for the propagation of the Buddhist faith there. It may be noted here that the great Indian King Asoka was a contemporary of Devānaṁpiyatissa and that they were in friendly terms. Asoka sent a branch of the Bodhi-tree of the Tathāgata to Laṅkā which was planted with great honour at Anurādhapura.

After the death of Devānaṁpiyatissa Buddhism was not in a flourishing condition. The immediate successors of the king were weak. The Damiḷas came over to Laṅkā from Southern India and occupied the country. The people were tired of the foreign yoke. They found in Duṭṭhagāmaṇi, a prince of the royal family, who could liberate the country from the foreign domination. Duṭṭhagāmaṇi at the head of a huge army drove the Damiḷas out of the country. He was the greatest of the Sinhalese kings. Whether as a warrior or a ruler, Duṭṭhagāmaṇi appears equally great. He espoused the cause of Buddhism and built the Lohapāsāda, nine storeys in height, the Mahāthūpa, and many other vihāras. Indeed Buddhism was in its most flourishing condition during the reign of this great king.

Duṭṭhagāmaṇi was followed by a number of kings, among them Vaṭṭagāmaṇi was the greatest. His reign is highly important for the history of Buddhist literature. It was during his reign that the bhikkhus recorded in written books the text of the three piṭakas and also the Aṭṭhakathā. Vaṭṭagāmaṇi was also succeeded by a number of unimportant kings. The account of the kings of Ceylon is brought down to the reign of King Mahāsena who reigned for 27 years from *circa* 325 to 352 A.D.

At the close of the 4th century A.D. there existed in Ceylon, an older work, a sort of chronicle of the history of the island from very early times.

Mahāvaṁsa—its sources.

The work was a part of the Aṭṭhakathā which was composed in old Sinhalese prose mingled with Pāli verses. The work existed in the different monasteries of Ceylon and on it the Mahāvaṁsa is based. The chronicle must have originally come down to the arrival of Mahinda in Ceylon; but it was later carried down to the reign of Mahāsena (4th century A.D.) with whose reign the Mahāvaṁsa comes to an end. Of this work, the Dīpavaṁsa presents the first clumsy redaction in Pāli verses. The Mahāvaṁsa is thus a conscious and intentional rearrangement of the Dīpavaṁsa as a sort of commentary on the latter.

Author.

The author of the Mahāvaṁsa is known as Mahānāman.[1]

Date.

A well-known passage of the later Cūḷavaṁsa alludes to the fact that King Dhātusena bestowed a thousand pieces of gold and gave orders to write a dīpikā on the Dīpavaṁsa. This dīpikā has been identified by Fleet with the Mahāvaṁsa; and if this identification be correct, then the date of its origin is more precisely fixed. Dhātusena reigned at the beginning of the 6th century A.D., and about this time the Mahāvaṁsa was composed.

Historicity of the work.

The historicity of the work is established by the following facts :—

(*a*) As to the list of kings before Asoka, namely, the nine Nandas, Candagutta, and Bimbisāra, the statements concerning Bimbisāra and Ajātasattu as contemporaries of the Buddha agree with canonical writings, and, in respect of the names, with those of the Brahmanic tradition. In the number of years of Candagutta's reign, the Ceylonese tradition agrees with the Indian. Candagutta's councillor Cāṇaka (Cāṇakya) is also known.

---

[1] Read 'Mahānāma in the Pāli Literature' by Rev. R. Siddhartha, published in I.H.Q., Vol. VIII, No. 3, pp. 462–465.

(*b*) The conversion of Ceylon, according to the chronicles, was the work of Mahinda, son of Asoka, and this is confirmed to a considerable extent by the fact that Asoka twice in his inscriptions (Rock Edicts XIII and II) mentions Ceylon to be one of the countries where he sent his religious missionaries and provided for distribution of medicines. It receives further support from Hiuen Tsang who mentions Mahendra, a brother of Asoka, expressly as the man by whom the true doctrine was preached in Sinhala. Even before Mahinda, relations existed between India and Ceylon, for the chronicles relate that Asoka sent to Devānaṁpiyatissa presents for his sacred consecration as the king of Ceylon.

(*c*) An inscription from a relic-casket from Tope No. 2 of the Sāñci group gives us the name of Sapurisasa Mogaliputasa who, according to the tradition, presided over the Third Council under Asoka's rule. There is no doubt that he is identical with Moggaliputta Tissa of the Ceylonese chronicles.

(*d*) The narrative of the transplanting of a branch of the sacred Bodhi-tree from Uruvelā to Ceylon finds interesting confirmation in a representation of the story on the reliefs of the lower and middle architrave of the East gate of the Sāñci Stūpa.

(*e*) The contemporaneity of Devānaṁpiyatissa with Asoka is established on the internal evidence of the Dīpavaṁsa and the Mahāvaṁsa, as well as by archæological evidence. Another contemporaneity of King Meghavarman reigning from *c.* 352–379 A.D. with Samudragupta is established by the Chinese account of Wang Hiuentse.

(*f*) There is a general historical reminiscence underlying the stories of the three Buddhist Councils recorded in the chronicles.

But the historical statements are not always infallible ; and the longer the interval between the time of the events and the time when they are related, the greater the possibility of an error, and the more will be the influence of legend noticeable. As regards the period from Vijaya to Devānaṁpiyatissa, there is a considerable distrust of tradition and traditional chronology. Also during the period from Devānaṁpiyatissa to Duṭṭhagāmaṇi there is matter for doubt. But in later periods we encounter no such difficulties and impossibilities. The chronology is credible, the numbers appear less artificial, and the accounts more trustworthy.

Text—the visit of the Tathāgata.

In the ninth month after Buddhahood, when the Lord Buddha was dwelling at Uruvelā, he one day personally went to Laṅkā and converted a large assembly of Yakkhas as well as a large number of other living beings. After this, he came back to Uruvelā but, again in the fifth year of his Buddhahood when he was residing in the Jetavana, he, in an early morning out of compassion for the nāgas went to the Nāgadīpa (apparently the north-western part of Ceylon) where he preached the five moral precepts and established the three refuges and converted many nāgas. The Lord then came back to Jetavana, but, again in the eighth year of his Buddhahood the Teacher, while dwelling in the Jetavana, went to Kalyāṇī and preached the Dhamma, and then came back to Jetavana.

The Race of Mahāsammata.

The Chapter II gives a long list of kings beginning with Mahāsammata from whose race sprang the Great Sage, the Tathāgata. Descendants of this race of kings ruled in Kusāvatī, Rājagaha, and Mithilā, and they reigned in groups in their due order. One group whose chief was Okkāka ruled at Kapilavatthu and was known as the Sākyas. In this line was born Yasodharā, a daughter of King Jayasena, and she was married to Sakka Añjana. They had two daughters, Māyā and Pajāpatī, who were both married to Suddhodana, a grandson of Jayasena and son of Sīhahanu. The son of Suddhodana and Māyā was the Lord Buddha whose consort was Bhaddakaccānā, son was Rāhula, great friend was Bimbisāra, and another contemporary was Bimbisāra's son, Ajātasattu.

The three Buddhist Councils.

The First Buddhist Council[1] was convened three months after the parinirvāṇa of the Buddha (at Kuśīnārā) in the Sattapaṇṇi Cave at Rājagaha where his nearest disciples followed by seven hundred thousand bhikkhus and a large number of laymen assembled to establish the most important rules of the Order as, according to their recollection, the Master himself had laid down. The work of the compilation was entrusted to Thera Ānanda and Thera Upāli. Thera Upāli spoke for the Vinaya, and Thera Ānanda for the rest of the Dhamma; and Thera Mahākassapa seated on the thera's chair asked questions touching the Vinaya. Both of them expounded them in detail and the theras repeated what they had said. The work of the First Council took seven months to be completed, and the Council rose after it had finished compilation of the Dhamma, and the Canon came to be known as thera tradition.

A century after the parinibbāna of the Buddha when Kālāsoka was the reigning king, there were at Vaiśālī many bhikkhus of the Vajji clan who used to preach the Ten points of Buddhism. But the theras of Pāvā and Avanti with their leader, the great Thera Revata, declared that these Ten points were unlawful, and wanted to bring the dispute to a peaceful end. All of them followed by a large number of bhikkhus then went to Vaiśālī and there met the bhikkhus of the Vajji clan. Kālāsoka too went there, and, hearing both sides, decided in favour of the true faith, held out by the theras of Pāvā and Avanti. The brotherhood then came together finally to decide, and Revata resolved to settle the matter by an *Ubbāhikā* wherein

---

[1] Prof. Przyluski's Le Concile de Rājagriha, pt. I, pp. 8, 30, 66, and 116 should be consulted. Read also Buddhist Councils by Dr. R. C. Majumdar published in the Buddhistic Studies, edited by Dr. B. C. Law. *Vide* The Buddhist Councils held at Rājagriha and Vesālī translated from Chinese by S. Beal.

four from each of the two parties were represented. Thera Revata, in order to hold a Council, chose also seven hundred out of all that troop of bhikkhus, and all of them met in the Vālikārāma and compiled the Dhamma in eight months. The heretical bhikkhus who taught the wrong doctrine founded another school which came to bear the name Mahāsāṅghika.

The Third Council was held under better circumstances during the reign of King Asoka at the Asokārāma in Pāṭaliputta under the guidance and presidentship of Thera Moggalliputta Tissa. Within a hundred years from the compilation of the doctrine in the Second Council, there arose eighteen different sects in the Buddhist Order with their respective schools and systems, and another schism in the Church was threatened. At this time, 218 years from the parinibbāna of the Buddha, Asoka came to the throne, and after a reign of four years, he consecrated himself as king in Pāṭaliputta. And, not long after, Sāmaṇera Nigrodha preached the doctrine to the king, and confirmed him with many of his followers in the refuges and precepts of duty. Thereupon the king became bountiful to the bhikkhus and eventually entered the doctrines. From that time the revenue of the brotherhood was on the increase but the heretics became envious, and they too, taking the yellow robe and dwelling along with the bhikkhus, began to proclaim their own doctrine as the doctrine of the Buddha, and carry out their own practices even as they wished. They became so unruly that King Asoka was obliged to arrange an assembly of the community of bhikkhus in its full numbers at the splendid Asokārāma under the presidency of Thera Moggalliputta Tissa. Then did the king question one by one on the teachings of the Buddha. The heretical bhikkhus expounded their wrong doctrine, upon which the king caused to be expelled from the Order all such bhikkhus and their followers. Only the rightly believing bhikkhus answered that the Lord taught the

Vibhajja-doctrine, and this was supported and confirmed by Thera Moggalliputta Tissa. Three thousand learned bhikkhus were then selected to make a compilation of the true doctrine under the guidance of the great thera, and they completed their work at the Asokārāma in nine months.

The coming and consecration of Vijaya and others.

Vijaya of evil conduct was the son and prince regent of King Sīhabāhu, ruler of the kingdom of Lāḷa; but he was banished from the kingdom by his father for his many intolerable deeds of violence. Boarded on a ship with his large number of followers with their wives and children, Vijaya first landed at Suppāraka, but afterwards, embarking again, landed in Laṅkā in the region called Tambapaṇṇi, where he eventually married and consecrated himself as king and built cities. After his death, he was succeeded by his brother's son Paṇḍuvāsudeva who married Subhaddakaccānā, and consecrated himself as king. He was in his turn succeeded by his son Abhaya who was followed by Paṇḍukābhaya. Between Paṇḍukābhaya and Abhaya there was no king for 17 years.

Devanāṁpiyatissa.

Paṇḍukābhaya's son Muṭasiva followed his father and was succeeded by his second son Devānaṁpiyatissa whose friend was Dhammāsoka whom he had never seen, but to whom he was pleased to send a priceless treasure as a gift. Dhammāsoka appreciated the gift, and sent as a return-gift another treasure to Devānaṁpiyatissa who was now consecrated as king of Laṅkā.

After the termination of the Third Council, Moggalliputta Tissa Thera, in order to establish the religion in adjacent countries, sent out learned and renowned missionaries to Kasmīr, Gandhāra, Mahīsamaṇḍala, Vanavāsa, Aparāntaka, Mahāraṭṭha, Suvaṇṇabhūmi (Burma), and to the Yona country. To the lovely island of Laṅkā, he sent Mahinda, the theras Iṭṭhiya, Uttiya, Sambala, and Bhaddasāla to preach the religion.

Mahinda.

Mahinda came out to Laṅkā with four theras and Saṅghamittā's son Sumana, the gifted sāmaṇera. Even on their landing many devas, nāgas, and supaṇṇas were converted to the doctrine, and he with his followers entered the capital city where people thronged to see him, and he preached the true faith unto them. The wise King Devānaṁpiyatissa heard him explain some of the miracles and teachings and episodes of the life of the Buddha, and became one of his most devoted patrons. The king then built for the great thera the Mahāvihāra, henceforth known as the Mahāmeghavanārāma, which the thera accepted. Next the king built for him and his followers another vihāra on the Cetiyapabbata, henceforth known as the Cetiyapabbata-vihāra, which too the thera accepted. The wise king then became eager to enshrine one of the relics of the Great Lord the Buddha in a stūpa, so that he and the followers of the faith might behold the Conqueror in his relics and worship him. At his request Mahinda sent Sumana to King Dhammāsoka with the instruction to bring from him the relics of the Sage and the alms-bowl of the Master, and then to go to Sakka in the fair city of the gods to bring the collar-bone of the Master from him. Sumana faithfully carried out the instruction, and when he landed down on the Missaka mountain with the relics, the king and the people were all filled with joy, and thirty thousand of them received the pabbajjā of the Conqueror's doctrine. Later on the king sent his nephew and minister Ariṭṭha again to Dhammāsoka to bring the Bodhi-tree which at Dhammāsoka's approach severed of itself and transplanted itself in the vase provided for the purpose. Ariṭṭha then came back on board a ship across the ocean to the capital with the holy tree and a gay rejoicing began. With the Bodhi-tree came also Therī Saṅghamittā with eleven followers. The Tree and its Saplings were planted with due ceremony at different places, and royal consecration was bestowed on them. Under the direction of the Thera Mahinda who converted the island, Devānaṁpiyatissa continued to build vihāras and thūpas one after another, and thus ruled for 40 years, after which he died. He was succeeded on the throne by his son, Prince Uttiya ; but in the eighth year of his reign, the great Thera Mahinda, who had brought light to the island of Laṅkā, died at the age of sixty ; and the whole island was struck with sorrow at his death, and the funeral rights were observed with great ceremony.

Duṭṭhagāmaṇi.

After a reign of ten years Uttiya died, and was followed by Mahāsiva, Sūratissa, two Damiḷas, Sena and Guttaka, Asela and Eḷāra, a Damiḷa from the Cola country, in succession. Eḷāra was killed by Duṭṭhagāmaṇi who succeeded the former as king.

Gāmaṇi, for such was his original name, was born of Prince Kākavaṇṇatissa, overlord of Mahāgāma, and Vihāradevī, daughter of the king of Kalyāṇī. Gāmaṇi was thus descended through the dynasty of Mahānāga, second brother of Devānaṁpiyatissa. Kākavaṇṇatissa had another son by Vihāradevī named Tissa, and both Gāmaṇi and Tissa grew up together. Now when they were ten and twelve years old, Kākavaṇṇatissa, who was a believing Buddhist, wanted his sons to make three promises ; first, they would never turn away from the bhikkhus, secondly, the two brothers would ever be friendly towards each other, and, thirdly, never would they fight the Damiḷas. The two brothers made the first two promises but turned back to make the third, upon which their father became sorry. Gāmaṇi gradually grew up to sixteen years, vigorous, renowned, intelligent, majestic, and mighty. He gathered round him mighty and great warriors from far and near villages, as well as from the royal and noble families. Gāmaṇi developed a strong hatred towards the Damiḷas who had more than once usurped the throne of Laṅkā, and became determined to quell them down. Now he had gathered a strong army of brave and sturdy warriors round him, he approached his father for permission to make war on the Damiḷas. But the king, though repeatedly requested, declined to give any such permission. As a pious Buddhist devoted to the cult of ahiṁsā, he could not give permission for war that would result in bloodshed and cruelty. He also dissuaded the warriors to fight for his sons. Gāmaṇi, thereupon, became disgusted with his father, and went to Malaya; and because of his anger and disgust towards his father, he was named as Duṭṭhagāmaṇi. In the meantime King Kākavaṇṇatissa died, and there arose a deadly scramble for the throne between the two brothers, Duṭṭhagāmaṇi and Tissa. Two battles were fought with considerable loss of life, and Duṭṭhagāmaṇi eventually became victorious. Peace was then concluded and the two brothers began to live together again. He took some time to provide for his people who had suffered during the last wars, and then went out to fight against the Damiḷas. He overpowered Damiḷa Chattā, conquered Damiḷa Titthamba and many other mighty Damiḷa princes and kings. Deadly were the wars that he fought with them, but eventually he came out victorious, and united the whole of Laṅkā into one kingdom. Gāmaṇi was then consecrated with great pomp, and not long after he himself consecrated the Maricavaṭṭi vihāra which he had built up. Next took place the consecration of the Lohapāsāda; but the building up of the Great Thūpa was now to be taken up. He took some time to the obtaining of the wherewithal, i.e., the materials of the thūpa from different quarters, and then began the work in which masons and workmen from far and near did take part, and at the beginning of which a great assemblage of theras from different countries took place. When the work of the building had considerably advanced, the king ordered the making of the Relic-chamber in which the relics were afterwards enshrined with due eclat, pomp, and ceremony. But ere yet the making of the chatta and the plaster work of the monument was finished, the king fell ill which later on proved fatal. He sent for his younger brother Tissa, and asked him to complete the thūpa, which Tissa did. The ill king passed round the Cetiya on a palanquin and did homage to it, and left with Tissa the charge of doing all the work that still remained to be done towards it. He then enumerated some of the pious works he had done in his life to the theras and bhikkhus assembled round his bed, and one of the theras spoke to him on the unconquerable foe of death. Then the king became silent, and he saw that a golden chariot came down from the Tusita heaven. Then he breathed his last, and was immediately seen reborn and standing in celestial form in a car that had come down from the Tusita heaven.

A Long Line of Kings.—Ten kings.

Duṭṭhagāmaṇi was succeeded by his brother Saddhātissa who ruled for 18 years, and built many cetiyas and vihāras. He was followed by Thūlathana, Lañjatissa, Khallāṭanāga, and Vaṭṭagāmaṇi. The last named was a famous king during whose reign the Damiḷas became powerful and again usurped the throne. Vaṭṭagāmaṇi was thus followed by Damiḷa Pulahattha, Damiḷa Bāhiya, Damiḷa Panayamāraka, Damiḷa Piḷayamāraka, and Damiḷa Dāṭhika. But the Damiḷas were dispossessed of their power not long after by Vaṭṭagāmaṇi, who now ruled for a few more years.

Eleven kings.

After his death, his adopted son Mahācūḷī Mahātissa reigned for 14 years with piety and justice. He was followed by Coranāga, Tissa, Siva, Damiḷa Vaṭuka, Brahmin Niliya, Queen Anulā, Kūṭakaṇṇa Tissa, Bhātikābhaya, and Mahādāṭhika Mahānāga.[1] All of them had short reigns and were builders of vihāras

[1] In the list of Ancient Kings of Ceylon the name of Dārubhatikatissa appears after Damiḷa Vaṭuka (*vide* Geiger, Mahāvaṁsa, Introduction, p. xxxvii).

and cetiyas. Anulā was a notorious queen and to her love intrigues at least four kings, Siva, Tissa, Damiḷa Vaṭuka, and Brahmin Niliya, lost their lives. Except Tissa, they were all upstarts and they rightly deserved the fate that had been theirs.

Twelve kings.

After Mahādāṭhika's death, Āmaṇḍagāmaṇi Abhaya, his son, followed him on the throne. He was followed by Kaṇirajānutissa, Cūḷābhaya, Queen Sīvalī, Iḷanāga, Candamukha Siva, Yasalālakatissa, Subharāja, Vaṅkanāsikatissaka, Gajabāhukagāmaṇi, and Mahallaka Nāga in succession. Most of these kings were worthless, and their merit lay only in the building or extension of vihāras and other religious establishments and in court-intrigues. Two of them, Iḷanāga and Subharāja were, however, comparatively more noted for their acts of bravery and valour exhibited mostly in local wars.

Thirteen kings.

After the death of Mahallanāga, his son Bhātikatissaka reigned for 24 years. He was followed in succession by Kaniṭṭhatissaka, Khujjanāga, Kuñcanāga, Sirināga, Tissa, Abhayanāga, Sirināga, Vijayakumāraka, Saṁghatissa, Sirisamghabodhi, Goṭhābhaya, and Jeṭṭhatissa who are grouped together in a chapter entitled "Thirteen Kings" in the Mahāvaṁsa. Scarcely there is anything important enough to be recorded about these kings, besides the fact that most of them ruled as pious Buddhists, always trying to further the cause of the religion by the foundation and extension of religious establishments, and that they carried out the affairs of the kingdom through wars, intrigues, rebellions, and local feuds.

King Mahāsena.

King Jeṭṭhatissa was succeeded by his younger brother, Mahāsena, who ruled for 27 years and during whose reign, most probably, the Mahāvaṁsa was given its present form. Originally it ended with the death of King Duṭṭhagāmaṇi, but now it was probably brought up-to-date.

On his accession to the throne, he forbade the

people to give food to any bhikkhu dwelling in the Mahāvihāra on penalty of a fine of hundred pieces of money. The bhikkhus thus fell in want, and they left the vihāra which remained empty for nine years. It was then destroyed by the ill-advisers of the king and its riches were removed to enrich the Abhayagirivihāra. The king wrought many a deed of wrong upon which his minister Meghavaṇṇābhaya became angry and became a rebel. A battle was imminent, but the two former friends met, and the king, repentant of his misdeeds, promised to make good all the harm done to the religious establishments of Laṅkā. The king rebuilt the Mahāvihāra, and founded amongst others two new vihāras, the Jetavanavihāra and the Maṇihīravihāra. He was also the builder of the famous Thūpārāmavihāra, as well as of two other nunneries. He also excavated many tanks and did many other works of merit.

Dr. Kern says in his Manual of Indian Buddhism that the Mahāvaṁsa deserves a special notice on account of its being so highly important for the religious history of Ceylon. Dr. Geiger who has made a thorough study of the Pāli chronicles, has edited the text of the Mahāvaṁsa for the P.T.S., London, and has ably translated it into English for the same society, with the assistance of the late Dr. M. H. Bode. G. Turnour's edition and translation of this text are now out of date. Prof. Geiger has translated it into German. Mrs. Bode has retranslated it into English and Dr. Geiger himself has revised the English translation. There is a commentary on the Mahāvaṁsa known as the Mahāvaṁsaṭikā (Waṁsatthapakāsinī revised and edited by Baṭuwantudawe and Ñānissara, Colombo, 1895) written by Mahānāma of Anurādhapura. This commentary is helpful in reading the text. It contains many additional data not found in the text. Readers are referred to the Mahāwanse, ed. by Turnour, Ceylon, 1837, Mahāvaṁsa revised and edited by H. Sumaṅgala Baṭuwantudawe, Colombo, 1883, and Cambodjan Mahāvaṁsa by E. Hardy, J.R.A.S., 1902. There is a Sinhalese translation by Wijesinha, Colombo, 1889 (chapter and verse).

Dīpavaṁsa and Mahāvaṁsa compared.

It has long been ascertained that both Dīpavaṁsa and Mahāvaṁsa owe their origin to a common source—the Aṭṭhakathā-Mahāvaṁsa of the Mahāvihāra monastery, which, evidently was a sort of chronicle of the history of the island from very early times, and must have formed an introductory part of the old theological commentary (aṭṭhakathā) on the canonical writings of the Buddhists. Both Oldenberg and Geiger, the celebrated editors of the Dīpavaṁsa and Mahāvaṁsa respectively, are of opinion that this Aṭṭhakathā-Mahāvaṁsa was composed in Sinhalese prose, interspersed, no doubt with verse in the Pāli language. This book (Mahāvaṁsa-aṭṭhakathā) existed in various recensions in the different monasteries of the island, and the authors of both Dīpavaṁsa and Mahāvaṁsa borrowed the materials of their works from one or other of the various recensions of that Aṭṭhakathā. This borrowing presumably was independent, and quite in their own way ; but even then, in the main, they are nothing but two different versions of the same thing. But as the Dīpavaṁsa had been composed at least one century and a half earlier than the Mahāvaṁsa, it shows perhaps more faithfulness to the original, i.e., to the Aṭṭhakathā, for, as Oldenberg points out, that the " author of the Dīpavaṁsa borrowed not only the materials of his own work but also the mode of expression, and even whole lines, word for word, from the Aṭṭhakathā. In fact, a great part of the Dīpavaṁsa has the appearance not of an independent, continual work, but of a composition of such single stanzas extracted from a work or works like the Aṭṭhakathā ".[1] But the author of

[1] Dīpavaṁsa (Oldenberg), Introduction, p. 6.

the Mahāvaṁsa is not so fettered in his style or execution. Coming as he did at least one century and a half later (i.e., the beginning of the 6th century A.D.) than the author of the Dīpavaṁsa when the islanders had attained much more freedom in their learning and writing of the Pāli language he evidently showed greater ease and skill in his use of the language, as well as in his style and composition, and finally, a more free and liberal use of the material of his original.

It is well known that Mahānāman was the author of the Mahāvaṁsa, whereas we are completely in the dark as to the name of the author of the Dīpavaṁsa. A further proof of the fact that both the authors were indebted to a common source is provided by a very striking coincidence of the two narratives, namely, that both the chronicles finish their accounts with the death of King Mahāsena who flourished about the beginning of the 4th century A.D. It was not much later that the Dīpavaṁsa was composed, but as the Mahāvaṁsa was composed still later, we might as well expect the bringing down of the narrative to a later date. But this was not the case, apparently for the fact that their common source, the Aṭṭhakathā-Mahāvaṁsa of the Mahāvihāra monastery, as shown by Oldenberg, was very intimately connected with King Mahāsena with whose reign the glorious destinies of the monastery came practically to an end, and there the Aṭṭhakathā could only logically stop its account.[1]

But the historical writers of the Mahāvihāra fraternity did not at once bring down their account to the reign of Mahāsena. The Aṭṭhakathā-Mahāvaṁsa seems to have originally brought down its account only to the arrival of Mahinda in Ceylon; but it was later on continued and brought down to the reign of Mahāsena, where both the Dīpavaṁsa and the Mahāvaṁsa as already noticed, came to an end.

---

[1] Dīpavaṁsa (Oldenberg), Intro., p. 8.

That the Dīpavaṁsa was well known to the author of the Mahāvaṁsa is evident from the very arrangement of the chapters and events of the narrative, so much so that the Mahāvaṁsa seems to be more an explanatory commentary on the earlier chronicle. The account in the Dīpavaṁsa is condensed, and the sequence of events and characters presents the form more of a list and catalogue than of any connected account. The Mahāvaṁsa, on the other hand, is elaborate, more embellished, and seems rather to explain the catalogue of events and characters of the earlier chronicle so as to give it the form of a connected narrative. Geiger rightly thinks in this connection that "the quotation of the Mahāvaṁsa of the ancients in the prooemium of our Mahāvaṁsa refers precisely to the Dīpavaṁsa".[1] The well-known passage of the Cūḷavaṁsa (38. 59) "datvā sahassaṁ dīpetuṁ Dīpavaṁsaṁ samādisi" which Fleet translates as "he (King Dhātusena) bestowed a thousand (pieces of gold) and gave orders to write a *dīpikā* on the Dīpavaṁsa" also lends support to this view,[2] for this Dīpikā, Fleet says, is identical with Mahāvaṁsa.

It is interesting to compare the more important chapters of the two chronicles to see how their subject-matters agree or differ. We have already indicated that their contents are almost identical; in the Dīpavaṁsa they are condensed, and in the Mahāvaṁsa, elaborate. After an identical account of the race of Mahāsammata, both the earlier and later chronicles proceed to give a more or less detailed account of the three Buddhist Councils. The account of the First Council is almost the same. Five hundred chosen bhikkhus assembled under the leadership of Mahākassapa in the Sattapaṇṇa cave at Rājagaha and composed the collection of the Dhamma and the Vinaya. The Dīpa-

---

[1] Mahāvaṁsa (Geiger), Intro., p. xi.

[2] Mahāvaṁsa (Geiger), Intro., p. xi, where Geiger quotes Fleet.

vaṁsa mentions the fourth month after the Master's death as the time at which the First Council was held. This was the second Vassa-month, i.e., Sāvaṇa. This date is substantially confirmed by that provided by the Mahāvaṁsa which mentions the bright half of Āsāḍa, the fourth month of the year as the beginning of the Council. But as the first month was spent in preparations, the actual proceedings did not begin till the month of Sāvaṇa. The account of the Second Council too is substantially the same. It was brought about by the dasa-vatthūni of the Vajjians of Vesālī, a relaxation of monastic discipline; and 700 bhikkhus took part in the discussion of the Council. It was held in the 11th year of the reign of Kālāsoka; there is, however, a slight discrepancy about the locality where the Council was held. The Mahāvaṁsa mentions the Vālikārāma, whereas the Dīpavaṁsa mentions the Kūṭāgārasālā of the Mahāvana monastery as the place of the Council. The tradition of a schism in the Second Council is also identical in the two chronicles. The Dīpavaṁsa states that the heretical monks held a separate Council called the Mahāsaṁgīti, and prepared a different redaction of the Scriptures. The tradition is also noticed in the Mahāvaṁsa where it is related that they formed a separate sect under the name Mahāsāṁghika. The account of the Third Council is also identical. It was held at Pāṭaliputta under the presidency of Tissa Moggaliputta and lasted for nine months.

The list of Indian kings before Asoka and pieces of historical account connected with them, the traditional date of the Buddha's parinirvāna, and the duration of reigns of individual Indian kings are always almost identical in both the chronicles. The story of the conversion of Ceylon, that of the coming of Vijaya and his consecration, the list and account of Ceylonese kings up to Devānaṁpiyatissa and that of the latter's contemporaneity with King Dhammāsoka, are for all practical purposes the same. But before the two chronicles take up the account of Mahinda's coming to Ceylon, the Mahāvaṁsa inserts a somewhat elaborate account of the converting of different countries under the efficient missionary organisation of Moggaliputta Thera. The Mahāvaṁsa thus rightly stresses the fact that it was a part of the religious policy of the great thera that Mahinda came to Ceylon. Here again the accounts of the Dīpavaṁsa and the Mahāvaṁsa are identical; then follow the identical accounts of Mahinda's entry into the capital, his acceptance of the Mahāvihāra and that of the Cetiyapabbata-vihāra, the arrival of the relics, the receiving and coming of the Bodhi tree, and the Nibbāna of the Thera Mahinda. From Vijaya to Devānaṁpiyatissa the tradition and traditional chronology are almost identical; there is only a discrepancy about the date of Devānaṁpiyatissa himself. The earlier chronicle states that King Devānaṁpiyatissa was consecrated king in the 237th year after the Buddha's death, whereas the Mahāvaṁsa places it on the first day of the bright half of the ninth month, Maggasira (Oct.-Nov.), showing a discrepancy involved probably in the chronological arrangement itself.[1]

The account of the kings from the death of Devānaṁpiyatissa to Duṭṭhagāmaṇi is also identical in the two chronicles. But the Mahāvaṁsa is much more detailed and elaborate in its account of King Duṭṭhagāmaṇi, giving as it does in separate chapters the topics of the birth of Prince Gāmaṇi, the levying of the warriors for the war of the two brothers, Gāmaṇi and Tissa, the victory of Duṭṭhagāmaṇi, the consecrating of the Maricavaṭṭi vihāra, the consecrating of the Lohapāsāda, the obtaining of the wherewithal to build the Mahāthūpa, the beginning of the Mahāthūpa, the making of the relic-chamber for the Mahāthūpa, the enshrining of the relics and finally his death: whereas the

[1] See Mahāvaṁsa (Geiger), Intro., pp. xxxi foll.

Dīpavaṁsa touches, and that also in brief, the two accounts only in their main outline.

The list and account of the later kings from Duṭṭhagāmaṇi to Mahāsena in the Dīpavaṁsa are very brief. In the Mahāvaṁsa, however, though the essential points and topics are the same, the accounts differ considerably in their detail which may be due to the more liberal use by the author of the original as well as of other historical and traditional sources than the Aṭṭhakathā-Mahāvaṁsa. He might have also used those indigenous historical literature and tradition that might have grown up after the author of the Dīpavaṁsa had laid aside his pen. This is apparent from a comparison of the respective accounts of any individual king, say, the last King Mahāsena. Thus the Dīpavaṁsa relates that while he was in search of really good and modest bhikkhus, he met some wicked bhikkhus ; and knowing them not he asked them the sense of Buddhism and the true doctrine. Those bhikkhus, for their own advantage, taught him that the true doctrine was a false doctrine. In consequence of his intercourse with those wicked persons, he performed evil as well as good deeds, and then died. The Mahāvaṁsa account is otherwise. It gives the story of his consecration by Saṅghamittā, the account of the vicissitudes of the Mahāvihāra, how it was left desolate for nine years, how a hostile party succeeded in obtaining the king's sanction for destroying the monastery, why for this fault of the king the minister became a rebel, how the Mahāvihāra was reconstructed and came to be again inhabited by bhikkhus, how an offence of the gravest kind was made against Thera Tissa and how he was expelled, how the king built the Maṇihīra-vihāra, destroying the temples of some brahmanical gods, and how he built many other ārāmas and vihāras, and a number of tanks and canals for the good of his subjects.

One such instance as just noticed is sufficient to explain the nature of the difference in the accounts of individual kings as given in the two chronicles. The duration of ruling years as given to individual kings is in most cases identical; there are only a few discrepancies, e.g., with regard to the reigns of Sena and Gutta, Lajjitissa (the Mahāvaṁsa gives the name as Lañjatissa), Niliya, Tissa Yasalāla, Abhaya, and Tissa. In the case of Sena and Gutta, the Dīpavaṁsa gives the duration of rule as 12 years, whereas the Mahāvaṁsa gives it as 22 years. The Dīpavaṁsa gives 9 years 6 months to Lajjitissa, whereas the later chronicle gives 9 years 8 months. Niliya is given 3 months in the earlier chronicle, but in the later chronicle he is given 6 months. Tissa Yasalāla is given 8 years 7 months, and 7 years and 8 months respectively; and the order of rule of Abhaya and Tissa of the Dīpavaṁsa is transposed in the Mahāvaṁsa as Tissa and Abhaya, and Abhaya is given only 8 years in place of 22 as given by the Dīpavaṁsa.

The value of the Ceylonese chronicles.

In the early days of the study of the Ceylonese chronicles, scholars were sceptical about their value as sources of authentic historical tradition and information. But now after lapse of years when the study of Indian and Ceylonese history has far advanced, it is now comparatively easy for us to estimate their real value.

Like all chronicles, the Dīpavaṁsa and the Mahāvaṁsa contain germs of historical truth buried deep under a mesh of absurd fables and marvellous tales. But if they do contain mainly myths and marvels and read more like fantasies, they are like other chronicles of their time. This, however, should not be used as any argument for completely rejecting the chronicles as positively false and untrustworthy. It is, however, important that one should read them with a critical eye as all records of popular and ecclesiastical tradition deserve to be read. Buried in the illumination of myths, miracles, and legends, there are indeed germs which go to make up facts of history, but they can only be gleaned by a very careful elimination of all mythical and unessential details which the pious sentiment of the believer gathered round the nucleus. "If we pause", Geiger rightly says, "first at internal evidence then the Ceylonese chronicles will assuredly at once win approval in that they at least wished to write the truth. Certainly the writers could not go beyond the ideas determined by their age and their social position, and beheld the events of a past time in the mirror of a one-sided tradition. But they certainly did not intend to deceive hearers or readers."[1]

The very fact that both Dīpavaṁsa and Mahāvaṁsa are based on the earlier Aṭṭhakathā-Mahāvaṁsa, a sort of a chronicle which itself was based upon still earlier chronicles, ensures us in our belief that they contain real historical facts, for, with the Aṭṭhakathā, the tradition goes back several centuries, and becomes almost contemporary with the historical incidents narrated in the chronicle.

Even in the very introductory chapters, there are statements which agree with other canonical writings, and find confirmation in our already known facts of history. Such are the statements that Bimbisāra was a great friend of Buddha, and both Bimbisāra and Ajātasattu were contemporaries of the Master. There does not seem to be any ground for rejecting the tradition of the chronicles that Gotama was five years older than Bimbisāra, though the duration of rule ascribed to each of them disagrees with that ascribed by the Purāṇas. But whatever that might be, there can hardly be any doubt as to the authenticity of the list of Indian kings from Bimbisāra to Asoka provided by the chronicles. The Jain tradition has, no doubt, other names; "this", as pointed out by Geiger, "does not affect the actual agreement. There can be no doubt that the nine Nandas as well as the two forerunners of Asoka, Candagutta

---

[1] Mahāvaṁsa—Geiger, Intro., p. xv.

and Bindusāra, were altogether historical personages." But more than this is the complete agreement of the Ceylonese and Pauranic tradition in the duration of reign, namely 24, ascribed to Candagutta. The discrepancy of the two traditions in respect of regnal duration of Bindusāra and Asoka, namely 3 years and 1 year respectively, is almost negligible. Still more interesting is the name of Canakka (Cāṇakya), the brahmin minister of Candagutta, who was known to the authors of the Dīpavaṁsa and the Mahāvaṁsa.

So much with regard to the historical value of the Ceylonese chronicles in respect of Indian history. But more valuable are the chronicles with regard to the history of Ceylon. As regards the oldest period from Vijaya to Devānaṁpiyatissa the chronicles are certainly untrustworthy to the extent that the duration of years ascribed to each reign seems incredible in view of the fact that they appear to be calculated according to a set scheme, and present certain insuperable difficulties of chronology with regard to one or two reigns, e.g., of King Paṇḍukābhaya and Muṭasiva. Moreover, the day of Vijaya's arrival in Ceylon has been made to synchronise with the date of Buddha's death, which itself is liable to create a distrust in our mind. But even in the first and the earliest period of Ceylonese history, there are certain elements of truth which can hardly be questioned. Thus there is no ground for doubting the authenticity of the list of kings from Vijaya to Devānaṁpiyatissa; nor is there any reason for rejecting the account of Paṇḍukābhaya's campaigns, as well as the detailed account of the reign of Devānaṁpiyatissa, which seem decidedly to be historical. We have also sufficient reason to believe the contemporaneity and friendship of Tissa and Asoka who exchanged greetings of gifts between themselves.

As for the period from Devānaṁpiyatissa to Mahāsena, the chronicles may safely but intelligently be utilised as of value. There are no doubt gaps in the traditional chronology which have been carelessly filled in, notably in the period from Devānaṁpiyatissa to Duṭṭhagāmaṇi, but after Duṭṭhagāmaṇi there is no such careless and fictitious filling in of gaps, nor any set-up system of chronology, and on the whole the list of kings and their duration of reigns are credible. But even where the chronology is doubtful, there is no ground whatsoever for doubting the kernel of historical truth that lies mixed up with mythical tales in respect of the account of each individual reign, say, for example, of the reign of Duṭṭhagāmaṇi. It may, therefore, be safely asserted that the Ceylonese chronicles can be utilised, if not as an independent historical source, at least as a repository of historical tradition in which we can find important confirmatory evidence of our information with regard to early Indian and contemporary Ceylonese history.

But the chronicles must be considered to be of more value for the ecclesiastical history not only of Ceylon but of India as well. With regard to this there are certain notices in the chronicles that have helped us to start with almost definite chronological points which are equally important in respect of the political history of the continent and its island. One such fixed point is provided by the chronicles where it has been stated that 218 years after the Sambuddha had passed into Nirvāṇa when Asoka was consecrated. This corner stone has helped us to ascertain one of the most knotty and at the same time most useful starting points of Indian history, namely, the year of the Buddha's parinirvāṇa and his birth, which, according to the calculation based on the date just cited are 483 B.C. and 563 B.C. respectively.[1]

Next in point of importance with regard to the history of Buddhism is the conversion of the island by Mahinda, who is represented in the chronicles as a son of Asoka. Historians have doubted the

---

[1] See Mahāvaṁsa (Geiger), Secs. 5 and 6. Introduction.

tradition in view of the fact that there is no mention of it in the numerous edicts and inscriptions of Asoka. Geiger has very ably shown that this argument is at least an *argumentum e silentio* and can hardly be conclusive. The tradition of the chronicles is unanimously supported by the tradition of the country itself, and finds further confirmation in the account of Yuan Chwang who expressly states that the conversion of Ceylon was the work of Mahendra or Mahinda, who is, however, represented as a brother of Asoka. But it must not be understood that Ceylon was converted all on a sudden by Mahendra or Mahinda. Similar mission must have been sent earlier; "a hint that Mahinda's mission was preceded by similar missions to Ceylon is to be found even in Dīpavaṁsa and Mahāvaṁsa when they relate that Asoka, sending to Devānaṁpiyatissa with presents for his second consecration as king, exhorted him to adhere to the doctrine of the Buddha."[1]

Geiger has also been able to find very striking confirmation of the history of the religious missions as related in the chronicles in the relic-inscriptions of the Sañchi stūpa, No. 2.[2] He has thus pointed out that Majjhima who is named in the Mahāvaṁsa as the teacher who converted the Himalaya region and Kassapagotta who appears as his companion in the Dīpavaṁsa are also mentioned in one of the inscriptions just referred to as 'pious Majjhima' and 'pious Kassapagotta, the teacher of the Himalaya'. In another inscription also Kassapagotta is mentioned as the teacher of the Himalaya. Dundubhissāra who is also mentioned in the chronicles as one of the theras who won the Himalaya countries to Buddhism, is mentioned in another inscription as Dadabhisara along with Gotiputta (i.e., Kotiputta Kassapagotta). The thera, i.e., Moggaliputta Tissa, who is described in the chronicles

---

[1] Mahāvaṁsa, p. xix.
[2] *Ibid.*, pp. xix-xx.

as having presided over the Third Buddhist Council, is also mentioned in another inscription as Mogaliputta. These facts are guarantee enough for carefully utilising the chronicles as an important source of information for the early history of Buddhism.

This would be far more evident when we would consider the accounts of the three Buddhist Councils as related in the two chronicles. The authenticity of the accounts of these Councils had during the early days of the study of the two chronicles often been doubted. But it is simply impossible to doubt that there must lie a kernel of historical truth at the bottom of these accounts. As to the First Council, both the northern and southern traditions agree as to the place and occasion and the President of the Council. As to the Second Council, both traditions agree as to the occasion and cause of the first schism in the Church, namely, the relaxation of monastic discipline brought about by the Vajjian monks. As to the place of the Council, the northern tradition is uncertain, but the southern tradition is definite inasmuch as it states that it was held in Vesālī under King Kālāsoka in 383/2 B.C. and led to the separation of the Mahāsāṁghikas from the Theravāda. The Ceylonese tradition speaks of a Third Council at Pāṭaliputra in the year 247 B.C. under King Dhammāsoka which led to the expulsion of certain disintegrating elements from the community. The northern tradition has, however, no record of a Third Council, but that is no reason why we should doubt its authenticity. Geiger has successfully shown that the "distinction between two separate Councils is in fact correct. The Northern Buddhists have mistakenly fused the two into one as they confounded the kings, Kālāsoka and Dhammāsoka, one with another. But traces of the right tradition are still preserved in the wavering uncertain statements as to the time and place of the Council."[1]

---

[1] Mahāvaṁsa (Geiger's Tr.), pp. lix-lx and ff.

The succession of teachers from Upāli to Mahinda as provided by the chronicles is also interesting from the view-point of the history of early Buddhism. The succession list which includes Upāli, the great authority on Vinaya at the time of the Buddha, Dāsaka, Sonaka, Siggava, Moggaliputta Tissa, and Mahinda, may not represent the whole truth, they even might not all be Vinayapāmokkhā, i.e., authorities on Vinaya; but the list presents at least an aspect of truth, and is interesting, presenting, as it does, "a continuous synchronological connexion between the history of Ceylon and that of India". The list can thus be utilised for ascertaining the chronological arrangement of early Indian history as well as of the teachers of early Buddhism.

The chronicles can still more profitably be utilised as a very faithful record of the origin and growth of the numerous religious establishments of Ceylon. They are so very elaborately described and the catalogue seems to be so complete that a careful study may enable us to frame out a history of the various kinds of religious and monastic establishments, e.g., stūpas, vihāras, cetiyas, etc., of Ceylon. Thus the history of the Mahāvihāra, the Abhayagiri vihāra, the Thūpārāma, Mahāmeghavanārāma, and of a host of others is recorded in elaborate detail. Incidentally they refer to the social and religious life led by the monks of the Order as well as by the lay people. It is easy to gather from the chronicles that the great architectural activity of the island began as early as the reign of Devānaṁpiyatissa and continued unabated during each succeeding reign till the death of Mahāsena. The numerous edifices, tanks, and canals whose ruins now cover the old capitals of the island were built during that period, and their history is unmistakably recorded in the chronicles. Religious ceremonies and processions are often vividly described, and they give us glimpses of the life and conditions of the time. Not less interesting is the fact, often times related as a part of the account of these religious edifices, of very close intercourse with more or less important religious centres of India, namely, Rājagaha, Kosambī, Vesālī, Ujjenī, Pupphapura, Pallava, Alasanda (Alexandria), and other countries. Every important function was attended by brother monks and teachers from the main land to which the Ceylonese kings and people turned for inspiration whenever any question of bringing and enshrining a relic arose. There are also incidental and stray references which are no less valuable. The Mahāvaṁsa informs us that King Mahāsena built the Maṇihīravihāra and founded three other vihāras, destroying temples of the (brahmanical) gods. It shows that brahmanical temples existed side by side, and religious toleration was not always the practice.

As for the internal political history and foreign political relations with South India, specially with the Damiḷas, the chronicles seem to preserve very faithful records. No less faithful is the geographical information of India and Ceylon as supported by them. But most of all, as we have hinted above, is the information contained in them, in respect of the history of Buddhism and Buddhist establishments of the island. There is hardly any reason to doubt the historicity of such information.

Cūḷavaṁsa.

The Cūḷavaṁsa[1] is not an uniform and homogeneous work. It is a series of additions to, and continuations of, the Mahāvaṁsa. The Mahāvaṁsa is the work of one man—Mahānāma, who compiled the work during the reign of Dhātusena in the 6th century A.D. But the single parts of the Cūḷavaṁsa are of different character, written by different authors at different times. The first who continued the chronicle was according to Sinhalese tradition the Thera Dham-

---

[1] Edited by Dr. W. Geiger in two volumes for the P.T.S., London, translated into English by Geiger and Mrs. R. Rickmers, 1930.

makitti. He came from Burma to Ceylon during the reign of King Parakkamabāhu II in the 13th century A.D.

Between the Chapters 37 and 79 no trace is found of the commencement of a new section. This part of the chronicle seems to be the work of the same author. So it is clear, if the Sinhalese tradition is authentic, then about three quarters of what we call the Cūḷavaṁsa (pages 443 out of 592 pages of Geiger's edition of the Cūḷavaṁsa) were composed by Dhammakitti.

The second section of the Cūḷavaṁsa begins with the reign of Vijayabāhu II, the successor of Parakkamabāhu I, and ends with that of Parakkamabāhu IV. Hence it follows, the second part of the Cūḷavaṁsa consists of the Chapters from 80 to 90, both inclusive.

The third portion begins with the Chapter 91 and ends with the Chapter 100.

The Mahāvaṁsa gives us a list of kings from Vijaya, the first crowned king of Ceylon, to Mahāsena. Mahānāma simply followed here his chief source, the Dīpavaṁsa, which also ends with King Mahāsena. The Cūḷavaṁsa, however, begins with the reign of King Sirimeghavaṇṇa, son of King Mahāsena, and ends with Sirivikkamarājasīha.

The first section of the Cūḷavaṁsa begins with Sirimeghavaṇṇa and ends with Parakkamabāhu I. Evidently this portion gives a chronological account of 78 kings of Ceylon. Altogether eighteen paricchedas are devoted to the glorification of the great national hero of the Sinhalese people, Parakkamabāhu I. Revd. R. S. Copleston has called this portion of the Cūḷavaṁsa the "epic of Parakkama". This king was noted for his charity. He not only made gifts of alms to the needy, but also to the bhikkhus. As a warrior this king also stands out pre-eminent. The Coḷas and Damiḷas came to Laṅkā from Southern India and occupied Anurādhapura. Parakkama fought many battles with them and drove them out of the country and became king of the united Laṅkā. He then espoused the cause of the Buddhist Saṁgha. He built many great vihāras and thūpas. He also constructed many vāpis and uyyānas.

The second portion of the Cūḷavaṁsa begins with Vijayabāhu II and ends with Parakkamabāhu IV. Thus it refers to 23 kings of Ceylon.

The third section begins with Bhuvanekabāhu III and ends with Kittisirirājasīha. Thus it refers to 24 kings.

The last chapter gives a brief account of the last two kings, e.g., Sirirājādhirājasīha and Sirivikkamarājasīha.

List of Pāli texts in the Ceylonese chronicles.

There are in both the chronicles, the Dīpavaṁsa and the Mahāvaṁsa, interesting references to Pāli texts affording very useful materials for the history of Pāli literature as well as of early Buddhism in Ceylon.

In the Dīpavaṁsa references are not only made to Vinaya texts, the five collections of Sutta Piṭaka, the three Piṭakas, the five Nikāyas (they are not separately mentioned), and the ninefold doctrine of the Teacher comprising the Sutta, Geyya, Veyyākaraṇa, Gāthā, Udāna, Itivuttaka, Jātaka, Abbhuta, and Vedalla, but also to the seven sections of the Abhidhamma, the Paṭisaṁbhidā, the Niddesa, the Piṭaka of the Āgamas and the different sections, namely, Vaggas, Paññāsakas, Saṁyuttas, and Nipātas into which the Dīgha, Majjhima, Saṁyutta, and Aṅguttara Nikāyas are respectively divided. Mention is also made separately of the two Vibhaṅgas of Vinaya, namely, Parivāra and Khandhaka, the Cariyāpiṭaka, the Vinaya Piṭaka, the Pātimokkha, and the Aṭṭhakathā. We find further mention of the Kathāvatthu of the Abhidhamma, the Petavatthu, the Saccasaṁyutta, and the Vimānavatthu. Of Suttas and Suttantas separate mention is made of the Devadūta Sutta, Bālapaṇḍita Suttanta, Aggikkhaṇḍa Suttanta, Āsivisa Suttanta, Āsivisūpama Suttanta, Anamataggiya Sutta, Gomayapiṇḍaovāda Suttanta, Dhammacakkapavattana Suttanta, and the Mahāsamaya Suttanta.

*Index of Pāli texts in the Dīpavaṁsa*

Vimānavatthu, 12, 85.
Bālapaṇḍita Suttanta, 13, 13.
Vinaya Piṭaka, 18, 19 ; 18, 33 ; 18, 37.
Vibhaṅgas, 7, 43.
Mahāsamaya Suttanta, 14, 53.
Sutta, 4, 15 ; 4, 16.
Sutta Piṭaka (pañcanikāye), 18, 19 : 18, 33.
Saṁyuttas, 4, 16.

In the Mahāvaṁsa too we find numerous mentions of Pāli texts. But, curiously enough, references to independent texts are much less comprehensive than that of the earlier chronicle; though mentions of Suttas and Suttantas mainly of the three Nikāyas, the Aṅguttara, the Majjhima, and the Saṁyutta, as well as of the Sutta Nipāta and the Vinaya Piṭaka are much more numerous. There are also several references to Jātakas. The three piṭakas are often mentioned as important texts, but only the Abhidhamma and the Vinaya are mentioned by name, and that too only once or twice in each case.

*Index of Pāli Texts in the Mahāvaṁsa*

Abhidhamma Piṭaka, 5, 150.
Āsivisūpamā Sutta (Aṅguttara Nikāya), 12, 26.
Anamatagga Saṁyutta (Saṁyutta Nikāya), 12, 31.
Aggikkhandopama Sutta (Aṅguttara), 12, 34.
Kapi Jātaka, 35, 31.
Kālakārāma Suttanta, 12, 39.
Khajjaniya Suttanta (Saṁyutta N.), 15, 195.
Khandhakas (Sections of the Mahāvagga and Cullavagga of the Vinaya Piṭaka), 36, 68.
Gomayapiṇḍisutta (Saṁ. N.), 15, 197.
Cūlahatthipadūpama Suttanta (Majjhima N.), 14, 22.
Cittayamaka (Ref. Yamakappakaraṇa of the Abhidhamma), 5, 146.
Jātaka (tales), 27, 34 ; 30, 88.
Tīpiṭaka, 4, 62 ; 5, 84 ; 5, 112 ; 5, 118 and 119 ; 5, 210 ; 27, 44.

Tittira Jātaka, 5, 264.
Devadūta Suttanta (Majjhima N.), 12, 29.
Dhammacakkapavattana-suttanta (Mahāvagga of the V.P.), 12, 41; 15, 199.
Bālapaṇḍita Suttanta (Saṁyutta N.), 15, 4.
Brahmajāla Suttanta, 12, 51.
Vessantara Jātaka, 30, 88.
Vinaya, 5, 151.
Mahā-nārada-Kassapa Jātaka, 12, 37.
Mahāppamāda-suttanta (Saṁyutta N.), 16, 3.
Maṅgala Sutta (Sutta Nipāta), 32, 43.
Mahāmaṅgala Sutta (Sutta N.), 30, 83.
Mahāsamaya Suttanta (Dīgha Nikāya), 30, 83.
Samacitta Sutta (Samacittavagga in the Duka Nipāta of the Aṅguttara Nikāya), 14, 39.
Sutta Piṭaka, 5, 150.

Geographical references in the Ceylonese chronicles.

The Ceylonese chronicles incidentally refer to a large number of countries and localities, important in the history of Buddhism, in India and Ceylon. Most of them come in for mention as a result of their association with the life and religion of the Buddha, or in connection with the historical interrelation, or the part played by them in the history of India and Ceylon. Most of these places and countries are already known from other, mainly Buddhist, sources, and few of them require any new identification. Even then, they add to our geographical knowledge, and not a few of the references are of more than passing usual interest. Such are, for example, the references to Alasanda in the city of the Yonas in the Mahāvaṁsa, or to Yonaka in the Dīpavaṁsa in connection with the building of the Great Thūpa, and the sending of Missions by Moggalliputta respectively. Alasanda, as is well known, is Alexandria in the land of the Yonas, probably the town founded by Alexander in the country of the Paropanisadæ near Kabul. The chronicles refer in common to the following places and countries in India and Ceylon:

*North and North-West India*—

Gāndhāra—modern Peshawar and Rawalpindi districts.

Yona or Yonaka—The foreign settlements on the North-Western Frontier, perhaps identical with the Græco-Bactrian kingdom.

Anotatta laka—One of the seven great lakes in the Himalayas.

*Western India*—

Aparāntaka—comprises modern Gujrat, Kathiawar and the sea-coast districts.

Suppāra (Dīp) or Suppāraka (Mah)—Surpāraka (Sans), modern Sopāra in the Thānā district, north of Bombay.

Mahāraṭṭha—modern Mahārāṣṭra.

*Mid-India and Eastern India*—

Kapilavatthu—the birth place of Gotama, and capital of the Śākya tribe in Nepal.

Kusāvatī—identical with later Kuśīnārā.

Kusīnārā—a town of the clan of the Mallas in modern Nepal.

Giribbaja—or Rājāgriha, modern Rājgir in Bihar.

Jetavana—a park and monastery near Sāvatthī in the Kosala country.

Madhurā—another name for Mathurā, modern Muttra.

Ujjenī—now Ujjain in the Gwalior State; old capital of Avantī.

Uruvelā—in ancient Buddha-Gayā in Gayā district.

Kāsī—modern Benares district.

Isipatana—the famous deer park of Benares where Buddha first turned the Wheel of Law.

Tāmalitiya (Dīp) or Tāmalittī (Mah)—Tāmralipti, modern Tamluk in the district of Midnapur, Bengal.

Pāṭaliputta—identical with modern Patna and the adjoining region.

Pupphapura—Puṣpapura, identical with ancient Pāṭaliputra.

Bārāṇasī—modern Benares.

Mithilā—modern Tirhut in Bihar.

Rājagaha—modern Rājgir in Bihar.

Vaṅgā (Dīp) or Vaṅga (Mah)—identical roughly with Eastern Bengal.

Vesālī—modern Basār in Muzaffarpur, north of Patna.

*The Deccan and South India*—

Viñjhā (Dīp), Viñjhāṭavī (Mah)—The Vindhya mountain with its dense forests.

Damiḷa—The Tamil country.

*Ceylon*—

Suvaṇṇabhūmi—not in Ceylon, generally identified with Lower Burma comprising the Rammaññadesa.

Malaya—Central mountain region in the interior of Ceylon.

Abhayagiri—outside the north gate of Anurādhapura.

Dīghavāpī—probably the modern Kandiya-Kattu tank in the Eastern Province.

Sīlakūṭa—northern peak of the Mihintāla mountain.

Jetavana—a park and monastery near Sāvatthī in the Kosala country.

Kalyāṇī—modern Kælani, the river that flows into the sea near Colombo.

Cetiyapabbata—the later name of the Missaka mountain.

Nandanavana—between Mahāmeghavana where the Mahāvihāra now stands and the southern wall of the city of Anurādhapura.

Laṅkā is identified with the island of Ceylon.

Missakagiri (Dīp),—pabbata (Mah)—modern Mihintāla mountain, east of Anurādhapura.

The Dīpavaṁsa, however, exclusively mentions several countries and places which are not mentioned in the Mahāvaṁsa.

*North and North-West India*—

Kurudīpa—probably identical with Uttarakuru.

Takkasīlā—modern Taxila in the N. W. frontier province.

Sāgala (reading doubtful)—modern Sialkot in the Punjab.

*Western India*—

Bharukaccha—modern Broach, an ancient sea-port in Kathiawar.

Lāḷaraṭṭha—identical either with Lāṭa in modern Gujerat or Rāḍha in Bengal.

Sīhapura—capital city of Lāṭa or Rāḍha country.

*Mid-India and Eastern India*—

Aṅgā—identical with modern Bhagalpur region in Bihar.

Campā—modern Pātharghāṭā in the district of Bhāgalpur.

Magadhā—a tribe dwelling in the territory now represented by modern Patna and Gayā districts in Bihar.

Mallā—a republican tribe of ancient Kusīnārā and Pāvā.

Vardhamānapura—Vardhamānabhukti of inscriptions: modern Burdwan.

Veḷuvana—the famous bamboo-garden monastery in Rājagriha, modern Rājgir.

Vedissa—Vidisā, modern Bhilsā in the Gwalior State.

Hatthipura—Hastināpura (Sans)—generally identified with an old town in Mawāna Tahsil, Meerut.

Indapaṭṭa—Indraprastha, near modern Delhi.

It may be noticed in this connection that in the Dīpavaṁsa, Aṅgā, Magadhā, Vaṅgā, and Mallā are mentioned in the plural, not as Vaṅga in the singular as in the Mahāvaṁsa. The tribal significance has been maintained in the Dīpavaṁsa, whereas in the later chronicle it has been overlooked.

*Ceylon*—

Anurādhapura—ancient capital of Ceylon, now in ruins.

Ariṭṭhapura—in North Central province, north of Habarana.

Naggadīpa—probably an island in the Arabian Sea.

Tambapaṇṇi—most probably identical with the island of Ceylon.

The Mahāvaṁsa likewise refers exclusively to several countries and places not mentioned in the Dīpavaṁsa.

*North and North-West India*—

Alasanda—Alexandria, the town founded by Alexander in the Paropanisadæ country.

Uttarakuru—a country north of Kāśmīra, mentioned in Vedic and Paurānic literature.

Kāśmīra—modern Kashmir.

*Mid-India and Eastern India*—

Avantī—the region round modern Ujjain in Gwalior.

Madda—the country lay between the Ravi and the Chenab, roughly identical with the country round the modern district of Sialkot.

Mahāvana—a monastery in the ancient Vajji country mentioned also by Fā-Hien.

Dakkhiṇagiri vihāra—a vihāra in Ujjenī.

Payāga—modern Allahabad.

Pāvā—a republican state inhabited by the Mallas.

Kosambī—modern Kosam in Allahabad, on the Jumnā, capital of the Vatsas.

*South India and the Deccan*—

Coḷa—the ancient Choḷa country whose capital was Kāñchipuraṁ, modern Conjeeveram.

Mahisamaṇḍala—identical with Mandhāta island on the Narbadā, ancient capital—Māhiṣmatī, a district south of the Vindhyā.

Vanavāsin—modern Vanavāsī in north Kanara, preserves the older name.

*Ceylon*—

Ākāsa Cetiya—situated on the summit of a rock not very far from the Cittalapabbata monastery.

Kadamba nadī—modern Malwaṭṭe-oya by the ruins of Anurādhapura (Kadambaka nadī in the Dīpavaṁsa).

Karinda nadī—modern Kirindu-oya in the Southern province where must be located the Pañjali-pabbata.

Kāla Vāpī—built by Dhātusena by banking up the river Kaḷu-oya or Goṇa nadī.

Gambhīra nadī—7 or 8 miles north of Anurādhapura.

Goṇa nadī—modern Kalu-oya river.

Jetavanārāma near Abhayagiri dagoba in Anurādhapura.

Tissamahāvihāra—in South Ceylon, north-east of Hambanṭota.

Tissavāpī—a tank near Mahāgāma.

Thūpārāma—a monastery in Anurādhapura.

Paṭhama Cetiya—outside the eastern gate of Anurādhapura.

Manihīrā—now Minneriya, a tank near Pulonnaruwa.

Mahāgaṅgā—identical with Mahāwæligaṅgā river.

Mahātittha—identical with modern Mantota opposite the island of Manaar.

Mahāmeghavana—south of the capital Anurādhapura.

Dvāramaṇḍala—near Cetiyapabbata (Mihintale), east of Anurādhapura.

Pulindā—a barbarous tribe dwelling in the country inland between Colombo, Kalutara, Galle and the mountains (Geiger-Mahāvaṁsa, p. 60, Note 5).

Ambatthala—immediately below the Mihintale mountain.

Besides these, there are many other references to countries and places of Ceylon of lesser importance. They have all been noticed and identified in Geiger's edition of the Mahāvaṁsa to which we are indebted for the identification of places in Ceylon noticed above.

Buddhaghosuppatti.

The Buddhaghosuppatti deals with the life and career of Buddhaghosa, the famous commentator, less authentic than the account contained in the Cūḷavaṁsa. It gives us an account of Buddhaghosa's boyhood, his admission to the priesthood, his father's conversion, voyage to Ceylon, Buddhaghosa as a witness, permission to translate scriptures, his object attained, return to India, and his passing away. The book is written in an easy language. It is more or less a historical romance. As to the historical value of this work readers are referred to my work, 'The Life and Work of Buddhaghosa' (Ch. II, pp. 43-44). The Buddhaghosuppatti has been edited by James Grey and published by Messrs. Luzac & Co., London. Grey has also translated the book into English.

The stories in the Milinda Pañha, the Mahāvaṁsa and the Buddhaghosuppatti are so similar that one doubts it very much that the author of this work borrowed the incidents from the Milinda Pañha and the Mahāvaṁsa and grafted them on to his own.

A critical study of the Buddhaghosuppatti does not help us much in elucidating the history of

Buddhaghosa. The author had little authentic knowledge of the great commentator. He only collected the legends which centred round the remarkable man by the time when his work was written. Those legends are mostly valueless from the strict historical point of view. Grey truly says in his introduction to the Buddhaghosuppatti that the work reads like an "Arthurian. Romance". The accounts given by the Buddhaghosuppatti about the birth, early life, conversion, etc., of Buddhaghosa bear a great similarity to those of Milinda and Moggaliputta Tissa. In the interview which took place between Buddhaghosa and Buddhadatta, the latter is said to have told Buddhaghosa thus, "I went before you to compile Buddha's word. I am old, have not long to live and shall not, therefore, be able to accomplish my purpose. You carry out the work satisfactorily".

In Buddhadatta's Vinayavinicchaya we read that Buddhadatta requested Buddhaghosa to send him the commentaries when finished that he might summarise them. This request was complied with by Buddhaghosa. Buddhadatta summarised the commentary on the Abhidhamma in the Abhidhammāvatāra and the commentary on the Vinaya in the Vinayavinicchaya. The above statement in the Vinayavinicchaya which is more authoritative than the Buddhaghosuppatti is in direct contradiction to the statement in the latter book. The author has made a mistake in the sixth chapter of the Buddhaghosuppatti in which it is stated that Buddhaghosa rendered the Buddhist scriptures into Māgadhī. In the seventh chapter of the same book we read that after the lapse of three months when he completed his task, the works of Mahinda were piled up and burnt. Buddhaghosa translated the Sinhalese commentaries into Māgadhī and not the texts themselves. Had it been so there would not have been any occasion for burning the works of Mahinda. On the other hand they would have been carefully preserved as the only reliable and authentic interpretation of the sacred texts. It has been distinctly stated in the Mahāvaṁsa that the texts only existed in the Jambudīpa and Buddhaghosa was sent to Ceylon to translate the Sinhalese commentaries into Māgadhī. If the tradition recorded in the Mahāvaṁsa is to be believed, then only we can get an explanation for the destruction of Mahinda's works.

Saddhammasaṁgaha.

The Saddhammasaṁgaha is a collection of good sayings and teachings of the Master. There are prose and poetry portions in it. It consists of nine chapters. It was written by Dhammakityābhidhāna Thera. It has been edited by Nedimāle Saddhānanda for the P.T.S., London. The Dīgha, Majjhima, Saṁyutta, Aṅguttara, and Khuddaka Nikāyas are mentioned in it. The books of the Abhidhamma Piṭaka are referred to in this work. There are references in it to the Vajjiputtakas of Vesālī and Yasa's stay in the Kūṭāgārasālā in the Mahāvana. It is mentioned in this book that Moggaliputta Tissa recited the Kathāvatthu in order to refute the doctrines of others. This treatise contains an account of the missionaries sent to various places to establish the Buddha's religion. Thera Majjhantika was sent to Kashmir and Gandhāra, Mahādeva Thera to Mahisamaṇḍala, Rakkhita Thera to Vanavāsī, Yonaka-Dhammarakkhita Thera to Aparāntaka, Mahādhammarakkhita Thera to Mahāraṭṭha, Mahārakkhita Thera to the Yonaka region, Majjhima Thera to the Himalayan region, Sonaka and Uttara to Suvaṇṇabhūmi, and Mahinda Thera to Laṅkā with four other theras, Itthiya, Uttiya, Sambala, and Bhaddasāla. Besides, there is a reference to the Buddha preaching his Dhamma to the inhabitants of the city of Campaka (Campakanagaravāsinaṁ).

Sandesa-Kathā.

The Sandesa-Kathā has been edited by Minayeff in J.P.T.S., 1885. It is written mostly in prose. It dilates on many points, e.g., the composition of Abhidhammatthasaṁgaha by Thera Anuruddha, the composition of a commentary known as the Abhidhammatthavibhāvinī by Thera Sumaṅgalasāmī, etc. It refers to many kingdoms, e.g., Suvaṇṇabhūmi, Rāmañña, Jayavaḍḍhana, Ayuddhaya, Kamboja, Sivi, Cīna, etc.

Mahābodhivaṁsa.

The Mahābodhivaṁsa has been edited by Mr. Strong for the P.T.S., London. This work was written by Upatissa (Upatissatheravarena viracito). The Sinhalese edition by Upatissa and revised by Sarandada, Colombo, 1891, deserves mention. There is a Sinhalese translation of this work in twelve chapters. Prof. Geiger says that the date of the composition of the Mahābodhivaṁsa is the 10th century A.D. (Dīpavaṁsa and Mahāvaṁsa, p. 79). According to some it was composed within the last quarter of the 4th century A.D. Strong points out in the preface to his edition of the Mahābodhivaṁsa that the author has treated his subject with freedom and prolixity. Most of the events in the early history of Buddhism pass under the shadow of the Bo-tree. The author has borrowed largely from the sources as well as from the actual text of the Mahāvaṁsa, but there is abundant evidence that he employed other materials as well. This work contains discourses on the attainment of bodhi (enlightenment), the attainment of bodhi by Ānanda, passing away of the Buddha who was endowed with ten potentialities, the first three Buddhist convocations (saṅgīti), landing of Mahinda at Laṅkā, accepting Mahāvihāra and Cetiyagiri, things worshipped by the Buddhas, advent of Duminda, etc.

The following manuscripts of the Mahābodhivaṁsa are available :—

(1) A manuscript on paper in the Sinhalese character in possession of the P.T.S., England.

(2) A palm-leaf manuscript in the Sinhalese character in possession of the P.T.S., England.

(3) A palm-leaf manuscript in the Sinhalese character in the Library of the British Museum.

(4) A palm-leaf manuscript in the Burmese character in the Library of the India Office.

Thūpavaṁsa.

The Thūpavaṁsa contains an account of the thūpas or dagobas built over the relics of the Buddha. Readers' attention is invited to a paper on this book by Don Martino de Zilva Wickremasinghe (J.R.A.S., 1898). This work has not yet been edited by the P.T.S., London. A Sinhalese edition of this work is available (ed. by Dhammaratana, Paeliyagoda, 1896).

Historical allusions in the Thūpavaṁsa.

In the Thūpavaṁsa we are told that the Thera Moggaliputta Tissa sent theras (elders) to different parts of India for the propagation of the Buddhist faith. He sent Majjhantikathera to Kasmīra and Gandhāra, Mahādevathera to Mahiṁsakamaṇḍala, Rakkhitathera to Vanavāsi, Yonaka-dhammarakkhitathera to Aparāntaka, Mahādhammarakkhitathera to Mahāraṭṭha, Mahārakkhitathera to Yonakaloka, Majjhimathera to Himavanta, Sonathera and Uttarathera to Suvaṇṇabhumī, and Mahinda and four other theras to Tamba-Paṇṇidīpa. It may be added here that the Thera Mahinda and the Therī Saṅghamittā, son and daughter respectively of Asoka, were instrumental in propagating Buddhism in Ceylon. The Mahāvaṁsa also states the same thing, and it further says that Moggaliputta Tissathera was a contemporary of Asoka and that he presided over the Buddhist Council which was held under the patronage of this great monarch.

It appears from both the Mahāvaṁsa and the Thūpavaṁsa that the Thera Moggaliputta Tissa sent these theras to different parts of India at his own initiative. There is no mention of Asoka having taken any part in this activity, though such an important event occurred during his time and in his own kingdom mainly. But in his Rock Edict XIII, Asoka says that he despatched ambassadors to countries in and outside India. He further says in his Rock Edict II that he provided for the distribution of medicines in different countries. In both the Edicts Asoka mentions Ceylon (Tāmbraparṇi). But how to reconcile these two accounts which we find in the Mahāvaṁsa and the Thūpavaṁsa on the one hand and the lithic records of Asoka on the other? Dr. Geiger in his introduction to his translation of the Mahāvaṁsa (pp. xvi–xx) says that before Mahinda relations existed between continental India and Ceylon and efforts were made to transplant the Buddhist doctrine to Ceylon. But with Mahinda this process came to a successful end. Besides, Mahinda's mission was preceded by similar missions to Ceylon. The Dīpavaṁsa and the Mahāvaṁsa relate that Asoka, sending to Devānaṁpiyatissa with presents for his second consecration as king, exhorted him to adhere to the doctrine of the Buddha.

The history of the missions as related in Dīpavaṁsa, Mahāvaṁsa, and Thūpavaṁsa receives most striking confirmation in the inscriptions. The names of the theras Majjhima and Kassapagotto (who appears as Majjhima's companion in the Dīpavaṁsa) occur in the Bhilsa Topes (Sāñchi group and Sonāri group) as teachers of the Himalayas. The name of Moggaliputta Tissa also occurs in the Sāñchi group. Further, according to Grünwedel, the transplanting of a branch of the sacred Bodhi-tree from Uruvelā to Ceylon is represented in the East Gate of the Sāñchi Topes.

Dr. Geiger has successfully proved the trustworthiness of the Ceylonese chronicles. He in an ingenious and convincing way has shown that the two accounts, which we find in the inscriptions of Asoka and the Ceylonese chronicles, are not untrustworthy. Asoka strove to propagate Buddhism in and outside India. Moggaliputta Tissathera also played an important part in spreading Buddhism in countries within India. The conversion of

Ceylon was achieved by Mahinda and his followers, who were despatched by Moggaliputta Tissathera, and also by Mahinda's sister Saṅghamittā.

It is thus clear from what Geiger says that there were two separate attempts to propagate Buddhism in the time of Asoka. The first attempt was made by the king himself who sent ambassadors to countries both in and outside India. The second attempt was made by Moggaliputta Tissathera, the then head of the Buddhist Church, after the Third Council was over. But this attempt was confined to India only.

That the success of Buddhism both in India and outside countries was largely due to the support it got from kings like Bimbisāra, Pasenadi, Asoka, Kanishka, and Harshavardhan and also from the Pāla kings of Bengal, nobody can dispute. If it did not receive royal patronage, it would have surely met the same fate as Jainism did. Taking this important fact into consideration, we shall not be unjustified to say that Asoka must have lent ungrudging help to Moggaliputta Tissathera.

From what has been stated above and from the grounds which we will state below it will not be unreasonable to say that there were no two separate attempts, but a single attempt for the propagation of the Buddhist Faith, and that in this attempt both Asoka and Moggaliputta Tissathera played important parts. But why the names of Asoka and Moggaliputta Tissathera are absent respectively from the Ceylonese chronicles and the inscriptions of Asoka ? In a general way Asoka says that he sent ambassadors, who were undoubtedly Buddhist monks, to different countries. He does not even make mention of his own son and daughter who did great service to the cause of Buddhism. He must have sent ambassadors in collaboration with the leading theras of the time. It will be unjust to accuse such a great king like Asoka that he intentionally out of self-complacency and self-conceit did not mention Moggaliputta Tissathera and other leading theras. But such is not the case with the authors of the Ceylonese chronicles. They have intentionally excluded the name of Asoka, and thereby have enhanced the position of the Buddhist Saṁgha, and the prestige of its leaders. There is no lack of fables and tales in the chronicles. There are also statements which are untenable. But these are meant for the glorification of the Buddha, His Dhamma, and His Saṁgha only.

Geographical Data.

*Tāmalitti*, a harbour in the region at the mouth of the Ganges, now Tamluk. At Tāmalitti the Chinese pilgrim Fā-Hien embarked for Ceylon in the beginning of the 5th century A.D.

*Gandhāra* comprises the districts of Peshāwar and Rāwalpiṇḍi in the northern Punjab.

*Kasmīra* is the modern Kāshmīr.

*Mahiṁsakamaṇḍala* is generally taken as the modern Mysore. Fleet takes it as the territory of Māhisha of which the capital was Māhiṣmatī. Agreeing with Pargiter he places this capital on the island of the Narbadā river, now called Mandhātā. Mahiṁsakamaṇḍala is, therefore, a district south of the Vindhya mountains.

*Vanavāsī*—The Vanavāsakas or Vanavāsins are mentioned in the Mahābhārata and Harivaṁśa, as a people dwelling in Southern India. There is also a modern town Vanavāsī in North Kanara which seems to have preserved the old name.

*Aparāntaka,* the western ends, comprising the territory of Northern Gujarat, Kathiawar, Kachcha, and Sind.

*Mahāraṭṭha,* the country of the Maraṭhās.

*Yonaloka*—The Yonas are also mentioned together with the Kambojas, in the Rock Edicts V and XIII of Asoka. V. Smith says that they must mean the clans of foreign race (not necessarily Greek) on the north-western frontier, included in the Empire of Asoka.

*Suvaṇṇabhūmi*—The general opinion is that Suvaṇṇabhūmi is lower Burma with adjacent districts. Fleet says that it might be the country in Bengal called Karṇasuvarṇa, or else the country along the river Son, a river in Central India, and tributary of the Ganges on its right bank, which is called Hiraṇyavāha 'the gold bearer'.

*Vedisa* is the modern Bhilsa in Gwalior State, situated 26 miles north-east of Bhopal.

*Rāmagāma*—The Koliyas of Rāmagāma were a tribe related to the Sākiyas. The river Rohiṇī flowed between the territories of the Koliyas and Sākyas. In the Sumaṅgalavilāsinī the capital of the Koliyas is called Vyagghapajja.

*Pāvā* was the capital of the Mallas. Missaka Pabbata, now the mountain Mihintale, 8 miles to the east of Anurādhapura, is also called the Cetiyapabbata.

Three chapters of the Text and their résumé.

The text of the Thūpavaṁsa may be conveniently divided into three main chapters. The first chapter comprises the previous births of the Buddha. The second chapter deals with the life of the Buddha from his birth to the attainment of his Mahāparinibbāna and also the distribution of the bodily relics of the Buddha by the brahmin Doṇa and the building of a great thūpa at the south-eastern part of Rājagaha by Ajātasattu of Magadha at the instance of the Thera Mahākassapa in which the bodily relics of the Buddha from Vesālī, Kapilavatthu, Allakappa, Veṭhadīpa, Pāvā, Kusīnārā, and Rājagaha were deposited. The third or the last chapter treats of the later history of the relics.

Chapter I.

The author justifies his composition of the Thūpavaṁsa in Pāli, when there are already two other versions of the same text, one in the Sinhalese language and the other in the Māgadhī, by saying that the Sinhalese version is not conducive to the good of all, and that the Māgadhī version is full of contradictory words and that it is not exhaustive.

The author goes to explain what is meant by a

thūpa. He says that there are four kinds of persons who are worthy of thūpas: Tathāgato, Pacceka-Buddha, Tathāgata-sāvako, and Rāja-cakkavattī. A thūpa is a cetiya in which the relics of any one of the above four have been deposited. As for example, the Kañcanamālika Mahāthūpo contains the relics of Gotama Buddha who has fulfilled the thirty pāramitās, attained the supreme knowledge, set rolling the wheel of law, and performed other duties and won the anupādisesa-nibbāna.

The author then gives a detailed account of the Buddhas who appeared in this earth for the salvation of mankind. He speaks of the Buddhas who preceded Gotama Buddha and the thūpas that were erected in honour of them. He then sums up the life of Gotama Buddha in a masterly way and gives a detailed account of the thūpas, that were erected over the relics of Gotama Buddha, with their later history.

We shall now deal with the story of Sumedha Tāpasa who was born as the Bodhisatta several times during the period in which the twenty-four Buddhas appeared in this earth for the welfare of the worldly beings and who himself appeared in this earth as the 25th Buddha, called Gotama Buddha.

In the time of the Buddha Dīpaṅkara, the brahmin Sumedha lived in the city of Amarāvatī. He was versed in the Brahmanical lore. He lost his parents in his boyhood. When he came of age he inherited a vast fortune. But knowing that the world is full of miseries and that money is the source of misery, he made up his mind to distribute his wealth among the needy. One day he gave away his wealth to the poor and left the world and dwelt in the Himavanta.

Meanwhile the Buddha Dīpaṅkara came to Rammanagara and the inhabitants of the city invited the Blessed One and his followers to take their meal at a certain place highly decorated for the purpose. The people began repairing the road connecting the proposed place and the Vihāra in which the Lord dwelt. Sumedha heard the news and offered his service. He was given a muddy place to cleanse. Before the place was cleansed the Buddha with his followers reached the place. Sumedha at once fell flat on the muddy place with the determined desire to become a Buddha in a later birth and the Buddha and his followers crossed the muddy place treading over his body. The Blessed One while crossing the muddy place over Sumedha's body predicted that Sumedha would surely become Gotama Buddha in future. The Buddha Dīpaṅkara went to the place where he had been invited, took his meal, and exhorted all to do good deeds and went away. The Blessed One attained anupādisesanibbāna in the Nandārāma and the people raised a great thūpa.

In the time of the Buddha Kondañña, the Bodhisatta was born as a great king named Vijitāvī. He made immense gifts to the Bhikkhu Saṁgha with the Buddha at its head. The Lord predicted that the Bodhisatta was destined to become Gotama Buddha in future. When the king heard the Buddha preaching he made up his mind to renounce the worldly life. He did leave the world. He performed many meritorious acts and was born in the Brahmaloka. The Buddha attained Parinibbāna in the delightful Candārāma and a cetiya, measuring 7 yojanas in extent, was raised by the people.

In the time of the Buddha Maṅgala, the Bodhisatta was born as a brahmin named Suruci. He invited the Buddha to his house for seven days and heard the Blessed One preaching. The Lord predicted that the Bodhisatta would become Gotama Buddha in future. When the Bodhisatta heard this prediction, he left the worldly life and adopted the life of a monk. In due course he was born in the Brahmaloka. The Buddha won Parinibbāna in due course and the people raised a great thūpa.

In the time of the Buddha Sumana, the Great

Being was born as a Nāga king named Atula. He invited the Buddha and his followers to his house and served them with dainty dishes. The Lord predicted that he would be the Buddha Gotama in future. The Blessed One attained Parinibbāna in due course and a thūpa was raised.

In the time of the Buddha Revata, the Bodhisatta was born as a brahmin named Atideva. He heard the Buddha preaching and was established in the sīlas. The Blessed One predicted that he would be Gotama Buddha in future.

In the time of the Buddha Sobhita, the Bodhisatta was born as a brāhmaṇa named Ajita. He heard the Buddha preaching and was established in the sīlas. The Lord predicted that he would be the Buddha Gotama in future.

In the time of the Buddha Anomadassī, the Bodhisatta was born as a Yakkhasenāpati. He made immense gifts to the Bhikkhu Saṁgha with the Buddha at its head. The Buddha predicted that he was destined to be the Buddha Gotama.

In the time of the Buddha Paduma, the Bodhisatta was born as a lion who for seven days without going out in search of food saw the Buddha engaged in the Nirodha-samāpatti. The Blessed One predicted that the lion would be born as the Buddha Gotama in future.

In the time of Buddha Nārada, the Bodhisatta renounced the worldly life and invited the Buddha and his followers to a sumptuous feast. The Buddha predicted that he would be the Buddha Gotama in future.

In the time of the Buddha Padumuttaro, the Bodhisatta was born as a great king named Jaṭila. He made immense gifts to the Buddha and his followers. The Buddha predicted that he would be the Buddha Gotama in future.

In the time of the Buddha Sumedha, the Bodhisatta was born as a youth named Māṇavo possessing immense riches. He distributed his wealth and made immense gifts to the Buddha and his followers and heard the Buddha preaching and was established in the saraṇas or refuges. The Buddha predicted that he would be the Buddha Gotama in the near future.

In the time of the Buddha Sujāta, the Bodhisatta was born as a great king. He heard the preaching of the Buddha and distributed in charity his riches to the Buddha and his Saṁgha. He renounced the world and always made great gifts. The Buddha predicted that he would be the Buddha Gotama in future.

In the time of the Buddha Piyadassī, the Bodhisatta was born as a youth named Kassapa. He mastered the three Vedas. Once he heard the discourses of the Buddha and distributed his immense riches. He was established in the sīlas and saraṇas. The Buddha predicted that he would be the Buddha Gotama in future.

In the time of the Buddha Atthadassī, the Bodhisatta was born as a great ascetic named Susīma. He heard the religious discourses of the Buddha and worshipped the lord with great honour. The Blessed One predicted that Susīma was destined to become a Buddha in future.

In the time of the Buddha Dhammadassī, the Bodhisatta was born as Sakka, the king of gods. He worshipped the lord with great honour. The Blessed One predicted that he would be a Buddha in future.

In the time of the Buddha Siddhattha, the Bodhisatta was born as a great ascetic named Maṅgala. He picked up jambu fruits and offered them to the Buddha. The Blessed One predicted that he would be the Buddha Gotama in future.

In the time of the Buddha Tissa, the Bodhisatta was born as a Khattiya of great fame and wealth. He renounced the worldly life. He worshipped the Buddha with great honour. The Blessed One predicted that he would be a Buddha in future.

In the time of the Buddha Phussa, the Bodhisatta was born as a Khattiya king named Vijitāvī.

He gave up the worldly life, learnt the three piṭakas, and performed the sīlas and pāramitās. The Buddha predicted that he was destined to be a Buddha in future.

In the time of the Buddha Vipassī, the Bodhisatta was born as a Nāga king named Atula. He made a gift to the Buddha of the great golden throne adorned with seven kinds of gems. The Blessed One predicted that he would become a Buddha in future.

In the time of the Buddha Sikhi, the Bodhisatta was born as a king named Arindamo. He made immense gifts to the Bhikkhu Saṁgha with the Buddha at its head. The Blessed One predicted that he would be a Buddha in future.

In the time of the Buddha Vessabhu, the Bodhisatta was born as King Sudassana. He made immense gifts to the Buddha and his Saṁgha. The Blessed One predicted that Sudassana would be born as Buddha in future.

In the time of the Buddha Kakusandha, the Bodhisatta was born as King Khema. He made immense gifts to the Buddha and his Bhikkhu Saṁgha, heard the discourses of the Buddha, and gave up the worldly life. The great teacher predicted that he should be a Buddha in future.

In the time of the Buddha Konāgamana, the Bodhisatta was born as a king named Pabbata. He accompanied by his ministers went to the teacher and heard the Master preaching. He made many gifts by way of charity to the Bhikkhu Saṁgha with the Buddha at its head. Afterwards he received ordination from the Buddha. The Blessed One predicted that the King Pabbata would be a Buddha in future.

In the time of the Buddha Kassapa, the Bodhisatta was born as a youth named Jotipāla. He was well versed in the three Vedas. He with Ghaṭikāra went to the place where the Buddha was. He heard the Master preaching. He took pabbajjā and learnt the three piṭakas. The teacher predicted that he was destined to be a Buddha.

Chapter II.

The Buddha Gotama having passed through successive births during the period in which the twenty-four Buddhas beginning with Dīpaṅkara appeared in this earth was born as King Vessantara having performed the Pāramitās. He was then born in the Tusita heaven. He was entreated by the Devatās to be born among men in order to work out their salvation. The Buddha consented to their proposal and observing the time, the island, the country, the family, and the extent of lifetime of her who will bear him, he was born in the Sākya family. He was bred and brought up in luxury. On four occasions while going out to enjoy in the gardens he saw an old man, a diseased person, a dead man, and a samaṇa respectively. Seeing the miseries of the world he was bent upon renouncing the world. He left the world leaving behind his wife and only son. On the bank of the Anomā he cut off his hairs and wore the robes of a monk forsaking his royal garments. He first went to Āḷāva and Uddaka and being unsatisfied with their discourses went to the river Nerañjarā and sat at the foot of the Bodhi tree meditating. He was fully enlightened. He became the Buddha. Being entreated by Brahmā to preach the doctrine he evolved, he went to Benares and preached the doctrine there to the Pañcavaggiya bhikkhus. Thousands of men and women gradually became his followers. The Blessed One attained Mahāparinibbāna at Kusīnagara in the Upavattana of the Mallas. The body was wrapped up with corded cotton and new cloth and was kept in an iron trough containing oil and was covered with another iron trough. Four Malla chiefs followed by others tried to light up the coffin but failed in their attempt. It was then told by Anuruddha that the coffin could not be lighted before the Thera Mahākassapa, who with his followers was on the way to Kusīnārā from Pāvā, would arrive at the place and pay his obeisance to the Lord. In due course the thera arrived. Fire was set to the coffin. When the body was burnt and the fire extinguished, the bones from the coffin were taken out to be distributed. The claimants for the bodily relics of the great teacher were the Mallas of Kusīnārā, King Ajātasattu of Magadha, the Licchavis of Vesālī, the Sākya rulers of Kapilavatthu, the Bulis of Allakappa, the Koliyas of Rāmagāma, a brāhmaṇa of Veṭhadīpaka, and the Mallas of Pāvā. At first the Mallas of Kusīnārā were unwilling to part with any portion of the relics. A strife became imminent. But the brahmin Doṇa by an impressive speech succeeded in bringing about reconciliation among those present. The relics were divided into eight equal portions. The Brāhmaṇa Doṇa kept for himself the teeth of the Master without telling others about it. But Sakka, the king of gods, stole the teeth and brought the same to the heaven of gods. When Doṇa, after distributing the relics, did not find the teeth, he took the bowl in which the relics were originally kept. The Moriyas of Pipphalivana who came late had to content themselves with the ashes only.

Eight great thūpas were built over the relics of the Buddha at the following places: Rājagaha, Vesālī, Kapilavatthu, Allakappa, Rāmagāma, Veṭhadīpa, Pāvā, and Kusīnārā. But the relics which were deposited at Rāmagāma were taken and kept by the Nāgas with great care and honour. These relics (of Rāmagāma) were afterwards taken to Ceylon.

At the suggestion of the Thera Mahākassapa King Ajātasattu collected the bodily relics of the Buddha from Vesālī, Kapilavatthu, Allakappa, Veṭhadīpa, Pāvā, and Kusīnārā and deposited them together with the relics at Rājagaha under a great thūpa at the south-eastern part of Rājagaha.

At the time of Asoka, eighty-four thousand cetiyas were built over the relics of the Buddha.

Chapter III.

We shall now proceed to give a detailed account of the same. King Bindusāra had one hundred sons. At the time when Bindusāra was ill, Asoka, who was Governor of Ujjenī, hurried to Rājagaha, the capital of the Magadha kingdom, to usurp the throne. Bindusāra died and Asoka having killed all his brothers except Tissa Kumāra took possession of the royal throne. But Asoka's consecration took place four years after. At first Asoka was not a patron of the Buddhists. He like his father supported the brahmins and other sects. One day he noticed the improper conduct of them while taking meals. He became highly dissatisfied with them. Thenceforth he began to feed the Buddhist monks and became their great patron.

One day the king saw his nephew Nigrodha Sāmaṇera, son of Sumana, who was Asoka's elder brother, passing through the royal courtyards. The king was highly satisfied with Nigrodha's calm demeanour. The king sent his minister for the Sāmaṇera. When Nigrodha came, the king received him with great honour. The Sāmaṇera admonished the king by reciting the Appamādavagga of the Dhammapada. The king with his followers was established in the three saraṇas and five sīlas. Throughout his kingdom he built 84,000 vihāras in 84,000 cities. He found out the relics that were deposited in the south-eastern part of Rājagaha by King Ajātasattu and deposited them in the 84,000 vihāras that he built. He further became a 'dāyāda' of the Dhamma by allowing his son Mahinda and his daughter Saṅghamittā to become members of the Buddhist Saṁgha.

Meanwhile the Thera Moggaliputta Tissa in order to propagate the Buddha's Dhamma sent Majjhantikathera to Kasmīra and Gandhāra, Mahādevathera to Mahiṁsakamaṇḍala, Rakkhitathera to Vanavāsī, Yonakadhammarakkhitathera to Aparāntaka, Mahādhammarakkhitathera to Mahāraṭṭha, Mahārakkhitathera to Yonakalokam, Majjhimathera to the Himavantadesa, the theras Soṇa and Uttara to Suvaṇṇabhūmi, and the theras Mahinda, Ittiya, Uttiya, and Bhaddasāla to the

Tambapaṇṇidīpa. All the theras succeeded in their mission. The Thera Mahinda together with his companions went to Ceylon when Devānaṁpiyatissa was ruling there. King Devānaṁpiyatissa was a great friend of Asoka, though the two had never seen each other. The Ceylonese king knowing that the theras were disciples of the Buddha received them with great honour. The people of Ceylon together with their king became followers of the Buddha. Many were established in the saraṇas.

The king with his 500 wives was established in the first stage of sanctification when they heard the Thera Mahinda preaching the Vimānavatthu, Petavatthu, and Saccasaṁyutta. When the thera preached the Devadūta Suttanta to the masses, they were also placed in the first stage of sanctification.

At the request of the Thera Mahinda the King Devānaṁpiyatissa sent the Sāmaṇera Sumana to King Asoka in order to have relics so that he could build a thūpa. Sumana went to Pāṭaliputta and got from King Asoka relics contained in the bowl used by the Buddha. He then saw Sakka, the king of gods, and got from him the Buddha's right eye. Sumana came back to Laṅkā with the relics. The relics were received by Devānaṁpiyatissa with great care and honour. A great vihāra was built and the right eye of the Buddha was placed in it.

Anulādevī, Devānaṁpiyatissa's brother's wife, became desirous of receiving pabbajjā. At the suggestion of the Thera Mahinda, Devānaṁpiyatissa sent his nephew Ariṭṭha to Asoka in order to bring a branch of the Bodhi tree to Ceylon and also to bring the Therī Saṅghamittā who would give pabbajjā to Anulā. King Asoka received Ariṭṭha with great honour when the latter came to Pāṭaliputta. The king readily consented to send a branch of the Bodhi tree and the Therī Saṅghamittā to Ceylon. In course of time Ariṭṭha came back to Ceylon with the branch and Saṅghamittā. The branch was transplanted at Anurādhapura with great honour. Anulādevī with five hundred young ladies received the pabbajjā ordination from the then Saṅghamittā. They gradually attained arahatship.

The great King Devānaṁpiyatissa built thūpas throughout Tambapaṇṇidīpa at the interval of a yojana.

Devānaṁpiyatissa was followed by a succession of rulers: Uttiya, Mahāsīva, and Sūratissa. But Sūratissa was defeated by the Damiḷas who usurped the throne of Laṅkā for some time. But the Damiḷas were overpowered by Asela, a son of Mūṭasiva. But a Damiḷa named Eḷāra came over to Laṅkā from the Choḷa country, defeated and killed Asela and became king of Ceylon. Eḷāra, however, could not rule for long, for he was killed and defeated by King Duṭṭhagāmaṇi.

King Devānaṁpiyatissa's second brother was Uparājā Mahānāga. The king's wife desiring that her son should be king, tried every means to put an end to Mahānāga's life. Mahānāga accompanied by his wife and followers fled to Rohaṇa and thence to Mahāgāma and began to rule there. His wife bore him two sons, Yaṭṭhālatissa and Tissa. After Mahānāga's death Yaṭṭhālatissa ruled over Mahāgāma. After Yaṭṭhālatissa's death his son Goṭhābhaya became king. Goṭhābhaya was succeeded by Kākavaṇṇatissa who had two sons, Gāmini Abhaya and Tissa.

The country was under the yoke of the Damiḷas. Duṭṭhagāmaṇi, when he came of age, expressed his desire to fight with the Damiḷas. But his father did not permit him to do so out of affection. But Duṭṭhagāmaṇi became very turbulent and repeatedly expressed his desire to free the country from the yoke of the Damiḷas. He fled from Mahāgāma as he was angry with his father. He was accordingly called Duṭṭhagāmaṇi. After the death of Kākavaṇṇatissa, Tissa, who was then at Dīghavāpi, came to Mahāgāma and performed his duties to the departed soul. He being afraid of his brother came back to Dīghavāpi with his mother and the elephant Kaṇḍula. Duṭṭhagāmaṇi came back to Mahāgāma and became king. On his accession to the throne he sent messengers to his brother demanding his mother and the elephant. Tissa refused to accede to the demand. The two brothers met in the battle-field. Duṭṭhagāmaṇi was defeated in the battle. Duṭṭhagāmaṇi again marched with a huge army against his brother. This time he came out successful. The theras of the island brought about reconciliation between the two brothers.

Duṭṭhagāmaṇi then decided to drive the Damiḷas out of the island. He marched with a mighty army against the Damiḷas. He first went to Mahiyaṅgana and inflicted a crushing defeat upon the Damiḷas and built the Kañcuka thūpa at Mahiyaṅgana. The past history of this thūpa may be told here. At the time of the Buddha's visit to Laṅkā at the ninth month of His Enlightenment, Sumana, the Lord of gods, got from the Buddha his (the Blessed One's) hairs as relics to worship. A thūpa was raised 7 cubits in height over the relics at Mahiyaṅgana, the place which the Buddha visited. After the Buddha's Mahāparinibbāna, Sarabhū, Sāriputta's disciple, came to Laṅkā with the collar-bone of the Buddha and deposited it in the same cetiya which was made 12 cubits in height. Devānaṁpiyatissa's brother Cūḷābhaya made the cetiya 30 cubits in height and Duṭṭhagāmaṇi after defeating the Damiḷas made the cetiya 80 cubits high.

Duṭṭhagāmaṇi succeeded in defeating and killing the thirty-two Damiḷa kings, the greatest of them being Eḷāra, and thus freed the country from the foreign domination. He then became the undisputed ruler of the country. He rewarded those who served him in his enterprise against the Damiḷas. He then devoted himself to promote the weal and happiness of his subjects and the interests of the Buddhist Saṁgha. The king built the Māricavaṭṭi-vihāra over the spear with the relic, with which he marched against the Damiḷas and routed them. The vihāra was dedicated to the Buddhist Saṁgha.

Duṭṭhagāmaṇi then made known his desire to build the great thūpa, the splendid Sovaṇṇamāli, a hundred and twenty cubits in height, and an uposatha house, the Lohapāsāda, making it nine storeys high. The Lohapāsāda was built after the design of the Palace of the gods. There were one thousand chambers in the pāsāda. On the pillars were figures of lions, tigers, and shapes of devatās. Some Jataka-tales were also fitly placed here and there. When the vihāra was finished, the king dedicated the same to the Buddhist Saṁgha.

Duṭṭhagāmaṇi then resolved to build the Mahāthūpa without oppressing the people by levying taxes from them. He was very anxious how to get the materials to build the great thūpa. But the gods came to his rescue. He was provided with all the materials by the gods. The building of the Mahāthūpa was begun on the full-moon day of the month Vesākha. The foundation stone of the Great Cetiya was laid with great care and magnificence in presence of the bhikkhus who assembled there from different parts of Jambudīpa. In the relic-chamber the king placed a Bodhi tree, made up of jewels. Over it a beautiful canopy was raised. The figures of the sun, moon, and stars and different lotus-flowers, made up of jewels, were fastened to the canopy. In the relic-chamber were depicted the setting in motion of the wheel of the doctrine by the Buddha, the preaching in the heaven of gods, the Mahāsamaya Suttanta, the exhortation to Rāhula, the Mahāmaṅgalasutta, the distribution of the relics by Doṇa, and many other scenes connected with the life of the Buddha.

One of the eight doṇas of the bodily relics of the Buddha, which was adored by the Koliyas of Rāmagāma and which was taken thence to the Nāga kingdom, was brought to Laṅkā to be deposited in the Mahāthūpa. The relics were then enshrined with great honour.

But before the making of the chatta and the plaster-work on the cetiya was finished, Duṭṭhagāmaṇi fell seriously ill. The king sent for his younger brother Tissa from Dīghavāpi and told him to complete the work of the thūpa that was left unfinished. Lying on a palanquin the king passed round the cetiya and paid his homage to it. He bade the scribe read aloud the book of meritorious deeds. It is stated that the king built 99 vihāras of which the Maricavaṭṭi-vihāra, the Lohapāsāda, and the Mahāthūpa were his greatest works. The great king passed into the Tusita heaven.

Hatthavanagalla-vihāra-vaṁsa.

The Hatthavanagalla-vihāra-vaṁsa or the history of the temple of Attanagalla consists of eleven chapters written in simple Pāli. Eight chapters deal with an account of King Siri-Saṁghabodhi and the last three chapters deal with the erection of various monumental and religious edifices on the spot where the king spent his last days. It reads like an historical novel. J. D'Alwis' English translation with notes and annotations deserves mention. Dr. G. P. Malalasekera has undertaken to prepare an edition and English translation of this work in the Indian Historical Quarterly. There is an edition of this work published in Colombo, 1909, under the title, "Attanagalu-vihāra-vaṁsaya".

Dāṭhāvaṁsa.

The Dāṭhāvaṁsa or the Dantadhātuvaṁsa means an account of the tooth-relic of the Buddha Gautama. Vaṁsa means chronicle, history, tradition, etc. Literally it means lineage, dynasty, etc. The Dāṭhāvaṁsa is a quasi-religious historical record written with the intention of edifying and at the same time giving an interesting story of the past. This work is noteworthy because it shows us Pāli as a medium of epic poetry.

The Author.

The work was written by Mahāthera Dhammakitti of the city of Pulatti. He was a disciple of Sāriputta, the author of the Sāratthadīpanī-ṭīkā, Sāratthamañjūsā-ṭīkā, Ratanapañcika-ṭīkā on the Candravyākaraṇa and the Vinayasaṅgraha. He was well versed in

Sanskrit, Māgadhībhāsā, tarkaśāstra (logic), vyākaraṇa (grammar), kāvya (poetry), āgama (religious literature), etc. He was fortunate enough to secure the post of a Rājaguru. Two vaṁsas of the Pāli Buddhist literature, the Sāsanavaṁsa and the Gandhavaṁsa, tell us that it was he who composed the Dāṭhāvaṁsa (P.T.S. Ed., p. 34 and J.P.T.S., 1886, p. 62). We know from the Dāṭhāvaṁsa that originally it was written by the poets in the Sinhalese language and later on rendered into Māgadhībhāsā by Dhammakitti for the benefit of the people of the other countries at the request of Parakkamo, the Commander-in-chief of Ceylon, who placed Līlāvatī on the vacant throne of Ceylon. This Līlāvatī, later on, became the queen of Parākramabāhu, the king of Ceylon. (Verses 4–10.)

Date of Composition.

The Dāṭhāvaṁsa was written in the Buddha era 845 during the reign of King Kittisirimeghavaṇṇa of Ceylon. Kern says that it is also known as Daḷadāvaṁsa composed about 310 A.D. It was translated into Pāli in A.D. 1200 under the title of Dāṭhāvaṁsa (Manual of Indian Buddhism, p. 89).

Importance.

The Dāṭhāvaṁsa is an important contribution to the history of Pāli Buddhist literature. It is an historical record of the incidents connected with the tooth-relic of the Buddha. It is as important as the Mahāvaṁsa and the Dīpavaṁsa. The history of Ceylon would be incomplete without it.

Style.

The Dāṭhāvaṁsa is a specimen of fine poetry. It contains Pāli and some debased Sinhalese words. Its vocabulary is rich. Kern rightly remarks that it belongs to the class of compendiums and contains repetitions of passages from more ancient works with more or less apocryphal additions (Manual of Indian Buddhism, p. 9). In the first chapter, stanzas are written in jagatichanda. Sixty stanzas are written in vaṁsastha vritta and the last two in śragdharā vritta; in the second chapter, stanzas are written in anuṣṭupachanda in pathyavaktra vritta and in mandākrānta vritta ; in the third chapter, the stanzas are written in triṣṭhupachanda in upajāta, indravajrā, upendravajrā, and śikhariṇī vrittas ; in the fourth chapter, stanzas are written in atiśakvarīchanda in mālinī, sāddulavikriḍita vrittas ; and in the last chapter, stanzas are written in śakvarīchanda in vasantatilaka and śragdharā vrittas.

Subject-matter.

The Dāṭhāvaṁsa gives an account of the tooth-relic of the Buddha which is said to have been brought to Ceylon by Dantakumāra, prince of Kaliṅga, from Dantapura, the capital of Kaliṅga. It consists of five chapters, a brief summary of which is given below.

Chapter I. While the Buddha Dīpaṅkara was coming to the city of Rammavatī at the invitation of the people of the city, a hermit named Sumedha showed his devotion by laying himself down on the muddy road which the Buddha was to cross. The Buddha walked over his body with his disciples. Sumedha prayed to the Buddha Dīpaṅkara that he might be a Buddha himself in future. Dīpaṅkara granted him the boon whereupon he set himself in all earnestness, to fulfil the ten pāramitās (perfections). The hermit was in heaven prior to his last birth. At the instance of the gods, he was reborn in Kapilavastu in the family of Suddhodana and in the womb of Mahāmāyā. As soon as he was reborn, he stood up and looked round and was worshipped by men and gods. He went seven steps northwards. He was named Siddhatthakumāra. Three palaces, suitable for the three seasons of the year, were built for him. While going to the garden, he saw an old man, a diseased man, a dead man, and a hermit. He then made up his mind to renounce the worldly life. With the help of the gods he left the palace and reached the river Anomā and on the banks of the river, he cut off his hair and threw it upwards to the sky. Indra got the hair and built a caitya over it which is still known as Cūḷamaṇi Caitya. A potter brought a yellow robe, a beggar's bowl, etc., for him. He put on the yellow robe and left for Rājagaha. Thence he went to Uruvelā and made strenuous efforts for six years to acquire bodhi (enlightenment). In the evening of the full-moon day of Vaiśākh, he went to the foot of the Bodhi tree and sat on a seat made of straw and defeated Māra's army. In the last watch of the night he acquired supreme knowledge. After the attainment of bodhi, he spent a week, seated on the same seat at the foot of the Bo-tree, enjoying the bliss of emancipation. He spent another week, looking at the Bodhi tree with steadfast eyes. Another week was spent by him at a place called Ratanaghara near the Bodhi tree, meditating upon paṭiccasamuppāda (dependent origination). He then went to the foot of the Ajapālanigrodha tree where he spent a week in meditation. He went to Mucalinda nāgabhavana where he was saved by the nāga from hailstorm. He then visited the Rājāyatana. Thence he started for Isipatanamigadāva to preach his first sermon known as Dhammacakkapavattana, but on the way two merchants, Tapussa and Bhallika, offered him madhupiṇḍika (a kind of food prepared with honey and molasses). The Buddha placed them in two refuges. He then reached Isipatana on the full-moon day of the month of Āṣāḍha. He preached the Dhammacakkapavattana Sutta to the first band of five disciples headed by Aññakondañña.

Chapter II. The Buddha was thinking of doing good to the world. Nine months after his attainment of bodhi, the Buddha made an aerial voyage to Laṅkā to fulfil his mission and descended on the garden named Mahānāgavana. Then he went to the meeting of the yakkhas and terrified them by creating storm, darkness, and heavy rains. The yakkhas having been greatly troubled by these, came to the Buddha and asked for protection. In the midst of the meeting he sat down on a seat of leather but by his miraculous power he made the seat very hot and owing to the excessive heat radiating from the seat, the yakkhas became very much distressed and the leather expanded so as to cover the whole of the island of Laṅkā and the yakkhas gathered together on the coast, unable to bear the excessive heat. The Giridīpa which was full of shady trees, was brought close to the island of Laṅkā by the Buddha and the yakkhas, to save themselves from the extreme heat, went into the Giridīpa which was again set on its former site and thus the island of Laṅkā was rid of the yakkhas. As soon as the yakkhas left the island of Laṅkā, he stopped his miracle and many a god came to the island and surrounded him. The Buddha preached to the devas Dhamma and gave one of his hairs to God Sumana who built a caitya over it on the top of the Sumanakūṭa Hill and worshipped it. Then the Buddha returned to Jetavana. Again he went to Laṅkā five years after his enlightenment and pacified the contest between Cūḷodara and Mahodara for a jewelled throne. Again he came to the island of Laṅkā eight years after his enlightenment being invited by a nāga named Maṇiakkhika. The Buddha with five hundred disciples went to the house of Maṇiakkhika in Kalyāṇī. A caitya built over the seat offered by Maṇiakkhika and used and left by the Buddha, was worshipped by the nāgas there. This caitya was named Kalyāṇī Caitya. The Buddha then visited the Sumanakūṭa Hill and left his footprints there. Thence he went to Dīghavāpī where he sat in meditation for some time. Thence he visited the site of the Bodhi tree at Anurādhapura where also he sat in meditation for some time. Thence he visited the Thūpārāma and finished his work in Ceylon. He preached Dhamma for forty-five years and obtained parinibbāna on the full-moon day of the month of Vaiśākha in the garden named Upavattana of the Malla kings near Kusīnārā. In the first watch of the night of his parinibbāna, he preached Dhamma to the Mallas, in the middle watch he made Subhadda an arahat, and in the last watch he instructed the bhikkhus to be ardent and strenuous. Early in the morning he rose up from meditation and passed away. Many miracles were seen after his parinibbāna, e.g., the earth quaked from end to end, celestial music was played, all trees became adorned with flowers, though it was not the time for flowers to bloom. The body of the Buddha was wrapped up in new clothes and cotton, five hundred times. It was put into a golden pot, full of oil. A funeral pyre was prepared with scented wood such as sandal, twenty cubits in height, and the Malla chiefs put the oil-pot in the pyre. As Mahākassapa did not arrive, fire could not be kindled because it was desired by the gods that the Buddha's body must not be burnt before Mahākassapa had worshipped it. As soon as Mahākassapa came and worshipped the dead body of the Buddha, fire was kindled. The dead body was so completely burnt as to leave no ashes or charcoal. Only the bones of the Buddha of the colour of pearl and gold remained. On account of the Buddha's desire the bones became separated excepting the four bones of the head, two collar-bones, and teeth. Sarabhu, a disciple of Sāriputta, went to Mahiaṅgana in Ceylon taking with him one of the collar-bones of the Buddha and built a caitya. An arahat named Khema took a left tooth-relic of the Buddha and over the remaining bone-relics, kings of eight countries began to quarrel. Doṇa settled the dispute and divided the bones equally among the eight countries. The kings after having received the relics, took them to their respective kingdoms, built caityas over them, and worshipped them. One tooth-relic taken by Khema was given to Brahmadatta, king of Kaliṅga, who built a caitya over it and worshipped it. Brahmadatta's son, Kāsīrāja, succeeded his father and worshipped, like his dead father, the caitya built over the tooth-relic of the Buddha. Kāsīrāja's son, Sunanda, succeeded him and did the same. Sunanda's son, Guhasīva, succeeded him to the throne and did the same. Guhasīva's minister, who was a false believer, asked the king whether there was anything supernatural in the tooth-relic of the Buddha which the king worshipped and for which valuable offerings were given by him. The king then narrated the various qualities of the tooth-relic which showed miracles when prayed for. The minister gave up his false belief and became a follower of the Buddha. The heretics seeing this became very much dissatisfied. Guhasīva ordered all the nigaṇṭhas to be driven out of the kingdom. The nigaṇṭhas went to King Paṇḍu of Pāṭaliputta, who was then a very powerful king of Jambudīpa. They complained to Paṇḍu that King Guhasīva being a king subordinate to him (Paṇḍu) worshipped the bone of a dead person (that is, Buddha's relic) without worshipping Brahmā, Siva, and others whom he (Paṇḍu) worshipped and they further complained that Guhasīva ridiculed the deities worshipped by him (Paṇḍu). Hearing this King Paṇḍu grew angry and sent one of his subordinate kings called Cittayāna with a fourfold army to arrest and bring Guhasīva with the tooth-relic. Cittayāna informed Guhasīva of his mission and Guhasīva welcomed him cordially, showed him the tooth-relic of the Buddha, and narrated to him the virtues possessed by it. Cittayāna became very much pleased with him and became a follower of the Buddha.

Chapter III. Cittayāna then informed Guhasīva of the order of King Paṇḍu. Guhasīva with the tooth-relic on his head, followed by a large number of followers with valuable presents for King Paṇḍu, went to Pāṭaliputta. The nigaṇṭhas requested King Paṇḍu not to offer any seat to Guhasīva, and they also requested him to set fire to the tooth-relic. A big pit of burning charcoal was dug by the king's command and the heretics after taking away the tooth-relic, threw it into the fire. As soon as it came in contact with fire, fire became as cool as the winter breeze and a lotus blossomed in the fire and in the midst of the lotus, the tooth-relic was placed. Seeing this wonder, many heretics gave up false beliefs, but the king himself being a false believer for a long time, could not give up false belief and ordered the tooth-relic to be destroyed by stone, which found its place in the sky. The nigaṇṭhas asked the king not to attach great importance to the miracles as they were not unprecedented. The tooth-relic was put in a casket and the nigaṇṭhas were asked to take it out and throw it away, but none could do so. The king declared that he who would be able to take out the tooth-relic, would be rewarded. Anāthapiṇḍika's great grandson recollecting the virtues of the Buddha and the deeds done by his great grandfather for the Buddha, was very much pleased to know of the declaration and went to take the tooth-relic out of the casket. He praised the tooth-relic much and then the tooth-relic rose up to the sky and then came down to rest on the head of the great grandson of Anāthapiṇḍika. The nigaṇṭhas told King Paṇḍu that due to the influence of Anāthapiṇḍika's great grandson the tooth-relic could rise up to the sky and come down to rest on the head of the great grandson. The nigaṇṭhas denied the influence of the tooth-relic which displayed various miracles according to the desire of Anāthapiṇḍika's great grandson. The tooth-relic was thrown into a moat. Cittayāna advised the king that he should follow Dhamma of the Buddha because by worshipping the tooth-relic, Bimbisāra and other kings attained nirvāṇa. Thus advised he gave up false belief and brought the tooth-relic with great pomp. King Guhasīva was cordially received by King Paṇḍu and both of them did many meritorious deeds.

Chapter IV. A king named Khiradhāra came to fight with King Paṇḍu who became victorious. Paṇḍu after re-establishing peace in his kingdom, sent back Guhasīva with Buddha's tooth-relic to Kaliṅga. Dantakumāra, son of the king of Ujjain, came to Kaliṅga to worship the tooth-relic. Guhasīva cordially welcomed him and became pleased to hear the qualities of Dantakumāra and afterwards gave his daughter in marriage to Dantakumāra. After the defeat of Dantakumāra, his sons and nephews came to Malayavana, a town near Dantapura, to take away the tooth-relic by force. Fully realising the danger, Guhasīva asked his son-in-law and daughter to go to Ceylon with the tooth-relic. As the king of Ceylon and his subjects were faithful to the Buddha, he thought Ceylon would be the best and safest place for the relic. At this time Mahāsena, a friend of Guhasīva, was the king of Ceylon. The son-in-law and the daughter with the relic sailed by a merchant ship from the port of Tāmbralipti. The ship reached Ceylon safely with the relic.

Chapter V. Dantakumāra and his wife with the relic went to a village near the eastern gate of Anurādhapura in the ninth year of the reign of Kittisirimegha, son of Mahādisena. Dantakumāra met an arahat and informed him of the tooth-relic which he brought to Ceylon for its safety. The arahat after hearing this, went to the king and informed him of the matter. Mahādisena, the preceding king of Ceylon, was a friend of Guhasīva, king of Kaliṅga, who did not know that Mahādisena had died and his son, Kittisirimegha, was on the throne of Ceylon. Dantakumāra and his wife became very much grieved to know that Mahādisena was no more and his son Kittisirimegha had succeeded him on the throne. The king of Ceylon after learning from the arahat that the tooth-relic was brought to Ceylon for its safety by Dantakumāra and his wife, became very much pleased. The king and the queen of Ceylon went barefooted to Meghagirivihāra, residence of the arahat, to receive the relic. They brought the relic to the palace and placed it on the throne with great devotion. The citizens of Ceylon, the bhikkhus well-versed in the Tripiṭakas, and the arahats came to worship it. The king knew that the colour of the relic was as white as the morning star. But finding it not to be so when it was taken out of the casket, suspicion arose in the mind of the king, but his suspicion was soon removed when the relic displayed several miracles. The king built a special temple and kept it there. All the Sinhalese monks and householders assembled at Anurādhapura to worship the tooth-relic. At this time a question arose as to the section of the monks to whom the tooth-relic would be entrusted for its safety and management. The king decided that the tooth-relic would select its own abode. The tooth-relic placed on a fully decorated elephant was taken round the city and was brought to the place where the Thera Mahinda preached his first sermon after reaching Ceylon. The king of Ceylon ruled that the relic would be taken round the city once in a year in spring. The temple where it was kept, was extended at the cost of nine lacs. After the death of Kittisirimegha, his successors such as Buddhadāsa worshipped it with devotion and protected it.[1]

Cha-kesa-dhātu-vaṁsa.

The Cha-kesa-dhātu-vaṁsa has been edited by Minayeff of St. Petersburg in J.P.T.S., 1885. It is a work by a modern Burmese author of unknown date. It is a mixture of prose and poetry. The language is simple and the diction noteworthy. It contains an account of the thūpas raised by Sakka, Pajjunna, Maṇimekhalā, Addhikanāvika, Varuṇa-

[1] The Dāṭhāvaṁsa has been edited in Devanāgarī character and translated into English by Dr. B. C. Law and published by Messrs. Motilal Banarsidas, proprietors of the Punjab Sanskrit Book Depot, Lahore. Besides, there are two Sinhalese editions (by Terunnanse and Silālaṅkāra), and a P.T.S. (London) edition published in 1884 in J.P.T.S. There is another English translation of this work by Mutu Coomaraswami, published by Messrs. Trübner and Co., London. A French version of this work appeared in Paris in 1884 under the name "Le Dāṭhāvaṅça; ou, Histoire de la dent relique du Buddha Gotama: poème èpique pali de Dhammakitti'. There is a commentary on the Dāṭhāvaṁsa known as the Dāṭhādhātuvaṁsaṭīkā mentioned in an inscription of the 15th century A.D. *Vide* also G. Turnour—Account of the Tooth-Relic of Ceylon (J.A.S.B. vi.).

nāgarāja, and Sattanāvika over the hair relics of the Buddha.

Gandhavaṁsa.

The Gandhavaṁsa has been edited by Minayeff. His edition is based on Burmese manuscripts. It is a small and interesting outline of the history of Pāli books. It is written mostly in prose. Besides the books of the canon, there is contained in it a sketch of the history of more modern Pāli works far more detailed than that in the Sāsanavaṁsa. A list of authors and their works as stated in the Gandhavaṁsa is given below :—

Mahākaccāyana :—Kaccāyanagandho, Mahāniruttigandho, Cullaniruttigandho, Nettigandho, Peṭakopadesagandho, Vaṇṇanītigandho.

Buddhaghosa :—Visuddhimaggo, Sumaṅgalavilāsinī, Papañcasūdanī, Sāratthapakāsinī, Manorathapūraṇī, Samantapāsādikā, Paramatthakathā, Kaṅkhāvitaraṇī, Dhammapadaṭṭhakathā, Jātakaṭṭhakathā, Khuddakapāṭhaṭṭhakathā, Apadānaṭṭhakathā.

Buddhadatta :—Vinayavinicchayo, Uttaravinicchayo, Abhidhammāvatāro, Madhuraṭṭhavilāsinī.

Ānanda :—Mūlaṭīkaṁ.

Dhammapāla :—Nettipakaraṇaṭṭhakathā, Itivuttaka-aṭṭhakathā, Udānaṭṭhakathā, Cariyāpiṭaka-aṭṭhakathā, Theragāthāṭṭhakathā, Vimānavatthussa Vimalavilāsinī nāma aṭṭhakathā, Petavatthussa Vimalavilāsinī nāma aṭṭhakathā, Paramatthamañjūsā, Dīghanikāyaṭṭhakathādīnaṁ catunnaṁ aṭṭhakathānaṁ Līnatthapakāsinī nāma ṭīkā, Jātakaṭṭhakathāya Līnatthapakāsinī nāma ṭīkā, Paramatthadīpanī, Līnatthavaṇṇanā.

Mahāvajirabuddhi :—Vinayagaṇḍhi.

Vimalabuddhi :—Mukhamattadīpanī.

Cullavajiro :—Atthabyakkhyānaṁ.

Dīpaṁkaro :—Rūpasiddhipakaraṇaṁ, Rūpasiddhiṭīkaṁ Summapañcasuttaṁ.

Culladhammapālo :—Saccasaṁkhepaı

Kassapo :—Mohavicchedanī, Vima|

Buddhavaṁsa. Anāgatavaṁsa.

Mahānāma :—Saddhammapakāsanī, Mahāvaṁsa, Cullavaṁsaṁ.

Upasena :—Saddhammaṭṭhitikaṁ.

Moggallāna :—Moggallānabyākaraṇaṁ.

Saṁgharakkhita :—Subodhālaṁkāraṁ.

Vuttodayakāra :—Vuttodaya, Saṁbandhacintā, Navaṭīkaṁ.

Dhammasiri :—Khuddasikkhaṁ.

Anuruddha :—Khuddasikkhaṁ.

Anuruddha :—Paramatthavinicchayaṁ, Nāmarūparicchedaṁ, Abhidhammatthasaṁgahapakaraṇaṁ.

Khema :—Khemaṁ.

Sāriputta :—Sāratthadīpanī, Vinayasaṁgahapakaraṇaṁ, Sāratthamañjūsaṁ, Pañcakaṁ.

Buddhanāga :—Vinayatthamañjūsaṁ.

Navo Moggallāna :—Abhidhānappadīpikaṁ.

Vācissaro :—Sambandhacintāṭīkā, Moggallānabyākaraṇassaṭīkā, Nāmarūparicchedaṭīkā, Padarūpavibhāvanaṁ, Khemapakaraṇassaṭīkā, Mūlasikkhāyaṭīkā, Vuttodayavivaranaṁ, Sumaṅgalapasādanī, Bālāvatāro, Yogavinicchayo, Sīmālaṅkāra, Rūpārūpavibhāga, Paccayasaṁgaho.

Sumaṅgala :—Abhidhammatthavikāsanī, Abhidhammattha-Vibhāvanī.

Dhammakitti :—Dantadhātupakaraṇaṁ.

Medhaṁkaro :—Jinacaritaṁ.

Saddhammasiri :—Saddatthabhedacintā.

Devo :—Sumaṇakūṭavaṇṇanā.

Cullabuddhaghoso :—Jātattagīnidānaṁ, Sotattagīnidānaṁ.

Raṭṭhapāla :—Madhurasavāhinī.

Aggavaṁsa :—Saddanītipakaraṇaṁ.

Vimalabuddhi :—Mahāṭīkaṁ.

Uttama :—Bālāvatāraṭīkaṁ, Liṅgatthavivaraṇaṭīkaṁ.

Kyacvārañño :—Saddabindu, Paramatthabindupakaraṇaṁ.

Saddhammaguru :—Saddavuttipakāsanaṁ.

Aggapaṇḍita :—Lokuppatti.

Saddhammajotipāla :—Sīmālaṁkārassaṭīkā,

Mātikatthadīpanī, Vinayasamuṭṭhānadīpanī, Gandhasāro, Paṭṭhānagaṇanānayo, Saṁkhepavaṇṇanā, Suttaniddeso, Pātimokkhavisodhanī.

Nava Vimalabuddhi :—Abhidhammapaṇṇarasaṭṭhānaṁ.

Vepullabuddhi :—Saddasāratthajāliniyāṭīkā, Vuttodayaṭīkā, Paramatthamañjūsā, Dasagaṇḍhivaṇṇanā, Magadhabhūtāvidaggaṁ, Vidadhimukkhamaṇḍanaṭīkā.

Ariyavaṁsa :—Maṇisāramañjūsaṁ, Maṇidīpaṁ, Gaṇḍābharanaṁ, Mahānissaraṁ, Jātakavisodhanaṁ.

Cīvaro :—Jaṅghadāsassa ṭīkaṁ.

Nava medhaṁkaro :—Lokadīpakasāraṁ.

Sāriputto :—Saddavuttipakāsakassaṭīkaṁ.

Saddhammaguru :—Saddavuttipakāsanaṁ.

Dhammasenāpati :—Kārikaṁ, Etimāsamidīpakaṁ, and Manohāraṁ.

Ñāṇasāgaro :—Liṅgatthavivaraṇapakāsanaṁ.

Abhaya :—Saddatthabhedacintāya mahāṭīkaṁ.

Guṇasāgaro :—Mukhamattasāraṁ taṭ-ṭīkaṁ.

Subhūtacandana :—Liṅgatthavivaraṇapakaranaṁ.

Udumbaranāmācariyo :—Peṭakopadesassa ṭīkaṁ.

Upatissācariya :—Anāgatavaṁsassa aṭṭhakathā.

Buddhapiya :—Sāratthasaṁgahanāmagandho.

Dhammānandācariya :—Kaccāyanasāro, Kaccāyanabhedaṁ, and Kaccāyanasārassaṭīkā.

Gandhācariyo :—Kurundigandha.

Nāgītācariya :—Saddasāratthajālinī.

Works of unknown authors mentioned in the Gandhavaṁsa are stated below :—

Mahāpaccariyaṁ, Pūrāṇaṭīkā, Mūlasikkhāṭīkā, Līnatthapakāsinī, Nisandeho, Dhammānusāraṇī, Ñeyyāsandati, Ñeyyāsandatiyā ṭīkā, Sumahāvatāro, Lokapaññattipakaraṇaṁ, Tathāgatupattipakaraṇaṁ, Nalātadhātuvaṇṇanā, Sīhalavatthu, Dhammadīpako, Paṭipattisaṁgaho, Visuddhimaggagandhi, Abhidhammagandhi, Nettipakaraṇagandhi, Visuddhimaggacullanavaṭīkā, Sotappamālinī, Pasādajananī, Subodhālaṅkārassa Navaṭīkā, Gūḷhatthaṭīkaṁ, Bālappabodhanaṁ, Saddatthabhedacintāya majjhimaṭīkaṁ, Kārikāyaṭīkaṁ, Etimāsamidīpikāyaṭīkaṁ, Dīpavaṁsa, Thūpavaṁsa, and Bodhivaṁsa.

Sāsanavaṁsa.

The author of the Sāsanavaṁsa gives an outline of Buddha's life and briefly deals with the three Buddhist Councils held during the reigns of the three Indian kings, Ajātasattu, Kālāsoka, and Asoka. After the Third Council was over, Moggaliputta Tissathera sent Buddhist missionaries to different countries for the propagation of the Buddhist faith. Paññāsāmī, the author of the Sāsanavaṁsa, speaks of the nine regions visited by the missionaries. But of these nine, five are placed in Indo-China. Dr. Mabel Bode is of opinion that the author's horizon seems to be limited, first by an orthodox desire to claim most of the early teachers for the countries of the South (and hence to prove the purest possible sources for the Southern doctrines), and secondly by a certain feeling of national pride. According to this account, Mahā-Moggaliputta Tissa (as if with a special care for the religious future of Maramma) sent two separate missionaries to neighbouring regions in the valley of the Irawaddy—besides three others, who visited Laos and Pegu.

The Thera Mahinda went to Ceylon for the propagation of the faith during the reign of the Sinhalese King Devānaṁpiyatissa who was a contemporary of the Indian King Asoka.

Sona and Uttara visited Suvaṇṇabhūmi (Sudhammapura—that is, Thaton at the mouth of the Sittaung River). The author holds that even before the sending out of the missionaries to Suvaṇṇabhūmi by Moggaliputta Tissathera, the President of the Third Buddhist Council, Buddha came here personally with a number of bhikkhus to preach his doctrines.

Mahārakkhita Thera spread Buddhism in the

Yona country (the country of the Shan tribes about Zimmé).

Yonakarakkhita Thera visited the country of Vanavāsī (the region round Prome) and propagated Buddhism there.

Majjhantika visited Kasmīra and Gandhāra (the Gandhāra country) lay on the right bank of the Indus, south of Kabul, and the whole country became a strong Buddhist hold.

It was through Mahā-Revata Thera that Buddhism found its way into Mahiṁsakamaṇḍala (Andhra country).

Mahā-Dhammarakkhita Thera went to Mahāraṭṭha (Mahānagara-raṭṭha or Siam) and spread Buddhism there.

Majjhima Thera spread the Buddhist faith in Cīnaraṭṭha (the Himavantapadesa of the Ceylon books).

Now we shall deal with the history of the spread of Buddhism in Aparantaraṭṭha which (placed by European scholars west of the Punjab) is no other than the Sunāparanta of the Burmese, i.e., the region lying west of the upper Irawaddy.

The Sāsanavaṁsa brings before us a picture of the relations of State and Saṁgha in Burma from the time of Anuruddha, with his constant adviser, Arahanta, to the time of Meng-Dun-Meng, with his Council of Mahātheras. Those relations were one of mutual dependence. The Order, though enriched by the gifts of pious laymen, yet depends, in the last resort, upon the king. The peaceful, easy life dear to the Burmese bhikkhu, the necessary calm for study or the writing of books, the land or water to be set apart for ecclesiastical ceremonies, all these are only secured by the king's favour and protection. This accounts for the general loyalty of the Saṁgha to the head of the State. The king's despotism is also held in check.

" At the lowest, the royal gifts of vihāras and the building of cetiyas are either the price paid down for desired prosperity and victory, or the atonement for bloodshed and plunder; and the despot dares not risk the terrors, the degradation, that later births, in coming time, may hold in store for him, if he injures or neglects the Saṁgha." As a rule, the king was the recognised authority in ecclesiastical affairs. This is evident from Anuruddha's vigorous reforms. The Saṁgharāja is not the elected Head of the Order. He is appointed by the king, whose favourite and tutor he usually is. It appears from the Pārupana Ekaṁsika controversy that the king's power to settle a religious question by royal decree is fully recognised by the Saṁgha. But we also see the king himself under his ācariya's influence, so far as to ensure his favouring the orthodox or unorthodox school, according to the views of the Saṁgharāja.

The history of religion in Mramma is nothing more than the history of the Buddhist Order in Sunāparanta and Tambadīpa. The history of the Burmese as a nation centres in a group of cities—Pugān, Sagain, Ava, Panyā, Amarapura, Mandalay—each, in its turn, the seat of kings.

The early Buddhist stronghold in Burma was at Sudhammapura, the capital of Manohari, king of Pegu. Anuruddha, king of Pugān, at the instance of Arahanta, a great thera who came from Sudhammapura to Pugān, made war with Manohari and brought the sacred relics and books to Pugān. All the members of the Saṁgha in Thatōn (Sudhammapura) were also transferred to Pugān. Anuruddha further sent for copies from Ceylon, which Arahanta compared with those of Pegu, to settle the readings.

During the reign of Narapatisisu, the celebrated teacher, Uttarājīva, came from Sudhammapura to Arimaddana and established religion there. His pupil Chapada who spent ten years studying in Ceylon returned with four colleagues to the capital. After the death of Chapada separate schools came into existence, having their origin in certain differences that arose between the three surviving teachers—Sīvali, Tamalinda, and Ānanda. The schools are together known as Pacchāgaṇa to distinguish them from the earlier school in Arimaddana (Purimagana) founded by Arahanta.

The reign of Kyocvā is highly important for the history of Buddhism. He was himself the author of two manuals—Paramatthabindu and Saddabindu, for the use of his wives, and one of his daughters wrote the Vibhatyattha. We are told of the science and zeal of the women of Arimaddana, and anecdotes are told of their skill in grammar and the keenness of their wit.

In the reign of Bureng Naung religion thrived most. It is recorded of him that he even forced Buddhism on the Shāns and Muslims in the north of his kingdom.

In the reign of Siri-Mahāsīhasūrasudhammarājā begins a new chapter in the history of Burmese Buddhism—the Pārupana-Ekaṁsika controversy. The rise and many phases of the dispute are set forth at length by the author of the Sāsanavaṁsa. Two sects arose—the Ekaṁsika sect (it was named so for going about in the village with one shoulder uncovered by the upper garment) and the Pārupana sect (this school strictly observed the wearing of the upper garment on both shoulders, during the village rounds). During the reign of Bodoah Prā the question was settled for good. A royal decree established the Pārupana practices for the whole of the kingdom.

During the reign of Meng-dun-Meng we come to the last controversy, perhaps recorded because it points to the influence of the Burmese Saṁgha in Ceylon. An ancient Sīmā in the island (Ceylon) was the subject of dispute. The matter was brought for judgment to the Saṁgharājā at Mandalay, by deputations from both sides. The Saṁgharājā gave judgment after consulting various sacred texts. The members of both sides received presents from the king. Thus the history of religion in Aparanta closes.

The edition of the Sāsanavaṁsa[1] is based on two palm-leaf MSS. in the British Museum. It is a non-canonical book and is a text of Burmese authorship. It is a very interesting historical work. The author Paññaswāmi, who dates his book 1223 of the Burmese Common Era 1861 A.D., was the tutor of the then reigning king of Burma and himself a pupil of the head of the Order at Mandalay. The table of contents promises a general history of Buddhism drawn from a few well-known Pāli works, e.g., Aṭṭhakathā, Vinaya Piṭaka, Mahāvaṁsa, and Dīpavaṁsa. Events are brought up to the time of the Third Council in the time of Asoka and the sending forth of missionaries by the Thera Mahā-Moggaliputta Tissa. The later history of religion consists of nine chapters, which falls into two parts. The first part consists of a few legends strung together with quotations from Buddhaghosa and Dīpavaṁsa. The accounts of Ceylon and Burma seem to be more careful and complete than those of other matters of this group. The second part covers three-fifths of the book and treats solely of the history of Buddhism in Burma proper. In part one, the section dealing with the missions strikes the key-note of the Sāsanavaṁsa. A few geographical notes explained the nine regions visited by the first missionaries. A careful study of this work shows the author's intimate acquaintance with the commentaries. The style imitates that of Buddhaghosa and his successors. There are no points of philological interest. The book gives us an interesting record of the part played by the Buddha's religion in the social and intellectual life. Paññaswāmi's history is a purely ecclesiastical piece of work. This work has been edited by Mabel Bode, Ph.D., for the P.T.S., London.

[1] Read Sāsanavaṁsadīpa edited by Jñanatilaka Nāyaka Punnānse and Sāsanavaṁsadīpaya by Vimalasāra Unnānse. Read also "The author of the Sāsanavaṁsa" by M. Bode, J.R.A.S., 1899, pp. 674–676.

## CHAPTER VII

# PĀLI MANUALS

### Introduction

*Saṅgaha* is an earlier Pāli nomenclature for both a compilation and a manual. The later term *Atthasāra* is precisely an equivalent of the English handbook or manual. The Buddhist teachers had indeed developed the art of manual writing much earlier, the Khuddakapāṭha, the Pātimokkha, and the Abhidhamma treatises, all partaking of the character of manuals. The manuals were written in both prose and verse and in some cases in the form of Kārikās. As a matter of fact most of the works of Thera Buddhadatta represent so many manuals in the shape of Kārikās. Buddhaghosa's writings are conspicuous by the absence of such manuals with the solitary exception of the Visuddhimagga. The same holds true in the case of Dhammapāla's writings. The art continued nevertheless and coming to somewhat later times we have a number of works that deserve to be classed under manuals. Although the subject-matters of these manuals vary, one predominant feature of each of them is this that it presents its theme systematically in a somewhat terse and concise form, purporting to be used as a handbook of constant reference.

Saccasaṁkhepa.

The *Saccasaṁkhepa* is a religious work on truth written by Dhammapāla Thera. Malalasekera points out that there seems to be some uncertainty as to the authorship and date of the Saccasaṁkhepa. The Saddhammasaṁgaha assigns it to Ānanda.[1] The Saccasaṁkhepa has been edited by Dhammārāma Bhikkhu. There are five chapters in it dealing with rūpa (form),

[1] The Pāli Literature of Ceylon, p. 202.

vedanā (feeling), cittapavatti (thought), pakiṇṇakasaṁgaha, and nibbāna. It is known as the summary of the truth, published by the P.T.S. in J.P.T.S., 1917–1919. It consists of 387 stanzas. Rūpa or form is one of the five khandhas. The destruction of the four elements means the destruction of rūpa. There are three kinds of vedanā or feelings, feeling that is pleasant, feeling that is unpleasant, and feeling that is neither pleasant nor unpleasant, i.e., indifferent. All the three vedanās are to be done away with, for they are painful. Citta or thought when attached to rāga or passion leads to repeated births which are full of misery. When citta is detached from passion there is no rebirth for a being. The Pakiṇṇakasaṁgahavibhāga treats of miscellaneous subjects, e.g., pride, sloth, niggardliness, and their evil effects. The last chapter deals with nirvāṇa which means destruction of all passions and desires and avoidance of all worldly miseries.

Abhidhammattha-Saṅgaha

The *Abhidhammattha-Saṅgaha* [1] has served for probably eight centuries as a primer of psychology and philosophy in Burma and Ceylon, and a whole literature of exegesis has grown up around it, the latest additions to which are but of yesterday. The manual is ascribed to a teacher named Anuruddha; but nothing is known about him except the fact that he had compiled two other treatises on philosophy, and one of them was written while the author was at Kāñcipura or Conjeeveram. Burmese tradition asserts that he was a thera of Ceylon and wrote the compendium at the Sinhalese vihāra founded by Somadevī, queen of King Vaṭṭagāmaṇī who flourished between 88–76 B.C., a date fictitiously early for the book. In fact, Anuruddha is believed to have lived earlier than 12th but later than the

[1] Abhidhammattha-Saṅgaha-im Compendium Buddhistischer Philosophie und Psychologie, Vol. I, by Brahmacārī Govinda deserves mention.

8th century A.D. Sāriputta compiled a paraphrase to this book. The Abhidhammattha-Saṅgaha has been edited and published in J.P.T.S., 1883, and translated with notes by Shwe Zan Aung and revised by Mrs. Rhys Davids under the name of the Compendium of Philosophy included in the P.T.S. translation series.

Other contemporary philosophical manuals.

The Abhidhammattha-Saṅgaha is classed in Burmese bibliography under a classified list of Philosophical manuals, nine in number. They are :—

1. Abhidhammattha-Saṅgaha, by Anuruddha, 2. Paramattha Vinicchaya, by Anuruddha, 3. Abhidhammāvatāra, by Buddhadatta, 4. Rūpārūpavibhāga, by Buddhadatta, 5. Saccasaṁkhepa, by Dhammapāla, 6. Mohavicchedanī, by Kassapa, 7. Khemapakaraṇa, by Khema, 8. Nāmacāradīpaka, by Saddhamma Jotipāla, and 9. Nāmarūpaparicched, by Anuruddha.

Exegetical literature on the book.

The Abhidhammattha-Saṅgaha, because of its exclusively condensed treatment, stimulated a large growth of ancillary works, of which the following have uptill now been known.

A. Four ṭikās or commentaries : 1. Porāṇaṭīkā, by Navavimāla Buddhi of Ceylon, 2. Abhidhammattha-vibhāvanī, by Sumaṅgala of Ceylon, 3. Saṅkhepa-vaṇṇanā, by Saddhamma Jotipāla of Burma, and 4. Paramattha-dīpanī-ṭīkā, by Ledi Sadaw of Burma.

B. A 'Key' to the Ṭīkā-gyaw, entitled Maṇisāramañju, by Ariyavaṁsa of Sagaing, Burma.

C. A commentary entitled Madhu-Sāratthadīpanī, by Mahānanda of Hanthawaddy, Burma.

D. A number of works, not in Pāli, but in Burmese :

1. Abhidhammattha-saṅgaha-madhu, a modern work by Mogaung Sadaw, 2. Abhidhammatthasaṅgaha-gandhi, a modern work by Payagyi Sadaw, 3. Paramattha-Sarūpa-bhedanī, by Visuddhārāma Sadaw, 4. Abhidhammattha-Sarūpa-dīpaka, by

Sadaw, 4. Abhidhammattha-Sarūpa-dīpaka, by the late Myobyingyi, and 5. a number of analytical works entitled Akauk.

The Abhidhammattha-Saṅgaha and the Visuddhimagga.

The Abhidhammattha-Saṅgaha covers very largely the same range of subject-matter as that of the Visuddhimagga, though the amplitude of treatment and the order and emphasis of treatment in each are different. But they are to some extent complimentary, and as such still hold the field as modern text-books for students of Buddhism in Buddhist countries.

The Abhidhammattha-Saṅgaha is so highly condensed that it consists, for the most part, of terse, jejune sentences, which are not easily intelligible to lay readers. It is, therefore, profitable to have a résumé of the main topics and problems of the whole work as a Manual of Buddhist Psychology and Philosophy.

Mind.

Mind is ordinarily defined as that which is conscious of an object; and the Buddhists have tried to frame their definition with the help of fifty-two mental attributes or properties enumerated in Part II of the Abhidhammattha-Saṅgaha. But the definition of mind is also a division of mind, and our author's division into vedanā, ñāṇa, and saṅkhāra corresponds to Bain's division of the mind into feeling, thought or intellect, and will or volition.

Consciousness (viññāna) has, therefore, been defined as the relation between ārammaṇika (subject) and ārammaṇa (object). In this relation the object presented is termed paccaya (the relating thing) and the subject, paccayuppanna (the thing related). The two terms are thus relative.

The object of Consciousness is either object of Sense or object of Thought. Object of sense subdivides itself into five classes—sight, sound, smell, taste, and touch, which are collectively termed pañcārammaṇa (fivefold object). The object of thought also consists of five sub-clauses: citta (mind), cetasika (mental properties), pasāda, rūpa and sukhumarūpa (sensitive and subtle qualities of body), paññati (name, idea, notion, concept), and nibbāna. These are collectively termed dhammārammaṇa.

Paññatti.

The Paññatti object consists of several subclauses. Paññatti is either (1) that which makes known (paññāpetīti); or (2) that which is made known (paññāpiyatīti), corresponding to our author's terminology—Saddapaññatti and Atthapaññatti which are undoubtedly relative terms. Saddapaññatti is a name (of a thing) which, when expressed in words, or represented by a sign is called a 'term'. It is synonymous with nāma-paññatti. Atthapaññatti is the idea or notion of the attributes of a thing made known or represented by a name. In other words, it is equivalent to 'concept' and is subdivided into various classes. Paññatti has been distinguished from Paramattha in the sense that the former is nominal and conceptual whereas the latter is real.

The object comprehending, as it does, the subject, is wider, more extensive than the latter. This is probably one reason why greater prominence is given to the object paṭṭhāna. In Buddhism there is no actor apart from the action, no percipient apart from perception. In other words, there is no conscious subject behind consciousness.

Life and Ancient view.

'Like the current of the river' (nadi soto viya) is the Buddhist idea of existence. For no two consecutive moments is the fabric of the body the same, and this theory of the ceaseless change or flux is called anicca-dhamma which is applied alike to the body and the mind, or the Being and thought respectively. The dividing line between these two is termed mano-dvāra, the Threshold of Consciousness. Life, then, in the Buddhist view of things, is like an ever-changing river, having its source in birth, its goal in death, receiving from the tributary streams of sense constant accretions to its flood, and ever-dispensing to the world around it the thought-stuff it has gathered by the way.

Primary classification of Consciousness.

Subliminal consciousness is either kāma, rūpa or arūpa. Supraliminal consciousness is normal, supernormal, and transcendental. Normal consciousness is termed kāmacitta, so called because desire or kāma prevails on the plane of existence. Supernormal consciousness is termed Mahaggatācitta because it has reached the sublime state, and is further distinguished as rūpa, or arūpacitta.

Universal mental properties and classes of Consciousness.

Consciousness in this fourfold classification is primarily composed of seven mental properties (cetasikas)—namely, contact (phassa), feeling (vedanā), perception (saññā), will or volition (cetanā), oneness of object (ekaggatā), psychic life (jīvitindriya), and attention (manasikāra). These seven mental properties are termed sabbacitta-sādhāraṇa or universals, because they are common to every class and state of consciousness, or every separate act of mind or thought. There are forty-five different properties distinguishing one class from another. And those, in varying combinations, give rise to the eighty-nine classes of consciousness enumerated in Part I of the Abhidhammattha-Saṅgaha, or according to a broader classification, one hundred and twenty-one. The seven mental properties have been enumerated above ; there are, besides these, six particular specific or accidental properties. These are vitakka, vicāra, adhimokkha, viriya, pīti, and chanda. The four universal bad cetasikas or properties are moha, ahirika, anottappa, and uddhacca. Besides these, there are also two specific cetasikas or properties, lobha and diṭṭhi. All these properties are discussed and explained in the body of the book.

Of these and other classes of consciousness making up a total of eighty-nine, some function as causes or karma, some as resultants or vipāka,

Classes and orders of Consciousness grouped.

and some are non-causal or kriyā. Besides these three classes, there are two elements in every consciousness, the Constant and the Variable. The form of consciousness is the constant element, and is opposed to the matter of consciousness which constitutes the variable element. But in Buddhism, both subject and object are variable at every moment; and there are several forms of consciousness each of which may be designated a 'process of thought' whenever it takes place as a fact. To every separate state of consciousness which takes part in a process of thought as a functional state, either in the subjective form of the stream of being, or in the objective form of a conscious act of mind or thought, there are three phases—genesis (uppāda), development (thiti), and dissolution (bhaṅga)—each of which is explained and discussed by the author in his Manual in all its processes and stages.

Internal Intuition and Reflection proper (Suddhamanodvāravithi).

The possibility of the 'internal' presentation of all the six classes of objects mentioned above is that a sensation can be experienced, the Buddhists believe, without the corresponding objective stimulus. The possibility of Reflection proper is attributed to the relation termed 'proximate sufficient cause' by virtue of which (*a*) a sense impression once experienced in a sense cognition by way of the five doors, or (*b*) a previous experience of all internal intuition or cognition by way of the mind-door, or (*c*) the idea once formed in the sequels of either, can never be lost. There are different processes of reflection in connection with Things Seen (diṭṭha). But when an object that has not been actually sensed is constructed out of, and connected with these seen objects, it is termed 'object associated with things seen' (diṭṭhi-saṁbandha). And the process of thought connected therewith is classed in the category of objects associated with things seen. The object constructed out of and connected with Things Heard (suta object) is termed 'object associated with things heard' (suta-saṁbandha). Any object constructed out of Things Cogitated (viññāta) and connected therewith is termed 'associated with things cogitated' (viññāta-saṁbandha). Any object in the category of Things Seen, Heard or Cogitated may either be past, present or future. When it is present, it is intuited as a vivid reality. The same forms hold good for all kinds of thought or reflection.

Memory and Changing Personality.

How is memory possible, if the object be not the same for any two consecutive moments in life? The answer is given in detail by the author. Each mental state is related to the next in at least four different modes of relation (paccaya):—Proximity (anantara), Contiguity (samanantara), Absence (natthi), and Abeyance (avigata). This fourfold relation is understood to mean that each expired state renders service to the next. In other words, each, on passing away, gives up the whole of its energy to its successor: and this is how the memory is helped and retained.

The ethical aspect of apperception of Javana.

The stage of apperception pertains to that active side of an existence (kamma-bhāva), which determines the passive side (upapatti-bhāva) of the next existence. The apperceptional act is thus a free, determining, causal act of thought, as distinguished from the mental states, which are fixed, determined and resultant acts (vipāka) of kamma. Volition, under favourable circumstances, is transformed into kamma. But volition (cetanā) in apperception on occasion of sense (pañca-dvārika-javana) cannot possibly become kamma. Hence we must look to the volition involved in reflective or representative apperception (manodvārika-javana) for kamma, which according to the different characters of volition is classed in different types or varieties with distinct characteristics.

Interesting though is the phenomenon of dream,

it is conspicuous in the Abhidhammattha-Saṅgaha by its absence. Scattered references and sometimes systematic explanations have here and there been made in Buddhist works regarding forms of dream-thought, dreams-classified, theories of dreams, relation of dream to sleep, etc.

Dream Consciousness.

The first essential qualification of the process of thought transition from the normal to the super-normal is 'purity of virtue or morals'. The next is meditation and concentration of thought. There are four moments of apperception during the transitional stage from normal to super-normal consciousness. The first is termed 'preparation', the second 'success', which is followed by the third called 'adaptation'. After the last moment of 'adoption' normal consciousness is cut off by the super-normal, and the transitional stage is superseded by the latter, known as the first Jhāna, and for one thought-moment, the person attaining it experiences ecstacy. Attainment in Jhāna is thus a very important psychological moment, marking an epoch in his mental experience for the person who succeeds in commanding it. Jhāna is usually classified in five stages, and in the fifth stage ecstatic concentration reaches its full development with the help of the continued voluntary exercise of the mind on an after-image to which it has been directed.

Higher consciousness or rūpacitta.

To attain super-intellectual powers (abhiññā) for an adept in the Fifth Jhāna, it will be necessary for him to go through a course of mental training in fourteen processes. Super-normal powers of will or Iddhi-vidhā may then be developed by means of the so-called four bases of Iddhi which involve respectively the development of Four dominant or predominant principles of purpose, effort, knowledge, and wisdom. There are ten classes of Iddhi known to Buddhism, the last three of which

Mental training and iddhi-pāda.

constitute the Iddhi-vidhā, and are used as a basis for the willing process.

Arūpa Jhānas.

With a slight difference in procedure in mental attitudes and mood of thought, the same forms of the transitional, inductive, or sustained and retrospective processes of Fifth Rūpa-Jhāna obtain in the case of the Four Arūpa-Jhānas. When an adept in the Fifth Rūpa-Jhāna, who has repeatedly induced the same through any one of the ten circles, with the exception of space, erroneously believes that all physical pain and misery are due to the existence of the body, and reflects on the relative grossness of this Jhāna, he wishes to attain the First Arūpa-Jhāna, which he considers to be very calm and serene.

Way to emancipation.

A person who wishes to transcend the experience of this conditioned world must first of all cultivate 'purity of views' or diṭṭhi-visuddi. Next, he must cultivate in succession, 'purity of transcending doubt' or Kaṅkhā-vitaraṇa-visuddhi, 'Ten modes of Insight' or Vipassanā-ñāṇas or in other words the contemplative insight, enumerated and explained in the Text. All these ten kinds of insight are collectively termed 'purity of intellectual culture'. The matured insight of equanimity receives the special designation of 'insight of discernment leading to uprising', because it invariably leads to the Path, conceived as a 'Rising out of'. It is also styled as the 'mouth or gate of Emancipation' (Vimokkha-mukha).

Emancipation.

Emancipation has a triple designation, namely, the 'Signless' or animitta, the 'Undesired' or appaṇihita, and the 'void' or suññatā. Emancipation itself, whether of the Path, the Fruit, or Nibbāna, also receives the same triad of names, according as it is preceded by the contemplation of things by 'uprising discernment' as either impermanent, or evil, or substantial.

The purity of insight which is the gateway of

Emancipation is also called Path-insight. One who has attained perfect purity of insight cuts off the heritage of the average man and evolves the lineage of the Transcendental. It is followed by a single moment of Path-consciousness by which the first of the Four Noble Truths is clearly discerned. Error and doubt are got rid of, Nibbāna is intuited, and the eightfold Path-constituents are cultivated. These four simultaneous functions correspond to the Four Noble Truths. Just like the Four Noble Truths, there are four stages of the Path, which are called Four Paths. The attainer of the first is termed Sotāpanna who will have as yet to undergo seven more rebirths in the Kāmaloka ; the attainer of the second is termed Sakadāgamī who will have one more such rebirth. But the complete destruction of these two does not permit of another rebirth in the case of the Anāgāmī or Never returner of the Third Path. The wisdom of the Highest or Supreme Path is the same mental order of intelligence developed into the Perfected view of the highest order and is the last stage of 'purity of insight'.

**Path Consciousness.**

Death is assigned to one of four causes: (1) the exhaustion of the force of the reproductive (janaka) kamma that has given rise to the existence in question, (2) the expiry of the maximum life-term possible for this particular generation, (3) the combination of both these causes, (4) the action of a stronger arresting kamma that suddenly cuts off the reproductive kamma before the latter's force is spent or before the expiry of the life-term.

**Death.**

The decease of the Arhant is according to Buddhist philosophy, the Final Death. If the Arhant be of the class known as 'dry-visioned' (sukkha-vipassaka) who does not practise Jhāna, his final death, which takes place on the kāma plane, occurs after apperception or retention of impressions. If he be proficient in Jhāna, final death may occur (*a*) after sustained

**Final Death.**

Jhāna; or (*b*) after apperception in subsequent retrospect; or (*c*) after the moment of 'super-intellectual' knowledge (abhiññā); or finally, (*d*) after retrospection following the attainment of the Topmost Fruit.

Nāmarūpaparic-cheda.

The Nāmarūpaparicheda is another Abhidhamma manual written by Anuruddha Mahāthera. It consists of 1,885 stanzas dealing with name and form.

Nāmarūpasamāsa.

The Nāmarūpasamāsa was written by Thera Khemācariya mostly in prose. It deals with citta and cetasikakathā.

Sutta Saṁgaha.

The Sutta Saṁgaha is a later manual or compendium of select suttas and is primarily intended for those beginners who desire to have a knowledge of the Pāli scriptural texts in a nut-shell.

Paritta.

The Paritta or Mahāparitta, a small collection of texts gathered from the Sutta Piṭaka, is more widely known by the Burmese laity of all classes than any other Pāli book. The Paritta, learned by heart and recited on appropriate occasions, is to conjure various evils, physical and moral. Some of the miscellaneous extracts that make up the collection are of purely religious and ethical character. The use of the Paritta is said to have had the Buddha's sanction. The victory of the holy men was accomplished by the Paritta (Mabel Bode, The Pāli Literature of Burma, pp. 3-4).

The Kammavācā[1] is a convenient title for the collection of certain set forms of speech followed or to be followed in conducting the business of the Saṁgha either at the time of conferring ordination or at the time of holding a synod or a council.

[1] *Cf.* "A new Kammavācā" by T. W. Rhys Davids and Clauson, F. Speigel's Kammavākya, Palice et Latine ed. Vgl Ferner Dickson, J.R.A.S., Vol. VII, New Series; Upasampadā-kammavācā, a Pāli text with a translation and notes by J. F. Dickson, J.R.A.S., 1875.

These set forms are but excerpts from the Vinaya Mahāvagga and Cullavagga, the utility of the Kammavācā text being no other than this, namely, that we have in it all put together in a handy and systematic form. There are various manuscripts of this text available in Burma, Ceylon, and Siam; some of the Mandalay manuscripts being very handsome written as they are in Burmese ritual or tamarind seed letters printed, with a thick black resinous gum. There is a collection of Kammavācās made by Herbert Baynes (*vide* J.R.A.S., 1892, Art. III). In Burmese Pāli collections we find no less frequently than the Paritta of the laity, the Kammavācā of the mendicant order. It goes without saying that the text of Kammavācā is a text of a purely Buddhist ecclesiastical use.

Sīmālaṅkārapakaraṇa.

In the Kalyāṇī stone inscriptions of Dhamma Bedi of Pegu, we find mention of the Sīmālaṅkārapakaraṇa amongst the earlier authoritative texts bearing upon the subject of sīmā or sanctified boundary of the Buddhist ecclesiastical order. It is not quite clear from the reference if the Sīmālaṅkārapakaraṇa was not the same work as the Sīmālaṅkārasaṁgaha mentioned in the same lithic record of the 15th century A.D. It is evident from these records as well as from a later work, the Sīmāvivādavinicchayakathā that the proper erection and the determination of the sanctified boundary came to be considered as an effective means of the purification of the Buddhist holy order.

Khuddakasikkhā and Mūlasikkhā.

The Khuddakasikkhā and the Mūlasikkhā are the two short Vinaya manuals, written mostly in verse, a few passages occurring in prose. The Thera Dhammasiri, evidently a Sinhalese priest, is the author of the Khuddakasikkhā. But in the Burmese history of the piṭakas the Mūlasikkhā is ascribed to Dhammasiri and the Khuddakasikkhā, to another Sinhalese priest, Mahāsāmī by name. The authorship of the Khuddakasikkhā cannot be reasonably ascribed to any other person than Dhammasiri in view of the author's own statement in the following stanza :

> "Tena Dhammasirīkena Taṁbapaṇṇiyaketunā therena racitā Dhammavinayaññupasaṁsitā."

If we are to give credence to the Burmese tradition, there is no other alternative than regarding the Mūlasikkhā as a work not of Dhammasiri but of Mahāsāmī. It is also difficult to accept the Burmese tradition according to which the two manuals were written about 920 years after the demise of the Buddha.[1] Judged by the language and general style of the two manuals, these would seem to be literary productions of a much later age. We have already given an idea of their contents (ante p. 79). Only one important point which remains to be noticed is the significance of the Mūlasikkhā used as a title of one of the two manuals. It is suggested in the opening stanza of the Mūlasikkhā that the title has no other significance than this, that the manual presents the necessary lessons on the Vinaya rules and discipline in the language of the original texts, that is to say, in Pāli which is the language of the piṭakas :

> "Bhikkhunā navakenādo mūlabhāsāya sikkhitum yannimittaṁ pavesanto bhikkhu maggattaye cuto."

---

[1] J.P.T.S., 1882, p. 87.

CHAPTER VIII

# PĀLI LITERARY PIECES

## Introduction

In the present chapter we have to deal with seven metrical compositions, the Anāgatavaṁsa, the Jinacarita, the Telakaṭāhagāthā, the Pajjamadhu, the Rasavāhinī, the Saddhammopāyana, and the Pañcagatidīpana, which were evidently the literary productions of Ceylon[1] and which belonged mostly to the closing period of Pāli literary activities of Ceylon ranging from the tenth or eleventh to the fourteenth or fifteenth century A.D. Amongst them the Anāgatavaṁsa stands as a supplement to the canonical work, Buddhavaṁsa ; the Jinacarita occupies the same place in Pāli as the Buddhacarita in the Sanskrit Buddhist literature, the Telakaṭāhagāthā and the Pajjamadhu represent two interesting examples of the Śataka type of poetry, the Pañcagatidīpana and the Saddhamopāyana are written for the edification of certain select topics of Buddhism and the Rasavāhinī is a most charming book of folk-tales narrated in elegant and simple style, in prose and in verse. Most of these works show a tendency towards the sanskritisation of Pāli and display that amount of literary excellence and poetic imagination as may be expected from the people of Ceylon in general and the Buddhist monks in particular.

Anāgatavaṁsa.

The Anāgatavaṁsa edited by Minayeff for the P.T.S., is based upon four Burmese manuscripts which do not agree in their contents. One manuscript embodies recension of this work in prose and in verse, and in another

[1] It is only in the case of the Anāgatavaṁsa that opinions may differ.

we have it entirely in verse while in a third we have quite a different work in prose dealing with ten future Buddhas including Metteyya and devoting a chapter to each of them. The possibility of the last mentioned work is suggested in the closing verses of that mixed recension of the Anāgatavaṁsa which is found in prose and in verse :—

> " Metteyyo, Uttamo, Rāmo, Pasenadi Kosalo'-bhibhū
> Dīghasoṇī ca Saṁkacco Subho Todeyya brāhmaṇo
> Nāḷāgiripalaleyyo Bodhisattā ime dasa
> Anukkamena sambodhiṁ pāpuṇissanti'nāgate'ti ".
>
> (Anāgatavaṁsa, J.P.T.S., 1886, p. 37.)

So far as the mixed recension goes, this text is written in prose style of the suttas in the nikāyas. The prose passages are intervened or followed by certain verses, the general tenor of which is somewhat different from those generally met with in the nikāyas. The text is composed of a dialogue between Sāriputta and Buddha and deals with the subject of gradual decline and disappearance of Buddhism, its literature, glory, and influence in time to come rather than with the life and career of the future Buddha, Metteyya. Viewed in this light, this text of the Anāgatavaṁsa may justly be regarded as a supplement or sequel to the suttas dealing with Anāgatabhayāni, " future dangers of the faith ", the discourses recommended by King Asoka in his Bhābrū Edict for a constant study by the Buddhists, both monks and laity. Whether such a prose dialogue as this was at any time incorporated in the nikāyas is a question to which no decisive answer may yet be given. It may suffice here to treat as a sequel to the Anāgatabhayasuttas and the texts dealing with the ten future Buddhas.

The text with which we are concerned is a work in verse. It is completed in 142 stanzas and which deals with the life and career of the future Buddha Metteyya. According to the Gandhavaṁsa the original Anāgatavaṁsa was the work of an elder named Kassapa (presumably the Citrakathi Kumāra Kassapa). The ascription of authorship to Kassapa is not however justified by the text itself, which is set forth as a dialogue between Sāriputta and the Buddha. It is composed apparently in the manner and style of the Buddhavaṁsa to which it was meant to serve, no doubt, as a supplement. A comparison between the following verses quoted from the two works may make their interconnection clear :—

1. Buddhavaṁsa—With regard to Buddha Vipassi :—

"Nagaraṁ Bandhumatī nāma Bandhumo nāma khattiyo mātā Bandhumatī nāma Vipassissa mahesino." (xx. v. 23.)

2. Anāgatavaṁsa :—

"Saṁgho nāma upāsako Saṁghā nāma upāsikā paccupessanti saṁbuddhaṁ caturāsītisahassato." (v. 61, J.P.T.S., 1886.)

Seeing that the account of future Buddha Metteyya is precluded from the extant Buddhavaṁsa scheme of the lives of 26 Buddhas including Metteyya, it will be reasonable to enquire if the Anāgatavaṁsa in its present form was not a later elaboration of a shorter account of Metteyya forming the closing section of the Buddhavaṁsa in its original form.

At the request of Sāriputta who desired to know about the future Buddha, the Buddha Gautama spoke in brief about Metteyya Buddha. The future Buddha would be born in India at Ketumatī in a brahmin family. He would be named Ajita and would possess immense wealth. He would enjoy worldly life for eight thousand years and then would forsake the world after having seen the four nimittas (Omens). Thousands of men and women would renounce the world with him. On the day of his retirement he would proceed to the great Bodhi tree. He would attain supreme enlightenment and then would set rolling the Wheel of Law. Many would escape worldly miseries by following the Dhamma which would be preached by the Buddha Metteyya.

Jinacarita. Jinacarita is a Pāli Kāvya consisting of more than 470 stanzas composed in different metres, some stanzas being of the atijagatī class, consisting of 13 syllables. It represents a poetic development in Pāli similar to that represented by the Buddhacarita in the Sanskrit Buddhist literature. Its theme, like that of the Buddhacarita, is the life of the Buddha and the narrative is chiefly based upon the Jātaka-nidānakathā. The slavish dependence on the prose narrative of the Nidānakathā has proved a handicap to a free expression of the poetic sentiment.

Mon. Duroiselle, to whom we owe the English edition and translation of the text, has aptly remarked that the poet has risen to heights placing him in the foremost rank among poets only in those places where he has broken through the slavish imitation and written from the depths of his own inspiration. In the opinion of Mon. Duroiselle, " the charm of the Jinacarita lies in its lighter style ; in the author's choice of graceful, and sometimes forcible, images ; in the art of his descriptions, the richness and, in some passages, the delicacy of his expressions ; qualities which go to make its reading refreshing and welcome after the laborious reading of heavy didactic poetry ". (Jinacarita, Introduction, p. ii.)

The influence of the Sanskrit Kavya poetry of India, particularly of the works of Kālidāsa, cannot be denied. We meet indeed in the Pāli Kavya with some images and comparisons " which are seldom found in Pāli, but are of frequent occurrence in Sanskrit works (e.g., the Kumārasambhava and Meghadūta). In a few instances Mon. Duroiselle has found also an echo of some of verses of the Mahābhārata:

Jinacarita—" Ko yaṁ Sakko nu kho Brahmā
Māro nāgo ti ādinā."
Mahābhārata—" Ko 'yan devo 'thavā yakṣo
gandharvo vā bhaviṣyati ?"
(III. 6, 52, Vanaparva.)

Without denying the intimate acquaintance of the author of the Jinacarita with classical Sanskrit poetry, we may point out that the type of stanzas quoted from the Mahābhārata is not such as not to be frequently met with in the Jātaka literature. And as far as the indebtedness of our author to Kālidāsa or to Aśvaghosa who paved the way for the former is concerned, we may equally maintain that the style of poetry developed either in the Buddhacarita of Aśvaghosa or in the Kumārasambhava of Kālidāsa, leads us back to the gāthās forming the prologue of the Nālakasutta in the Sutta Nipāta for its model.

In the Gandhavaṁsa and Saddhamma-saṅgaha the work has been ascribed to one Medhaṅkara. He was called Vanaratana Medhaṅkara, and was also the author of another Pāli book 'Payogasiddhi' and flourished under Bhuvaneka Bāhu 1st (1277-1288 A.D.[1]).

Its importance.

The Jinacarita, however, throws no new light on the life of the Master; and we can hardly expect such a thing from a purely devotional work such as this. But what is strikingly surprising is that the Jinacarita is unknown both in Burma and Siam.

[1] Jour. P.T.S., 1904-5, p. iv, Note on Medhaṅkara by T. W. Rhys Davids. But Mon. Charles Duroiselle thinks that " the poem was written in the monastery built by Vijayabāhu II, who ascended the throne in A.D. 1186 and was the immediate successor of the famous King Parākramabāhu ". Jinacarita, p. iii (edited and translated by C. Duroiselle, Rangoon, 1906). Read also " Jinacarita ", edited and translated by Dr. W. H. D. Rouse in the J.P.T.S., 1904-1905.

The Poem.

In the beautiful city of Amara, there was a Brahman youth, wise and compassionate, handsome and pleasant, by name Sumedha. Hankering after wealth and treasures he had none, for this bodily frame he had no attachment. He, therefore, left his pleasant house, went to the Himalayas, and there discovered the eight implements necessary for an ascetic. He put on the ascetic garb and within a week obtained the five High Powers and the eight Attainments, enjoying the bliss of mystic meditation. One day he came down from the sky, and lay himself down in a muddy portion of a road through which the Dīpaṅkara Buddha with his disciples was to pass. He, the Dīpaṅkara Buddha, was delighted at it, and foretold that the ascetic Sumedha, in times to come, should become a fully enlightened Buddha, by name Gotama. Sumedha did him homage, and then seated in meditation, he investigated those conditions that go to make a Buddha. Sumedha, searching for Nirvāṇa, endured many hardships while going through the continued succession of existences, fulfilling the virtue of charity. He fulfilled, moreover, the Perfections of Morality, of Self-abnegation, of wisdom, and all others, and came to the existence of Vessantara. Passing away thence, he was reborn in the city of Tusita, and afterwards had another rebirth in the city of Kapila through the noble King Suddhodana, and his Queen Māyā. He approached the bosom of Māyā, and at the time of his conception, various wonders took place all over the world. In her tenth month, while she was proceeding to the house of her relative, she brought forth the Sage in the Lumbini garden while she kept standing under a Sāla tree catching hold of a branch. The god Brahmā approached and received the child in a golden net, the child that was born unsullied as a priceless gem. From the hands of Brahmā and the angels, he stepped on to the ground, and gods and men approached and made offerings to him. Accompanied by a concourse of gods and men, he went to Kapilavastu and there a rejoicing of nature and men ensued for days and nights. In the Tāvatiṁsa heaven the hosts of angels rejoiced and sported and predicted that he, the child, would sit upon the Throne of Wisdom and become a Buddha. The ascetic Kalādeva, the spiritual adviser of King Suddhodana, went to the Tāvatiṁsa heaven, heard the cause of their rejoicings, came down to Suddhodana's palace, and wanted to see the child. The child was brought and instantly, the lotus-feet of the prince were fixed on the ascetic's head. Upon this, both Kalādeva and Suddhodana reverenced the soft lotus-feet. A second act of reverence was done by Suddhodana and other men and women of the royal house during the sowing festival when the child, the Wise One, had performed a miracle. The prince then began to grow day by day living as he did in three magnificent mansions provided for him. One day as he came out on chariot on the royal road, he saw in succession the representation of an old man, of a diseased man, and of a dead man. He then became free from attachment to the three forms of existence and on the fourth occasion, delighted in seeing pleasant representation of a monk. He then came back home and laid himself down on a costly couch, and nymph-like women surrounded him and performed various kinds of dances and songs. The Sage, however, did not relish them; and while the dancers fell asleep he bent upon retirement into solitude and free from attachment to the five worldly pleasures, called his minister and friend Channa to harness his horse. He then went to his wife's apartment and saw the sleeping son and mother and silently took leave of them. Descending from the palace he mounted his horse and silently came out of the gate which was opened up by the gods inhabiting it. Māra then came to thwart him from going by saying that on the seventh day hence, the divine wheel of a universal monarch should appear unto him. But, he, the Wise of the World, did not desire any sovereignty, but wanted to become a Buddha. Upon this Māra disappeared, and he proceeded towards the bank of the river Anomā where he dismounted himself and asked Channa to go back home with the horse and his ornaments. He then cut off his knot of hair with a sword ; the hair rose up into the air and Sakra received it with bent head and placed it in a gold casket to worship it. Next he put up the eight requisites of a monk and having spent seven days in the Anupiya mango grove in the joy of having left the world, went to Rājagaha and made his round for alms just enough for his sustenance. Leaving the town he went to the Pāṇḍava mountain and took the food. He was repeatedly approached by King Bimbisāra and offered the kingdom, but he declined it ; and retiring to a cloister practised unmatched hardships. All this was of no avail ; he, therefore, partook of material food and regaining bodily perfection, went to the foot of the Ajapāla banyan tree where he sat facing the east. Sujātā, a beautiful woman, mistook him for a sylvan deity and offered him a gold vessel of milk rice. The Sage took it, and having gone to the bank of the Nerañjarā river he ate the food, took his rest, and then in the evening went to the Bo-tree which he circumambulated keeping the tree to his right. To his astonishment, a throne appeared, on which he took his seat facing the east, and promised that he would give up his efforts to attain Supreme Enlightenment even if his flesh, blood, bones, sinews, and skin dried up. On his head the Mahā-Brahmā held an umbrella. Suyāma, the king of gods, fanned a splendid yak's tail, and god Pañcasikha, the snake-king Kāla and thirty-two nymphs all kept standing and serving the Sage. Māra, then, creating unto himself a thousand dreadful arms, and surrounding himself by a manifold faced army, approached the Bo-tree. And at his approach the gods made good their escape. Māra created a terrific wind with a fierce roar, then the terrible torrent of large rocks, and brought on a most dreadful darkness, but each in succession was of little avail. All these turned to good account and the Blessed One did not even show any sign of consternation. The Evil One then threw his disc, hurled rocky peaks, yet the Unconquerable sat motionless as before. Baffled in his attempts he approached the All-Merciful and asked him to rise from his seat. The Blessed One enquired of the witness about his seat and Māra, showing his army, told that they were his witnesses and asked in his turn who had been the witness of Siddhārtha. Siddhārtha then stretched his hands towards the earth and called the earth goddess to witness. She gave forth thousands of roars and Māra caught by the fear fled with his army. Having dispersed Māra's hosts, he remained seated still on the immoveable seat, and in the first watch of the night he obtained the excellent knowledge of the past, and in the middle watch the Eye Divine. In the last watch, he gained thorough knowledge of the concatenation of causes and effects, and at dawn he became perfectly Enlightened Buddha. Yet he did not rise up from his seat, but to remove the doubts of the gods remained seated there for seven days and performed a double miracle. Then after the investigation of the Pure Law, he at the foot of the goat-herd's banyan tree, caused to wither the face of Māra's daughter, and, at the foot of the Mucalinda tree, caused to blossom the mind of the snake-king. And, at last, at the foot of the Rājāyatana tree, he enjoyed the bliss of meditation. Then the king of the Law, entreated by Brahmā Sahaṁpati, wanted to fill the world with the free gift of the nectar of the Good Law. With this object, he travelled to the splendid Deer Park where the sages and mendicants made him a saint, and came to acknowledge him as the Sanctified, the Perfectly Enlightened, the Tathāgata. To the Elders of the Park, he delivered a discourse on the establishment of the kingdom of Truth, and dispelled their ignorance. He thus set the Wheel of the Law in motion for the good of the world by delivering the people from the mighty bond of transmigration. On his way next to Uruvela, he gave to some thirty Bhaddavaggiya princes the immortal draught of the Three Paths ; and conferred on them the gift of ordination. He then went to Laṭṭhivana Park and there presented King Bimbisāra with the immortal draught of true doctrine. Thence he proceeded to the Veluvana Park and dwelt there in a hermitage. Then King Suddhodana, having heard that his own son had attained to Supreme Knowledge, sent his minister Udāyi to bring his son back to him. Udāyi came with a thousand followers and hearing the Master preach renounced the world and entered upon the path to sainthood. He then made known to the Master the desire of Suddhodana to see him, and requested to preach the Law to his kith and kin. The Buddha agreed to it and went to Kapilavastu where he was worshipped by Suddhodana and his relatives. But seeing that the young ones did not greet him, he performed a miracle at the sight of which Suddhodana was filled with joy. Then he went to the royal palace and preached the sweet doctrines to the king and hundreds of fair royal women. Next he extinguished the great grief in the heart of Bimbā or Yasodharā, his wife ; and ordained prince Nanda even before the three festivals, marriage, ceremonial sprinkling and entering on the house, had taken place. When his own son Rāhula followed next for the sake of an inheritance, the Wise One ordained him too.

After this he went to Sītāvana at Rājagaha where he preached to a merchant of Sāvatthī, named Sudatta, who attained the fruit of the First Path. Sudatta then went back to Sāvatthī, and there selected a park of Prince Jeta for the residence of the Blessed One. He (better known as Anāthapiṇḍika) bought this for a crore of gold pieces for the Teacher's sake alone, and built there a chamber and a noble monastery for the abode of the Master and his followers. He also beautified it with tanks and gardens, etc., and then inviting the Teacher to the spot dedicated to him the park and the monastery. The Buddha accepted the gift and thanked Sudatta for it, preaching to him the great benefit which lies in the giving of monasteries.

Residing there, he spent his days going here and there and beating the great drum of the Law. In the first season, he dwelt in the Deer Park in the Benares city. In the second, third, and fourth seasons he dwelt in the lovely Veluvana at Rājagaha. In the fifth season, he made his abode in the great wood near Vesālī. In the sixth, he dwelt on the great mountain Makula, and in the seventh in the cool and spacious rocky seat of Indra. In the eighth, ninth, tenth, eleventh, and twelfth seasons, he dwelt respectively in the delightful wood of Bhesakalā, in the Kosambī silk cotton wood, in goodly Pāraleyya, and in the Brahman villages of Nālā and Verañjā. In the thirteenth season, he lived on the beautiful Cāliya mountain, and in the fourteenth, in fair and lovely Jetavana. In the fifteenth, sixteenth, seventeenth, eighteenth, and nineteenth seasons, the Wise One made his abode respectively in the great Nigrodha monastery on a large hill at Kapilavatthu in the city of Ālavaka, in Rājagaha, and twice on the great mount Cāliya. In the twentieth season, he took up his abode in Rājagaha; and for the rest twenty-five years of his life, he made his abode in Sāvatthī and Jetavana. Thus for forty-five years, the Blessed One preached his sweet doctrine, bringing happiness to men, and freeing all the world and the gods from the great bond of transmigration.

The book ends with a prayer of the author in which he gives out his pious wishes to be born in the Tusita heaven, to be born contemporaneously with the great being, the future Buddha, to be able to give food, drink, alms, and monasteries to the Wise One and so forth, and to become at least a Buddha himself.

Telakaṭāhagāthā.

The Telakaṭāhagāthā is a small poem in 98 stanzas on the vanity of human life. It contains some of the fundamental doctrines of Buddhism. The verses are written in chaste language. They represent the religious meditations and exhortations of a great thera named Kalyāṇiya who was condemned to be cast into a cauldron of boiling oil on suspicion of his having been accessory to an intrigue with the Queen-consort of King Kalani Tissa who reigned at Kelaṇiya in 306–207 B.C.[1] A reference to this story can be traced in the Mahāvaṁsa, the Rasavāhinī and the Sinhalese work, the Saddhammālaṅkāra, which is a compilation from the Rasavāhinī.[2] The incident on which the poem is based is somewhat differently narrated also in the Kākavaṇṇatissāraññavatthu. The author of this work is unknown. A careful study of the poem shows that the author was well acquainted with the texts and commentaries of the Buddhist scriptures. This work mentions the three refuges, death, impermanence, sorrows, soullessness of beings, evils of committing bad deeds, fourfold protection, and exhorts all to practise dhamma strenuously and attain salvation. It then discusses paṭiccasamuppāda (dependent origination) and points out that nothing happens in this world without any cause. Avijjā or ignorance is the cause of bad deed which leads to birth and which in turn is the cause of manifold miseries such as old age and death. So every one should practise dhamma by doing good deeds and thus escape from worldly miseries.

The charm of the style of composition lies in the balanced rhythm of the lines and alliterations, a literary art that may be seen developing itself through the stanzas of such earlier poems as Ratana

[1] G. P. Malalasekera, The Pāli Literature of Ceylon, p. 162.
[2] J.P.T.S., 1884, p. 49.

Sutta in the Khuddakapāṭha and Sutta Nipāta and the Narasīhagāthā presupposed by the Jātaka commentaries.

(1) Telakaṭāhagāthā, stanza No. 3:

> Sopānamālaṁ amalaṁ tidasālayassa
> Saṁsārasāgarasamuttaranāya setuṁ
> Sabbāgatībhayavivajjitakhemamaggaṁ
> Dhammaṁ namassatha sadā muninā
> paṇītaṁ.

(2) Ratana Sutta, v. 222:

> Yānīdha bhūtāni samāgatāni
> bhummāni vā yāni va antalikkhe,
> sabbe va bhūtā sumanā bhavantu,
> atho pi sakkacca suṇantu bhāsitaṁ.

Though in Goonaratne's edition published in J.P.T.S., 1884, the poem contains 98 stanzas, it may be presumed from its general style and purpose that it was meant to represent a Pāli sataka consisting of a hundred stanzas. The poem, as we now have it, is divided into nine sections, each section dealing with a particular topic of Buddhism, Ratanattaya, Maraṇānussati, Aniccalakkhaṇa, Dukkhalakkhaṇa, Anattalakkhaṇa, Asubhalakkhaṇa, Duccarita-ādinavā, Caturārakkhā, and Paṭiccasamuppāda. The sataka type of poetry came into vogue with the popularity of the three famous satakas, the Sriṅgāra, the Vairāgya, and Nirvāṇa, composed by so great a poet as Bhartrihari. Among the Buddhist satakas, the one which may rank as a high class of poetry is no doubt the Bodhicaryāvatāra of Śāntideva. Although the aim of the satakas, whether found in Sanskrit or in Pāli is didactic like that of the Pāli Dhammapada or the Śāntiparva of the Mahābhārata, the characteristic difference of the *Centuries* lies in their conscious attempt to give expression to individual moral or religious experiences. This differential feature of the satakas has been well brought out in the following apology of Śāntideva in the opening verses of his Bodhicaryāvatāra.

> " Na me parārtha cintā, samano vāsayituṁ
> kritaṁ mamedaṁ
> Mama tāvadanena yāti vriddhiṁ, kuśalaṁ
> bhāvayituṁ prasādavegaḥ
> Atha matsamadhātureva paśyed aparo'
> pyenamato'pi sārthako'yaṁ."

By this one must understand that the object of a sataka is not so much to instruct others as to manifest one's own self in the hope that those " who are like-natured, like-minded, and like-visioned will care to look at the (matter as the author has) viewed it and may, perhaps, derive some benefit from it " (Barua's Gaya and Buddhagaya, p. xi). We mean to say that in the satakas, the didactic aim has been subservient to the purpose of self-expression, a feature which is noticeable in certain Psalms of early Buddhist Brethren and Sisters.

Pajjamadhu.

The Pajjamadhu is a poem composed of 104 stanzas in praise of the Buddha. Buddhappiya, a pupil of Ānanda, is the author of this work. He is also the author of the Pāli grammar known as the Rūpasiddhi. " We may safely premise ", says Goonaratne, " that it was composed at the same time as the Rūpasiddhi to which scholars give 1100 A.D. as the probable date".[1] The author has given his name and pupilage in verse 103 of this poem :

> " Ānanda raññā ratanādi mahā yatinda
> Niccappa buddha padumappiya sevi naṅgī
> Buddhappiyena ghana buddha guṇappiyena
> Therālinā racita Pajjamadhum pi bantu."

The language is sanskritised Pāli and some of the verses are puzzling. There is a gloss in Sinhalese on the entire poem but it is verbose and rather diffuse in its explanations. This poem may be

---

[1] J.P.T.S., 1887, p. 1.

regarded as another example of sataka in Pāli with four stanzas in excess. The first 69 verses describe the beauty of the Buddha and the remaining verses are written in praise of his wisdom concluded with a panegyric on the order and nirvāṇa. It is lacking in the vigour of poetical imagination and its style is laboured and artificial and is far from fulfilling the promise of sweetness of poetry suggested in its title Pajjamadhu.

Rasavāhinī.

The Rasavāhinī is a collection of 103 tales written in easy Pāli, the first forty relating to the incidents which happened in Jambudīpa and the rest in Ceylon. A Sinhalese edition of this work has been brought out by M. S. Unnanse. The text with Sinhalese interpretation by B. Devarakkhita has been published in Colombo, 1917. The P.T.S., London, has undertaken to bring out an edition of this work in Roman character. Its date is unknown, but at the conclusion the author gives us a clue which helps us in determining it to be in all probability in the first half of the 14th century A.D. It is considered to be a revision of an old Pāli translation made from an original compilation by Raṭṭhapāla Thera of the Mahāvihāra in Ceylon. Vedeha, the author of the Rasavāhinī, gives us an account of the Vanavāsī School to which he belonged.[1] The late H. Nevill suggests that the Sahassavatthuppakaraṇa still extant in Burma, formed the basis for the Pāli Rasavāhinī.[2] This work throws much light on the manners, customs, and social conditions of ancient India and Ceylon. It contains materials of historical importance and as such is widely read in Ceylon. This work has been edited and translated by P. E. Pavolini.[3] There is a glossary on the Rasavāhinī called the Rasavāhinīgaṇṭhi. The verses of this text with a word-for-word Sinhalese

[1] Malalasekera, The Pāli Literature of Ceylon, p. 210.
[2] *Ibid.*, p. 129.
[3] Societe Asiatica Italiana, 1896.

translation by Dharmaratna have been published in 1913.

Literature on the Rasavāhinī.

Buddhist legends of Asoka and his time translated from the Pāli of the Rasavāhinī by Lakṣmaṇa Śāstrī with a prefatory note by H. C. Norman (J.R.A.S., 1910) and Zwei Erzahlungen aus der Rasavāhinī, Von. Sten Kono (Deutsche morgenlandische Gesellschaft, Zeitschrift, Leipzig)—II settimo capitolo della Rasavāhinī by P. E. Pavolini (Societe Asiatica Italiana, Giornale, Firanze, 1895), should be consulted. Die Zweite dekade der Rasavāhinī (M. and W. Geiger), Munchen, 1918, with translation deserves mention.

Saddhammopāyana.

The Saddhammopāyana edited for the P.T.S. by Richard Morris and published in the J.P.T.S., 1887, is a most notable work on Buddhism. It is written entirely in verse and completed in 629 stanzas. It begins with a prologue and is closed with an epilogue, the author introducing himself in the prologue under the name and designation of Brahmacārī Buddhasomapiya.[1] He was undoubtedly a Buddhist teacher of Ceylon. The work, as its title implies, deals with the Way of the Good Faith. We can broadly divide it into two parts, the first of which contains an edification of the dangers or disadvantages of things moral and the second, that the rewards or advantages (ānisaṁsa) of things moral. The author dwells on such topics of the saddhamma as akkhaṇa, dasa akusala, petadukkha, pāpādinava, puññaphala, dānānisaṁsa, and the rest. Though the views of the author are not in any way new, the manner of treatment of each topic is masterly, and his style is at once easy, dignified, and restrained. Such a treatment of the subject cannot be expected from one who had not long pondered over it and thoroughly assimilated the fundamental

[1] Nāmato Buddhasomassa piyasabrahmacārino—Saddhammopāyana, verse 3.

principles of Buddhism. He has nowhere slavishly followed any earlier authority—a fact which may be clearly brought home to the reader by a comparison between the Praises of sīla (sīlānisaṁsa) in Buddhaghosa's Visuddhimagga and those in the Saddhammopāyana :—

(1) Visuddhimagga—

"Na Gaṅgā, Yamunā cāpi, Sarabhū vā Sarasvatī,
ninnagā vā' ciravatī Mahī vā pi mahānadī
Sakkuṇanti visodhetuṁ taṁ malaṁ idha pāṇinaṁ,
Visodhayati sattānaṁ yaṁ ve sīlajalaṁ malaṁ."

(Vol. I, p. 10.)

(2) Saddhammopāyana—

Idaṁ hi sīlaratanaṁ idhaloke parattha ca
ānisaṁsavare datvā pacchā pāpeti nibbutiṁ
Paccakkhaṁ hīnajaccaṁ hi accantoḷāravaṁsajā
narindā sīlasampannaṁ namassantīha bhāvato.

(Verses 415–416.)

Pañcagatidīpana.

The Pañcagatidīpana has been edited by M. Leon Feer (J.P.T.S., 1884, pp. 152–161). It is written in 114 stanzas. This work tells us of the five destinies which are in store of beings according as they commit good or bad deeds in this world by body, mind, etc. This text furnishes us with an interesting piece of information regarding different hells, namely, Sañjīva, Kālasutta, Saṁghāta, Roruva, Mahāroruva, Tapa, Mahātapa, and Avīci. Those who kill and cause living beings to be killed out of avarice, delusion, fear, and anger must go to the Sañjīva hell. For one thousand years they suffer in this hell being subjected to continual torments without losing life and consciousness. Those who cause injury or do harmful deeds to friends and parents, speak falsehood and backbite others must go to the Kālasutta hell.

In this hell they are cut to pieces with burning saws. Those who kill goats, sheep, jackals, hares, deer, pigs, etc., are consigned to the Sanghāta hell, where they are huddled up in one place and then beaten to death. Those who cause mental and bodily pain to others or cheat others or are misers have to go to the Roruva hell, where they make terrible noise while being burnt in the terrific fire of hell. Those who steal things belonging to gods, brahmans, and preceptors, those who misappropriate the property of others kept in trust with them, and those who destroy things entrusted to their care are cast into the Mahāroruva hell, where they make a more terrible noise while being consumed by a fire fiercer than that in the Roruva hell. Those who cause the death of living beings by throwing them into the Dāvadaha fire, etc., have to go to the Tapa hell, where they have to suffer being burnt in a dreadful fire. Those who cause the death of beings by throwing them into greater Dāvadaha fire must go to the Mahātapa hell, where they have to suffer still more by being burnt in a greater fire. Those who injure men of great virtue and those who kill parents, arahats, or preceptors must sink into the Avīci hell, where they suffer being burnt in such a terrible fire that would consume even the hardest things. In this hell there is not a least wave of happiness, it is therefore called the Avīci or waveless. Besides these hells, mention is made of a hell called the Patāpana, where people suffer by being burnt in fires that are much more terrific than those of the Tapa and Mahātapa hells. Each hell has four Ussadanirayas, viz., Miḷhakūpa, Kukkula, Asipattavana, and Nadi. Those who are in the Mahāniraya have to proceed to Miḷhakūpa when released. In this terrible hell they are bitten by a host of worms. Thence they go to Kukkula where they are fried like mustard seeds on a burning pan. Coming out of Kukkula they find before them a beautiful tree of fruits and flowers where they take shelter for relief from torments. As soon as they reach the tree they are attacked by birds of prey such as vultures, owls, etc. They are killed by these animals which they make a repast on their flesh. Those who are traitors must go to the Asipattavana where they are torn and eaten up by bitches, vultures, owls, etc. Those who steal money will also suffer in this hell by being compelled to swallow iron balls and molten brass. Those who kill cows and oxen, suffer in this hell by being eaten up by dogs having large teeth. Those who kill aquatic animals will have to go to the fearful Vaitaraṇī river where the water is as hot as a molten brass. Those who prostitute justice by accepting bribes will be cut to pieces in an iron wheel. Those who destroy paddy have to suffer in the Kukkula hell. Those who cherish anger in their heart are reborn as swans and pigeons. Those who are haughty and angry are reborn as snakes. Those who are jealous and miserly are reborn as monkeys. Those who are miserly, irritable, and fond of backbiting are reborn as tigers, bears, cats, etc. Those who are charitable but angry at the same time are reborn as big Garuḍas. Those who are deceitful and charitable are reborn as great Asuras. Those who neglect their friends on account of their pride are reborn as dogs and asses. Those who are envious, cherish anger, or become happy at sight of sufferings of others are reborn in Yamaloka and the demon world. (Cf. the description of hell in the Mārkaṇḍeya Purāṇa.)

There is nothing new to be learnt from this poem, new in the sense of that which is different from what we read in some of the Jātakas and suttas and particularly in the canonical text, Petavatthu. The real literary value of this poem consists in the simplicity of its diction and the handy form which is peculiar to a later digest of doctrines that are old.

## CHAPTER IX

# PĀLI GRAMMARS, LEXICOGRAPHIES, AND WORKS ON PROSODY, ETC.

Vyākaraṇa is the accepted Indian term to denote a book of grammar. This very term was used to denote one of the six Vedāṅgas, or sciences or treatises auxiliary to the four Vedas. We have in the ancient vocabulary another term to denote another amongst the six Vedāṅgas, namely, the Chandas or treatise or treatises on metre or prosody. The treatises on Alaṅkāra or Poetics were later offshoots of the treatises on grammar. The beginnings of lexicography (abhidhāna) can similarly be traced in the Nigraṇṭha sections of the treatises on exegetical etymology—the Nirukta denoting another amongst the six Vedāṅgas. Corresponding to the Sanskrit Vyākaraṇa we have the Pāli Veyyākaraṇa, counted among the nine types of literary texts or compositions (navaṅgaṁ satthu-sāsanaṁ). But the Pāli term, as explained by Buddhaghosa and other Buddhist commentators, was far from signifying any treatise on grammar. They have taken it to represent that distinct literary type which is characterised by prose exegeses, the Abhidhamma books being mentioned as chief examples of such a type.[1] There is indeed another Pāli word, Vyākaraṇa, which is phonetically the exact equivalent of the Sanskrit Vyākaraṇa, but in Buddhist terminology it means 'announcement or prediction'. The term 'Veyyākaraṇa' means 'exposition or explanation, the function of which is to make things explicit or clear'. If this term be applied to a treatise on grammar, we can understand that the main function of grammar is to

---

[1] Sumaṅgalavilāsinī, part I, p. 24. "Sakalaṁ Abhidhamma Piṭakaṁ niggāthaka-suttaṁ....tam veyyākaraṇan ti veditabbam."

help expositions of texts by clearing up the connections of letters, words, sentences, their sequence, and the rest. The importance of grammar has been sufficiently emphasized in early Buddhism in a verse of the Dhammapada which reads :—

"Vītataṇho anādāno niruttipadakovido
akkharānaṁ sannipātaṁ jaññā pubbāparānica
sa ve antimasārīro mahāpañño (mahāpuriso)
ti [1] vuccati."

In this important dictum a great man or a man of knowledge is expected to be conversant with the rules of construction of sentences, combination of letters or syllables in words, and determination of sequence or syntax. Here the most important term is nirutti which may be taken to mean 'verbal analysis', 'glossology', 'use or expression of a language', or 'grammatical and logical explanation of the words or text of the Buddhist scriptures' (Childers, Pāli Dictionary, *Subvoce Nirutti*). Thus we may understand that the need of grammatical analysis and grammatical treatises came to be felt by the exigency of exposition, and this point has been well brought out in the Nettipakaraṇa (pp. 8-9). Pada, akkara, vyañjana, ākāra, nirutti are the terms that are of use in a treatise on grammar. Saṅkāsanā, pakāsanā, vivaraṇā, and the rest are the terms that are of use in an exegetical treatise. The Netti says "Bhagavā akkharehi saṅkāseti, padehi pakāseti, byañjanehi vivarati, ākārehi vibhajati, niruttīhi uttānikaroti, niddesehi paññāpeti : akkharehi ca padehica ugghaṭeti, byañjanehi ca ākārehi ca vipañcayati, niruttīhi niddesehi ca vitthāreti."

So far as Buddhism is concerned, the development of grammar, lexicography, and works on prosody took place long after the development of literature itself and it appears that no need of a separate book of grammar for the teaching or learn-

---

[1] Dhammapada, v. 352.

ing of Pāli was felt so long as India remained the home of the language. There were certainly some codified rules of grammar to which the language of the Pāli piṭakas conformed. It cannot surely be doubted that a wonderful linguistic genius has been displayed in the coinage and manipulation of many new technical terms and expressions which could not have been possible but for a close and intimate acquaintance with the fundamental principles of grammar and phonology. We may venture to suggest that there was no book of Pāli grammar in existence till the time of the three great Pāli commentators, Buddhadatta, Buddhaghosa, and Dhammapāla. All of them appear to have explained the grammatical construction of Pāli words by the rules of Pāṇini quoted verbatim in Pāli, e.g., Sutta Nipāta commentary, Vol. I, p. 23, vattamānasamīpe vattamāna vacanalakkhaṇa, Pāṇini, III. 3. 131. It appears that Buddhaghosa studied the great grammar of Pāṇini. In the Visuddhimagga (P.T.S. Edition, pp. 491-492, 'Indriyasaccaniddeso') we read :—

"Ko pana nesaṁ indriyaṭṭho nāmāti ? Indaliṅgaṭṭho indriyaṭṭho; indadesitaṭṭho indriyaṭṭho; indadiṭṭhaṭṭho indriyaṭṭho ; indasiṭṭhaṭṭho indriyaṭṭho ; indajuṭṭhaṭṭho indriyaṭṭho : so sabbo pi idha yathāyogaṁ yujjati. Bhagavā hi sammāsambuddho paramissariyabhāvato indo, kusalākusalaṁ ca kammam, kammesu kassaci issariyābhāvato. Ten' ev'ettha kammasañjanitāni tāva indriyāni kusalākusalakammaṁ ullingenti. Tena ca siṭṭhānīti indalingaṭṭhena indasiṭṭhaṭṭhena ca indriyāni. Sabbān eva pan' etāni Bhagavatā yathābhūtato pakāsitāni abhisambuddhāni cā ti indadesitaṭṭhena indadiṭṭhaṭṭhena ca indriyāni. Ten'eva Bhagavatā munindena kānici gocarāsevanāya, kānici bhāvanāsevanāya sevitānīti indajuṭṭhaṭṭhenāpi etāni indriyāni."

Buddhaghosa goes on to add :—

"Api ca ādhipaccasaṅkhātena issariyaṭṭhena pi etāni indriyāni. Cakkhuviññāṇādippavattiyam hi cakkhādīnaṁ siddhaṁ ādhipaccaṁ, tasmiṁ tikkhe tikkhattā, mande mandattāti. Ayaṁ tāv' ettha atthato vinicchayo."

These explanations of 'Indriya' are evidently a reminiscence of Pāṇini, V. 2, 93. "Indriyaṁ indraliṅgaṁ indradṛṣṭaṁ indrajuṣṭaṁ indradattaṁ iti vā."

In the grammar of Pāṇini, there is a mention of *āpatti* in the sense of *prāpti* and in this sense too, āpatti occurs several times in the Samantapāsādikā. This seems also to show that Buddhaghosa knew of and utilised the work of Pāṇini.

If Pāṇini had remained the standard grammatical authority with the Buddhist scholiasts who flourished in the 5th or 6th century A.D., the ascription of the first Pāli grammar to the authorship of Kaccāyana or Mahākaccāyana, an immediate disciple of the Buddha, becomes unjustifiable on account of the anachronism that it involves. If any authoritative book of Pāli grammar were in existence when Buddhaghosa and Dhammapāla wrote their commentaries, there is no reason why they should seek guidance from the rules of Pāṇini rather than from those of Kaccāyana. We may indeed maintain that the first Pāli grammar, attributed to Kaccāyana, was a compilation made by some Buddhist teachers of Ceylon and that the ascription of its authorship to Kaccāyana cannot be justified except on the ground that the necessity for grammatical study of the Pāli texts was particularly felt in the tradition of Kaccāyana who even according to Buddha's own estimate was a past master in the art and method of exegesis or analytical exposition. Even as regards Kaccāyana's grammar, the unknown Pāli compiler of Ceylon can hardly claim any originality in view of the fact that barring certain special rules introduced to meet certain exceptional cases, the bulk of the treatise is based verbatim on the Sanskrit grammar of Kātantra. The indebtedness of the Pāli grammar to some such Sanskrit authority is frankly admitted in the aphorism, 1. 1. 8. (Parasamaññāpayoge), and clearly brought out in the vutti or gloss of the same :

"Yā ca pana sakkatagandhesu samaññā ....pajuññate."

The next standard book of Pāli grammar to be noted is the Rūpasiddhi or Mahārūpasiddhi based on Kaccāyana's work. The Bālāvatāra is the second important work that was produced in Ceylon on the lines of Kaccāyana's work and its only importance lies in the re-arrangement of the aphorisms of Kaccāyana. Passing over the ṭīkās and glosses on Kaccāyana's grammar, the Rūpasiddhi and Bālāvatāra, we have to mention the Saddanīti and the Mukhamatthadīpanī as the two later grammatical works of outstanding merit.

The earliest known Pāli lexicography is the Abhidhānappadīpikā which too must stand to the credit of the Pāli scholars of Ceylon. The plan of this lexicography seems to have been conceived on the model of the Sanskrit koṣa of Amarasingha who is taken, for some good reasons, to be a Buddhist by faith. The Abhidhānappadīpikā just like its Sanskrit prototype is a dictionary of synonyms. It is far from having any alphabetical arrangement of words, which was adopted in some later works, such as Ekakkharakosa and the Abhidhānappadīpikā sūci. The beginnings of Pāli lexicography may, however, be clearly traced in the Vevacanahāra chapter of the Nettipakaraṇa and the Peṭakopadesa. The dictionary method of making the meaning of a term or word clear is indeed extensively used in the Pāli Abhidhamma books and in some portions of the nikāyas.

Pāli literature is conspicuous by the absence of any noteworthy work on Poetics. If there be any such work, we may safely take it to be based on some Sanskrit authority. There are a few Pāli works on metre notably the Vuttodaya and the Subodhālaṅkāra. With regard to all these works on prosody, it may suffice to say that they are far from being original productions.

The three principal grammarians are Kaccāyana, Moggallāna, and the author of the Saddanīti.

Books of grammar.

Kaccāyana's Pāli grammar [1]—Kaccāyana is reported to be the author of the first Pāli grammar called Susandhikappa. There are many suttas in Kaccāyana's grammar which are identical with those of the Kātantravyākaraṇa. This grammar is said to have been carried into Burma early in the fifth century A.D.

As helps to the grammar of Kaccāyana, there are Rūpasiddhi [2], Bālāvatāra [3], which consists of 7 chapters, Mahānirutti, Cūlanirutti, Niruttipiṭaka, and Mañjūsaṭīkāvyākhyā.

As helps to the grammar of Moggallāna, there are Payogasiddhi, Moggallāyanavutti, Susaddasiddhi and Padasādhana [4] or Moggallāna Saddattharatnā-

[1] The oldest and best commentary on Kaccāyana's Pāli grammar is Mukhattadīpanī written by Ācārya Vimalabuddhi. This work is commonly known as Nyāsa. There is a paper entitled "Note on the Pāli Grammarian, Kaccāyana" (Proceedings of the Asiatic Society of Bengal, 1882). The late Dr. Satish Chandra Vidyābhūṣaṇa edited Kaccāyana's grammar. Mason's edition of this grammar is noteworthy.

[2] Rūpasiddhi-ṭīkā ascribed to Dīpaṁkara should be read along with the text to get a clear idea of the Pāli grammar. Grunwedel's Rūpasiddhi, Berlin, 1883, is noteworthy. There are editions containing Burmese interpretations of the Rūpasiddhi (*vide* supplementary catalogue of Sanskrit, Pāli, and Prakrit Books in the British Museum, p. 442, compiled by L. D. Barnett, 1928).

[3] Bālāvatāra by Dharmakitti; Bālāvatāra, ed. Sri Dharmārāma; Bālāvatāra with ṭīkā, ed. Sumaṅgala, Colombo, 1893. It is a work on Pāli grammar and is the most exhaustively used handbook in Ceylon on the subject. It is the smallest grammar extant and based on Kaccāyana's work.

There is an abridgement of the Bālāvatāra with Pāli sūtras and Sinhalese commentary composed by Revd. Sitinamaluwa Dhammajoti and edited by Jinaratana Thera and D. A. DeSilva, Batuwantudava, second edition, Colombo, 1913. There is a word-for-word Burmese interpretation of the Bālāvatāra, Rangoon, 1915. The Bālāvatāra has been translated into English by Mr. H. T. DeSilva with the co-operation of the Rev. Katane Oopatissa Thera and revised by Woodward, Pegu, 1915.

[4] There is a commentary on Padasādhana, a Pāli grammatical work on the system of Moggallāna, written by Sri Rāhula Thera and discovered by Louis De Zoysa.

kara which consists of six sections dealing with sadda, sandhi, samāsa, verbs, prefixes, and suffixes.

As helps to the grammar called Saddanīti [1], there is only one work called Cūlasaddanīti. The Saddanīti is still regarded as a classic in Burma.

Among other treatises on Pāli grammar may be counted the following :—

Sambandhacintā, Saddasāratthajālinī (a good book on Pāli Philology), Kaccāyanabheda, Saddatthabhedacintā, Kārika, Kārikavutti, Vibhattyattha, Gandhatthi, Vācakopadesa, Nāyalakkhaṇavibhāvanī, Niruttisaṅgha, Kaccāyanasāra, Vibhattyatthadīpanī, Sanvannanayadīpanī, Vaccavācaka, Saddavutti, Balappabodhana [2], Kārakapupphamañjarī, Kaccāyanadīpanī, Guḷhatthadīpanī, Mukhamattasāra, Saddavindu [3], Saddakalika, Saddaviniccaya, Bijaṅga, Dhātupāṭha, Sudhiramukhamandandana [4], etc., with their commentaries and supplementary commentaries.

Kaccāyana, as we have already pointed out, is the oldest of all Pāli grammarians. Readers are referred to Kaccāyana's Sandhikappa [5] (J.P.T.S., 1882).

Nepatikavaṇṇanā is a work on Pāli indeclinable participles. Saddamālā is a comprehensive Pāli grammar based on the grammar of Kaccāyana.

[1] There is a book named Dhātuatthadīpanī, by Hiṅgulwala Jinaratana, which contains a re-arrangement in material form of the roots mentioned in Aggavaṁsa's Saddanīti. Saddanīti, La Grammaire Pāli de' Aggavaṁsa by Helmer Smith in 3 vols. is worth perusal. The date of this grammar is traditionally given as the 12th century A.D. This grammar consists of three parts, Padamālā, Dhātumālā (root numbers) and Suttamālā (sūtra number). It gives many quotations from the Pāli canon as examples of grammatical rules. It is no doubt a standard work on Pāli grammar and philology. It is undoubtedly a scholarly edition prepared by Helmer Smith.

[2] It is a grammar for beginners.

[3] It was written by Nārada Thera.

[4] It is a work on samāsa of Pāli compound nouns written by Attaragāmavandararājaguru.

[5] On sandhi in Pāli by R. C. Childers, J.R.A.S., new series, Vol. II, 1879.

The development of grammar is a comparatively late phase of Pāli literature, as late as the sixth or seventh century A.D., if not later still. Even in the grammar of Kaccāyana, the debt to Sanskrit is freely acknowledged in one of the introductory aphorisms. Uptill the time of Buddhaghosa and Dhammapāla, the Buddhist teachers as already pointed out, followed the authority of the grammar of Pāṇini. It has only recently been detected that the Pāli commentators have freely quoted the rules of Pāṇini in accounting for grammatical formations of Pāli words.

Lexicons.

Abhidhānappadīpikā (by Moggallāna Thera, ed. by W. Subhuti, 2nd edition, Colombo, 1883)[1] and Ekakkhara-kosa[2] are the two well-known Pāli lexicons. The Abhidhānappadīpikā was written by Moggallāna in the reign of Parākramabāhu the Great. It is the only ancient Pāli dictionary in Ceylon and it follows the style and method of the Sanskrit Amarakoṣa (*vide*, Malalasekera, The Pāli Literature of Ceylon, pp. 188-189). This work consists of three parts dealing with celestial, terrestrial, and miscellaneous objects and each part is subdivided into several sections. The whole book is a dictionary of synonyms. The last two sections of the last part are devoted to homonyms and indeclinable particles. This work is held in the highest esteem both in Burma and Ceylon (*Ibid.*, p. 189). Subhuti's edition of this dictionary with English and Sinhalese interpretations together with a complete Index of all the Pāli words giving their meanings in Sinhalese deserves mention. R. C. Childers has published a very useful dictionary of the Pāli language. In 1921, T. W. Rhys Davids and W. Stede brought out a Pāli dictionary compiled mainly from collection by the former for 40 years which is a

---

[1] Ferner, A complete Index to the Abhidhānappadīpikā is a useful publication.

[2] It is a small work on Pāli lexicography, a vocabulary of words of one letter by Saddhammakitti Thera of Burma.

publication of the P.T.S., London. Quite recently a critical dictionary begun by V. Trenckner and revised, continued, and edited by Dines Anderson and Helmer Smith has appeared in two parts (1924 and 1929).

The beginnings of Indian lexicons are to be traced mainly in the Nighaṇṭu section of Yāṣka's Nirukta. The Nettipakaraṇa stands to the Pāli canon in the same relation in which Yāṣka's Nirukta stands to the Vedas. And it is in the Vevacanahāra of the Netti, the chapter on homonyms, that the historians can clearly trace the early model of later lexicons.

Works on prosody.

Vuttodaya[1] written by Saṅgharakkhita Thera, Kāmaṇḍakī, and Chandoviciti are Pāli works on metres. Subodhālaṅkāra[2] is a work on rhetoric by Saṅgharakkhita Thera. Kavisārapakaraṇaṁ and Kavisāraṭikānissaya are the two good books on prosody.

Modern Works.

A number of scholars, both European and Indian, have made a study of Pāli grammars and have embodied their researches in their treatises on Pāli grammars. These treatises are named below :—

(1) E. Burnouf—observations grammaticales sur quelques passages de l' Essai sur le Pāli de Burnouf et Lassen—Paris, 1827.

(2) B. Clough—compendious Pāli grammar with a copious vocabulary in the same language—Colombo, 1824.

(3) J. Minayeff—Grammaire Pālie, traduite par St. Guyard, Paris, 1874.

(4) J. Minayeff—Pāli Grammar, a phonetic and morphological sketch of the Pāli language, with an introductory essay

[1] Vuttodaya (exposition of metre) by Saṅgharakkhita Thera, J.A.S.B., Vol. XLVI, pt. I, (Col. G. E. Fryer).

[2] Analysis and Text of Subodhālaṅkāra or Easy Rhetoric by Saṅgharakkhita Thera, J.A.S.B., Vol. XLIV, pt. I, (Col. G. E. Fryer).

on its form and character by J. M., 1872; translation from Russian into French by M. St. Guyard, 1874, rendered into English by Ch. G. Adams, 1882.

(5) E. Kuhn—Beitrage Zur Pāli Grammatik, Berlin, 1875.

(6) O. Frankfurter—Handbook of Pāli being an elementary grammar, 1883.

(7) E. Muller—A simplified grammar of the Pāli language, London, 1884.

(8) V. Henry—Precis de Grammaire Pālie accompague d' um choix de textes Graduis, Paris, 1894.

(9) Geiger—Pāli Literatur und sprache (Grundriss der Indo Arischen Philologie and Altertumskunde).

(10) E. Windisch, uber den sprachlichen charakter des Pāli, Paris, 1906.

(11) H. H. Tilbe—Pāli Grammar, Rangoon, 1899.

(12) J. Grey—Elementary Pāli Grammar, Calcutta, 1905.

(13) Charles Duroiselle—A Practical Grammar of the Pāli Language, Rangoon, 1906.

(14) Senart—Kaccāyanappakaranāni (1868–70).

(15) E. Kuhn—Kaccāyanappakaranae Specimen, Halle, 1869.

(16) Nyanatilaka—Kleine systematische Pāli Grammatik, Breslau, 1911.

(17) Grunwedel—Rūpasiddhi, Berlin, 1883.

(18) Tha Do Oung—A Grammar of the Pāli language (after Kaccāyana), Vols. I, II, III, and IV.

(19) Subhuti—Nāmamālā.

(20) Sri Dharmārāma—Bālāvatāra by Dharmakirti.

(21) H. Sumangala—Bālāvatāra with ṭīkā, Colombo, 1893.

(22) Chakravarty and Ghosh—Pāli Grammar.

(23) Pe Maung Tin—Pāli Grammar.
(24) Vidhusekhar Śāstrī—Pāli Prakāsa.
(25) J. Takakusu—A Pāli Chrestomathy, Tokyo, 1900.

Of all these works on Pāli grammar, Mr. Tha Do Oung has treated this subject exhaustively. The first volume deals with sandhi, nāma, kāraka, and samāsa ; the second volume contains taddhita, kita, uṇādi, ākhyāta, upasagga, and nipāta participles ; the third and fourth volumes deal with word roots, ten figures of speech and 40 modes of expression, and prosody. Pāli grammar by Muller and Duroiselle are also very useful. Prof. Chakravartty's grammar is worth perusal. Paṇḍit Vidhusekhar Śāstrī's work is a compilation and as such it is useful.

The following are the noteworthy publications :

Morris—Notes and Queries, J.P.T.S., 1884, 1885, 1886, 1887, 1889, and 1891–93.

E. Muller—A glossary of Pāli proper names, J.P.T.S., 1888.

Morris—Contributions to Pāli Lexicography, Academy, 1890-91.

Mabel Bode—Index to Pāli words discussed in translations, J.P.T.S., 1897–1901.

J. Takakusu—A Pāli Chrestomathy with notes and glossary giving Sanskrit and Chinese equivalents, Tokyo, 1900.

E. Windisch—Uber den Sprachlichen charakter des Pāli Actes du XIVe. Congress Internat des Orientalistes, Paris, 1906.

Mrs. Rhys Davids, Similes in the Nikāyas, J.P.T.S., 1907-8 and Mrs. Rhys Davids, Sākya or Buddhist origins, chapter XVII, pp. 314 foll.

Surendranath Majumdar, Shastri.

The Dative Plural in Pāli (published in Sir Asutosh Mookerjee Silver Jubilee volumes, Vol. III, Orientalia—Pt. 2, pp. 31–34). It is a valuable paper and should attract the attention of scholars interested in Pāli grammar and philology. Prof. Majumdar has shown in it that in the inscriptions of Asoka and of his grandson there are ten instances of the use of dative plural in 'Epigraphic Pāli'. These occur not only in one version or at one place but at such distant places as Dhauli, Jaugaḍā, Barābar hills, Nāgārjuni hills, Kālsi, Manserā, and Girnār. In Barābar and Nāgārjuni cave inscriptions the dative is the only form in use showing that the old form was better preserved in the Māgadhī. As for the Rock Edicts some versions use the dative and some the genitive. The Shāhbāzgarhi text is the only version which has not used even once the dative form. Majumdar sums up his argument by saying that we find promiscuous use of the dative and genitive plurals in 'Epigraphic Pāli'. If the old Buddhist and Jaina texts be carefully examined in this light, some instances of the dative plural will be found in literary Pāli and Prakrit also. When the genitive plural began to be used for the dative plural, their singular forms also came to be confused in use. This confusion in the singular was also helped by the fact that in the language of the later Vedic texts the dative singular of feminine nouns was used for the genitive. But as the dative singular Prakritic form had not been confused in shape with any other form, it lingered longer than the dative plural. Dative singular is almost as common in Asokan dialects as in Sanskrit. It lingered in literary Pāli but died out in the Prakrits of the dramas.

# CONCLUSION

In the foregoing pages an attempt has been made to give a general survey of canonical and non-canonical Pāli literature. Some distinct types of literature came to be developed within a growing collection of texts of traditional authority. This collection came indeed to be closed at a certain date which is undoubtedly pre-Christian. The origin and development of even just one recension of the early corpus of Buddhist literature covered a pretty long period of about five centuries, which is very imperfectly known or understood by the meagre evidence of Sanskrit literature. The Pāli piṭakas coupled with the Jain āgama texts and some of the Sanskrit treatises like Pāṇini's grammar, Kātyāyana's Vārtika, Patañjali's Mahābhāṣya, and the contemporary inscriptions and coin-legends fill up a very important gap in the history of ancient Indian humanity. The particular literature with which we are concerned developed under ægis of religion which was destined to be a great civilising influence in the East, highly ethical in tone, dignified in the forms of expression, dramatic in setting, direct in narration, methodical in argument, and mechanical in arrangement. This wealth of literary output was shown forth in its perspicuity and grandeur in the garb of a new literary idiom having a place midway between the Vedic Sanskrit on one hand and classical Sanskrit and Ārdhamāgadhī on the other. In between the closing of the Pāli canon and the beginning of the great commentaries and chronicles we had to take note of an imperfectly known period of transition which became remarkable by the production of so great a work of literary merit and doctrinal importance as the Milinda Pañha occupying, as it does, the foremost place for its lucid, elegant, and rhythmical prose style in the whole range of Sanskrit and Sanskritic literature. The Pāli commentaries, as we have them, were produced at a period far beyond the Mauryan and Śūnga, the Kānva and the Kushāṇa. The Augustan period of Pāli literature began with these commentaries and closed with the earlier epic chronicles of Ceylon. The period which followed was a decadent one, and it became noted only for the compilation of some useful manuals, some books of grammar and lexicography chiefly in imitation of some Sanskrit works of India, and a few metrical compbsitions exhibiting the wealth of Ceylonese poetical imagination and plagiarism. Pāli literature would have been as dead but for its rejuvination in Burma, the Buddhist country, which has produced enormous literature of considerable importance during the last three or four centuries. From the geographical allusions it may be deduced that the main bulk of the Pāli canon developed within the territorial limits of the Middle Country and some parts of Western India, notably Mathurā and Ujjain. The Milinda Pañha is full of associations reminiscent of the life, manners, and customs of the north-western region of India, which became the meeting place of Indo-Aryan and Graeco-Bactrian civilisation. The commentaries clearly point to Kāñcipura, Kāveripaṭṭana, Madurā, and Anurādhapura as notable centres of Pāli Buddhism. Along with South India one has got to take Sirikhetta (modern Prome) in Burma as the centre of Pāli Abhidhamma culture. There is reason to believe that Pāli literature developed in one shape or another in Lower Burma giving rise to Pāli law codes, compiled more or less on the model of Manu's code. The inscriptions and sculptures are not without their important bearings on the history of Pāli literature. We can say that the lower limit of the evolution of Pāli literature is represented by the Kalyāṇī stone inscriptions of King Dhammaceti of Pegu. In dealing effectively with Pāli literature, one has got to consider the history of literary development in India, Ceylon, Burma, and Siam. It still remains a problem for modern historian and philologist to find out how far Pāli literature has influenced the vernaculars of these four countries. There is sufficient evidence to prove that Sinhalese developed as a vernacular with its wealth of literature as early as the 2nd century B.C.

Pāli literature is incomplete by itself. It is wanting in many works of secular interest, such as those on mathematics, astronomy, astrology, medicine, logic, and royal polity. The few such works that we have are of recent origin and as such, they do not fall within the scope of our present investigation. Even as a pure literature, it has just one work, the Jinacarita, which deserves the name of a Kāvya. The Jinacarita itself is chiefly based upon the Jātaka Nidāna-kathā which latter may be regarded as a Kāvya in prose, or in prose and verse.

There is hardly a drama or a novel, strictly so called. But there are a great many suttas, particularly those contained in the Dīgha Nikāya, the Brahmajāla, the Sāmaññaphala, the Sakkapañha, the Mahāparinibbāna, which have a dramatic setting. The literary art employed in the Sāmaññaphala Sutta has been extensively developed in the Milinda Pañha. In reading the suttas of the Sagātha-vagga of the Saṁyutta Nikāya one is apt to feel as though there is a stage-action in which one devaputta appears to test the knowledge of the Buddha and retires to make room for the next man waiting. In short, Pāli literature abounds in dramatic elements without having a single book of drama. The literary art employed in the historical narrative of the Mahāparinibbāna Suttanta and in those of the Milinda Pañha, the Udenavatthu and the Visākhāvatthu is a novelty.

There are several legendary and historical accounts of the life and career of the Buddha and his disciples and followers—Theras, Therīs, Upāsakas, and Upāsikās which are interesting biographical sketches without a rigorous biographical treatment.

Even if it be assumed that there are no biographies in the modern sense, there is no getting away from the fact that the Buddhist teachers successfully tried to conceive and develop a universal science of biography in the Jātaka Nidāna-kathā.

There is just one story of creation in the Pāli Aggañña Suttanta. The way in which it has been introduced goes to show that it was rather a citation for some purpose than an original production.

The early Buddhist attitude towards ornate poetry or imaginative literature was far from appreciative. Such poetry was viewed with disfavour, the superabundance of it being dreaded as a great future danger of the good faith (anāgata-bhaya) uptill the time of Asoka. The development of ornate poetry was sought to be accounted for in early Buddhism by an extraneous influence. A highly imaginative literature developed nevertheless within the four corners of Pāli Buddhism with its wealth of *gāthās* and *akkhānas*, highly ethical or spiritual in tone. We come across an example of song in the Sakkapañha Suttanta, which is said to have been sung by Pañcasikha, the heavenly minstrel. Other pieces described as songs in some of the Birth-stories and Buddhist legends are hardly distinguishable from the main body of *gāthās*. Some of the Psalms of the Early Brethren and Sisters, which are musings of emancipated hearts, e.g., the Tālapuṭa-thera-gāthā and the Ambapāli-gāthā, are truly musical in tone. One can say that Pāli literature is sufficiently rich in the wealth of lyrics and reflective poetry. The Dhammapada stands out as a remarkable literature in the field of didactic poetry.

Its richness consists also in the wealth of similes and parables deserving a separate and careful study as elements that apparently influenced the later Kāvya poetry of India and have their parallels in the early Gospels of Christianity.

To counteract the influence of the Mahābhārata and the Rāmāyaṇa, particularly that of the former, the Buddhists began to develop the Jātakas, supplying thereby so many interesting themes for artistic delineation and materials for Indian dramas and kāvyas.

So far as the epic and historical chronicles go, the position of Pāli literature is almost unique, the mediæval Kashmere chronicle, Rājataraṅginī, being the only notable Sanskrit work of their kind.

Pāli literature has no book on logic, but in the Kathāvatthu we have a great book of controversy, which lies at the immediate background of the entire Nyāya literature. Strictly speaking, there is no medical treatise in Pāli, but in the Buddhist study of the 32 parts of the human organism we have something which is of paramount interest to a student of medical science. Prior to the compilation of the Law codes, we meet with in Pāli the definitions of *karma*, murder, theft, and the rest which anticipate many points in modern jurisprudence. There may not be a Buddhacarita or a Kumārasambhava in Pāli, but there is certainly the Vatthugāthā of the Nālaka Sutta in the Sutta Nipāta to serve as a clear model of them. The manuals of psychological ethics must always be considered as notable contributions to Indian culture.

These and other points of interest and importance are left for future study and investigation. In spite of the fruitful labours of great many scholars, we are still on the threshold of the study of Pāli literature, to evaluate and appreciate which one has to look at it in different aspects, just as one looks at a gem by its facet.

It has still its immense possibilities as a means of developing modern literature, both in the East and the West. The Amitābha, the Jagajjyoti, the Buddhadevacarita, the Aśoka, the Ajātaśatru, and the Kinnarī are but the few works produced yet in modern Bengali utilising the materials of Pāli and Sanskrit Buddhist literature. As regards old Bengali literature, Pāli literature has its legacy in the plot of Vidyāsundara set forth in the story of the Mahā-ummagga-Jātaka and the song composed in praise of the princess Pañcālacaṇḍī. The creation of literary types is indeed the most distinctive feature of the literature, a bird's eye view of which is given in the present work.

# APPENDIX A

## HISTORICAL AND GEOGRAPHICAL REFERENCES IN THE PĀLI PIṬAKAS

### I.—In the Vinaya Piṭaka

The Vinaya Piṭaka is an important store-house of interesting geographical and historical information of the time of which it speaks. There is a very important reference to the four boundaries of the Middle Country or the Majjhimadesa as understood by the Buddhists, and to the various sites, towns, and villages included therein, and associated very intimately with the Buddha and Buddhism. Interesting sidelights are also thrown on the political history, and social and economic conditions of the time.

Historical, etc.

Bimbisāra is said to have ruled over 80,000 townships (Vinaya Texts, S.B.E., II, p. 1) and there were 80,000 overseers over the townships (*Ibid.*, II, p. 4). That the Magadha kings were in fear of the Vajjians is testified to by the fact that Sunīdha and Vassakāra are referred to as building a fort at Pāṭaliputta to crush the Vajjians (*Ibid.*, II, p. 101). The Magadha king had a royal physician, Jīvaka by name, who was asked by the king to cure a seṭṭhi who did good service to the king and to the merchants' guild (*Ibid.*, II, 181). Jīvaka also cured King Pradyota of Avanti of jaundice (*Ibid.*, II, pp. 187 ff.). His success in operating on the fistula of King Bimbisāra won for him the post of royal physician, and he was afterwards appointed by the king physician to the Buddha and the congregation of bhikkhus that lived with him. Once we are told Magadha was visited by five kinds of diseases (e.g., leprosy, goitre, asthma, dry leprosy, and apamāra), and Jīvaka had to treat the bhikkhu patients only suffering from those diseases (Vinaya Piṭaka, I, p. 71). Once we are told that King Bimbisāra went to have his bath in the river Tapoda that flew by this ancient city; when he reached the river, he saw the bhikkhus taking their bath. The city gate was closed and so he could not enter the city of Rājagaha. Next morning he came after taking his bath without proper dress to the Buddha who gave him instruction and advised the bhikkhus not to spend so much time in their bath (*Ibid.*, IV, 116-117). Bimbisāra's son was Ajātasattu, whose chief minister was Vassakāra who began the work of repairing the fort of Rājagaha in the kingdom of Magadha. He needed timber for the purpose and went to the reserved forest, but was informed that the wood was taken by a bhikkhu named

Dhaniya. Vassakāra complained to King Bimbisāra about it. It was brought to the notice of the Buddha who ordered the bhikkhus not to take anything not offered or presented to them (*Ibid.*, III, 41–45). There is a reference which suggests that the palace of Bimbisāra should be of gold (Vinaya Texts, S.B.E., II, p. 65). There was a sugar factory at Rājagaha (*Ibid.*, II, p. 67) ; and the country was rich in molasses (Vinaya Piṭaka, I, 226).

The town of Vaiśālī too was well provided with food, and was generally prosperous (Vinaya Texts, II, 117).

There is a reference to the dancing girls asked to dance and greeted with applause (Vinaya Texts, II, 349).

Of the notable bhikkhu disciples of the Master, mention is made of Sāriputta and Moggallāna (*Ibid.*, II, 318, 353), Upāli (*Ibid.*, II, 395) who discussed the mānatta discipline of a bhikkhu with the Master, and Ānanda through whose intercession Mahāpajāpatī Gotamī with other Sakya ladies obtained permission for ordination (III, p. 322). Kakudha, a Koliyan, was an attendant on Moggallāna (*Ibid.*, III, 234).

Of the heretical teachers mention is made of Makkhali Gosāla, Ajīta Kesakambalī, Pakudha Kaccāyana, Sañjaya Belaṭṭhiputta, and Nigaṇṭha Nāthaputta (*Ibid.*, III, p. 79).

References are made to Devadatta's attempt to create a disunion among the bhikkhus in the Bhikkhu Saṁgha (*Ibid.*, III, p. 251), and also to the two councils of Rājagaha and Vaisālī (*Ibid.*, III, 11th and 12th Khandhakas). When the First Great Council of the disciples of the Buddha was held after his parinirvāṇa to compile the teachings of the Master, Yasa sent messengers to the bhikkhus of Avanti inviting them to come, and settle what is Dhamma, what is Vinaya, and what is not, and to help the spread of Dhamma and Vinaya (III, p. 394).

Geographical.

To the east of the Middle Country or Majjhimadesa lay the town Kajañgala, and beyond it Mahāsālā, to the south-east the river Salalavatī, to the south, the town Setakaṇṇika, to the west the brāhmaṇa district of Thūna, and to the north, the mountain range called Usīradhvaja. Beyond these were the border countries and this side of these was the Middle Country (Vinaya Texts, II, pp. 38-39). One of the most important towns of the Madhyadeśa was Rājagaha (Rājagriha-Giribraja) where the Gijjhakūṭa was and the Buddha stayed there for some time (*Ibid.*, II, p. 1). From Rājagaha, a road lay to Andhakavinda which was once visited by 500 carts, all full of pots of sugar (*Ibid.*, II, p. 93). Rājagaha was the capital city of King Bimbisāra, while the court-physician Jīvaka is referred to as an inhabitant of this place (*Ibid.*, II, pp. 184-5). But his birth-place was Magadha (*Ibid.*, II, 173). Jīvaka was, however, educated at Taxila (*Ibid.*, II, p. 174). Rājagaha had a gate which was closed in the evening, and nobody, not even the king, was allowed to enter the city after the gate was closed (*Ibid.*, IV, 116-17). It was here at Rājagaha that Sāriputta learned Buddha's Dhamma from Assaji, one of the Pañcavaggiya bhikkhus. Sāriputta went to Rājagaha with his friend Moggallāna where the Buddha was, and both of them were converted by the Master (Vinaya Piṭaka, I, pp. 40 ff.). Rājagaha could boast of another physician (vejja) named Ākāsagotta (*Ibid.*, I, p. 215). Veluvana, the bamboo park of Rājagaha, has often been referred to as a residence of the Master. When once the Buddha was here, Devadatta's gain and fame were completely lost (Vinaya Piṭaka, IV, p. 71). The Kalandakanivāpa of Rājagaha has also been referred to as another residence of the Master. While he was once there, a party of six bhikkhus (chabbaggiyā bhikkhū) went to attend the Giraggasamajja, a highly popular music of the day (*Ibid.*, II, 107). A seṭṭhi of Rājagaha built a vihāra for the bhikkhus. He had to take consent of the Buddha as to the bhikkhus' dwelling in a vihāra (Vinaya Piṭaka, II, p. 146). References are made to a trader of Rājagaha who wanted to go to Patiyāloka (*Ibid.*, IV, pp. 79-80), to a Sākyaputta named Upananda who, while at Rājagaha, was invited by his supporters (*Ibid.*, IV, p. 98), to Upāli, the son of a rich trader of Rājagaha, who was ordained as bhikkhu at the initiative of his parents (*Ibid.*, IV, pp. 128-29). The Mahāvagga tells us of an occasion when the Blessed One on his way to Vesālī noticed bhikkhus with a superfluity of dress, and advised them as to the least quantity of robes a bhikkhu should require (*Ibid.*, II, pp. 210 foll.). The Cullavagga speaks of a seṭṭhi of Rājagaha who acquired a block of sandal wood, and made a bowl out of it for the bhikkhus (Vinaya Texts, III, p. 78).

Pāṭaligāma was another important locality which was once visited by the Buddha accompanied by a great number of bhikkhus (*Ibid.*, II, p. 97). Sunīdha and Vassakāra are referred to as building a fort at Pāṭaligāma to crush the Vajjians (*Ibid.*, II, p. 101).

No less important were Vesālī and Sāvatthī. The former was well provided with food, the harvest was good, alms were easy to obtain, one could very well get a living by gleaning or through favour (*Ibid.*, II, p. 117). There at Vesālī was the Gotamaka shrine (*Ibid.*, II, p. 210) where the Buddha stayed for some time. There lay a high road between Vesālī and Rājagaha (*Ibid.*, II, p. 210). The Buddha came to Vesālī from Kapilavastu whence a number of Sākya ladies came to receive, through the intercession of Ānanda, ordination from the Master who at that time resided at the Kūṭāgāra hall in the Mahāvana (*Ibid.*, III, pp. 320 foll.). The Cullavagga of the Vinaya Piṭaka tells us an occasion when the Enlightened One was staying at the peak-roofed hall in the Mahāvana (Cullavagga, VI, S.B.E., XX, p. 189). We are further told of a poor tailor of Vaisālī who was very much bent on building a house for the Saṁgha (*Ibid.*, pp. 190-91). In the 12th Khandhaka, there is the important reference to the Buddhist Council of Vesālī (*Ibid.*, III).

References are often made to the Jetavana of Anāthapiṇḍika at Sāvatthī (Vinaya Texts, S.B.E., I, p. 325) where the Buddha stayed. Another staying place of the Master there was the ārāma of Migāramātā (*Ibid.*, pt. III, p. 299).

Kāsī or Bārāṇasī (i.e., Benares) and Kosala (Vinaya Texts, I, pp. 226, 312) often find mention in the Vinaya Piṭaka. In course of his religious propaganda tour, the Master first went to Benares, then to Uruvelā and then he visited Gayāsīsa, Rājagaha, Kapilavatthu, and Sāvatthī (*Ibid.*, I, pp. 116, 136, 210). There lay a road from Sāketa to Sāvatthī (*Ibid.*, p. 220). A few bhikkhus travelling on the road in the Kosala country went off the road to a cemetery to get themselves paṁsukūla robes (Vinaya Texts, S.B.E., II, p. 197). Brahmadatta, the legendary king of Benares, is invariably alluded to while introducing a Jātaka. In his time there was a king of Kosala named Dīghīti who was not so wealthy as the king of Kāsī. Brahmadatta went to wage war against the king of Kosala, and thus ensued a series of vicissitudes in which the king of Kosala suffered most, though his son Dīghāvu ultimately brought the king of Kāsī to his knees, and friendship was restored (*Ibid.*, II, pp. 301 ff.). Yasa, a young nobleman of Benares, son of a seṭṭhi, had three places fixed for three seasons of the year (Vinaya Texts, I, pp. 102–108).

Kosambī was another important place where at Ghositārāma Buddha stayed from time to time (Vinaya Texts, II, p. 285 ; *Ibid.*, II, p. 376). There is a reference to the quarrelsome bhikkhus of Kosambī who came to Sāvatthī (Vinaya Texts, S.B.E., II, p. 318).

The republican states of Pāvā and Kusinārā are also mentioned (Vinaya Texts, III, 370 and *Ibid.*, pt. II, 135) and Roja, a member of the Mallas of Kusinārā, is said to have gone to welcome the Buddha (Vinaya Texts, S.B.E., pt. II, p. 135).

Of less important places and localities, mention is made of Campā inhabited by a seṭṭhi's son named Soṇa Koḷivisa (Vinaya Texts, S.B.E., II, p. 1), Avanti visited by Mahākaccāna, and where there was a hill called Kuraraghara (*Ibid.*, II, 32), Koṭigāma where Buddha resided for some time (*Ibid.*, II, p. 105), and Bhaddiyanagara where lived a householder named Meṇḍaka who was possessed of a miraculous power (*Ibid.*, II, p. 121). Reference is also made to Kiṭāgiri where dwelt the wicked bhikkhus who were the followers of Assaji and Punabbasu (*Ibid.*, II, p. 347), to Anupiyā, a town of the Mallas (*Ibid.*, III, p. 224), to Sāketa where dwelt a banker whose wife was suffering from head disease and who was treated by Jīvaka (*Ibid.*, II, pp.176 foll.), to the Gijjhakūṭa hill in Rājagaha which was visited by the Buddha (*Ibid.*, I, p. 239), and to Uttarakuru where Buddha is said to have gone to beg alms (*Ibid.*, I, p. 124).

Of important rivers, mention is made of Gaṅgā, Yamunā, Aciravatī, Mahī, and Sarabhu (Vinaya Texts, III, pp. 301-302).

## II.—In the Sutta Piṭaka

### *Historical*

In the Dīgha Nikāya of the Sutta Piṭaka.

The Sāmaññaphala Suttanta (Dīgha, I.) is important from a historical point of view; for it furnishes us with valuable information about the views of six leading thinkers (titthiyas) of the time: Pūraṇa Kassapa, Makkhali Gosāla, Ajitakesakambalī, Pukudha Kaccāyana, Sañjaya Belaṭṭhiputta, and Nigaṇṭha Nāthaputta. This sutta also gives us a list of crafts and occupations of the time, e.g., Dāsakaputtā (slaves), Kumbhakārā (potters), Mālākārā (garland-makers), Hatthārohā (elephant-riders), Assārohā (cavalry), Rathikā (charioteers), Danuggahā (archers), Āḷārikā (cooks), Kappakā (barbers), Nahāpakā (bath-attendants), Sudā (confectioners), Rajakā (washermen), Pesakārā (weavers), and Naḷakārā (basket-makers). Another important historical allusion in this sutta is the fact which refers to Jīvaka, the famous physician of the Buddha, and gives us an account of the visit paid to the Buddha by the patricide monarch of Magadha, the terrible Ajātasattu. In the concluding portion of the suttanta there is an allusion to the actual murder of Bimbisāra which his son Ajātasattu committed.

The Ambaṭṭha Suttanta (Dīgha, I.) refers to King Pasenadi of Kosala, as well as to some famous sages of the time, e.g., Yamataggi, Aṅgirasa, Bhāradvāja, Vāseṭṭha, Bhagu, and Vessāmitta. A famous brahmin teacher of Kosala and the teacher of Ambaṭṭha, Pokkharasādi, is said to have enjoyed the property given by King Pasenadi, the contemporary of the Buddha.

The Sonadaṇḍa Suttanta (Dīgha, I.) refers to Campā visited by the Buddha with 500 monks, to Gaggarā, a famous tank in Campā, and to King Bimbisāra of Magadha and King Pasenadi of Kosala. This suttanta also tells us how the Aṅga kingdom with its capital Campā was included in the Magadhan empire. While the Buddha was sojourning at Campā in the kingdom of Aṅga, a brahmin named Sonadaṇḍa was in the enjoyment of the revenues of the town as it was given to him by Bimbisāra of Magadha. Brahmin householders of Campā went to the Buddha. Sonadaṇḍa also accompanied them, and eventually all of them became lay supporters of the Buddha.

The Mahāli Suttanta (Dīgha, I.) refers to Buddha's dwelling at Vesālī in a Kūṭāgārasālā in Mahāvana.

The Lohicca Suttanta (Dīgha, I.) refers to king of Kosala, to Sālavatika inhabited by a brahmin named Lohicca, and to Pasenadi, king of Kāsī-Kosala, who used to collect taxes from the inhabitants of Kāsī-Kosala and to enjoy the income not alone but with his subordinates.

The Mahāpadāna Suttanta (Dīgha, II.) refers to the two famous disciples of the Buddha, Sāriputta and Moggallāna.

The Mahāparinibbāṇa Suttanta (Dīgha, II.) has a dramatic setting inasmuch as it represents King Ajātasattu of Magadha as appearing on a stage and indulging in a soliloquy giving an expression of his grim determination to annihilate his Vajjian rivals. It further relates that when the Buddha heard of this determination of the king, he remarked that so long as the Vajjians fulfilled the seven conditions of welfare, there would not be any danger for them. But, afterwards Ajātasattu is stated to have succeeded in annihilating the Vajjians with the help of his two ministers, Sunīdha and Vassakāra, when dissensions arose among the Vajjians. The suttanta also refers to some incidents of Buddha's life, e.g., the visit of Subhadda to Buddha, and his conversation with the Lord, the passing away of the Lord, the homage of the Mallas, cremation of Buddha's dead body, quarrel over the relics, the amicable distribution of relics by Doṇa, and erection of stūpas over them.

The Janavasabha Suttanta (Dīgha, II.) refers to King Bimbisāra of Magadha as a righteous king.

The Pāsādika Suttanta (Dīgha, III.) refers to the news of the demise of Mahāvīra to Ānanda at Sāmagāma in the Malla country.

The Āṭānāṭiya Suttanta (Dīgha, III.) states that the Blessed One dwelt in the Gijjhakūṭa mountain at Rājagaha.

The Sangīti Suttanta (Dīgha, III.) informs us that Mahāvīra, the founder of Jainism, died at Pāvā. It further tells us that the Mallas of Pāvā are addressed as the Vāseṭṭhas by the Buddha. This shows that the Mallas belonged to the Vaśiṣṭha gotra.

*Geographical*

The Ambaṭṭha Suttanta (Dīgha, I.) refers to a brahmin village of Kosala named Icchānaṅgala or Icchānaṅkala which was visited by the Buddha with a large retinue of 500 monks. It also refers to the Himalayan region.

The Kūṭadanta Suttanta (Dīgha, I.) refers to a brahmin village named Khānumata visited by the Buddha with 500 monks.

The Mahāli Suttanta (Dīgha, I.) refers to Vesālī inhabited by the brahmin messengers of Kosala and Magadha, and to a hermitage called Ghositārāma at Kosambī.

The Kevaddha Suttanta (Dīgha, I.) refers to Pāvārika mango grove at Nālandā where the Buddha dwelt. It speaks of the prosperity of Nālandā which was inhabited by many people.

The Tevijja Suttanta (Dīgha, I.) refers to a brahmin village in Kosala named Manasākaṭa which was visited by the Buddha with 500 monks, and to the north of which flowed the river Aciravatī. On the banks of this river there was a mango grove.

The Mahānidāna Suttanta (Dīgha, II.) refers to a Kuru country named Kammāssadhamma where the Buddha dwelt for some time.

The Mahāparinibbāṇa Suttanta (Dīgha, II.) states that the Exalted One went from Nālandā to Pāṭaligāma where Sunīdha and Vassakāra built a fort to crush the Vajjians. From Pāṭaligāma he went to Magadha where he had accepted the invitation of the two ministers, Sunīdha and Vassakāra. Thence he went to Koṭigāma; and further he proceeded to Nādikā where he dwelt at the Giñjaka abode. He then went to Vesālī where he had accepted the invitation of the famous courtesan, Ambapālī. The same suttanta refers to the Gijjhakūṭa-pabbata at Rājagaha where the Blessed One dwelt, to the river Gaṅgā where the Buddha approached at the time when it was overflowing, to Ajapāla banyan tree on the banks of the river Nerañjarā where the Buddha obtained Enlightenment, to Isigili, Sītavana, and Veluvana at Rājagaha. This sutta also speaks of Gotamakanigrodha, Corapapāta, Vebhārapassa, Sattapaṇṇiguhā, Kalandakanivāpa, and of Jīvaka's mango grove as beautiful. It further refers to the river Kakutthā, Upavattana, the Sālavana of the Mallas at Kusīnārā, and to the river named Hiraññavatī. This suttanta mentions Sāvatthī as a great city which was the resort of many wealthy nobles, brahmins, heads of houses, and believers in the Tathāgata. Great cities such as Campā, Rājagaha, Sāvatthī, Sāketa, Kosambī, and Bārāṇasī are suggested as the places where the Blessed One should obtain parinibbāṇa.

The Mahāsudassana Suttanta (Dīgha, II.) refers to the Sālavana of the Mallas called Upavattana at Kusīnārā and to Campā, Rājagaha, Sāketa, Sāvatthī, Kosambī, and Bārāṇasī. Kusīnārā was also named as Kusāvatī, the capital of the King Mahāsudassana. Kusāvatī was rich, prosperous, and full of many men. Alms could profusely be obtained there.

The Janavasabha Suttanta (Dīgha, II.) refers to Kāsī-Kosala, Vajji-Malla, Cedi-Vaṁsa; Kuru-Pañcāla, and Maccha-Sūrasena kingdoms.

The Mahāgovinda Suttanta (Dīgha, II.) refers to a number of great cities built by Govinda. They are: Dantapura of the Kaliṅgas, Potana of the Assakas, Māhissatī of the Avantis, Roruka of the Sovīras, Mithilā of the Videhas, Campā of the Aṅgas, and Bārāṇasī of the Kāsīs.

The Sakkapañha Suttanta (Dīgha, II.) points out that to the east of Rājagaha there was a brahmin village called Ambasaṇḍa, and to the north there was a cave called Indasāla in the Vediyaka mountain.

The Mahāsatipaṭṭhana Suttanta (Dīgha, II.) refers to the Buddha's dwelling among the Kurus. It mentions the Kammāssadhamma, a village of the Kurus.

The Pāyāsi Suttanta (Dīgha, II.) refers to King Pasenadi

of Kosala, and to a forest called Siṁsapāvana which lay to the north of the city, Setavya.

The Pāṭika Suttanta (Dīgha, III.) refers to Anupiya as the country of the Mallas where the Buddha went for alms. It also refers to Buddha's stay at Kūṭāgārasālā or the pinnacled house in the Mahāvana at Vesālī.

The Udumbarika Sīhanāda Suttanta (Dīgha, III.) refers to the Gijjhakūṭa-pabbata at Rājagaha visited by the Buddha.

The Cakkavattī Sīhanāda Suttanta (Dīgha, III.) mentions that the Blessed One dwelt at Mātula in the kingdom of Magadha. It refers to the capital called Ketumatī of King Saṁkha, and to Jambudīpa.

The Dasuttara Suttanta (Dīgha, III.) states that the Blessed One dwelt at Campā on the side of the tank called Gaggarā with 500 bhikkhus.

### *Historical*

In the Majjhima Nikāya of the Sutta Piṭaka.

Important historical references in the Majjhima Nikāya are mainly concerned with the life and itinerary of the Buddha and some of his disciples. Thus we are told that the Blessed One once stayed at the foot of a big Sāla tree in the Subhaga forest at Ukkaṭṭha (Vol. I, 1), at another time in the Jetavana hermitage of Anāthapiṇḍika at Sāvatthī (I, 12; II, 22), at Ukkācelā on the banks of the Ganges (I, 225), at Vesālī in the Kūṭāgārasālā at Mahāvana (I, 227), at Sāvatthī in the palace of Migāramātā at Pubbārāma (I, 251), at Veluvana at Rājagaha (I, 299) at Campā by the side of the tank Gaggarā (I, 339), at Nālandā in the mango grove of Pāvārika (I, 371), at Rājagaha in the Kalandakanivāpa at Veluvana, a hermitage of the paribbājakas called Moranivāpa (II, 1), at Mithilā in the mango grove of Makhādeva (II, 74), at Sāvatthī (II, 196; III, 1, 15, 20), at Kusīnārā in the thicket known as Baliharaṇa (II, 238), at Mahāvana in a pinnacled house (II, 252), at Kapilavatthu among the Sakkas in the Nigrodhārāma (III, 109), at Ghositārāma at Kosambī (III, 152), at Tapodārāma at Rājagaha (III, 192), at Nagaravinda, a brahmin village of the Kosalans where the Blessed One went with a large assembly of bhikkhus (III, 290) as well as at Mukheluvana at Kajaṅgala (III, 298). Of the places visited by the Buddha, mention is made of Mahāvana (I, 108). The Master also went to the Kosalans for alms with a large retinue of monks (II, 45), to the Kurus for the same purpose with a retinue of monks and to the Kuru country called Thullakoṭṭhita (II, 54), to Devadaha, a country of the Sakkas (II, 214), and to Kammassadhamma or Kammāssadhamma, a country of the Kurus (II, 261, 1, 55). Of his disciples and other prominent individuals, reference is made to Sāriputta and Moggallāna (I, 24-25), Kumārakassapa dwelling at Andhavana (I, 142), Ānanda living at Vesālī in the Veluva village (I, 349), Kassapa Buddha dwelling at Benares in the Deer Park at Isipatana where King Kiki of Benares came to see him (II, 49), Mahākaccāna dwelling at Gundāvana at Madhurā (II, 83), Aṅgulimāla, a bandit, dwelling in the kingdom of King Pasenadi of Kosala (II, 97) and entering Sāvatthī for alms (II, 103), Brahmāyu, an old brahmin of Mithilā (II, 133), Ānanda residing in the Kalandakanivāpa at Veluvana in Rājagaha shortly after the parinibbāṇa of the Buddha (III, 7), Ajātasattu, king of Magadha (III, 7), Mahāpajāpatī Gotamī who approached the place where the Buddha was, saluted him, and entreated him to instruct and give a religious discourse to the bhikkhuṇīs (III, 270), Sunakkhatta, a Licchavi (I, 68), and Mahānāma, a Sakka (I, 91).

Of other historical references, mention may be made of the allusions to the Vajjis and Mallas (I, 231), the Sākyas of Kapilavatthu (I, 353), the Kāsīs of Bārānasī (I, 473), the Aṅgas and the Magadhas (II, 2), to the heretical teachers, Pūraṇa Kassapa, Makkhali Gosāla, Ajitakesakambalī, Pakudha Kaccāyana, Sañjaya Belaṭṭhiputta, and Nigaṇṭha Nāthaputta (II, 2), and to Nigaṇṭha Nāthaputta's death at Pāvā (II, 243).

### *Geographical*

Important geographical references in the Majjhima Nikāya are few, and are already well known from other sources. Thus we have references to Bāhuka, Adhikakka, Gayā, Sundarikā, Sarassatī, Payāga, and Bāhumatī (I, 39), to Gosiṅgasālavana which was beautiful (I, 213), Vejayanta palace (I, 253), Assapura, a country of the Aṅgas (I, 271), Sālā, a brahmin village of the Kosalans (I, 285), Naḷakapāna, a palāsa forest (I, 462), Haliddavasana, a country of the Koliyas (I, 387), Suṁsumāra mountain in the Deer Park of Bhesakaḷāvana of the Bhaggas (II, 91), Medaḷumpa, a country of the Sākyas (II, 118), Opasāda, a brahmin village of the Kosalans visited by the Buddha along with the bhikkhus (II, 164), and to Sāmagāma of the Sakkas (II, 243).

### *In the Saṁyutta Nikāya of the Sutta Piṭaka*

Historical references.

The Saṁyutta Nikāya refers to King Pasenadi of Kosala, the capital of which was Sāvatthī. The whole of the Kosala-Saṁyutta is devoted to him. We are told that a war broke out between Ajātasattu, king of Magadha, and Pasenadi. Each claimed the possession of the township of Kāsī. At first Ajātasattu was victorious, but later on he was defeated and taken prisoner by Pasenadi. Pasenadi, however, married his daughter, Vajirā, to him and granted to him the township of Kāsī (I, 82–85). We are also told of the death of Pasenadi's grandmother (I, 97). The venerable Piṇḍolabhāradvāja who dwelt at Kosambī in the Ghositārāma gave answer to King Udena's questions. Udena was highly pleased with his answers and declared his faith in the Buddhist Triad (IV, 110).

Geographical references.

When the Master attained Supreme Enlightenment at Uruvelā under the Banyan tree on the bank of the river Nerañjarā, he was unwilling to preach the doctrine. Brahmā requested him to set rolling the Wheel of Law for the good of all. The Blessed One after much deliberation consented to the proposal (I, 136-137).

The Lord, while dwelling at Rājagaha in Veluvana in the Kalandakanivāpa, converted the brāhmaṇa Bhāradvāja and many other brāhmaṇas of the Bhāradvājagotta (I, 160–163).

The Blessed One once dwelt in the country of the Bhaggas at the Suṁsumāragiri in the Deer Park of Bhesakaḷāvana where he gave to the householder Nakulapitā religious discourses (III, 1).

The Blessed One dwelt at the city of Devadaha of the Sākyas (III, 5).

Mahākaccāna dwelt at Avanti on the mountain called Kuraraghara (III, 12). When the Lord was residing in Vesālī at Mahāvana in the Kūṭāgārasālā, he refuted the heretical views of Pūraṇa Kassapa which had been put to him by Mahāli, a Licchavi (III, 68-69).

The Lord once dwelt at Kapilavatthu in the Nigrodhārāma (III, 91).

At Sāvatthī Vacchagotta, a wanderer, put to the Buddha some heretical questions (whether the world is eternal or non-eternal, etc). The Buddha explained the origin of wrong views (III, 258).

Sāriputta while dwelling at the village of Nālaka in Magadha explained to the wanderer Jambukhādaka the Eightfold Path leading to the attainment of nibbāṇa (IV, 251).

Sāriputta while dwelling in the country of the Vajjis in Ukkavelā on the bank of the river Gaṅgā addressed a religious discourse to the wanderer Sāmaṇḍaka (IV, 261).

The Blessed One once went to Nālandā from Kosala and converted Gāmaṇi, Asibandhakaputto (IV, 323).

Once the Lord dwelt at the Deer Park of Añcanavana at Sāketa (V, 73).

The Lord resided at the city of Setaka in Sumbha (V, 89).

The Lord dwelt at the city of Haliddavasana in the country of the Koliyas (V, 115).

The Blessed One visited the brāhmaṇa village of Sālā in Kosala (V, 144).

The Lord visited with a company of the bhikkhus the brāhmaṇa village of Veḷudvāra in Kosala (V, 352).

The Blessed One visited Koṭigāma in the Vajji country (V, 431). Ānanda and Bhadda lived at the Kukkuṭārāma in Pāṭaliputta (V, 171).

### *In the Aṅguttara Nikāya of the Sutta Piṭaka*

Historical references.

There were sixteen Mahājanapadas, viz., Aṅga, Magadha, Kāsī, Kosala, Vajji, Malla, Cetī, Vaṁsa, Kuru, Pañcāla, Maccha, Sūrasena, Assaka, Avanti, Gandhāra, and Kamboja. It is worthy of notice that the names are names of people and not of countries (I, 213 ; IV, 252).

We are also told of King Pasenadi of Kosala and his Queen Mallikādevī (III, 57).

While the Lord was staying at Rājagaha on the Gijjhakūṭapabbata, Vassakāra the brahmin minister of King Ajātasattu of Magadha, as directed by his royal master, came to the Buddha for advice concerning the king's desire for leading an expedition to the Vajji country. After a talk with the Buddha, Vassakāra realised that the only means of subjugating the Vajjis lay in sowing the seeds of mutual jealousy among them (IV, 17–21).

Geographical references.

Mahākaccāna while dwelling at Madhurā in the Gundāvana explained the evils of sensual pleasures to the Brāhmaṇa Kaṇḍarāyana who professed his faith in the Buddhist Triad (I, 67).

Once the Blessed One went to the brāhmaṇa village of Venāgapura in Kosala where he addressed a religious discourse to the brāhmaṇas who took their refuge in the Buddha, the Dhamma, and the Saṁgha (I, 180).

The Master once visited the township of Kesaputta of the Kālāmas who were converted by him (I, 188).

The Buddha visited the township of Paṅkadhā in Kosala and from Paṅkadhā went to Rājagaha and dwelt at the Gijjhakūṭa (I, 236, 237).

There are references in the Aṅguttara Nikāya to Bhaṇḍagāma in the kingdom of the Vajjis visited by the Buddha (II, I), Ajapālanigrodha (*Ibid.*, 22), Madhurā and Verañji (*Ibid.*, 57), the Master dwelling among the Bhaggas in the Deer Park of Bhesakaḷāvana (*Ibid.*, 61), Kusinārā where the Buddha dwelt between the twin sāla trees of the Mallas at Upavattana (*Ibid.*, 79), the hermitage of Anāthapiṇḍika at Jetavana in Sāvatthī (III, 1), a brahmin village of the Kosalans called the Icchānaṅgala visited by the Buddha (*Ibid.*, 30), the Blessed One dwelling among the Bhaddiyas (*Ibid.*, 36), the Master dwelling at the pinnacled house in the Mahāvana in Vesālī (*Ibid.*, 38), Nārada dwelling at the Kukkutārāma in Pāṭaliputta (*Ibid.*, 57), the young Licchavi roaming about in the Mahāvana armed with bows and arrows accompanied by dogs (*Ibid.*, 75), Sārandadacetiya (*Ibid.*, 168), the bhikkhus dwelling in the Deer Park at

Benares (*Ibid.*, 320), the Buddha dwelling at Rājagaha on the Gijjhakūṭa mountain (*Ibid.*, 366).

While dwelling at Vesālī in the Sārandada Cetiya the Blessed One spoke to the Licchavis on the seven conditions, by following which, they were sure to thrive (IV, 16).

The Venerable Uttara is said to have dwelt at Mahisavatthu on the mount Saṁkheyyaka (IV, 162).

The Blessed One while dwelling at Verañjā under Naḷerupucimandamūla converted the Brāhmaṇa Verañja (IV, 172).

There were five great rivers, Gaṅgā, Yamunā, Aciravatī, Sarabhu, and Mahī (IV, 202).

The Lord dwelt at the Aggāḷava Cetiya in Āḷaviya (IV, 218).

The Buddha once visited the township of Kakkarapatta of the Koliyas (IV, 281).

The Lord also went to the brahmin village of Icchānaṅgala in Kosala and there he converted the brahmin householders (IV, 340), to the township of Uruvelakappa of the Mallas (IV, 438), to Kammāsadhamma in the Kuru country (V, 29-30), to Sahajāti in the Cetī country (V, 41), to Kajaṅgala and dwelt there at the Veḷuvana (V, 54).

The township of Kāsī was in the possession of Pasenadi, king of Kosala (V, 59).

The Lord once went to the township of Naḷakapāna in Kosala and dwelt at the Palāsavana (V, 122).

A certain householder, Dasama by name, came to Pāṭaliputta from Aṭṭhakanagara on some business. He went to Kukkuṭārāma, which was in Pāṭaliputta, in order to see the Thera Ānanda. But he was informed that Ānanda was then dwelling at Vesālī in Veluvagāma. He then after finishing his business went to Veluvagāma (V, 342).

### *Historical and geographical references in the Khuddaka Nikāya*

Devadatta was destined to go to Hell (Itivuttaka, p. 85).

Historical. King Bimbisāra of Magadha and King Pasenadi of Kosala have been referred to in the Udāna (p. 11) and there is a mention in it of Suppavāsā, a daughter of the Koliyas (p. 15). There are references in the Udāna to Pasenadi and his wife Mallikā (p. 47), Cunda (p. 81), and King Udena who went to a garden. When he went there, a harem was built and 500 women headed by Sāmāvatī died (p. 79). The Udāna further refers to Visākhā, mother of Migāra (p. 91), and Dabba, a Mallian (p. 93).

The Sutta Nipāta refers to the Buddha dwelling among the Magadhas in a brahmin village named Ekanālā at Dakkhināgiri (p. 13) and to the Master dwelling at Āḷavī in the abode of the Yakkha Āḷavaka (p. 31). There are references in the Petavatthu to King Brahmadatta of Pañcāla (p. 32) and King Piṅgalaka of the kingdom of Suraṭṭha and the Moriyas (p. 57).

We shall briefly state some facts from the Jātakas regarding the political history of ancient India. From the Jātakas we know that Aṅga was once a powerful kingdom. Magadha was once under the sway of Aṅgarājā (Jātaka, Fausboll, VI, p. 272). It is said (Jātaka, V, pp. 312–316) that King Manoja of Brahmavardhana (another name of Benares) conquered Aṅga and Magadha. It appears from the Jātakas (Jātaka, III, pp. 115 foll.; Jātaka, I, pp. 262 foll.) that before the Buddha's time Kāsī was the most powerful kingdom in the whole of Northern India. In the Jātakas (Vol. II, p. 237; IV, pp. 342 foll.) we find that Mahākosala, father of King Pasenadi of Kosala, gave his daughter in marriage to King Bimbisāra of Magadha. The pin-money was the village of Kāsī yielding a revenue of a hundred thousand for bath and perfume. We are also told that there took place many a fierce fight between the sons of Mahākosala and Bimbisāra, Pasenadi, and Ajātasattu respectively. In one of the Jātakas (Jāt., IV, pp. 144 ff.) we are told that Viḍūḍabha, in order to crush the Sakiyas who deceived his father Pasenadi by giving him a daughter of a slave girl to marry, deposed his father and became king. He marched out with a large army and succeeded in annihilating the Sakiyas. But he with his army met also with destruction. The river Rohiṇī was the boundary between the Sākya and Koliya countries. A quarrel broke out among the Sakiyas and Koliyas regarding the possession of the river. But the Buddha succeeded in restoring peace among his kinsfolk (Jāt., I, pp. 327 foll.—Rukkhadhamma Jātaka; Jāt., IV, pp. 207 foll.—Phandana Jātaka). A king of Benares attacked the kingdom of Kosala and took the king prisoner. The king of Kosala had a son named Chatta who fled while his father was taken prisoner. Afterwards Chatta recovered his kingdom (Jātaka, III, pp. 115 foll.). The kingdom of Benares was seized by a king of Sāvatthī named Vaṅka. But it was soon restored to the king of Benares (Jātaka, III, pp. 168-69).

Besides there are other historical references. A king of Benares had a gardener who could make sweet mangoes bitter and bitter mangoes sweet (Jātaka, V, p. 3). Fine cloths widely known as Kāsī cloths were manufactured (Jātaka, V, p. 377). There was a great town of carpenters in Benares containing a thousand families (Jātaka, IV, p. 159). There were in Benares snake-charmers (Jātaka, III, p. 198). Slaughter of deer, swine, and other animals for making offerings to goblins was in vogue in Benares (Jātaka, IV, p. 115). There was a king named Assaka in Potali. He was instructed by a Bodhisatta (Jātaka, II, pp. 155 foll.). There was a festival at Rājagaha where people drank wine, ate flesh, danced, and sang (Jātaka I, p. 489). Pilindiyavaccha turned the palace of Rājagaha into gold with the result that he was given an abundant supply of the five eatables, e.g., sugar, butter, ghee, honey, and oil (Jātaka, III, pp. 363-364). A meeting was held in a Saṅthāgāra at Rājagaha where the people met and discussed the means of welfare but they could not arrive at any definite conclusion and the matter was referred to the Buddha who settled it finally by preaching the Maṅgala Sutta of the Khuddakapāṭha (*Ibid.*, IV, pp. 72 foll.). In the Vepulla mountain surrounding Rājagaha there was a gem used by an universal monarch by which Dhanañjaya, the Kaurava king, might be defeated in playing dice (*Ibid.*, VI, p. 271).

Geographical.

The Gijjhakūṭa-pabbata has been described as a big mountain in Giribbaja of the Magadhas (Itivuttaka, p. 17). The Udāna mentions the Bo-tree at the foot of which the Buddha first obtained enlightenment on the bank of the river Nerañjarā at Uruvelā (p. 1). Jetavana where the Buddha dwelt (p. 3), Gayāsisa at Gayā where the Master dwelt (p. 6), Pipphali cave where Mahākassapa dwelt (p. 29), Upavattana, the sāla forest of the Mallas (p. 37), Kalandakanivāpa at Veluvana at Rājagaha visited by the Buddha (p. 39), and Kosambī visited by the Buddha (p. 41). There are references in it to Gaṅgā, Yamunā, Aciravatī, and Mahī (pp. 53, 55), Mahāvana where the Master dwelt (p. 62), and to the five Cetiyas, Cāpāla, Udena, Gotamaka, Sattambaka, Bahuputta, and Sārandada (p. 62). Kusīnārā and Pāṭaligāma are also referred to in it (pp. 82 and 85).

The Sutta Nipāta refers to the Gijjhakūṭa-pabbata (p. 86), Rājagaha (p. 86) visited by the Buddha, Veluvana, and Kalandakanivāpa (p. 91), Icchānaṅkala (p. 115), Sāvatthī (p. 18), Pubbārāma where there was the palace of Migāramātā (p. 139), Dakkhiṇāpatha (p. 190), Kapilavatthu (p. 192) visited by the Buddha, Patiṭṭhāna, Māhissati, Ujjenī, Vedisā, Kosambī, Setavya, Kusīnārā, Magadha, and the Cetiya Pāsānaka (p. 194). This work refers to the rivers Godāvarī (p. 190), Gaṅgā (p. 32), and Sundarikā (p. 79).

The Vimānavatthu refers to Cittalatāvana which was beautiful (p. 16) and the Petavatthu refers to Gaṅgā (pp. 28 and 29) and to two famous cities of Vesālī and Sāvatthī (pp. 45 and 63).

There are many geographical allusions in the Jātakas. It is said that Campā, the capital of the kingdom of Aṅga, was at a distance of 60 yojanas from Mithilā (Jāt., VI, p. 32). In the Assaka Jātaka (Jāt., II, p. 155) we are told of the Assaka territory, the capital city of which was Potali. In the Bhīmasena Jātaka (Jāt., I, pp. 356 ff.) Takkasilā is referred to as a great centre of learning. In the Cetiya Jātaka (Jāt., III, p. 460) we are told that the four sons of the king of Ceti built five cities : Hatthipura, Assapura, Sīhapura, Uttara-Pañcāla, and Daddarapura. From the Sivi Jātaka (Jāt., IV, p. 401) we know that Ariṭṭhapura was the capital of the Sivi kingdom. The kingdom of Bāveru is referred to in the Bāveru Jātaka (Jāt., III, p. 126).

Bharukaccha, a seaport town, is referred to in the Sussondi Jātaka (Jāt., III, pp. 187 ff.). In the Cetiya Jātaka (Jāt., III, p. 454) it is said that Sotthivatinagara was the capital of the kingdom of Ceti. In the Gandhāra Jātaka (Jāt., III, pp. 363–369) the Kasmīr-Gandhāra kingdom and the Videha kingdom are also mentioned. The kingdom of Kāsī is also referred to in the Jātakas. Its capital was Bārāṇasī. The extent of the city is mentioned as 12 yojanas (Jāt., IV, p. 160). There are also references to the Kosala kingdom (Jāt., III, p. 237 ; Jāt., III, pp. 211–213). The Kamboja kingdom is also referred to in the Jātakas (Jāt., IV, p. 208). There are innumerable references to the Magadha kingdom (Jāt., IV, pp. 454-455 ; Jāt., V, p. 316 ; Jāt., VI, p. 272). The city of Mithilā, the capital of the Videhas, was 7 leagues and the kingdom of Videha 300 leagues in extent (Cowell's Jāt., III, p. 222). We find a reference to the Maddaraṭṭha in the Kāliṅga-Bodhi Jātaka (Cowell's Jāt., IV, pp. 144-145). In the Kumbhakāra Jātaka (Cowell's Jāt., III, p. 230) we read that the capital of Uttara-Pañcāla was Kampilla. The city of Saṁkassa is referred to in the Kaṇha Jātaka (Jāt., Fausboll, I, p. 193). The country of Suraṭṭha is referred to in the Sarabhaṅga Jātaka (Jāt., V, p. 133). In the Sālittaka Jātaka (Jāt., I, p. 418) and in the Kurudhamma Jātaka (Jāt., II, p. 366) we find that the river Aciravatī was near Sāvatthī. In the Baka-Brahma Jātaka (Jāt., III, p. 361) the river Eṇī is referred to. The river Campā formed the boundary between Aṅga and Magadha (Campeyya Jātaka—Jāt., IV, p. 454). The river Godāvarī is near the Kaviṭṭha forest (Sarabhaṅga Jātaka—Jāt., V, p. 132). The Arañjara, a chain of mountains, is referred to in the Sarabhaṅga Jātaka (Jāt., V, p. 134). The Candaka mountain is referred to in the Saṁkhapāla Jātaka (Jāt., V, p. 162). In the Gaṅgamāla Jātaka (Jāt., III, p. 452) the Gandhamādana is mentioned. The Hiṅgula-pabbata is in the Himavanta-padesa (Jāt., V, p. 415).

The Niddesa contains some geographical information. It refers to Gumba, Takkola, Takkasilā, Kālamukha, Maraṇapāra, Vesuṅga, Verāpatha, Java, Tamali, Vaṅga [1], Eḷavaddana, Suvaṇṇakūṭa, Suvaṇṇabhūmī [2], Tambapaṇṇi [3], Suppāra [4], Bharukaccha [5], Suraṭṭha [6], Aṅgaṇeka, Gaṅgaṇa, Paramagaṅgana, Yona [7], Paramayona, Allasanda [8], Marukantāra, Jaṇṇupatha, Ajapatha, Meṇḍapatha, Saṅkupatha, Chattapatha, Vaṁsapatha, Sakuṇa-

---

1 Bengal.
2 Burma.
3 Ceylon.
4 Souppara (Pāli—Suppāraka), once a great seaport town.
5 Broach.
6 Surat.
7 Between the rivers Kophen and the Indus.
8 Alexandria.

patha, Mūsikapatha, Daripatha, Vettādhāra (Niddesa, I, pp. 154-155).

In the Niddesa (II, p. 1) we are told that once a certain brahmin named Bāvarī desirous of akiñcannaṁ (salvation) went to Dakkhiṇāpatha from the beautiful city of the Kosalans. He lived on the banks of the river Godāvarī in the kingdom of Assaka near Mulaka. In the same book (*Ibid.*, pp. 4-5) we find that there was a route, probably a trade route, from Patiṭṭhāna to Magadha. There are references to Muḷaka [1], Patiṭṭhāna [2], Māhissati [3], Ujjenī [4], Gonadham, Vedisā, Kosambī [5], Sāketa, Sāvatthī [6], Setavyam, Kapilavatthu [7], Kusinārā, Pāvā [8], Bhoganagara, Vesālī [9], and Magadha.[10]

The Paṭisaṁbhidāmagga mentions Sāvatthī as the place visited by the Master (Vol. II, pt. I, p. 177), Kosambī visited by Ānanda (Vol. II, p. 92), and Isipatana Migadāva at Benares visited by the Buddha (Vol. II, pp. 147, 159).

The Buddhavaṁsa refers to the city of Amarāvatī where lived a brahmin, Sumedha (p. 6), the city of Rammavatī (p. 17), the Himalayas (p. 49), Kusinārā, Vesālī, Kapilavatthu, Allakappa, Rāmagāma, Pāṭaliputta, Avantipura, and Mithilā (p. 68).

The Cariyāpiṭaka mentions the following cities—Indapatta ruled by Dhanañjaya, some brahmins from Kalinga came to him (p. 74). Kusāvatī (p. 75), Campeyya where the Bodhisatta was born as a snake king (p. 85), and Pañcāla where there was a king named Jayadissa in the city of Kappila (p. 90), and there is a reference to Gaṅgā in the Cariyāpiṭaka (p. 87).

The Apadāna refers to the cities of Hamsavatī famous for good flowers (p. 124), Bandhumatī (pp. 270, 295), Aruṇavatī (p. 282), and Ketumatī (II, p. 354). This work also refers to the following rivers :

[1] According to the Buddhists, Mūḷaka was a different town from Assaka. The countries of Muḷaka and Assaka were separated by the river Godāvarī.

[2] Paiṭhān. the capital of Assaka or Mahārāshtra on the Godāvarī.

[3] Maheśvara or Mahesh, on the right bank of the Nerbuda, 40 miles to the south of Indore. During the Buddhist period it was the capital of Avanti-Dakshināpatha.

[4] Capital of Mālava or Avanti on the Siprā.

[5] Kosaṁ, an old village on the Jumna, 30 miles S.-W. of Allahabad.

[6] Sahet-Mahet on the border of the Bhraich and Gonda districts of the Fyzabad division, U.P.

[7] The village of Piprāwā (Basti district) marks the site of Kapilavatthu.

[8] Between Pāvā (Fazilpur-Gorakhpur district) and Kusinagara (Kasia) was the river Kukuttha or Kuku.

[9] Vesali has been identified with the ruins at and near Besarhar Bazar (Muzaffarpur district, Bihar).

[10] The districts of Patna and Gaya formed this territory proper.

(1) Sindhu (p. 325), Candabhāgā (pp. 277, 291), Gaṅgā, Yamunā, Sarabhu, Mahī, Saraswatī (p. 27), and it mentions the following cetiyas—Buddha-cetiya (p. 71) and Sikhi-cetiya (p. 255). The Himalayan mountain has been mentioned in the Apadāna (pp. 15, 20, 50, 58, 160, 278, 279, 336, 411).

# APPENDIX B

## PĀLI TRACTS IN THE INSCRIPTIONS

Asoka's Bhābrū Edict.

Much light is thrown on the development of Pāli canonical literature by the lithic records of Asoka.

The first inscription that deserves notice in this connection is the Bhābrū Edict. It opens with a declaration of Asoka's deep and extensive faith in the Buddhist Triad and of his firm conviction that the utterances of Buddha are gospel truth. It then enumerates certain Dhammapariyāyas or canonical texts selected out of the Buddhist scriptures then known to him for the constant study and meditation not by the clericals only, but also by the laity and that with a view to making the good faith long endure. The texts referred to by Asoka are as follows :

(1) *Vinaya Samukase* or the exaltation of discipline, Pātimokkha (Rhys Davids, J.R.A.S., 1898).

| | | |
|---|---|---|
| Prof. Bhandarkar | .. | Tuvaṭṭhaka Sutta (Sutta Nipāta). |
| Mr. Mitra | .. | Sappurisa Sutta (Majjhima) and later, A Vinaya tract in the Aṅguttara, Vol. I. |
| Prof. Oldenberg | .. | The Pātimokkha. |
| ,, Barua | .. | Siṅgālovāda Sutta (Dīgha) called Gihivinaya and Anumāṇa Sutta (Majjhima) called Bhikkhuvinaya. |

(2) *Aliya-Vasāni*

| | | |
|---|---|---|
| ,, Kosambī | .. | Ariyavaṁsa (Aṅguttara), Vol. II, p. 27. |
| ,, Rhys Davids | .. | Ten Ariyavasāni enumerated in the Saṁgīti Suttanta (Dīgha), J.R.A.S., 1898. |

(3) *Anāgata b hayāni*

| | | |
|---|---|---|
| ,, Rhys Davids | .. | Anāgata bha yāni (Aṅguttara). |

(4) *Munigāthā*

| | | |
|---|---|---|
| ,, Rhys Davids | .. | Muni Sutta (Sutta Nipāta), I, 12, p. 36. |

(5) *Moneya Sūte*

| | | |
|---|---|---|
| ,, Kosambi | .. | Nālaka Sutta (Sutta Nipāta), iii, II, pp. 131-134. |

| | | |
|---|---|---|
| Prof. Barua | .. | Nālaka Sutta *minus* the Prologue. |
| ,, Rhys Davids | .. | Moneyya Sutta, J.R.A.S., 1898. |

(6) *Upatisa Pasine*

| | | |
|---|---|---|
| ,, Kosambī Barua. | and | Sāriputta Sutta (Sutta Nipāta), iv, 16, pp. 176–9. |
| ,, Neuman | .. | The questions of Upatissa in the Rathavinita Sutta (Majjhima). |

(7) *Lāghulovāde*

| | | |
|---|---|---|
| ,, Rhys Davids | .. | ' Rāhulovāda Sutta (Majjhima), ii, 2, 1, Vol. I, p. 414. |
| ,, M. Senart | .. | The Ambalaṭṭhika Rāhulovāda Sutta (Majjhima). |

These are the Dhammapariyāyas or canonical texts which have been identified differently with suttas of the Pāli canonical literature.

At the time of Asoka there was a Buddhist literature. Asoka selected out of this body of Buddhist literature seven Dhammapariyāyas which, in his opinion, would serve his purpose, that is, making the good faith long endure.

It is generally accepted by scholars that Buddhism is the basis and source of inspiration in regard to Asoka's Dhamma. The Siṅgālovāda Sutta of the Dīgha Nikāya and the Mahāmaṅgala Sutta of the Sutta Nipāta enumerate just those courses of conduct which Asoka was never tired of inculcating on the minds of his people and it is easy to understand how greatly the texts of the Rock Edicts, 9 and 11, were inspired by the Maṅgala Sutta. Now there are the two scriptural texts which have been particularly reserved by Buddhism for the lay people to read, contemplate, and practise.

The style of composition and the subject of discussion in the last portion of the Kālsī, Shāhbāzgarhi, and Mansherāh versions of R.E. IX are almost similar to those in the Kathāvatthu (composed by Moggaliputta Tissa in the third council held under the patronage of Asoka), and the Sāmaññaphala Sutta respectively. (Bhandarkar and Majumdar, Inscriptions of Asoka, pp. 34–36.)

M. Senart points out that the use of the phrase " Dhammadāna " must have been suggested to Asoka by a verse from the Dhammapada—" Sabbadānam dhammadānam jināti ".

References to Buddhist canonical literature.

On the monuments of the 2nd century B.C. the names of donors of different parts of the buildings are inscribed and in many cases with their titles. Some of these titles are very important because they have been derived from the well-known divisions of the Buddhist canonical literature. Among these epithets have been found the following : Dhammakathika, Peṭakin, Suttantika, Suttantakinī, and Pañcanekāyika which refer to the Buddhist books. They conclusively prove the existence of a Buddhist literature before the date of the inscriptions. This Buddhist literature had divisions known by the technical names of Piṭaka, Nikāya, Suttanta, and Jātaka. Again the Nikāya is said to have five divisions. There were not only the Piṭaka, the five Nikāyas and the Jātakas but also distinct groups of reciters known as the bhāṇakas.

Barhut Inscriptions.

The inscriptions on the Inner Railings and Gateways of the Buddhist Stūpa at Barhut in Central India throw interesting light on the development of Pāli literature. Barua and Sinha in their 'Barhut Inscriptions' have broadly distinguished the inscriptions as Votive Labels and Jātaka Labels, grouping the former as they occur on the Gateway-pillars, the Rail-pillars, the Rail-bars, the Coping-stones and the isolated Fragments, and grouping the latter as they are attached to different scenes in accordance with the accepted Jātaka-outlines of the Buddha's life.

That the bas-reliefs on the Barhut Tope illustrate several scenes from the Jātaka stories can be shown by the fact that the titles of the Jātakas inscribed on the bas-reliefs correspond to those in Pāli literature. The titles inscribed on the bas-reliefs, e.g., Vitura Punakiya, Miga, Nāga, Yavamajhakiya, Mugapakaya, Latuvā, Chadantiya, Isisingiya, Yaṃ bamaṇo avayesi, Hansa, Kinara, Isimigo, Janoko rājā, Sivalā devī, Uda, Secha, Sujato gahuto, Biḍala Jātaka, Kukuṭa Jātaka, Maghādeviya and Bhisa Haraniya, correspond to those found in the Pāli Jātaka books, e.g., Vidhūra Paṇḍita, Nigrodha, Kakkaṭa, Episode in Mahā-Ummagga, Mūgapakkha, Latukikā, Chaddanta, Alambusa, Andha-bhūta, Nacca, Caṇḍa Kinnara, Miga-potaka, Mahā-Janaka, Dabbha-Puppha, Dūbhiya-Makkaṭa, Sujāta, Kukkuṭa, Makhādeva, and Bhisa. Again, in the Barhut Stūpa we find some scenes which have got no title inscribed on the bas-relief. But a close examination of the pictures engraved on the railing enables us to identify some of the scenes with those in the Pāli Jātaka stories. The names of such Pāli Jātaka stories are, e.g., Kuruṅga-Miga, Sandhi-bheda, Asadisa, Dasaratha, Mahā-Kapi, Camma-Sataka, Ārāma-Dūsaka, and Kapota.

Pāli Inscriptions at the Sārnāth Museum.

The Museum at Sārnāth shelters a huge, more than life size image of a standing Bodhisattva. At the front and back of the pedestal of the image, as well as on the umbrella over his head, there are three Pāli inscriptions inscribed in the 3rd year of the reign of Kaniṣka, the great Kuṣāṇa king. The text of the inscription relates itself to the subject of the first sermon delivered by the Buddha to the five brāhmaṇas immediately after the sambodhi at Sārnāth. It is not exactly a quotation but is rather of the character of an abstract of the original subject from the Mahāvagga (1, 7, 6).

(*a*) "Chattār=imāni bhikkhave ar (i) ya-saccāni, (*b*) Katamāni (ca) ttāri dukkha (ṁ) di (bhi) kkhave arā (i) ya-saccaṁ, (*c*) dukkha-samuday (ō) ariya-saccāni dukkha-nirōdhō ariyasaccaṁ, (*d*) dukkha-nirōdhō-gāminī (cha) paṭipadā."

Translation :—" Four are the Noble Axioms, ye monks! And what are these four? The Noble Axiom about suffering, ye monks, the Noble Axiom about the origin of suffering, the Noble Axiom about the cessation of suffering, and the Noble Axiom about the way, leading to the cessation of suffering" [Catalogue of the Museum of Archæology at Sārnāth, No. D, (c) 11].

*Maunggan Gold plates*

Inscriptions found in Burma.

*Two gold plates* bearing inscription in Pāli, very closely allied to the Kadamba script of the 5th century A.D., of Southern India, were discovered at Maunggan, a village near old Prome, Burma. These two plates begin each with the well-known Buddhist formula : Ye dhammā hetuppabhavā tesaṁ hetu, etc., which is followed in the first, by *19 categories from the Abhidhamma in numerical order* and, in the second, by the no less well-known praise of the Triratana. (An. R.A.S., Burma, 1924, p. 21.)

*Bawbawgyi pagoda stone fragments*

In 1910-11, while clearing a small portion of the debris round the Bawbawgyi pagoda of Hmawza (old Prome) three fragments of a stone inscription were discovered. Their characters are the same as those of the Maunggan plates ; and the script may be referred to the 6th century A.D. It contains *an extract from the Vibhaṅga, a book of the Abhidhamma,* and corresponds to page 144 of Mrs. Rhys Davids' edition. (An. R.A.S., Burma, 1924, p. 21.)

The two gold plates and the stone fragments have been elaborately treated by Mon. Finot in his article "*Un nouvean document sur le buddhisme birman*"—a new document of Burmese Buddhism—published in the *Journal Asiatique, Vol. XX, Juillet-Aout*, 1912, *pages* 121 *ff*.

*Text of the two Gold plates*

I. (1) Ye dhammā hetuppabhavā tesaṁ hetu tathāgato āha tesañ ca yo nirodho evaṁvādi mahāsamano ti (2) Catvāro sammappadhānā catvāro satipaṭṭhānā catvāri ariyasaccāni cutuvesarajjāni pañcindriyāni pañca cakkhuni cha (3) asaddhā-raṇāni satta bojjhaṅga ariyo aṭṭhaṅgiko maggo navalokuttarā dhammā dasa balāni cuddasa buddhaññāni atthārasa buddha dhammā ti.

II. (1) Ye dhammā hetuppabhavā (te) sa (ṃ) hetu tathāgato āha tesāñ ca yo nirodho evambādi mahāsamano ti iti pi so bhagavā arahaṁ (2) Sammā saṁbuddho vijjācaraṇa-sampanno sugato lokavidū anuttaro purisadhamma sārathī satthā devamanussānaṁ buddho bhagavā ti (3) Sākhyāto bhagavatā dhammo sandiṭṭhiko akāliko ehipassiko opanāyiko paccattam veditavvo viññuhīti.

The first plaque begins with the well-known formula. After that it enumerates 19 categories in a progressively numerical order: 4 iddhipādas, bases of magical power, 4 Sammappadhānas, good deeds, 4 Satipaṭṭhānā, subjects of meditation, 4 ariyasaccāni, holy truths, 4 Vesārajjāni, confidences, 5 indriyāni, senses, 5 Cakkhuni, eyes, 6 asādhāraṇāni, special knowledges of Buddhism, 7 bojjhaṅgā, elements of the Bodhi, the noble way of the 8 elements, 9 lokuttarā dhammā, supernatural states, 10 balāni, powers, 14 Buddhañāṇāni, knowledges of the Buddha, and 18 Buddha dhammas.

The 2nd plaque begins in the same manner. It is followed by the well-known hymn (praise) of Triratna. See for example the Aṅguttara Nikāya, II, 56.

The script may at first sight be said to belong to Southern India—'Kanara-Telegu' script of Bühler, more particularly Kadamba.

*Text of the fragmentary stone inscription*

(1) ........nā samphus (i) tattam vedanākkhando saññākkhando saṅkkhārakhando............

(2) diṭṭhivipphanditam diṭṭhi ayam vuccati chaḷāyatanapaccayo phasso tattha katam (ā) (pha) ssa paccāya vedanā Ī yaṁ ceta (s) i .........

(3) Saññojanaṃ gā (ho) paṭilāho abhiniveso parāmāso kummaggo.

Translation :—

(1)..........(the contact), the fact of coming into contact, the Vedanākkhandha, the Saññākkhandha, the saṁkhārakhandha—constituent elements of sensation, perception, and confections; (2) quarrels of opinion, this is what people call opinion. (Diṭṭhi.) Touch comes from the six organs of sense. What is the sensation which is derived from touching. That which in thought........(3) Chain, inclination, contagion, bad path.........

This text is probably an extract from a canon, which is difficult to be traced. It presents considerable similarities with certain passages of the Dhammasaṅgaṇi. It could, therefore, be found in a treatise of the Abhidhamma, and perhaps one of those which are still unpublished.

### *A gold-leaf manuscript discovered at Hmawza, Prome*

A manuscript in every way similar to the palm-leaf manuscript so common in India and Burma but with leaves of gold, twenty in number with writing incised on one side, has been discovered within a relic chamber unearthed at Hmawza, a small village five miles north of Prome.

The writing is in characters of an early South Indian script of the Canara Telegu type, and may be assigned to the V-VIth century A.D.

The manuscript contains extracts from the Vinaya and Abhidhamma Piṭakas, together with those mentioned above, the earliest proofs of Pāli Buddhism in Burma. The MS. begins on the first page with an extract giving the chain of causation (Paṭiccasamuppāda) and ends on the last page with 'Itipi so Bhagavā arahaṁ Sammāsambuddho, etc.' enumerating the qualities of the Buddha. This manuscript may be assigned to the VI-VIIth century A.D. (Archæological Survey of India, Annual Report, 1926-27, p. 200).

### *An inscription of A.D.* 1442

The inscription of B.E. 804 (1442 A.D.) is among those collected by Forchhammer at Pagan. The Governor of Taungdwin and his wife made various gifts to the Buddhist Order and this inscription commemorates this memorable event. The pious donors not only made gifts of monastery, garden. paddy-lands, and slaves but also offered to the bhikkhus a collection of texts. The importance of the list of texts lies in the fact that it not only helps us in fixing the chronology of many Pāli works but also enables us to form some notion of the point reached by the Sanskrit scholars in Burma in the 15th century for the list contains a number of titles of Sanskrit works.

The list of texts contained in the inscription may be given here :

1. Pārājikakaṇḍa. 2. Pācittiya. 3. Bikkhuṇīvibhaṅga. 4. Vinayamahāvagga. 5. Vinayacūḷavagga. 6. Vinayaparivāra. 7. Pārājikakaṇḍa-aṭṭhakathā. 8. Pācittiyādi-aṭṭhakathā. 9. Pārājikakaṇḍa-ṭīkā. 10. Terasakaṇḍa-ṭīkā. 11. Vinayasangraha-aṭṭhakathā (the greater). 12. Vinayasangraha-aṭṭhakathā (the less). 13. Kaṅkhāvitaraṇī-aṭṭhakathā. 14. Khuddasikkhā-ṭīkā (ancient). 15. Khuddasikkhā-ṭīkā (new). 16. Kaṅkhā-ṭīkā (new). 17. Vinayagaṇṭhipada. 18. Vinayauttarasiñcaya-aṭṭhakathā. 19. Vinayasiñcaya-ṭīkā (later). 20. Vinayakandhaniddesa. 21. Dhammasaṅgaṇi. 22. Vibhaṅga. 23. Dhātukathā. 24. Puggalapaññatti. 25. Kathāvatthu. 26. Mūlayamaka. 27. Indriyayamaka. 28. Ṭīkāpaṭṭhāna. 29. Dukaṭīkapaṭṭhāna. 30. Dukapaṭṭhāna. 31. Atthasālinī-aṭṭhakathā. 32. Sammohavinodanī-aṭṭhakathā. 33. Pañcapakaraṇa-aṭṭhakathā. 34. Abhidhamma-anuṭīkā. 35. Abhidhammattha-

saṅgaha-aṭṭhakathā. 36. Abhidhammatthasaṅgaha-ṭīkā. 37. Abhidhammatthavibhāvanī-ṭīkā. 38. Sīlakkhandha. 39. Mahāvagga. 40. Pātheyya. 41. Sīlakkhandha-aṭṭhakathā. 42. Mahāvagga-aṭṭhakathā. 43. Pātheyya-aṭṭhakathā. 44. Sīlakkhandha-ṭīkā. 45. Mahāvagga-ṭīkā. 46. Pātheyya-ṭīkā. 47. Mūlapaṇṇāsa. 48. Mūlapaṇṇāsa-aṭṭhakathā. 49. Mūlapaṇṇāsa-ṭīkā. 50. Majjhimapaṇṇāsa. 51. Majjhimapaṇṇāsa-aṭṭhakathā. 52. Majjhimapaṇṇāsa-ṭīkā. 53. Uparipaṇṇāsa. 54. Uparipaṇṇāsa-aṭṭhakathā. 55. Uparipaṇṇāsa-ṭīkā. 56. Sagāthāvaggasaṁyutta. 57. Sagāthāvaggasamyutta-aṭṭhakathā. 58. Sagāthāvaggasaṁyutta-ṭīkā. 59. Nidānavaggasaṁyutta. 60. Nidānavaggasaṁyutta-aṭṭhakathā. 61. Khandhavaggasaṁyutta. 62. Khandhavaggasaṁyutta-ṭīkā. 63. Saḷāyatanavaggasaṁyutta. 64. Saḷāyatanavaggasaṁyutta-aṭṭhakathā. 65. Mahāvaggasaṁyutta. 66. Ekaduka-ṭīkā-aṅguttara. 67. Catukanipāta-aṅguttara. 68. Pañcanipāta-aṅguttara. 69. Chasattanipāta-aṅguttara. 70. Aṭṭha-navanipāta-aṅguttara. 71. Dasa-ekādasanipāta-aṅguttara. 72. Ekanipāta-aṅguttara-aṭṭhakathā. 73. Dukaṭīkācatukanipāta-aṅguttara aṭṭhakathā. 74. Pañcādi-aṅguttara-aṭṭhakathā. 75. Aṅguttara-ṭīkā. 76. Aṅguttara-ṭīkā. 77. Khuddakapāṭha text and aṭṭhakathā. 78. Dhammapada text and aṭṭhakathā. 79. Udāna text and aṭṭhakathā. 80. Itivuttaka text and aṭṭhakathā. 81. Suttanipāta text and aṭṭhakathā. 82. Vimānavatthu text and aṭṭhakathā. 83. Petavatthu text and aṭṭhakathā. 84. Thera(gāthā) text and aṭṭhakathā. 85. Therī(gāthā) text and aṭṭhakathā. 86. Pāṭhacariya. 87. Ekanipātajātaka-aṭṭhakathā. 88. Dukanipātajātaka-aṭṭhakathā. 89. Ṭikanipātajātaka-aṭṭhakathā. 90. Catuka-pañca-chanipātajātaka-aṭṭhakathā. 91. Satta-aṭṭhanavanipātajātaka-aṭṭhakathā. 92. Dasa-ekādasanipātajātaka-aṭṭhakathā. 93. Dvādasaterasa-pakiṇṇaka-nipātajātaka-aṭṭhakathā. 94. Vīsatijātaka-aṭṭhakathā. 95. Jātattakī-sotattakīnidāna-aṭṭhakathā. 96. Cūḷaniddesa. 97. Cūḷaniddesa-aṭṭhakathā. 98. Mahāniddesa. 99. Mahāniddesa. 100. Jātaka-ṭīkā. 101. Dumajātaka-aṭṭhakathā. 102. Apadāna. 103. Apadāna-aṭṭhakathā. 104. Paṭisambhidāmagga. 105. Paṭisambhidāmagga-aṭṭhakathā. 106. Paṭisambhidāmagga-gaṇṭhipada. 107. Visuddhimagga-aṭṭhakathā. 108. Visuddhimagga-ṭīkā. 109. Buddhavaṁsa-aṭṭhakathā. 110. Cariyāpiṭaka-aṭṭhakathā. 111. Nāmarūpaṭīkā (new). 112. Paramatthavinicchaya (new). 113. Mohavicchedanī. 114. Lokapaññatti. 115. Mohanayana. 116. Lokuppatti. 117. Aruṇavatī. 118. Chagatidīpanī. 119. Sahassaraṁsimālinī. 120. Dasavatthu. 121. Sahassavatthu. 122. Sīhaḷavatthu. 123. Peṭakopadesa. 124. Tathāgatuppatti. 125. Dhammacakka (? pavattanasutta). 126. Dhammacakkaṭīkā. 127. Dāṭhādhātuvaṁsa. 128. Dāṭhādhātuvaṁsa-ṭīkā. 129. Cūḷavaṁsa. 130. Dīpavaṁsa. 131. Thūpavaṁsa. 132. Anāgatavaṁsa. 133. Bodhivaṁsa. 134. Mahāvaṁsa. 135. Mahāvaṁsa-ṭīkā. 136. Dhammadāna (? in text dhammandan).

137. Mahākaccāyana. 138. Nyāsa. 139. Than-byan-ṭīkā. 140. Mahāthera-ṭīkā. 141. Rūpasiddhi-aṭṭhakathā. 142. Rūpasiddhi-ṭīkā. 143. Bālāvatāra. 144. Vuttimoggallāna. 145. Pañcika-Moggallāna. 146. Pañcika-Moggallāna-ṭīkā. 147. Kārikā. 148. Kārikā-ṭīkā. 149. Liṅgatthavivaraṇa. 150. Liṅgatthavivaraṇa-ṭīkā. 151. Mukhamattasāra. 152. Mukhamattasāra-ṭīkā. 153. Mahāgaṇa. 154. Cūḷagaṇa. 155. Abhidhāna. 156. Abhidhāna-ṭīkā. 157. Saddanīti. 158. Cūḷanirutti. 159. Cūḷasandhivisodhana. 160. Saddatthabhedacintā. 161. Saddatthabhedacintā-ṭīkā. 162. Padasodhana. 163. Sambandhacintā-ṭīkā. 164. Rūpāvatāra. 165. Saddāvatāra. 166. Saddhammadīpaka. 167. Sotamālinī. 168. Sambandhamālinī. 169. Padāvahāmahācakka (Padāvatāra ?). 170. Nvādi (Moggallāna). 171. Katacā (Kṛt-cakra ?). 172. Mahākā (Kappa or Kaccāyana ?). 173. Bālattajana (Bālāvatāraṇa ?). 174. Suttāvali. 175. Akkharasammohacchedanī. 176. Cetiddhīnemiparigāthā (*sic*) (?). 177. Samāsataddhitadīpanī. 178. Bījakkhyam. 179. Kaccāyanasāra. 180. Bālappabodhana. 181. Atthasālinī. 182. Atthasālinī-nissaya. 183. Kaccāyana-nissaya. 184. Rūpasiddhi-nissaya. 185. Jātaka-nissaya. 186. Jātakagaṇṭhi. 187. Dhammapada-gaṇṭhi-nissaya. 188. Kammavācā. 189. Dhammasatta. 190. Kalāpapañcikā (pañjikā). 191. Kalāpapañcikā-ṭīkā. 192. Kalāpasuttapratiññāsaku (? patiññāpaka) ṭīkā. 193. Priṇḍo-ṭīkā. 194. Rattamālā. 195. Rattamālā-ṭīkā. 196. Roganidāna. 197. Dabraguṇa. 198. Dabraguṇa-ṭīkā. 199. Chandoviciti. 200. Candaprutti (Cāndra-vṛtti). 201. Candrapañcikara (pañjikā). 202. Kāmandakī. 203. Dhammapaññāpakaraṇa. 204. Mahosaṭṭhi (Mahosadha ?). 205. Subodhālaṁkāra. 206. Subodhālaṁkāra-ṭīkā. 207. Tanogabuddhi (?). 208. Taṇḍi (Daṇḍin ?). 209. Taṇḍi-ṭīkā. 210. Caṅkadāsa. 211. Ariyasaccāvātara. 212. Vicitragandha. 213. Saddhammupāya. 214. Sārasaṅgaha. 215. Sārapiṇḍa. 216. Paṭipattisaṅgaha. 217. Sūlachāraka. 218. Pālatakka (bālatarka ?, logic for beginners ?). 219. Trakkabhāsā (Tarkabhāṣā). 220. Saddakārikā. 221. Kāsikāpruttipalini. 222. Saddhammadīpaka. 223. Satyatatvavabodha (?). 224. Bālappabodhanapruttikaraṇa. 225. Atthabyākhyam. 226. Cūḷaniruttimañjūsā. 227. Mañjūsāṭīkābyākhyam. 228. Anuṭīkābyākhyam. 229. Pakiṇṇakanikāya. 230. Catthapayoga (?). 231. Matthapayoga (?). 232. Rogayātrā (on medicine ?). 233. Rogayātrā-ṭīkā. 234. Satthekavipasvaprakāsa (?). 235. Rājamattanta. 236. Parāsava. 237. Koladdhaja. 238. Brihajjātaka. 239. Brihajjātaka-ṭīkā. 240. Dāṭhādhātuvaṁsa and ṭīkā. 241. Patigaviveka-ṭīkā. 242. Alaṁkāra-ṭīkā (on Subodhālaṁkāra ?). 243. Calindapañcikā (commentary on C° ?). 244. Vedavidhinimittanirutti-vaṇṇanā. 245. Niruttibyākhyaṁ. 246. Vuttodaya. 247. Vuttodaya-ṭīkā. 248. Milindapañha (in text Malinapañña). 249. Sāratthasaṅgaha. 250. Amarakosanissaya. 251. Piṇḍo nissaya. 252. Kalāpanissaya. 253. Roganidānabyākhyaṁ. 254. Dabbragaṇa-ṭīkā. 255. Amarakosa. 256.

Daṇḍi-ṭikā. 257. Daṇḍi-ṭīkā. 258. Daṇḍi-ṭīkā. 259. Koladhvaja-ṭīkā. 260 Alaṁkāra. 261. Alaṁkāra-ṭīkā. 262. Bhesajja-mañjūsā. 263. Yuddhajeyya (Yuddhā-dhyāya ?). 264. Yatana-prabha-ṭīkā (Ratana ?). 265. Viragdha. 266. Viragdha-ṭīkā. 267. Cūḷamaṇisāra. 268. Rājamattanta-ṭīkā.

269. Mṛtyuvañcana
270. Mahākālacakka } (Çaiva works ?).
271. Mahākālacakka-ṭīkā

272 Paraviveka (commentary on Parahita ?). 273. Kaccāyana-rūpāvatāra. 274. Pumbharasārī (or karasārī in text ?). 275. Taktāvatāra (Tattvāvatāra ?). 276. Taktāvatāra-ṭīkā. 277. Nyāyabindu. 278. Nyāyabindu-ṭīkā. 279. Hetubindu. 280. Hetubindu-ṭīkā. 281. Rikkaṇiyayātrā (?). 282. Rikkaṇiya-yātrā-ṭīkā. 283. Barittaratākara (Vṛttaratnākara ?). 284. Shyārāmitikabya (?). 285. Yuttisaṅgaha. 286. Yuttisaṅgaha-ṭīkā. 287. Sārasaṅgaha-nissaya. 288. Rogayātrā-nissaya. 289. Roganidāna-nissaya. 290. Saddatthabhedacintā-nissaya. 291. Pārānissaya. 292. Shyārāmitikabya-nissaya (?). 293. Brihajjātaka-nissaya (?). 294. Rattamālā. 295. Narayutti-saṅgaha.[1]

The Kalyāṇī inscriptions of Pegu—Introduction.

The Kalyāṇī inscriptions of Pegu (Burma)[2] were erected c. 1476 A.D. by Dhammaceti, king of Rāmaññadesa or ancient Pegu, and record the history of the establishment of Buddhism in Burma, and its gradual evolution through many vicissitudes of fortune. The main object in founding the Kalyāṇī-sīmā appears to have been to afford to the priesthood of Rāmaññadesa a duly consecrated place for the purpose of performing the uposatha, upasampadā, and other ecclesiastical ceremonies, and indirectly to secure continuity in their apostolic succession from Mahinda, the Buddhist apostle of Ceylon. The object of the Kalyāṇī inscriptions is to give an authoritative ruling on the varied opinions of scholars with regard to ordination, and to prescribe a ceremonial for the consecration of a sīmā.

The Kalyāṇī inscriptions are situated at the western suburbs of the town of Pegu. They comprise ten stone slabs, more or less broken to pieces and scattered about. The language of the first three stones is Pāli, and that of the rest is Talaing, being a translation of the Pāli text.

Interpretations of Pāli texts.

Owing to the want of a large number of priests well versed in Tripiṭaka, learned, wise and able, and who could after meeting and consulting together, investigate as to what was proper or not, disputations arose amongst the Buddhist Order of Pegu

---

[1] For details, readers are referred to M. H. Bode's 'The Pāli Literature of Burma', pp. 101–109.

[2] Taw Seim ko—A preliminary study of the Kalyāṇī inscriptions, Pegu, I.A., Vol. XXIII, 1893.

with regard to the performance of ecclesiastical ceremonies, such as the consecration of a sīmā and the upasampadā ordination. Each thera gave his own interpretation, and the king himself joined in the disputations. In course of these disputations citations were made from various Buddhist authorities, most important of which was the Aṭṭhakathā. The following tracts collected here were incidentally made use of by the theras and the king in their discussion as to the performance of ecclesiastical ceremonies of consecrating a sīmā and upasampadā ordination.

1. '*Anvaḍḍhamāsaṁ anudasāhaṁ anupañcāhanti*' *Aṭṭhakathāyaṁ*

Some theras could not rightly interpret these words mentioned in the Aṭṭhakathā, and would like in the excessively rainy region of Rāmaññadesa to perform the upasampadā ordination in an udakukkhepasīmā consecrated on a river or lake, which was devoid of its respective characteristics.

2. Dhammaceti, the king, in repeatedly investigating and considering the rule of the Vinaya as regards the consecration of a sīmā, as interpreted by the authors of the Aṭṭhakathās, ṭīkās, and pakaraṇas, consulted both the spirit and the letter of the following works, controlling the Aṭṭhakathā by means of the Pāli, the ṭīkā by means of the Aṭṭhakathā, and the pakaraṇa by one another, and at the same time, by collecting what was gone before, and what came after :—the Vinayapāli, the Vinayaṭṭhakathā, the vinayaṭīkā called the Sāratthadīpanī, the Vinayaṭīkā called the Vimativinodanī, the Vinayaṭīkā written by Vajirabuddhi-thera, the Mātikaṭṭhakathā called the Kaṅkhāvitaraṇī together with its ṭīkā, the Vinayaviniccayapakaraṇa together with its ṭīkā, the Vinayasaṅgahapakarana, the Sīmālaṅkārapakaraṇa, and the Sīmālaṅkārasaṅgaha To the king who repeatedly investigated and considered the question and interpreted the ruling of the Vinaya according to his light and knowledge.

3. "Yasmā hi vassānassa catūsu māsesu" iti aṭṭhakathāyāṁ. This short citation purports to say that the rainy season comprises four months, during which lakes and rivers become filled with water and during which season the under-robe of a bhikkhuṇī crossing a stream of such description at any place, is wetted. On such a mahānadī such a udakukkhepasīmā may be consecrated, and the upasampadā ordination performed in it will be valid and inviolable.

4. There existed an old sīmā whereon the Kalyāṇī-sīmā came to be built and consecrated later on. It was, therefore, necessary to desecrate the old sīmā, for otherwise the new sīmā would be null and void, because of the doubtful defeat of

the junction and overlapping of sīmās. The king accordingly had preparations made for performing the ceremony of desecrating the existing sīmā in accordance with the procedure expressly laid down in the Aṭṭhakathā. He then proceeds to interpret the passage of the Aṭṭhakathā in question.

5. With regard to this subject of desecration of an existing sīmā, and consequent consecration of a new one a question is made from the Vimativinôdaṇī :—

> " Keci pana īdisesu pi vihāresu chapañcamatte bhikkhu gahetvā, vihārakoṭito paṭṭhāya vihāraparikkhepassa anto ca bahi ca samantā leḍḍupāte tattha sabbattha mañcapamāne okāse nirantaraṁ ṭhatvā, paṭhamaṁ avippavāsasimaṁ tatosamānasaṁvāsakasīman ca samuhananavasena sīmāsamugghāte kate, tasmiṁ majjhagatā te bhikkhu tā samūhaneyyuṁ. Tato gāmasīmā eva avasisseyya. Na hettha sīmāya vā paricchedassa vā jānanam aṅgam hoti. Sīmāya pana anto ṭhānaṁ samuhanessāmāti, kammavācākaraṇañc'ettha aṅgaṁ. Aṭṭhakathāyāṁ kheṇḍasīmaṁ pana jānantā avippavāsaṁ ajānantā pi samūhatāya vuttattā gāmasimāy' eva ca avasitthāya tattha yathārucilakaṁ duvidhaṁ pi sīmaṁ bandhituñ c'eva upasampadādi-kammaṁ kātuñ ca vaṭṭatīti vadanti. Taṁ yuttaṁ viya dissati ; vimaṁsitvā gahetabban ti ".

Translation :—" There are some theras, who, in the case of such vihārasīmās, would convene a chapter of five or six priests, would station them in a continuous row of places, which are each about the size of a bedstead, and whose distances are determined by the fall, all round, of stones thrown, first from the extremity of a vihārasīmā, and then towards the inside and outside of its limits, and would successively desecrate an avippavāsasīmā, and a samānasaṁvāsakasīmā. If either a khaṇḍasīmā or a mahāsīmā exists on that vihāra, the priests standing, as they do, in the midst of these sīmās, would, from a mañcaṭṭhāna, certainly desecrate the sīmā, and the gāmasīmā would remain. In this manner it is not essential to know the sīmā on its extent. But it is necessary for the reciters of the kammavācā to say : ' We shall desecrate the inside of a sīmā (and act accordingly) '. It is stated in the Aṭṭhakathā that those who are aware of the existence of a khaṇḍasīmā, but not that of an avippavāsasīmā, are qualified to effect both desecration and consecration, and then thus, although the extent of a mahāsīmā is unknown, desecration may be effected. On the authority of this statement, they say that at any selected spot on the remaining gāmasīmā, it is appropriate to consecrate the two kinds of sīmās, and to perform the upasampadā ordination and such other ceremonies. This dictum appears to be correct ; but it should be accepted after due enquiry."

6. When the existence of an old sīmā is not known, it is said in the Aṭṭhakathā :—

"Aṭṭhakathāyañca purāṇa-sīmāya vijjamānattam vā paricchedaṁ vā ajānantānaṁ sīmāsanugghātassa dukkarattā mahantam vāyāmam akatvā yena vā tena vā vāyāmena samūhananavasena sīmāsamugghātaṁ sandhāya ye pana ubho pi na jānanti ; te n'eva samūhanituñ ca labhantīti vuttaṁ".

Purport :—'If both classes of sīmā are not known, the sīmā should not be desecrated or consecrated.' This dictum of the Aṭṭhakathā does not, however, mean to indicate that, although the existence of the sīmā to be desecrated may not be known, if great exertion is put forth that sīmā will not be desecrated.

References to Pāli texts.

Besides these quotations from and interpretations of Pāli texts, there are a good number of references to Pāli texts in the Kalyāṇī inscriptions in the way of adducing arguments or citing authorities. The three piṭakas are more than once mentioned the Vinaya having the honour of being mentioned most. But most often referred to is the Aṭṭhakathā of the Vinaya-piṭaka. Other texts are the Pātimokkha, the Khuddakasikkhā, the Vimativinodaṇī, the Vinayapāli, the Vinayaṭīkā called the Sāratthadīpaṇī, the Vinayaṭīkā written by Vajirabuddhi-thera, the Mātikaṭṭhakathā called the Kaṅkhāvitaraṇī together with its ṭīkā, the Vinayavinicchayapakaraṇa together with its ṭīkā, the Vinayasaṅgahapakaraṇa, the Sīmālaṅkārapakaraṇa, the Sīmālaṅkārasaṅgaha, and other texts relating to the Vinaya-piṭaka.

*Pāli texts referred to in the inscription of Parākramabāhu at Galwihāra, Ceylon*

1. The Vinaya books, 2. The Khuddakasikkhā, 3. The Pātimokkha, 4. The Dasadhammasutta, 5. The three Anumānasuttas, 6. The Mūlasikkhā, 7. The Heraṇasikkhā, and 8. The Sekhiya.

# INDEX

# ERRATA

| Page | Read | Instead of |
|---|---|---|
| 350 | *quietude* | *quietitude* |
| 355 | *perorations* | *prerorations* |
| 358 | *another* | *the another* |
| 399 | *Grimblot* | *Grimbolt* |
| 402 | *are* | *is* |
| 404 | *ghāna* | *jhāna* |
| 409 | *great* | *erudite* |
| 443 | *shone* | *shined* |
| 453 | *an interesting legend* | *legend* |
| 487 | *she* | *he* |
| 505 | *dropped* | *dripped* |
| 513 | *a banker's family* | *banker's family* |
| 520 | *Bindusāra* | *Bimbisāra* |
| 590 | Omit *Anuruddha—Khuddasikkhaṁ* | |
| 592 | *Pasādanī* | *Pasādajananī* |
| 616 | *her* | *his* |